2003 EDITION

PICTORIAL PRICE GUIDE TO

AMERICAN ANTIQUES

and objects made for the American market

ILLUSTRATED AND PRICED OBJECTS

by

Dorothy Hammond

First published 2002
© Dorothy Hammond
World copyright reserved

ISBN 1 85149 424 3

British Library Cataloguing-in-Publication Data
A catalogue record for this book is available from the British Library

Printed in Spain
Published in England by the Antique Collectors' Club Limited

Index

Introduction 5

A note to the reader 5

Acknowledgments 6

Abbreviations used in this book 7

Advertising 8

American Indian 14

Banks 18

Boxes 20

Clocks / Watches / Barometers 22

Firefighting 29

Folk Art 35

Furniture 38

Glass 88

Kitchen Collectibles 114

Lighting 119

Metals 131

Paintings / Pictures 146

Pottery / Porcelain 149

Textiles 198

Toys / Dolls 204

Miscellaneous 223

Index 254

Introduction

In the highly volatile and uncertain market for art, antiques, and collectibles, it is critical to have accurate and useful information about current prices and trends. This has never been more true than today, when prices are more volatile than at any time I can remember in my thirty plus years in the antiques and auction business.

Many of the price guides that are available, and I use ten or more on a regular basis, are based on shop or gallery prices. The most valuable information, however, is based on actual selling prices instead of the asking price. Dorothy Hammond has always worked hard to bring that information to her readers in the *Pictorial Price Guide to American Antiques and Objects made for the American Market.* The quality and quantity of her information is the result of many years of accumulating resources and contacts. Using these resources and contacts, Dorothy is able to bring to her audience, in one publication, the best cross section of information and prices available.

We have all heard that a picture is worth a thousand words, and it is nowhere more applicable than in the world of antiques and art. Seeing a picture of the object can prevent costly misunderstandings, especially for those not an expert in the field. Dorothy provides more pictures than any other price guide with which I am familiar.

We all know that condition can greatly impact the value of any object. Another great thing about Dorothy's guide is that it provides information about the condition of items that have sold. This goes a long way toward explaining variations in sales prices, and helps the reader make appropriate adjustments to the value of items in which they are interested.

Dealers are quite often specialists and real authorities in their field. However, all dealers have opportunities to buy outside their field. It is these occasions that require quick and valid information. Collectors, new to collecting or branching out into new areas, often need a user-friendly source of information. This new guide is the ideal reference tool for both collectors and dealers. It is a major resource for those who catalog major sales plus specialty sales.

My long professional relationship with Dorothy has been a pleasure and I feel honored to write this introduction. The 2003 edition is again a triumph and is perhaps unique in its use of selling prices, pictures, and condition reports. I am sure that everyone who uses it will find it as important and indispensable as I do.

— John C. Newcomer

A note to the reader

Like the title itself, this book holds something for everyone with an interest in or a curiosity about antiques and collectibles. It covers 17 different categories acquired from auction houses from coast to coast, reflecting the growth of interest in antiques and collectibles during 2001. Each entry is keyed to the auction house where the item actually sold, with the state abbreviation, because prices vary in different regions of the country. The year and month the item sold is also included.

Collecting has become a highly sociable pastime throughout the country. It is fascinating, enjoyable and educational because of the seemingly endless categories. In our fast-paced society, the material past will always hold its allure, and the mere survival of fine antiques will always command our respect. Collectibles produced during the late nineteenth century and well into the twentieth century continue to dominate a large segment of the market because of their availability. They can represent a gamble, a sound investment, a serious error, or a found fortune. New and growing trends range from the most humble of household collectibles to period furniture, because good early items in fine condition are so incredibly scarce. Centennial and early twentieth century items in all categories continue to increase in value. Folk art and early country furniture, especially painted pieces, bring record prices. Furniture and accessories from the Arts and Crafts movement which thrived from the late nineteenth century into the first quarter of the twentieth century, are currently one of the hottest trends in decorating. And in light of the events of last September 11th, the most widely appealing field is American antiques and collectibles.

Auction houses continued to enjoy another good year with healthy and diversified buyer response. To recognize a bargain ... and to avoid buying unwisely ... it is very important that the collector understand current market prices. Therefore, serious collectors look to auctions as the ultimate price determinant because they reflect market trends. When comparing similar pieces within this edition, consider that fluctuations in the market, the quality of an object, the region in which it is sold, and popularity of an item all determine the auction price.

Surprisingly, minor restoration and repairs to furniture have become more acceptable these days because of scarcity and demand. However, the original finish remains an important factor, regardless of the period or age of the piece of furniture. The quality of the finish can reduce the value substantially. And because of the quality of later mass-produced furniture, there has become an increased demand for custom-made furniture from all periods made by well recognized cabinetmakers. When these pieces find their way into the market place, they are well received for their quality and fetch strong prices.

Acknowledgments

I wish to express my sincere gratitude to my Publisher, Diana Steel, Managing Director of Antique Collectors' Club Ltd., Woodbridge, Suffolk IP12 4SD, for her many constructive suggestions which have all played an important part in the final form of the book. I am particularly indebted to Dan Farrell, Managing Director of Antique Collectors' Club, North America, for his commitment to this book, and his dedication to seeing it reach fruition.

All those whom I contacted in the process of assembling the book were more than generous in giving of their time and sharing their knowledge. I am very grateful to John C. Newcomer, for writing the introduction. John is an appraiser of antiques for York Town Auction, Inc., York, PA, and writes feature articles for The Magazine Antiques.

To Steve Philip, my project coordinator, I extend my deep appreciation for his patience and expertise for making this book a reality within five months. And a special thank you to his staff at Hi-Rz Graphics. Their help is gratefully acknowledged.

A book such as this one, covering a variety of areas and a multitude of objects required the assistance of many individuals and auction galleries. I wish to express my sincere gratitude to the following who have so generously provided pictorial and textual material for this edition:

Cover Image:
Courtesy of Ronald Bourgeault,
Northeast Auctions

Alderfer's Fine Art & Antiques
501 Fairgrounds Road
Hatfield, PA 19440
215-393-3000
www.alderferauction.com

Noel Barrett Antiques & Auction Ltd.
P.O. Box 300
Carversville, PA 18913
215-297-5109

Bertoia Auctions
2141 DeMarco Drive
Vineland, NJ 08360
856-692-1881
www.bertoiaauctions.com

Frank H. Boos Gallery
420 Enterprise Court
Bloomfield Hills, MI 48302
248-332-1500
www.boos.com

Brunk Auction Services, Inc.
P.O. Box 2135
Asheville, NC 28802
828-254-6846
www.rsbrunk.com

Butterfield's, Inc.
220 San Bruno Avenue
San Francisco, CA 94103
800-223-2854
www.butterfields.com

Carlton Hall Galleries, Inc.
912 Gervais Street
Columbia, SC 29201
803-779-5678
www.carltonhallauctions.com

Conestoga Auction Company, Inc.
P.O. Box 1
Manheim, PA 17545
717-898-7284
www.conestogaauction.com

Craftsman Auctions, Inc.
333 North Main Street
Lambertville, NJ 08530
609-397-9374
www.ragoarts.com

Doyle New York
175 East 87th Street
New York, NY 10128
203-618-9749
www.doylenewyork.com

Early Auction Company
123 Main Street
Milford, OH 45140
513-831-4833
www.earlyauctionco.com

Robert C. Eldred Company, Inc.
P.O. Box 796
East Dennis, MA 02641
508-385-3116
www.eldreds.com

Fontaines Auction Gallery
1485 West Housatonic Street
Pittsfield, MA 01201
413-448-8922
ww.fontaineauction.com

Garth's Auctions
P.O. Box 369
Delaware, OH 43015
740-362-4771
www.garths.com

Green Valley Auctions, Inc.
2259 Green Valley Lane
Mt. Crawford, VA 22841
540-434-4260
www.greenvalleyauctions.com

Harris Auction Center, Inc.
P.O. Box 476
Marshalltown, IA 50158
641-752-0600
www.geneharrisauctions.com

Hesse Galleries
53 Main Street
Otego, NY 13825
607-988-2523
www.hessegalleries.com

Horst Auction Center
50 Durlach Road
Ephrata, PA 17522
717-859-1331
www.horstauction.com

Jackson's International Auctioneers, Inc.
2229 Lincoln Street
Cedar Falls, IA 50613
319-277-2256
www.jacksonsauction.com

James D. Julia, Inc.
P.O. Box 830
Fairfield, ME 04937
207-453-7125
www.juliaauctions.com

Majolica Auctions, Inc.
P.O. Box 332
Wolcottville, IN 46795
260-854-2859
www.majolicaauctions.com

Northeast Auctions
93 Pleasant Street
Portsmouth, NH 03801
603-433-8400
www.northeastauctions.com

Pook & Pook, Inc.
P.O. Box 268
Downington, PA 19335
610-269-0695
www.pookandpook.com

Skinner, Inc.
The Heritage On The Garden
63 Park Plaza
Boston, MA 02116
617-350-5400
www.skinnerinc.com

Sloan's
4920 Wyaconda Road
North Bethesda, MD 20852
800-649-5066
www.sloansauction.com

Woody Auction
P.O. Box 618
Douglass, KS 67039
316-747-2694
www.woodyauction.com

York Town Auction, Inc.
1625 Haviland Road
York, PA 17404
717-751-0211
www.yorktownauction.com

Many of the auction galleries listed charge a buyer's premium which is a surcharge on the hammer or final bid price at auction. The premium can range from around 10% upward to 17½%. In most instances, the buyer's premium has been included with prices listed. For inquiries regarding buyer's premium, a complete address and website for each of the auction galleries listed has been included for readers' convenience.

All prices listed have been rounded off to the nearest dollar.

Although most auction houses give detailed catalog descriptions of items sold, others do not. Every effort has been made to include as much information as possible to ensure accuracy. However, neither the publisher nor the writer can assume responsibility for any errors that might be incurred as a result of typographical or other errors.

— Dorothy Hammond

Abbreviations

adv. . . . . .advertising
Am. . . . . .American
attrib. . . . . .attributed
C. . . . . .century
ca. . . . . .circa
circ. . . . . .circular
compo. . . . . .composition
const. . . . . .construction
D . . . . .depth
decor. . . . . . . .decorated/decoration
diam. . . . . .diameter
dov. . . . . .dovetail/dovetailed
DQ . . . . .Diamond Quilted
emb. . . . . .embossed
Eng. . . . . .England
engr. . . . . .engraved
escut. . . . . .escutcheon
ext. .exterior
Fr. . . . . .France/French
Ger. . . . . .German/Germany
GWTW . . . . .Gone With The Wind

H . . . . .height/high
illus. . . . . .illustrated/illustration
imp. . . . . .impressed
incl .include
int. .interior
irid. . . . . .iridescent
IVT . . . . .inverted thumbprint
L . . . . .length/long
litho. . . . . .lithograph
mah . . . . .mahogany
mech . . . . .mechanical
mfg. . . . . .manufactured
mkd. . . . . .marked
MOP . . . . .Mother Of Pearl
mrk. . . . . .mark
N. Eng. . . . . .New England
opal. . . . . .opalescent
orig. . . . . .original
pat. .patent
patt. . . . . .pattern
pc. . . . . .piece

pcs. .pieces
pr. . . . . .pair
prof. . . . . .professional
Q.A. . . . . .Queen Anne
reconst. . . . . .reconstructed
rect. . . . . .rectangular
ref. . . . . .refinished
replm . . . . .replacement
repr . . . . .repair/repaired
repro . . . . .reproduction
restor . . . . .restored/restoration
rev. .reverse
sgn. . . . . .signed
sq. .square
T. . . . . .tall
unmkd. . . . . .unmarked
unsgn. . . . . .unsigned
W. . . . . .width
wrt. . . . . .wrought
The common and accepted abbreviations
are used for states.

A-MA Mar. 2001   Robert C. Eldred Co.

Woolwork Picture, English, 19th C., w/ circular central image of a British ship flanked by American & British flags. Each corner w/ a smaller circular image of a sailing vessel or cannon, all surrounded by a green foliate border. Bird's-eye maple frame, 21″ square. **$9,200**

A-IA Aug. 2001   Gene Harris Antique
                       Auction Center, Inc.
Paper Sign Advertising, ca. 1898, 30" x
14½". **$1,000**

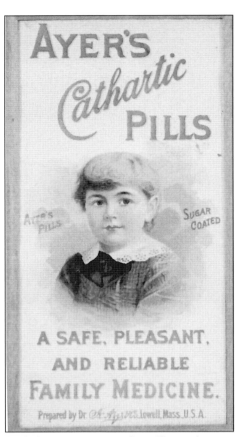

A-IA Aug. 2001   Gene Harris Antique
                       Auction Center, Inc.
Paper Sign Advertising, ca. 1890, by
J.C. Ayer Co., 27¼" x 13¾". **$1,000**

A-IA Aug. 2001   Gene Harris Antique
                       Auction Center, Inc.
Paper Sign Advertising, Dr. Harter's
Bitters, 28¼" x 13½". **$1,000**

A-IA Aug. 2001   Gene Harris Antique
                       Auction Center, Inc.
Silk Thread Cabinet, Corticelli thirteen-
drawer, oak. **$1,100**

A-IA Aug. 2001   Gene Harris Antique
                       Auction Center, Inc.
Silk Thread Cabinet, Corticelli nine-
drawer, oak. **$3,000**

A-IA Aug. 2001   Gene Harris Antique
                       Auction Center, Inc.
Silk Thread Cabinet, Corticelli twelve-
drawer, oak. **$700**

A-IA Aug. 2001   **Gene Harris Antique Auction Center, Inc.**

Corticelli Spool Silk Advertising Clock, modern. **$525**

A-IA Aug. 2001   **Gene Harris Antique Auction Center, Inc.**

Corticelli Advertising Clock, schoolhouse design by Sessions. **$600**

A-IA Oct. 2001   **Gene Harris Auction Center**

Sidney Advertising Clock w/ Seth Thomas movement, oak case, old advertisement. **$19,000**

A-IA Aug. 2001   **Gene Harris Antique Auction Center, Inc.**

Silk Thread Cabinet, Corticelli thirty-drawer w/ modern Corticelli glass inserts. **$1,300**

A-IA Aug. 2001   **Gene Harris Antique Auction Center, Inc.**

Spool Cabinet, Kerr & Co.'s Dollar Brand six-drawer. **$850**

A-IA Aug. 2001   **Gene Harris Antique Auction Center, Inc.**

Coca-Cola Cafe Sign, porcelain double side, 42½" H, 62½" W. **$1,050**

A-IA Aug. 2001   **Gene Harris Antique Auction Center, Inc.**

Tin Advertising Sign, De Laval in wood frame, 42" x 27". **$700**

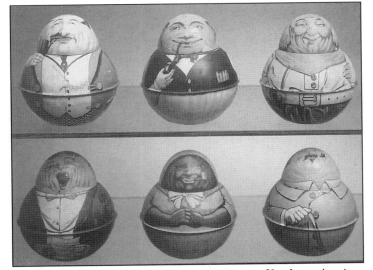

A-NH Mar. 2001   **Northeast Auctions**

Roly-Poly Mayo's Tobacco Advertising Tins, 6, 7" H. **$5,000**

A-ME Nov. 2001   James D. Julia, Inc.

Uncle Sam Banner, ca. 1935, red, white and blue cotton bunting, 112" x 30". **$80**

Litho & Calendar Print, (top) The Love of Freedom copyright 1917 by M.A. Stern, Chicago. Artist Ezio Anichini, Florence, Italy, 19½" x 15½". (second) Illustration of Uncle Sam. Artist Dean Cornwell. Copyright 1952, 22½" x 20½", **$86**

Uncle Sam, color cardboard, jointed, ca. 1944, 55" x 15¼". **$28**

Welcome Home Cloth Pennants, two, (top) W. W. I ca. 1919. 25¾" x 10¾". (second) Silk screen on paper, Made by B.B. Bonter, Chicago, IL USA. Copyright 1945, 43½" x 15". **$86**

Uncle Sam on Big Wheeled Bicycle, hand carved and hand painted. Bicycle made of cast iron with oak rim spoke wheels. Uncle Sam's jacket tails made of hand painted tin red, white and blue. Uncle Sam holding flag that says "Liberty". 20th Century, 52" H. **$1,800**

A-ME Nov. 2001   James D. Julia, Inc.

First Row

Uncle Sam Bisque Figurine, ca. 1870, blue jacket, gray top hat, red striped pants on a yellow toned base, 8¼" H. **$57**

Uncle Sam Celluloid Doll, ca. 1915, appears to have natural fading color due to age and exposure, 7" H. **$57**

Second Row

Uncle Sam Wax Doll, ca. 1900, red, white and blue cotton fabric clothing, 16½" H. **$230**

Uncle Sam Composition Doll, ca. 1892, cotton clothing, stuffed torso, 12" H. **$150**

Third Row

Uncle Sam Papier Mache Figure, ca. 1890-1893, blue coat, red vest, blue hat with stars on the band, on a blue base. Unger Doll & Toy Co., 12" H. **$345**

Uncle Sam Doll, w/ bisque head, grayish blonde hair and goatee, molded eye brows and glass eyes; blue felt jacket w/ red tails, red & white striped trousers, dark blue vest w/ white stars. Made by Schlaggenwald under the manufacturing firm Haas & Czjzek in 1892, 14½" H. **$575**

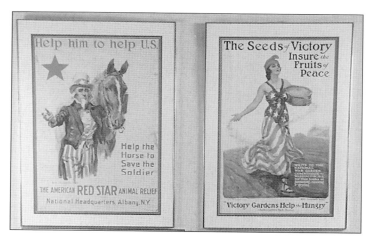

A-ME Nov. 2001   James D. Julia, Inc.

Poster, ca. 1918, Help Him to Help Us. Help the Horse to Save the Soldier. The American Red Star Animal Relief National Headquarters, Albany, NY. Artist James Montgomery Flagg, 33" x 23". **$460**

WW I Miss Liberty Poster, Copyright: 1918, "The Seeds of Victory Insure the Fruits of Peace". "Victory Gardens Help the Hungry". Artist: James Montgomery Flagg, 33" x 21". **$780**

Poster, "I Am Telling You". Artist James Montgomery Flagg. ca. 1917, 30" x 20". **$575**
Poster, artist James Montgomery Flagg, 34" x 24" **$345**
War Savings Stamp Poster, "Beware of the Wrath of a Patient Man!" Artist: James Montgomery Flagg. ca. 1918, 30" x 20". **$720**
Poster, "Hold on to Uncle Sam's Insurance" Artist: James Montgomery Flagg, ca. 1918, 33" x 23". **$143**

Poster, wood framed, "I Want You" Artist: James Montgomery Flagg. ca. 1952. 37½" x 25½". **$488**
Poster, "A Union in the Interest of Humanity - Civilization, Freedom and Peace for all time." ca. 1900, 38" x 27". **$747**

Poster, ca. 1917. "Some Backing!". The Empire State Needs Soldiers. Join the New York State Guard. Artist James Montgomery Flagg, 42" x 30". **$400**
Recruiting Poster, "I Want You for the US Army" Nearest recruiting Station. First issued as a poster in 1917 40" x 30". **$3,450**

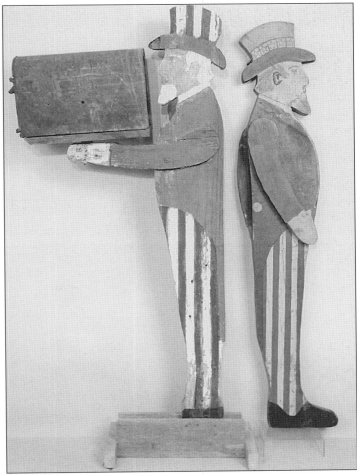

Uncle Sam Mailbox Holder, ca. 1918, all wood, orig. paint, paint loss, some restoration, piece missing in top hat, 60" H. **$747**
Uncle Sam Flag Pole Holder, ca. 1918-1920, all wood, orig. paint, loss to paint, scrapes and scuffs, 60" H. **$460**

ADVERTISING

First row

Adams One-Cent Gum Dispenser, stainless steel w/ divided racks, 10" W, 16" H. **$431**

Putnam Dye Cabinet, ca. 1920s, tin lithographed lid, 36 divided compartments, 19" W, and 14" H. **$201**

Glovers Dog Remedies Sign, ca. 1900, lithographed tin, minor oxidation, 13" diam. **$1,208**

Tin Litho Coffee Can, ca. 1900, green & gold, bail handle w/ dome lid, some losses, 10" H. **$58**

Second row

Hershey One-Cent Candy Dispenser, ca. 1930, glazed front w/ Hershey placard, 18" H. **$489**

Gold Dust Paper Container, orange & black, 2lb. 10 oz. size, minor losses, 9" H. **$46**

Pennsylvania Railroad First Aid Tin, red & black w/ logo, orig. contents, 5" H. **$35**

Schlitz Brewing Signs (pr.), ca. 1920, porcelain on metal w/ logo, blue, amber & red, 13" diam. **$431**

Monarch Peanut Butter Tin "Teenie Weenie", 1lb. size w/ lid & bail handle, 4" H. **$81**

Chicos Spanish Peanuts Countertop Container, glass w/ tin litho base & lid, minor losses, 12" H. **$230**

Third row

Gold Dust Cleanser Can, paper & tin, unopened, w/ child's miniature bucket, 5" H. **$104**

Horseshoe Tobacco Sign, porcelain on metal, blue & white on orange, minor loss, 18" W, 8" H. **$173**

Stollwerck Sign, porcelain on metal, cobalt blue & white, 9½" L, 2½" H. **$201**

Wrigley's Gum Display, ca. 1920s, 13" H. **$1,495**

Orsinger's Ice Cream Light Shade, red lettering on white opaque glass panels, metal frame w/ 6 colored jewels, 6" H. **$748**

Howels Orange Julep Dispenser, porcelain w/ orange ground, orig. dispenser, 15" H. **$920**

Oil Cans (2), "Simmons" blue jay & "Maytag", 8" H and 6½" H. **$35**

Fourth row

Tin Containers (4) "Popeye's" popcorn, "Lovell & Covel C." Peter Cottontail, "Sinclair" gasoline bank, Cities Service oil can bank. **$115**

Bevo Advertising Tray, ca. 1910, 13" W, 10½" H. **$115**

International Milk & Cream Sign, ca. 1920, cast aluminum, some losses, 14" diam. **$633**

Tin Bank, Century of Progress (sold w/ Parker Bros. "Tiddledy Winks" game in orig. box). **$17**

Akro Agate Marbles, ca. 1910, 3 sleeves, each containing 5 marbles, used as premiums w/ back stamp "Free w/ 1 lb. White Bear Coffee". 4" L. **$345**

Beer Drivers Union Souvenir Tray, ca. 1908, 14th anniversary, 10½" W, 13½" H. **$184**

Fifth row

Tin Lunch Pail, ca. 19th C., 5½" H. **$17**

Wrigley's Double Mint Gum Sign, ca. 1930, lithographed tin w/ red ground, 13" W, 6" H. **$863**

Tydol License Tag, embossed metal, black on yellow, 6" H. **$104**

Edelweiss Beer Tray, ca. 1913, lithographed metal, 13" diam. **$127**

Humo Cigar Display, blue & gold litho on tin w/ glass top, 9" L. **$58**

Tobacco Tins (3), "Lucky Strike", "Heidsieck" & "Drummond", 3" to 5" L. **$17**

Phez Juice Sign, ca. 1920, lithographed tin , 9" W, 6½" H. **$575**

Fan Tan Gum Tray, ca. 1920, lithographed tin, 13" W, 10½" H. **$127**

Cast Iron Cigar Cutter, ca. 1906, "El Commercio Havana Cigars", 9" L. **$661**

A-PA Sept. 2001   Pook & Pook, Inc.

Trade Sign, ca. 1870, painted poplar, retains salmon & black lettering on brown ground, 12½" H, 52½" L. **$2,250**

A-IA May 2001   **Jackson's International Auctioneers**

Case Logo Sign, ca. 1930, porcelain on metal in two parts, brilliant colors, 80" H. **$3,737**

A-ME Nov. 2001   James D. Julia, Inc.

"I Want You - FDR" Poster, ca. 1939. Stay and Finish the Job! Artist: James Montgomery Flagg, 24" x 18". **$603**

War Savings Stamp Poster, "Beware of the Wrath of a Patient Man!" Keep your War Savings Pledge. Artist: James Montgomery Flagg, ca. 1918. 30" x 20". **$287**

A-NC July 2001   Robert S. Brunk Auction Services, Inc.

Yei Rug, three corn dancers, border figure holding feather, red & br., minor soiling, 56" x 38". **$700**

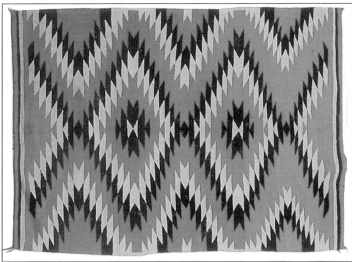

A-NC July 2001   Robert S. Brunk Auction Services, Inc.

Navajo Rug, red field, dk. outlines are blk., dk charcoal & blue/gray, slight selvedge breaks, minor soiling, slight bleeding, 45" x 64". **$1,500**

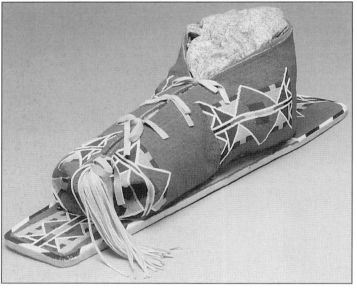

A-NC July 2001   Robert S. Brunk Auction Services, Inc.

Cradle Board, fully beaded, designs in red, gr., ivory pink on med. blue field, hide ties & fringe, modern construction, 35½" x 10½". **$600**

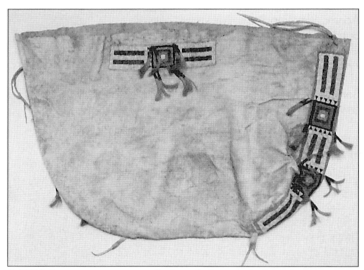

A-NC July 2001   Robert S. Brunk Auction Services, Inc.

Hide Bag, sinew-sewn w/ beaded panels of green vertical rectangles on white, alter. w/ yellow, blue, orange, white beads & tufted yellow tassels w/ tin ferrules, 19" x 21". **$1,700**

A-Apr. 2001   William Doyle Galleries

Apache Basket Bowl, w/ radiating diamonds, humans & dogs, 14" diam. **$6,325**
Pima Basket bowl, w/ radiating spiral design, 11½" diam. **$1,092**
Apache Basket Bowl, w/ friezes of humans, dogs & triangles, 14½" diam. **$2,300**

A-NC July 2001   Robert S. Brunk Auction Services, Inc.

Hopi Basket, coiled, polychrome & raised dec., six Kachina heads, br., amber & yel, 7" x 10". **$900**

A-Apr. 2001   William Doyle Galleries

Pottery
Santo Domingo Jar, w/ polychrome dec., 13″ H. **$115**
Hopi Jar, w/ polychrome dec. of plant & geometric designs, 8″ diam. **$1,150**
Santa Clara Carved Blackware Jar, w/ meander design, sgn. Toni Roller, 11½″ H. **$862**
Hopi Polychrome Pottery Jar, w/ frieze of feather design, sgn. Fannie Nampeyo, 5¼″
diam. **$690**
Acoma Black on White Jar, w/ fine line linear design, sgn. D. Torivio, 9″ diam. **$690**
San Ildefonso Blackware Pottery Jar, globular form, polished & matte, w/ frieze of
feathers, sgn. Maria Martinez & Popoui Da, 5¾″ diam. **$6,612**
Acoma Polychrome Jar, w/ deer, plants, feather & other designs, sgn. Jesse Garcia,
10½″ diam. **$632**
San Ildefonso Blackware Jar, w/ polished & matte red frieze of cloud, arrow & other
design, sgn. Adam & Santana Martinez, 6¾″ diam. **$1,840**

A-NC July 2001   Robert S. Brunk Auction
Services, Inc.

Plateau Beaded Fabric Vest, decor. w/
hearts arrows, flowers, arrowheads &
horse heads in varying colors, hand-sewn
fabric backing. Approx. 24″ x 21″. **$950**

A-PA Oct. 2001   York Town Auction, Inc.

Ephemeris (the assigned places of a celestial
body) **$250**
Taos, NM, drum, all orig. **$875**
Raven God Totem. **$700**

Broadside, Pawnee Bill's Wild West. **$525**
Pipe Bag, leather w/ decor. **$600**
Springfield Rifle, model 1812-1816. **$2,000**

A-OH Apr. 2001   Garth's Auctions, Inc.
Navajo Rug, Western regional w/
expanding serrate "X" design in gray, lt.
br. red, white & bl., fret border in lt. br.,
white & bl., 2′10″ x 5′41½″. **$247**

A-NC July 2001   Robert S. Brunk Auction
Services, Inc.

Horse Collar, finely beaded on canvas w/
elaborate pyramid diamond designs w/
blue, green, yellow & read beads. Approx.
37″ x 14½″ excl. hide ties. **$1,900**

A-Apr. 2001   William Doyle Galleries

Navajo Rug, Tec Nos Pas, 1920-30, w/ multi-colored diamonds & angular design, red, blk. white & ochre, approx.
7' x 5' **$747**

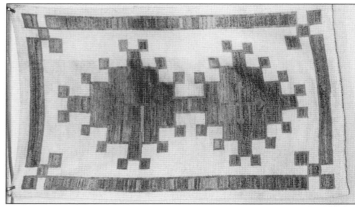

A-OH Apr. 2001   Garth's Auctions, Inc.

Navajo Rug, crystal regional weaving, hand carded wool in shaded gray/tan & natural white, minor wear & lt. stains, 4'6" x 7'4". **$962**

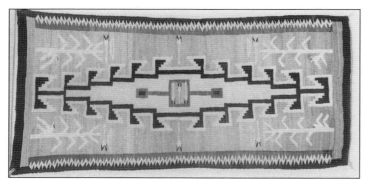

A-OH Jan. 2001   Garth's Auctions, Inc.

Navajo Rug, Klagetoh pictorial weaving, sacred corn & bow & arrow motifs, double dye red, dk. br. & natural carded white, 3' x 6'. **$550**

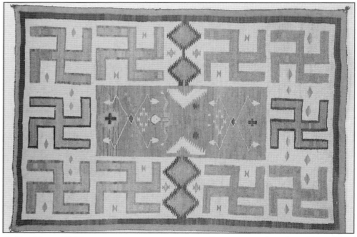

A-Pa Mar. 2001   Conestoga Auction Company

Navajo Wool Rug w/ sun symbols & geometric designs and central figure w/ outstretched arms, ca. 1900, 55" x 79". **$2,640**

A-OH Jan. 2001   Garth's Auctions, Inc.

Crow Beaded Belt, colorful design on sky blue ground, brass tack dec., metal buckle leather belt, missing tack, some bead loss, beaded area 3' L, overall 5'6" L. **$990**
Bandoleer Bag, Great Lakes, cloth, colorful & bold floral design in cut metallic beads on opales. bead ground, repl. velvet shoulder band, minor bead loss, pouch 12½" x 19" **$220**

A-NC July 2001   Robert S. Brunk Auction
                              Services, Inc.

Yokuts Basket, polychrome, fragments of attached feathers & red fabric, hashmarks may be maker's mark, losses to fabric, rim stitch missing, 9" x 16¾". **$3,100**

A-NC July 2001   Robert S. Brunk Auction
                              Services, Inc.

Apache Coiled Olla, woven of willow & blk. devil's claw, bottom w/ stylized flowers, minor wear & loss, 21¾" x 20".
$12,000

Navajo Tapestry, ca. 1970s, blk. gray, lt. & med blue & white yarn, 4'10" x 6'11". **$605**

Navajo Rug, two Grey Hills, fairly early w/ hand carded wool in gray, natural, bl. & tan, centered by stylized butterfly, edge damage, 3'2½" x 5'8". **$220**

Navajo Rug, early Ganado area, finely hand carded wool in bl. white & tan w/ double dye red cross center, fret & geometric design, 4'2" x 5'5". **$687**

Navajo Rug, two gray hills, bold geometric patt. in blk., natural, pale beige, w/ pale salmon accents, 71" x 88". **$2,900**

Navajo Rug, reg. weaving, outlined terraced diamonds in red, blk. soft tan, gray & natural white w/ carded gray ground, holes, 4' x 6'4". **$1,210**

Navajo Rug, two Grey Hills w/ elongated "sunrise" design in bl., white & gray, hand carded & spun wool, attached tag "Genuine Navajo Rug" by "Alfredia James Two Grey Hills…", 2'10" x 4'7". **$275**

Top Row

Mechanical Cast Iron Bank, "Trick Pony" by Shepherd Hardware, orig. paint, trap door missing, 7¾" L, 8" H. **$1,495**

Mechanical Cast Iron Bank, Kyser & Rex Lion & Monkeys, missing top monkey, trap & eyes 8¾" H. **$316**

Mechanical Cast Iron Bank, "Eagle & Eaglets" J&G Stevens, 95% paint. **$1,092**

Building Bank, cast Iron flat Iron 5½" H. **$259**

Andy Gump General Thrift Products Bank, cast metal 5¾" H. **$460**

General Pershing Cast Iron Bank, 7½" H. **$115**

Second Row

Cast Iron Bank, J.E. Stevens Co., broken hand 6½" H. **$69**

Novelty Cast Iron Bank, J.E. Stevens Co., missing door and figure 6½" H. **$92**

Hulls Excelsior Cast Iron Bank, J.E. Stevens Co., monkey missing. **$230**

Cast Iron Skyscraper Bank, A.C. Williams, 5½" H. **$57**

Moon & Star Safe Bank, cast iron, 5" H. **$34**

Cast Iron Still Bank, 4 stories w/ gold towers on each corner, orig. condition, 95% of paint. **$57**

Gothic Shaped Cast Iron Bank, 5¾" H. **$57**

Baby in Egg Cast Metal Bank, missing squeaker & trap, 7" H. **$69**

Third Row

Mutt & Jeff Cast Iron Bank, A.C. Williams, 5" H. **$69**

Hubley Puppy with Bee Bank, cast iron, 4¾" H. **$92**

Deckers Iowana Pig Bank, cast iron, 2" H. **$69**

Aunt Jemima w/ Spoon Bank, cast iron, gold version, 5½" H. **$103**

Hubley Aunt Jemima Bank, cast iron, 5¾" H. **$103**

A.C. Williams Graf Zepplin Bank, cast iron, 6¼" H. **$172**

Kenton Radio Bank, cast iron, 4¼" H. **$115**

State Bank, cast iron, 3⅞" H. **$34**

Mosque Banks, pr., cast iron, 3" H & 4⅝" H. **$34**

Mechanical Cast Iron Bank, Kilgore, ca. 1925, rabbits ears move when coin is deposited, trap door missing. **$230**

Arcade General Sheridan Bank, cast iron, broken tail, 5¾" H. **$57**

State Bank, cast iron, 4" H. **$69**

Kenton Hetrola Bank, cast iron, 4½" H. **$103**

Donkey Bank, A.C.Williams, cast iron, 3¾" H. **$46**

Arcade Rooster Bank, cast iron, 4¾" H. **$69**

Fourth Row

Animal Banks, pr., cast iron, rabbit, donkey & pig, 4¼" H & 4¾" H. **$23**

Colonial House Bank, A.C. Williams, cast iron, 3½" H. **$57**

Mail Box with Eagle Bank, cast iron, 3½" H. **$11**

Security Safe Bank, cast iron, 3¾" H. **$69**

Southern Comfort Mechanical Bank, pot metal. **$287**

Bull Bank, pr., cast iron, 3½" H. **$46**

Hubley Kitten Bank, cast iron, 4⅜" H. **$92**

Bear and Stump Bank, cast brass, ca. 1950s. **$69**

Building Banks, pr., cast iron, 4¼" H & 3" H. **$80**

Cast Iron Still Bank, silver building w/ gold dome, 3" H. **$23**

Snappit Cast Iron Bank, broken latch 4" H. **$80**

Fifth Row

Sheep Bank, pr., one cast iron, one pot metal no trap, marked "Feed My Sheep". **$34**

Elephant Mechanical Bank, pr., pot metal, 4¼" H. **$115**

Boston Terrier Bank, cast iron, still, repaint, 5¼" H, 5" L. **$34**

Book of Knowledge, Cat & Mouse Mechanical Bank, cast iron, 8" H. **$144**

St. Bernard Bank, cast iron, w/ pack, screw replaced, 5½" L, 3½" H. **$23**

Elmer Fudd Character Bank, cast metal, no trap, 5½" H. **$34**

Mail Box Banks, pr., one cast iron, one tin, overpainted, 3½" H. **$23**

"Save for a Home" Bank, pr., sheet metal, one overpainted, 3½" L. **$57**

Sixth Row

Lion Bank, three, cast iron, one overpainted, largest, 3½" H. **$103**

Elephant Bank, pr., cast iron, overpainted, 3½" H & 2¾" H. **$34**

Bulldog Bank, three, cast iron, 4⅜"H. **$46**

A-NH Mar. 2001

Northeast Auctions

Mechanical Banks, Cast Iron

First Row

I Always Did 'Spise A Mule by J. & E. Stevens Co., 7" H. **$1,000**

Cabin by J. & E. Stevens Co., 3½" H. **$650**

Stump Speaker by Shepard Hardware Co., 10" H. **$900**

I Always Did 'Spise A Mule, jockey, by J. & E. Stevens, 6" H. **$450**

Second Row

Bad Accident by J. & E. Stevens Co., 6" H. **$1,100**

Boy on Trapeze by J. Barton Smith Co., 9½" H. **$1,700**

Darktown Battery by J. & E. Stevens Co., 7" H. **$1,900**

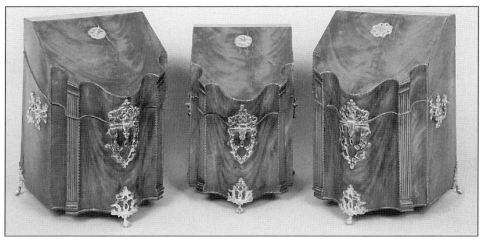

A-NH May, 2001   Northeast Auctions

Cutlery Boxes, Georgian, set of three 18th C. w/ inlay & silver mounts, each w/ serpentine front, slant lid opening & fitted interior, 13" H. **$40,000**

A-NH Mar. 2001   Northeast Auctions

Shaker Finger Lapped Oval Boxes, stack of 11 w/ colorful stain inc. yellow, blue, red, green and salmon. Length of smallest 3½", largest 15". **$62,500**

A-PA Mar. 2001   Conestoga Auction Company

Trinket Box, miniature, attrib. to Jacob Weber, Fivepointsville, Lancaster Co., PA, w/white, red & green house flanked by trees, green & red foreground, pegged const., 5¼" W, 2" D, 3"H. **$5,500**

A-PA Mar. 2001   Conestoga Auction Company

Salt Box, 19th C., w/ orig. smoke decor. over light brown ground, dovetailed & pegged case w/drawer. 8¼" W, 8¼" D, 11½" H. **$5,775**

A-MA Feb. 2001   Skinner, Inc.

Decorated Storage Box, New England, ca. 1830 w/ intricate foliate & scrollwork decor. & linear banding at edges, gr., red, yel., blue & blk. on yellow ground, minor imperfections, 5¼" x 11¼" x 6¼". **$4,600**

A-NY Nov. 2000   Hesse Galleries

Wooden Box, paint decor. floral & swag motif, snipe hinges, orig. lock & pull. 13" L, 8" H, 8" diam. **$1,045**

A-MA Feb. 2001   Skinner, Inc.

Hanging Cupboard, Southern, late 19th early 20th C., w/ old red stain, paint wear & other imper., 27½" H. **$920**

Decorated Box w/ polychrome decor., possibly PA, early 20 C., w/ hinged top, 6¼" H, 13" W, 7" D. **$2,350**

Miniature Apothecary or Spice Cabinet, possibly NH, ca. 1900, w/ 24 drawers, variegated finish and wooden pulls, 18" H, 8½" W. **$2,070**

Wall Box, painted, probably NY State, early 19th C., w/ open compartment & worn dark gray paint, 15" H, 7" W. **$2,760**

Storage Box w/ polychrome decoration, late 19th C., European, 7" H, 11½" W. **$345**

Hanging Open Cupboard, New England, early 19th C., w/ worn red paint, 29½" H, 18" W. **$2,644**

Barrel-Form Jar, Am., 19th C., ring-turned, painted red over earlier gray, 8½" H. **$460**

A-NH Mar. 2001   **Northeast Auctions**

Tea Caddies, Georgian, fruitwood apple 4½", pear 6½" H. **$11,000**

A-SC June 2001   Charlton Hall Galleries, Inc.

Tea Caddy, George III, walnut w/ inlay. Opening to divided interiors w/ covers, bun feet, 7½" H, 10½" W. **$225**

A-SC June 2001   Charlton Hall Galleries, Inc.

Tea Caddy, English, double, mah., ca. 1850, opening to divided & covered interiors, 5⅛" H, 7½" W. **$130**

A-SC June 2001   Charlton Hall Galleries, Inc.

Tea Caddy, tortoiseshell & bone inlaid, w/ silver inlaid cartouche, containing silver caddy spoon, 4" H, 4¼" W, 2¾" D. **$1,300**

Regency Jewelry Box, rosewood & M.O.P. w/ fitted int. & lift-out tray, 7" H, 12" W, 9" D. **$425**

Regency Double Tea Caddy, rosewood & M.O.P., first qtr. 19th C., w/ covered int., body w/ ring handles, 6⅛" H, 8" W, 5" D. **$350**

A-SC Dec. 2001   Charlton Hall Galleries, Inc.

Sewing Box, rosewood, brass inlaid, Eng., late 19th C., w/ secret compartment, some loss, 7¾" H, 14¼" W, 10" D. **$190**

A-PA Nov. 2001   Conestoga Auction Co.

Tall Case Clock w/ 8 day movement, walnut Chippendale case, mkd. "Martin Shreiner, Lancaster", rosettes possible old rest., ca. 1790s, 98" H. **$30,800**

A-PA Sept. 2001   Pook & Pook, Inc.

Tall Case Clock, 8-day, dial inscribed "S. Hill, Harrisburg", cherry case, ca. 1800, w/ polychrome inlaid eagle within an oval above notched corner door w/ line inlays, feet restored, 97" H, **$32,000**

A-PA Apr. 2001   Pook & Pook, Inc.

Tall Case Clock, PA, ca. 1780, broken arch bonnet w/ inlaid rosettes, oval inlaid fascia, 8-day works w/ moon phase, sgn. "Nathan Gulick", Easton, ogee feet, 96½" H. **$13,000**

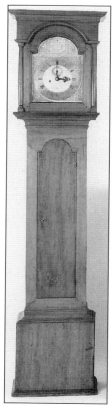

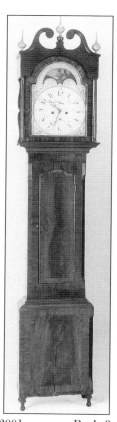

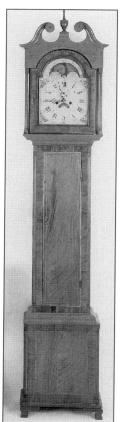

A-PA Sept. 2001   Pook & Pook, Inc.

Tall Case Clock, Q.A. cherry case, ca. 1760, dial sgn. "Cornelius Miller", w/ 8/day brass works, 85½" H. **$9,500**

A-PA Feb. 2001   Pook & Pook, Inc.

Tall Case Clock, Philadelphia, ca. 1805, mah. veneer, attrib. to David Weatherly, 92¼" H. **$5,000**

A-PA Feb. 2001   Pook & Pook, Inc.

Tall Case Clock, PA, mah., 1790, 8-day works, 98" H, restoration. **$4,000**

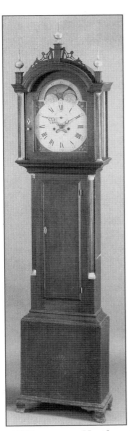

A-NH Aug. 2001   Northeast Auctions

Tall Case Clock, NH, by Chandler & Ward, Concord, 94" H. **$37,000**

A-NH Aug. 2001   Northeast Auctions

Tall Case Clock, Chippendale, walnut case, 91" H. **$3,750**

A-PA Feb. 2001   Pook & Pook, Inc.

Tall Case Clock, Georgian, mahogany, veneered, ca. 1800, 91½" H. **$2,300**

A-NH Aug. 2001   Northeast Auctions

Tall Case Clock, Chippendale, walnut case, 89" H. **$7,000**

A-NH Aug. 2001   Northeast Auctions

Tall Case Clock, Am. Chippendale, cherry case w/ English works by W. Burnett, 90" H. **$5,200**

A-PA Nov. 2001   Conestoga Auction Co.

Tall Case Clock w/ 8 day movement, mkd. "George Fisher" (1767-1809), walnut case. reduced feet. ca. 1790, 95" H. **$11,000**

A-IA Oct. 2001   Gene Harris Auction Center
Watch Co. of America, 14K hunting case, Paillards Pat. non-magnetic, size 18. **$395**

A-IA Oct. 2001   Gene Harris Auction Center
Romeo Chambert hunting case, 18K gold, presentation watch, dated 1875, size 16. **$1,400**

A-IA Oct. 2001   Gene Harris Auction Center
Waltham Vanguard, 21J, w/ up & down indicator, open face. **$700**

A-IA Oct. 2001   Gene Harris Auction Center
Ancre Lighe Droite, 14K, repeater, size 18, w/ moon phase, chronograph dial. **$2,500**

A-IA Oct. 2001   Gene Harris Auction Center
Rockford Indicator, 21J, 14K, open face w/ bridge movement, size 16. **$1,700**

A-IA Oct. 2001   Gene Harris Auction Center
Open Face Chronograph, 18K, pin set **$500**

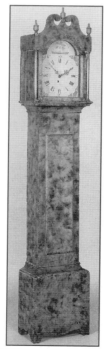

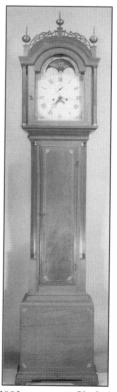

A-NH Mar, 2001   Northeast Auctions
Tall Case Clock, New England Chippendale, white enamel face w/ painted floral decor., w/ single long door having a raised sunburst carving on a plinth base ending in bracket feet, 86" H. **$8,000**

A-NH Mar. 2001   Northeast Auctions
Tall Case Clock, Silas Hoadley 1786-1870, Plymouth, CT, painted & smoke dec. w/ wooden works, hood w/ scrolled pediment, astragal glazed door, demilune panel w/ tree above Roman numerals, 88" H. **$18,000**

A-PA Apr. 2001   York Auction Inc.
Tall Case Clock sgn. Aaron Willard, Roxbury. Restoration to feet & fretwork. **$28,000**

A-lA Oct. 2001 Gene Harris Auction Center
Regulator Clock by Seth Thomas, No. 19 w/ walnut case, mercury pendulum. **$19,000**

A-PA Feb. 2001   Pook & Pook, Inc.
Banjo Clock, Federal, by Aaron Willard Sr., Boston, ca. 1810, 39½" H. **$3,000**

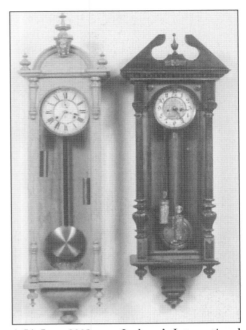

A-IA June 2001   Jackson's International Auctioneers

Left to Right
Ansonia Oak Regular Wall Clock w/ curved crest, 48" H. **$632**
Regulator Wall Clock by Gustave Becker, ca. 1890, walnut case, 48" H. **$633**

A-1A Oct. 2001 Gene Harris Auction Center
Shelf Clock by E. Howard & Co., No. 47, ca. 1873. **$70,000**

A-NH Aug. 2001   Northeast Auctions
Banjo Clock, Federal, giltwood, glass depicts the Boston Massacre on giltwood presentation bracket, dial inscribed Aaron Willard-Boston, 40" H. **$4,000**

A-NH Aug. 2001   Northeast Auctions

Left to Right
Banjo Clock, MA Federal, mah. w/ Roman numerals, inscribed S. Willard's Patent, 32" H. **$1,250**
Banjo Clock, lyre form, carved mah., dial inscribed Aaron Willard, Boston, 39" H. **$2,500**

A-IA Oct. 2001 Gene Harris Auction Center
E. N. Welch "Ardita", walnut case, double dial. **$1,500**
Gilbert "General", walnut case, time, strike & alarm. **$775**
Ithaca, No. 10, walnut case, double dial. **$675**

A-IA Oct. 2001 Gene Harris Auction Center
Ansonia, Davies Patent, no dome. **$600**
Ansonia, Louis XIV, walnut case. **$1,100**
Ansonia Crystal Palace, No. 1 w/ dome. **$900**

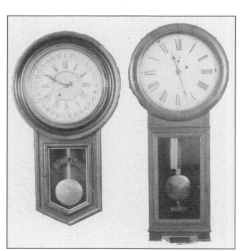

A-IA Oct. 2001 Gene Harris Auction Center
New Haven Regulator, No. 1, time & calendar, walnut case. **$375**
No. 2 w/ walnut case. **$1,100**

A-IA Oct. 2001 Gene Harris Auction Center
German Cuckoo w/ 3 weights, carved eagle, stag & dog, 31" L. **$500**

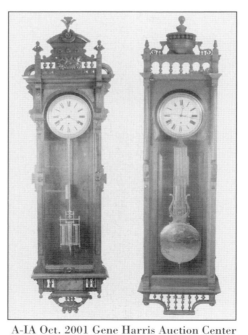

A-IA Oct. 2001 Gene Harris Auction Center
Swiss Jewelers Regulator, No. 48, ca. 1890-1910, mercury pendulum, walnut case. **$18,000**
Ansonia Jewelers Regulator, No. 18, ca. 1893-1895, cherry wood case. **$14,000**

A-IA Oct. 2001 Gene Harris Auction Center
Seth Thomas w/ time, strike & alarm, oak case. **$650**
Waterbury "Cincinnati" 30 day clock w/ oak case. **$850**
Atkins, octagon shape w/ short drop, rosewood case, time & strike. **$375**

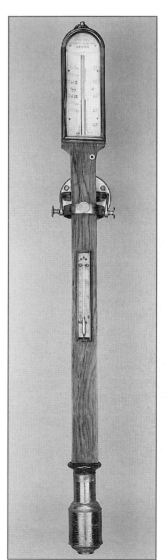

A-CA June 2001   Butterfields
George III Stick Barometer, early 19th C., rosewood w/ ivory & brass mounting gimbel, inscribed "Wm Alder/Nautical Stationer/Blyth", 38" H. **$3,884**

A-IA Oct. 2001 Gene Harris Auction Center
French Westminster 15 day clock, 6 pc. beveled glass door, fancy headboard, walnut case, good running order, ca. 1910, 43" H x 15¼" W x 9" D. **$650**

A-IA Oct. 2001 Gene Harris Auction Center
New Haven "Columbia", 30 day double spring, time only, seconds bit, cherry case, ca. 1890, 49" H. **$1,500**

A-IA Oct. 2001 Gene Harris Auction Center
Waterbury "Agusta", time and strike. **$2,900**

A-IA Oct. 2001 Gene Harris Auction Center
New Haven Jewelers Regulator, No. 8 w/ burled walnut case, mercury pendulum, ca. 1890-1910. **$8,000**
Railroad Regulator, E. Howard & Co., Model No. 89, oak case. **$9,500**

A-IA Oct. 2001 Gene Harris Auction Center
Vienna Regulator, 8 day, signed dial, time and strike, maple case, ca. 1865, dwarf size, 35" T. **$2,100**

A-IA Oct. 2001 Gene Harris Auction Center
New Haven Regulator, 8 day, time and strike. **$700**
German Vienna Regulator, 2 weight, 8 day time and strike. **$600**

A-IA Oct. 2001 Gene Harris Auction Center
Presentation Watch, C.H. Meylan Brassus, 18K, minute repeater, w/ hunting case. **$3,000**

A-IA Oct. 2001 Gene Harris Auction Center
U.S. Assay, John Hancock, 21J, 14K, open face, size 18, presentation, 1899. **$725**

A-NH Aug. 2001 **Northeast Auctions**
Shelf Clock, Federal, MA, mah. by Elnathan Taber, Roxbury, MA, w/ brass finial, white painted enamel dial inscribed "E. Taber", 37" H. **$13,000**

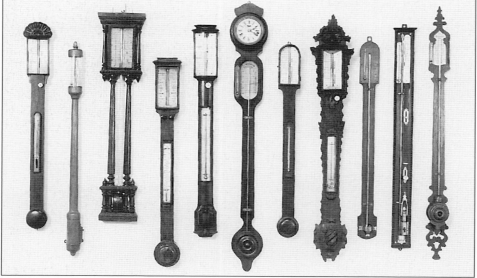

A-Apr. 2001 **William Doyle Galleries**

Barometers
Rosewood Stick, G. Tagliabue, NY, mid 19th C., w/ carved rosette crest, 37½" H. **$1,380**
Fruitwood Stick, Charles Wilder, Peterboro, VT, 2nd qtr. 19th C., (Woodruff's patent, of cylindrical form), 39" H. **$1,380**
Mahogany Stick, H.A. Glum, Rochester, NY, ca. 1860, w/ tabernacle face above two columns, lower sections w/ small column, 37½" H. **$1,035**
American Rosewood Stick, Benjamin Pike's Son & Co., NY, mid 19th C., w/ inscribed ivory meters, 38½" H. **$1,150**
Mahogany Stick, Benjamin Pike & Son, NY, w/ stepped cornice above convex face & standard, bottom set w/ urn, 39½" H. **$4,312**
Mahogany Stick, G. V. Mooney/A.S. Chubback's Son, Utica, NY, mid 19th C., of typical form w/ clock at top, 49" H. **$1,092**
Oak Stick, Benjamin Pike & Sons, 166 Broadway, NY, mid 19th C., 35" H. **$977**
Oak Stick, Benjamin Pike & Sons, NY, mid 19th C., w/ scrolling crest set w/ fruit, foliate carved standard, lower section w/ cartouche, 44" H. **$1,610**
Mahogany Stick, C.T. Ansler, Philadelphia, mid 19th C., simple form, 36" H. **$805**
Mahogany Stick, mid 19th C., flat rectangular form w/ brass fittings & carved molding, 40" H. **$1,725**
Walnut Stick, G.V. Mooney, NY, mid 19th C., w/ flat fret carved back & pointed crest, applied circular boss at bottom, 46½" H. **$1,092**

A-MA Feb. 2001 **Skinner, Inc.**
Federal Shelf Clock, mah., by Aaron Willard, Boston, ca. 1800, w/ diagonal inlaid banding, old finish, restoration, 36" H. **$8,050**

A-NH May 2001   **Northeast Auctions**

Four Currier & Ives Medium-Folio Lithographs of American Fireman, hand-colored. Includes "Always Ready", "Facing the Enemy", "Prompt to the Rescue" & "Rushing to the Conflict", all after L. Maurer, pub. 1858, in grain-painted frames. **$5,000**

A-NH Nov. 2001   **Northeast Auctions**

Left to Right

Fire Buckets, leather, early Am., painted & decor. w/ clasped hands & banners, 20" H, pr. **$4,000**
Trumpet, brass speaking, 20¼" H. **$500**
Fire Bucket, MA, leather, painted & decor., 13" H. **$3,500**

A-MA Nov. 2001   **Skinner, Inc.**

Dietz Fire Dept. Lanterns, pr., brass, red Fitz All Globes, one replacement filler cap. **$1,035**
Dietz Fire Dept. Lantern, nickel, minor dent bottom rim. **$460**
Presentation Lantern, brass, fixed cage, "NAHANT F.D.," pat. Oct. 24, 1854, "N.E. Glass Co." stamped on bottom of burner. (Restored & polished, glass has two minor cracks, does not affect engraving), 11½" H. **$977**
Lanterns, pr., brass, "T.M. Holmes Maker. 307 Race St, Phila." embossed on bottom. Burner missing, globe cracked, 15" H. **$747**

A-MA Nov. 2001   **Skinner, Inc.**

Wristlet Lantern, fixed etched globe, "Excelsior 1," damage to burner, 13" H. **$1,495**
Chief Engineer Lantern, engraved beveled glass lens. "White Mfg. Co. Pat. Feb. & Aug. 1874, Bridgeport, Conn.", 13" H. **$1,610**

A-MA Nov. 2001   **Skinner, Inc.**

Oil Reservoir, by Lunkenheimer, brass & glass, 12" H and an oil pressure chamber. **$201**
Hand Engine or Hose Carriage Bell, 9" H, 7" diam. **$373**
Steam Whistle, three-chamber domed, 2½" w/acorn finial & later metal & wood base, 10¾" H. **$316**
Steam Whistle, brass 2½" diam. single-chamber, by Morris, Toronto, 14½" H. **$287**

A-MA Nov. 2001   Skinner, Inc.

Leather Fire Bucket, red paint, replaced handle, repaint. **$575**
Leather Fire Bucket, dated "1821", 12" H. **$920**

Fiber Fire Bucket, by Hayward, Stoneham, MA., labeled "For Fire Only C.M. & L. R.R.", 12" H. **$747**

Leather Fire Bucket, brass riveted, 12" H. **$431**
Composition Fire Bucket, labeled "B.F.F.D.1," 11½" H. **$402**

A-MA Nov. 2001   Skinner, Inc.
Chief's-style Lantern, by F.O. Dewey Co., Boston, w/ green over clear lens, labeled "REEB", 19½" H. **$1610**

A-MA Nov. 2001   Skinner, Inc.
Lithograph, Hope Hose Co., hand colored, by George Heiss, 13" x 17", framed & glazed. **$747**

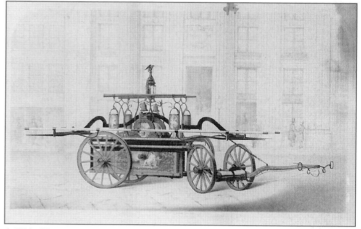

A-MA Nov. 2001   Skinner, Inc.
Advertising Lithograph, color, "Hunneman & Co., Builders, Boston Mass.," by L.H. Bradford & Co., damage, 27¼" x 37¼" framed & glazed. **$2,530**

A-MA Nov. 2001   Skinner, Inc.
United Fireman's Fire Mark, cast iron, traces of orig. paint. **$345**
Copper Fire Mark, English, "Protector". **$431**

A-MA Nov. 2001   Skinner, Inc.
Fireman's Top Hat, w/ pinned on panel & brass letters, maker's gold stamped label "McAlister 428 Broadway, Albany." **$460**
High Eagle Helmet, Cairns working-weight black leather w/ brass eagle front holder. Top painted red, missing liner. **$460**
Helmet Front, for a Jockey-style helmet. Black panel w/ white cut-out letters, 3½" H, 12" L. **$172**

A-MA Nov. 2001   Skinner, Inc.

High Eagle Helmet, black leather, sewn letters. **$287**

High Eagle Helmet, Cairns & Bro., eight comb black leather w/ canvas liner. 7⅜" dark red front w/ white painted letters. **$373**

Helmet, Belt and Dress Cap, ventilated Cairns black leather eight comb helmet w/ metal front. Black belt w/ sewn on white letters & meal Cairns maker's tag. Blue wool dress cap w/ "M" embroidered on front visor. **$1,265**

Ninety-six Comb Cairns Helmet, black, ventilated w/ metal front. Leather has been chemically treated, brim has minor crack. **$1,150**

Helmet and Matching Parade Belt, black leather w/ 6" sewn on front. Remnants of a paper mfg. label. Helmet never had metal front holder applied. Black belt w/ red panel and white cut-out letters. **$402**

A-MA Nov. 2001   Skinner, Inc.

Chemical Fire Extinguisher, Holloway Apparatus by American La France, 22" H. **$747**

Soca-Acid Extinguisher, Royal Apparatus, 25" H. **$63**

A-MA Nov. 2001   Skinner, Inc.

Half-plate Daguerreotype, The Union No. 2 Fire Co., c1850, w/ mat, in later frame **$9,200**

A-MA Nov. 2001   Skinner, Inc.

Breast Badges, set of three, **$546**

A-MA Nov. 2001   Skinner, Inc.

White Cairns Ninety-six Comb High Eagle Helmet, w/ aluminum front w/ brass "WC, AFD", canvas liner, repainted. **$690**
Sixty-four Comb White High Eagle Helmet, orig. 8" white front, red cut-out panels, early repaint to helmet. **$431**
Helmet & Matching Belt, Cairns aluminum helmet, never painted, felt liner, brass mfg. tag. Natural leather belt w/ red panel & metal letters. **$632**
Eight Comb White Leather High Eagle Helmet, 8" leather front w/ brass letters, new pins on front, minor paint loss, two glued spots. **$460**

A-MA Nov. 2001   Skinner, Inc.

Parade Top Hat, pressed wool, black w/ gilt lettering & red liner brim. "Friendship Fire Co., 5 Inst. March 4th 1848" w/ owner's initials "H.J." on top, 6½" H. **$2,990**
Parade Hat, w/ label "Warranted Waterproof Wool Hat Manufactured by Garvin & Cutter, East Cambridge Mass & No – 14 Fulton Street, Boston". Painted black w/ gold letters & green under brim, 16" L. **$4,887**
Parade Hat, red oil cloth & satin liner. **$1,265**

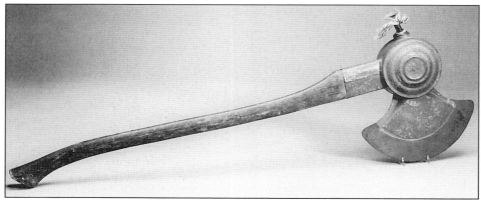

A-MA Nov. 2001   Skinner, Inc.
Axe-form Parade Torch, red painted tin head w/ reservoir, wood handle, 38" L. **$2,070**

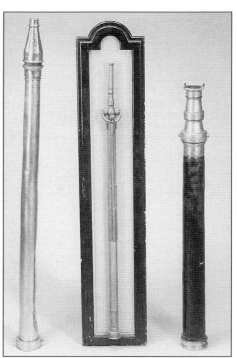

A-MA Nov. 2001   Skinner, Inc.

Steamer Play Pipe, brass & copper, 47" L. **$402**
Competition Nozzle, brass, mounted on wood board, 39" L. **$460**
Play Pipe Nozzle, leather wrapped, brass, mkd."C.F.D.", 39½" L. **$1,840**

A-MA Nov. 2001   Skinner, Inc.
Foam-type Extinguisher, Mack Apparatus, 2½ gal., 25" H. **$374**
Fire Extinguisher, Empire Apparatus, pat. Sept. 3, 1898, 21" H. **$345**

A-MA Nov. 2001   Skinner, Inc.
Breast Badges, set of three. **$230**

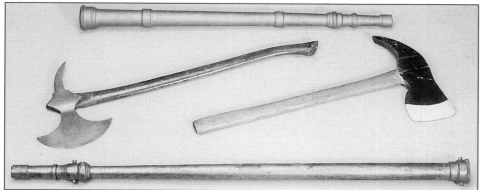

A-MA Nov. 2001   Skinner, Inc.
Wood Parade Nozzles, two Cumberland, Pennsylvania, couplings & tips painted gold, body black w/ red stenciled "Cumberland", 36" L & 36¾" L. **$287**
Parade Axes, two, one w/ aluminum head. **$575**

A-MA Nov. 2001   Skinner, Inc.
Boston Breast Badges, set of 4, **$201**

A-MA Nov. 2001   Skinner, Inc.
Presentation Trumpet, silver plated, "Lanesville, Engine Co. No 7", 19" H. **$690**
Presentation Trumpet, silver plated, 18" H. **$1,265**
Working Trumpet, brass, w/ red tassel, 17" H. **$466**
Presentation Trumpet, brass, w/ applied oval plaque, 19" H. **$1,035**

A-MA Nov. 2001   Skinner, Inc.
Badges, set of 2, helmet & breast, **$345**

A-MA Nov. 2001   Skinner, Inc.

Top Row
Excelsior Gong, Gamewell, wood case, 15¾" H. **$1,265**
Cast-iron Excelsior Alarm Box, Gamewell, 13¾" H. **$316**

Second Row
Muffin Bell, wood handle, 5" bell. **$489**
Muffin Bell, wood handle, 5½" bell. **$460**

A-MA Nov. 2001   Skinner, Inc.
Cast-iron Fire Alarm Box, Gamewell, 84" H. **$1,092**

A-MA Nov. 2001   Skinner, Inc.

Presentation Working Trumpet, brass, 2nd qtr. 19th C., copper mouthpiece, leather strap, remnants of red paint, engraved, old repairs & damages, 16" H **$1,092**
Working Fire Trumpet, nickel, orig. red cord & tassels, 19" H **$546**

A-MA Nov. 2001   Skinner, Inc.

Chromolithograph Advertising Print, Amoskeag Mfg. Co., Charles H. Crosby & Co., Boston. Creases, repairs & tears, 22½" x 29", framed & glazed. **$5,175**

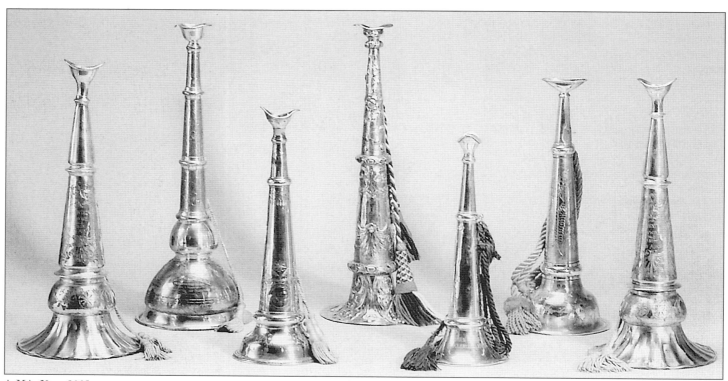

A-MA Nov. 2001   Skinner, Inc.

Presentation Trumpet, silver plated, early 20th C., engraved, gold rope & tassel. Worn, minor dent center, 21" H. **$1,495**
Presentation Trumpet, silver plated, 1914, engraved, w/ gold rope and tassel, 24⅛" H. **$2,645**
Trumpet, silver plated, late 19th C., engraved, gold rope & tassels, 19" H. **$690**

Presentation Horn, silver, by G. Bard & Son, 1859, engraved "Awarded to the Philadelphia Fire Co. by the Penn. State Agricultural Society for Best 2nd Class Fire Engine Distance Played 188 feet 3 in: 7/8 nozzle Oct. 1, 1859," red, white & blue wool rope and tassels, 24" H. **$12,650**

Presentation Trumpet, silver plated, 1862, engraved, blue cotton rope & tassels, 16⅞" H. **$805**
Presentation Trumpet, silver plated, late 19th C., scarlet rope & tassel, 20⅛" H. **$632**
Presentation Trumpet, silver plated, early 20th C., engraved, gold rope & tassel, 21" H. **$1,955**

A-MA Feb. 2001   Skinner, Inc.

Wood Whimsey, w/ gray, blue & salmon polychrome decor., dated 1881, wear, final missing, 20" H. **$2,760**

Wood Whimsey Tower, ca. 1876, surmounted w/ carved bust of George Wasington over tier enclosing sphere, natural surface, chip at base, 11¼" H. **$4,888**

Tramp Art Box, Am. ca. 1890-1910, painted blue & gold, hinged top opens to a mounted pincushion, on base w/ two concealed short drawers, 8¼" H, 14" W. **$805**

Tramp Art Christmas Tree, w/ polychrome decor., sgn., ca. 1900, on stepped base, minor paint wear, 25" H. **$2,070**

A-MA Feb. 2001 Skinner, Inc.

Figural Whirligig, carved & painted advertising figure, ca. 1910. Mounted on iron rod, minor imper., 33" H, including paddle & stand. **$18,400**

A-MA Feb. 2001   Skinner, Inc.

Red Slate Whimsey, New England, 19th C., w/ carved foliated decor. & heart motifs on stepped rectangular base, 17" H, 14¼" W. **$1,725**

A-MA Feb. 2001 Skinner, Inc.

Whirligig, carved pine w/ polychrome decor., late 19th C., w/ copper hat, bowtie, buttons & glass eyes w/ stand. Some paint wear, 20" H. **$10,925**

A-MA Feb. 2001   Skinner, Inc.

Carved & Polychrome Painted Figure of Lady, 19th C., possibly Quaker, w/ full length red dress, white apron & painted face, 20¼" H, w/ stand. **$17,250**

A-NY Nov. 2000　　　　　　　　　　Hesse Galleries
Carved Schimel Eaglets, pr., 6¹¹⁄₁₆″ H. $1,430

A-NY Nov. 2000　　　　　　　　　　Hesse Galleries
Carved Eagle, folk art, mkd. ROB PA. 14¾″ wing span, 10½″ H. $412

A-NH Mar. 2001　　　　　　　　　　Northeast Auctions

Carved & Painted Whirligigs

First Row
Sailor w/ tin hat, red & blue outfit, 17″ H. $2,000
Sailor w/ yel. hat & middy blouse w/ stars, 22″ H. $800
Sailor w/ scalloped middy blouse, 19″ H. $1,400
Sailor w/ blue & white middy blouse, red belt & red paddles, 18″ H. $1,500
Bearded Sailor w/ blue & white outfit, 20″ H. $3000

Second Row
Sailor w/ navy outfit, 16″ H. $1,200
Sailor w/ mustache, navy & white outfit, 15″ H. $3,250
Carved Boat & Sailor w/ blue & white outfit, 16″ H. $2,400
Large Sailor w/ yel. face & red/white/blue outfit, 16½″ H. $1,000

A-PA Apr. 2001   Pook & Pook, Inc.

Tramp Art

First Row

Picture Frame, w/ 14 layers, ca. 1900, w/ cut-out star & diamond patt. Old surface 18" x 24½" **$850**

Picture Frame, late 19th C., w/ circles & scalloped sides. Retains traces of old mustard painted surface, 14" W, 16½" H. **$300**

Carved Mirror, w/ inset mirror, the initials "W.T." and date 1897 over stylized flowers. Retains polychrome painted surface, 34" H, 25½" W. **$1,300**

Second Row

Sewing Box, w/ six layers, ca. 1900, w/ rectangular lid, w/ central pin cushion. Case w/ six small drawers & initialed "W.H.", 7" H, 12½" W. Together w/ box having a single drawer, applied brass eagle, and initialed "T.M.", and a small chestnut tramp art box initialed "A.E." **$325**

Vanity Box, late 19th C., dated "1895", & flanked by stylized flowers all on velvet over decorated case, enclosing mirror, retains old red painted surface, 6" H, 10½" W. **$150**

Minature Wardrobe, late 19th C., w/ double arched pediment, 2 arched doors open to 7 small drawers, 15" H, 10½" W. **$800**

Sewing Box, late 19th C., w/ large velvet pin cushion lid opening to comp. w/ smaller pin cushion & mirror, six small hidden drawers, 7" H, 13" W. **$200**

Storage Boxes, pr., late 19th C., w/ single drawer, retains traces of red paint, 6" H, 8½" W. **$500**

A-MA Feb. 2001   Skinner, Inc.

Carved Wooden Figural Group, VT, late 19th C., horse w/ feather harness, brass & copper fittings, pulling two-part sleigh, minor imperfections, 14" x 25" x 14¼". **$9,200.00**

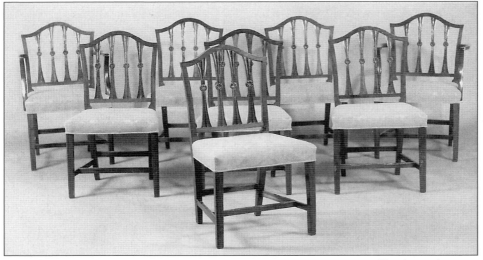

A-NH Aug. 2001   Northeast Auctions

Dining Chairs, Hepplewhite carved mah., w/ over-upholstered seat, set of eight. **$4,000**

A-NH Mar. 2001   Northeast Auctions

Classical Mahogany Dining Chairs, ca. 1815-20 w/ carved rail, reeded stiles & molded sabre legs. **$15,000**

A-NH Aug. 2001   Northeast Auctions

Dining Chairs Hepplewhite, set of 11 including two arm chairs (8 illus.). **$2,400**

A-MA March 2001   Skinner, Inc.

Easy Chair, mah., New England, early 19th C., molded & beaded tapering sq. front legs, raked rear chamfered legs, old ref., imper., 47¼" H. **$9,775**

A-MA Mar. 2001   Skinner, Inc.

Chippendale Easy Chair, mahogany upholstered, arched crest, shaped wings, rounded seat & frontal cabriole legs, claw & ball feet, sq. chamfered rear legs, old refinish, restored, 45" H. **$17,250**

A-MA Mar. 2001   Skinner, Inc.

Wing Chair, Q.A. mah. upholstered, MA, ca. 1760, arched crest, vertical out-scrolled arms, rounded seat, cabriole legs, pad feet, sq. raked rear legs by block, vase, & ring-turned stretchers, old ref., reprs., 47¾" H. **$34,500**

A-NH Mar. 2001   Northeast Auctions

Chippendale Side Chairs, set of six, Am., mahogany w/ serpentine crest above geometric pierced splat, square legs w/ beaded edge, recessed stretcher. **$4,000**

A-MA Mar. 2001   Skinner, Inc.

Roundabout Commode Chair, Q.A., walnut, PA, ca. 1740-60, shaped pillow back, sq. seat & deeply valanced seat rail, four cabriole legs ending in trifid feet, refinished, restrored, 31" H. **$3,105**

A-NH March 2001   Northeast Auctions

Classical Mahogany Chairs, set of 9 (7 illus.), attrib. to Duncan Phyfe, ca. 1800-1815, w/ scrolled tablet crest, taperings legs. **$50,000**

A-NH Mar, 2001   Northeast Auctions

Lolling Chair, MA, Hepplewhite, mah. w/ serpentine top. **$1,650**
Georgian Marlborough Chair, English, mah. w/ serpentine top. **$1,600**

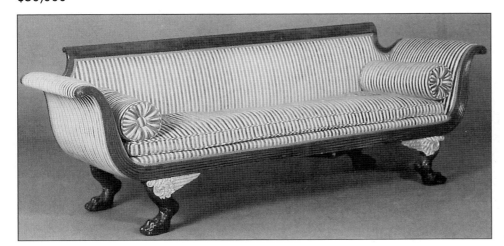

A-NH Aug. 2001   Northeast Auctions

Sofa, NY Classical, mah. & giltwood w/ reeded seat rail on gilded winged paw feet, 94" L. **$2,750**

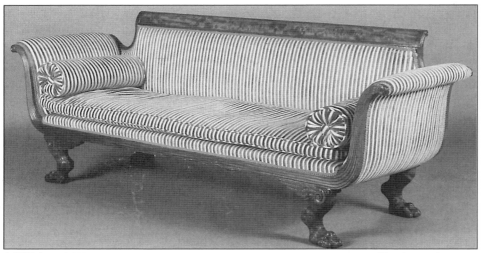

A-NH Aug. 2001   Northeast Auctions

Sofa, NY Classical, mah., w/ reeded seat rail on hairy paw feet w/ wing returns, 89" L. **$1,250**

A-MA Feb. 2001   Skinner, Inc.

Roundabout Chair, maple, New England, early 19th C., w/ rush seat, old surface, 30" H. **$920**

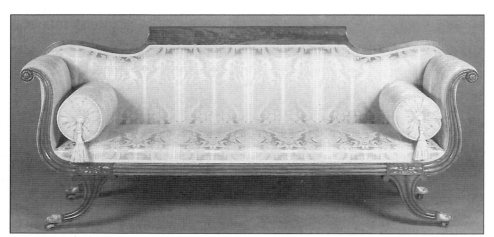

A-NH Aug. 2001   Northeast Auctions

Sofa, classical w/ scroll arm, reeded support continuing to a seat rail on stylized cornucopia legs, 86" L. **$1,500**

A-PA Sept. 2001   Pook & Pook Inc.

Q.A. Ladder Back Arm Chair, PA, ca. 1750, retains old reddish brown painted surface. **$2,000**

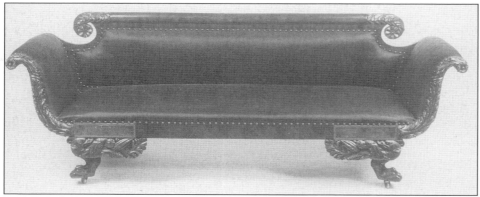

A-MA Mar. 2001   Skinner, Inc.

Sofa, carved mah. veneer, PA or Balt., ca. 1815-20, scrolled veneered crest rail ends & arm supports in leaf & foliate carving, leaf & carved legs, old ref. w/ blk. horsehair upholstery, imper., 90" L. 33½" H. **$1,350**

A-MA Oct. 2001   **Skinner, Inc.**

Settle Bench, painted pine, early 19th C., double-hinged lift-top seat, some orig. paint remains back & side, imper. **$2,415**

A-PA May 2001   **Horst Auction Center**

High Chair, mid-19th C., PA, w/ plank seat, painted brown w/ painted fruit & foliage motifs in yellow, red, green, white, blue & black, scrubbed seat. **$350**
Child's Rocker, mid-20th C., w/ black ground, hand painted flowers & gold striping, wear, 28" H. **$85**

A-KS Aug. 2001   **Woody Auction**

Salon Set (1 of 4 pcs.), sofa, arm chair & 2 side chairs, rosewood by John Jeliff. **$4,600**

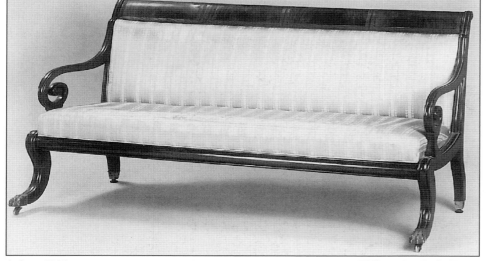

A-Apr. 2001

William Doyle Galleries

Classical Mahogany Settee, Boston, ca. 1825, upholstery w/ sabre legs ending in brass paw casters, 6' 3" L. **$3,450**

A-IA June 2001   **Jackson's International Auctioneers**

Victorian Platform Rocker w/ carved crest. **$80**

A-IA Mar. 2001   **Harris Auction Center, Inc.**

Renaissance Revival 7pc. Parlor Set (3 illus.), walnut attributed to John Jeliff. **$9,000**

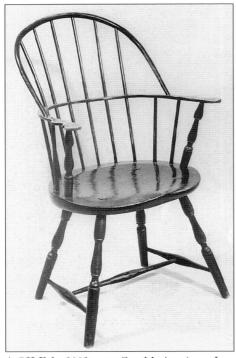

A-OH Feb. 2001   Garth's Auctions, Inc.

Windsor Sack Back Arm Chair, old blk. repaint w/ vase & ring turnings, well-shaped oval seat & scalloping on hand holds, wear & sm. pieced repr., 37" H. **$1,760**

A-MA Oct. 2001   Skinner, Inc.

Windsor Sack Back Chair, bl. painted, PA, ca. 1770-80, cut-out handholds on vase & ring-turned stiles, shaped seat on splayed base, old bl. paint, minor imper., 36¼" H. **$1,380**

A-MA Oct. 2001   Skinner, Inc.

Windsor Continuous Arm Chair, N.Y., ca. 1780-90, vase & ring-turned supports on shaped saddle seat w/ tail piece & splayed vase and ring-turned legs, old red paint over earlier gr., minor imper., 35¼" H. **$2,185**

A-PA Sept. 2001   Pook & Pook, Inc.

Comb Back Windsor Arm Chair, ca. 1790, New England, 41" H. **$1,900**

A-PA Feb. 2001   Pook & Pook, Inc.

Comb Back Windsor Chair, Phil. ca. 1770, retains later red/ brown painted surface. **$8,500**

A-PA Sept. 2001   Pook & Pook, Inc.

Brace Back / Fan Back Windsor Arm Chair, Nantucket, MA, ca. 1775, restored. **$1,700**

A-PA June 2001   Pook & Pook, Inc.

Windsor Sack Back Arm Chairs, CT, ca. 1790, retaining worn
varnished finish. **$7,500**

A-PA June 2001   Pook & Pook, Inc.

Windsor Chairs, PA w/ bamboo turnings, ca. 1810, 5 side &
one arm chair. **$950**

A-PA Sept. 2001   Pook & Pook, Inc.

Bow Back Windsor Chairs, PA, assembled set of 8 incl. 2 arm chairs & 6 side, all
retaining black painted surface. **$5,000**

A-OH Apr. 2001   Garth's Auctions, Inc.

Ladder Back High Chair, dark green w/
traces of earlier green, worn woven tape
seat. Small hole in center slat & poss.
repair to bottom slat, seat 20½" H, 38¼"
H. **$3,850**

A-PA Feb. 2001   Pook & Pook, Inc.

Balloon Back Dining Chairs, PA, set of 6 w/ fruit and butterfly stenciled decor. on a brown grained surface w/ yellow & green pinstriping, ca. 1870. **$1,400**

A-PA May 2001   Horst Auction Center

Chairs, set of 6, sgn. "J. Swint, Chairmaker", Lancaster, PA, w/ reddish-brown ground, black graining, yellow striping w/ stenciled fruit on crest. **$1,250**

A-MA Oct. 2001   Skinner, Inc.

Settee, PA, ca. 1825-35, painted & dec., shaped crest, curving arms, rolled plank seat, ring-turned legs, orig. yel. ground paint w/ fruit and leaf olive-gr. dec. w/ bl. & gr. striping, all orig. paint & dec. 78½" W, 34" H. **$3,737**

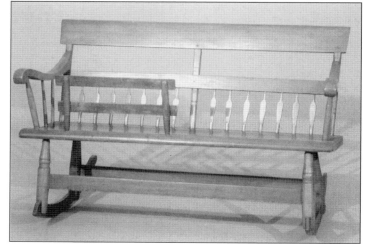

A-SC Sept. 2001   Charlton Hall Galleries, Inc.

Windsor Nanny's Bench, Am., mixed wood, ca. 1840, 48½" L. **$500**

A-OH Feb. 2001   Garth's Auctions, Inc.

Windsor Comb Back Rocking Chair w/ decor., branded initials "A S" under seat, orig. mustard paint w/ stenciled fruit dec. on crests, br. & blk. line detail, wear to paint but finely crafted, 44¼" H. **$935**

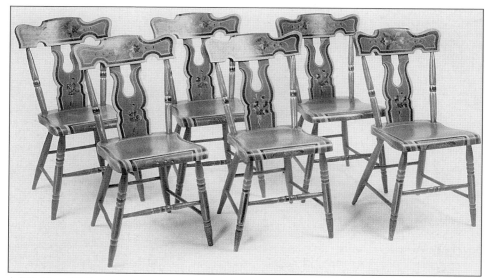

A-MA Mar. 2001   Skinner, Inc.

Side Chairs, set of six, polychrome painted, PA, ca. 1840-50, plank seats w/ rolled seat rails on front legs, & turned back legs, mustard-colored paint w/ floral dec. crests & splats w/ blk. & yel. accents, some paint enhanced, 33" H. **$1,955**

A-NC July 2001   Robert S. Brunk Auction Services, Inc.

Ladder Back High Chair, maple & hickory constr., later woven seat, old ref., 38" H. **$450**
Windsor High Chair, bentwood back w/ spindle supports, blk. paint, one spindle repr., 32" H. **$325**
Ladder Back High Chair, traces of old red paint, worn rounds, later woven seat, losses to arms, separations cracks, 34" H. **$325**

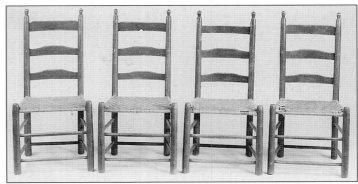

A-MA Oct. 2001   Skinner, Inc.

Side Chairs, set of four, red stained slat back, late 18th C., ring-turned stiles w/ urn finials above woven splint seats, orig. red stained surface, imperf., 38" H. **$805**

A-SC March 2001   Charlton Hall Galleries, Inc.

Hoop Back Windsor Side Chair, Am., ca. 1860. **$200**
Windsor Side Chair, Am., ca. 1840, w/ shaped top rail & plank seat. **$300**
Windsor Arm Chair, Am., ca. 1830, w/ shaped back rest on plank seat. **$425**
Windsor Claw Back Side Chair, Am., ca. 1850, w/ plank seat. **$160**

A-NC July 2001   Robert S. Brunk Auction Services, Inc.

Arm Chair, DE Valley, 18th C., repl. seat, old ref., 44½" H. **$2,500**

A-NH Aug. 2001   Northeast Auctions

Comb Back Writing Arm Chair in black paint. **$9,500**

A-NC July 2001   Robert S. Brunk Auction Services, Inc.

Windsor Comb Back Arm Chair, scrolled ears, shaped seat, multiple paint history, traces orig. gr. paint, old ref., 44" x 23½" x 22". **$4,200**

A-PA May 2001   Horst Auction Center

Side Chair, New England, painted yellow w/ black striping & gold banding, wear. **$90**
Table, pine w/ single board top, 2 drawers, 23" x 21" x 29¼" H. **$190**
Slipper Chair w/ yellowish-brown grain painted decor. **$40**

A-PA May 2001   Horst Auction Center

Sheraton Washstand, 19th C., PA, w/ early finish, some wear. 34½" H. **$450**
Rocker, PA, w/ plank seat, orig. brown paint w/ yellow striping & black banding. **$90**

A-MA Oct. 2001   Skinner, Inc.

Windsor Sack Back Chair, dk. stain, New England, ca. 1780, shaped handholds on carved saddle seat, ring-turned legs joined by swelled stretchers, 39¾" H. **$2,645**

A-PA May 2001   Horst Auction Center

Sack Back Windsor Rocking Chair, 18th C., w/ dark brown paint. **$2,300**

A-PA Sept. 2001   Pook & Pook Inc.

Sack Back Windsor Arm Chair, RI, ca. 1790, retains blackpainted surface. **$1,500**

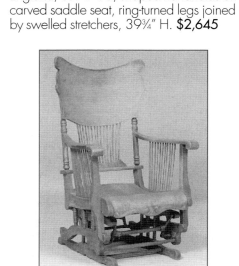

A-IA Dec. 2001   Jackson's International
                                    Auctioneers

Oak Rocker, ca. 1900 w/ spindle back & arms supported on glider base, 41" H. **$172**

A-IA Apr. 2001 Gene Harris Auction Center

Swivel Office Chair, w/mixed woods, & pressed floral design on back. **$250**

A-PA May 2001   Horst Auction Center

Sack Back Windsor Chair, late 18th C., w/ early dark red paint over earlier gray, over earlier green, left arm post broken at base. **$3,000**

A-NH May, 2001   Northeast Auctions

Q.A. Highboy, NH, tiger maple, in two parts, 75" H., lower case 38" W. **$17,000**

A-PA Apr. 2001   Pook & Pook, Inc.

Chippendale Highboy, DE Valley, walnut, ca. 1780, two-part, cabriole legs, ball & claw feet, highly figured drawer fronts, retain orig. bail & rosette brasses, 40" W, 73½" H. **$8,500**

A-SC March 2001   Charlton Hall Galleries, Inc.

High Chest of Drawers, Q.A., CT, cherry, ca. 1790, in two parts, 75" H, 41¼" W. **$23,000**

A-PA Nov. 2001   Conestoga Auction Company

Chest-on-Chest, Chippendale, New Eng., ca. 1760-1790, figured maple, hdw. repl. & some rest. to feet, 89" H, 40" W. **$9,900**

A-PA Apr. 2001   York Town Auction, Inc.

Chippendale Chest-on-Chest, walnut, Philadelphia. **$19,000**

A-NH Aug. 2001   Northeast Auctions

Highboy, N.H., attrib. to Dunlap Family, two parts, maple w/ carving, 87" H, 38¼" W, 18½" D. **$75,000**

A-NC July 2001   Robert S. Brunk Auction
Services, Inc.

High Chest, NC, late 18th C., birch, dov.
drawers, ogee bracket feet, poplar & yel.
pine secondary wood, brass pulls, old
ref., 76¾" H x 42½" W. **$60,000**

A-NH Nov. 2001   Northeast Auctions

Chippendale Tall Chest, tiger maple,
New England, 56½" H, 39½" W, 20"
D. **$16,000**

A-PA Nov. 2001   Conestoga Auction
Company

Chippendale Chest of Drawers, PA,
dovetailed const., fluted quarter columns,
ogee bracket feet, 61½" H, 43" W,
21½" D. **$6,325**

A-NY Nov. 2000   Hesse Galleries

Chest of Drawers, walnut w/ fluted corner
columns, dovetailed case & ogee bracket
feet. 61⅝" H. **$4,290**

A-PA May 2001   Horst Auction Center

Chest of Drawers, PA, early 20th C.,
walnut, top drawers have Quaker locks
(wooden strips mounted on the bottom of
drawer which are pushed up to open
drawer), front & sides of molded cornice
has band of herringbone inlay flanked by
inlaid stringing, 48½" W, 24½" D, 68¼"
H. **$3,800**

A-PA Apr. 2001   Pook & Pook, Inc.

Chippendale Chest-on-Chest, N.Y., ca.
1780, mah., upper section w/ dentil
molded cornice, blind fretwork frieze,
short cabriole front legs, ball & claw feet,
46½" W., 78¾" H. **$8,000**

A-PA May 2001   **Horst Auction Center**

Chest of Drawers, Empire, w/ reddish-orange feather-like grain painted decor., 41½" W, 46" H. **$500**

A-MA Oct. 2001   **Skinner, Inc.**

Bureau, mah. & mah. veneer, North Shore area, MA., 1820s, the top w/ attached scrolled backsplash, reeded columns, cock-beaded veneered drawers, turned tapered feet w/ casters, old ref., orig. pulls, minor height loss & imperf., 44½" W, 49" H. **$805**

A-NC July 2001   **Robert S. Brunk Auction Services, Inc.**

Chest, NC, ca. 1795-1830, inlaid walnut on frame, dov. drawers, yel. pine secondary wood, trifid feet, orig. brass pulls, old ref., restor., reprs. & losses, 43¾" x 42". **$18,000**

A-NH Mar. 2001   **Northeast Auctions**

Sheraton Stepback Chest, ME, painted & rosewood grain dec. w/ gr. & yel. highlights, w/ backsplash, 43" W, 51" H. **$1,100**

A-NH Aug. 2001   Northeast Auctions

Chippendale Reverse-Serpentine Chest of Drawers, MA, cherry, 34½" H., 39½" W., 22" D. **$16,500**

A-NH May, 2001   Northeast Auctions

Chippendale Blockfront Chest, New England, carved mahogany w/ shell drop on short cabriole legs ending in claw & ball feet, 30" W., 31" H. **$18,000**

A-NC July 2001   Robert S. Brunk Auction Services, Inc.

Chest, NC, walnut, ca. 1830, cockbeaded drawers, Fr. feet, yel. pine & poplar secondary woods, extensive barber pole inlay, red crayon loops on drawer backs & sides, orig. oval brasses w/ fan designs, attrib. to Swisegood School, lacking locks, backboards reattached, minor surface flaws, ref., 42" x 36¾" x 19". **$40,000**

A-OH Nov. 2001   Garth's Auctions, Inc.

Empire Chest of Drawers, cherry, pine & poplar w/ bird's eye maple veneer drawer fronts, imper., 52½" H, 42" W. **$1,155**

A-IA Dec. 2001   Jackson's International
Auctioneers

Sheraton Maple Chest of Drawers, ca.
1820 w/ orig. hardware, 43" W, 49" H.
$805

A-SC Dec. 2001   Charlton Hall
Galleries, Inc.

Bow-front Chest of Drawers, Georgian,
mah., mid 19th C., w/ bowed top, 50"
H, 45" W, 22" D. **$1,700**

A-OH Aug. 2001   Garth's Auctions, Inc.

Chest, cherry & tiger maple, well-turned
feet w/ rope twist carvings, dov. drawers
w/ solid tiger maple fronts & turned
walnut drawer pulls, inset end panels, two-
board top, repl. feet and pulls 40" W,
50½" H. **$1,320**

A-NH Mar. 2001   Northeast Auctions

Blanket Chest, New England, putty painted & dec. two-drawer,
hinged top above case w/ two drawers on cut-out feet, dec. in
russet & ochre fans w/ faux-flame mahogany drawers, 36" W,
37" H. **$16,00**

A-PA Sept. 2001   Pook & Pook Inc.

Blanket Chest, New England, William & Mary, ca. 1750, pine,
retains old red painted surface, 42" H, 37" W. **$550**

A-PA May 2001   Horst Auction Center

Bow-Front Bureau, late 19th C., veneered cherry w/ inlaid stringing, scalloped skirt w/ half round inlaid fan design in center, solid sides, 40½" W, 40" H. **$2,700**

A-CA June 2001   Butterfields

Bow-Front Chest, Federal, tiger maple w/ inlay, New England, ca. 1810, 39" W., 35" H. **$5,875**

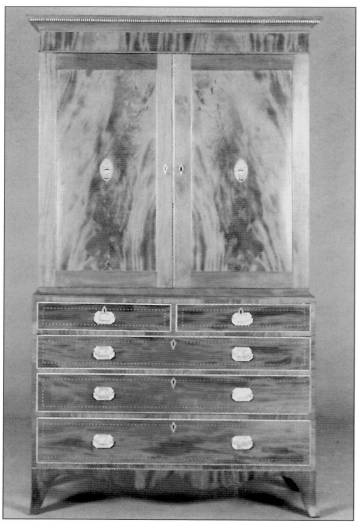

A-NH Aug. 2001   Northeast Auctions

Linen Press, Federal, NJ, mah., two parts w/ contrasting striped banding over case w/ eagle & shield brasses, 88" H, 48" W. **$11,500**

A-PA Apr. 2001   Pook & Pook, Inc.

Linen Press, New Jersey, Q.A., gumwood, ca. 1780, applied arched panels, flanked by applied arched panel pilasters, scalloped bracket feet, 48½" W, 72" H. **$4,500**

A-PA June 2001   Pook & Pook, Inc.

Schrank, Lancaster Co., PA, ca. 1790, walnut w/ orig. brass "H" hinges, removable stepped cove cornice, 93¾" H, 84" W, 24½" D. **$15,000**

A-PA Sept. 2001   Pook & Pook Inc.

Linen Press, NJ, Chippendale, gumwood, ca. 1770, 2 parts, 73" H, 48¼" W. **$10,000**

A-PA Nov. 2001   Conestoga Auction Company

Wardrobe, OH, softwood w/ feather grain painted decor., int. w/ shelves & pegs, ornate applied brass urn, grape, fruit & leaf key escutcheons, 86" H, 68½" W & 23" D. **$7,150**

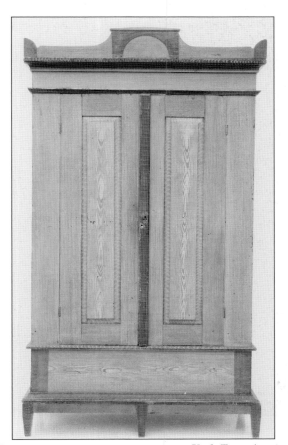

A-PA June 2001   York Town Auction, Inc.

Mennonite Wardrobe w/ original yellow graining. **$1,650**

A-Feb. 2001   Skinner, Inc.

Shaker Blanket Chest, w/ grain paint to simulate exotic wood, repl. pulls, surface imper., New Lebanon, NY, 1830-40, 36″ H, 40½″ W, 18½″ D. **$1,265**

A-NC July 2001   Robert S. Brunk Auction Services, Inc.

Pie Safe, TN, walnut, poplar secondary, dov. drawers, urn & grape punched tins w/ stars, finish losses, rodent chew, repl. hinge work, 48½″ x 53″ x 19″. **$2,900**

A-PA Nov. 2001   Pook & Pook, Inc.

Kas, PA, pine & poplar, ca. 1790, upper hinges repl., 50″ W, 79″ H. **$7,000**

A-NC July 2001   Robert S. Brunk Auction Services, Inc.

Chest, TN, 19th C., walnut, w/ dov. drawers, full-turned baluster columns, mortise-and-tenon constr., back w/ poplar boards w/ orig. cut nails, 48″ x 45″ x 21½″. **$1,600**

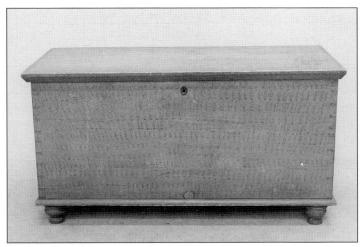

A-PA May 2001   Horst Auction Center

Blanket Chest, mid-19th C., w/ overall reddish-orange sponge decor, 44" x 22½" x 24¼" H. **$975**

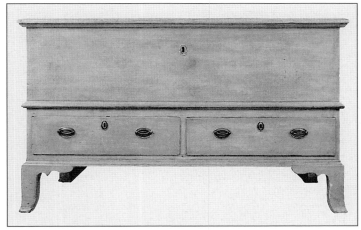

A-PA Nov. 2001   Conestoga Auction Company

Blanket Chest, PA., w/ orange & red paint, dovetail const., interior w/ wrought iron strap hinges & jaw lock, lid to till missing. 31½" H, 50" W. **$770**

A-PA June 2001   Pook & Pook, Inc.

Blanket Chest, Chippendale, PA, walnut, 18th C., w/ dovetailed case, dated 1794 over initials "E.M.", embellished with inlays, 31" H, 48" W, feet restored. **$5,750**

A-PA Apr. 2001   Pook & Pook, Inc.

Painted Dower Chest, PA, poplar, late 18th C., floral & tulip trees red & gr. pots on white ground, central panel w/ similar dec. on salmon ground, all on gr. reserve, minor rest., fitted w/ removable shoe feet, 47" W, 23" H. **$6,400**

A-NC July 2001   Robert S. Brunk Auction Services, Inc.

Blanket Chest, walnut, lidded till, two dov. drawers, orig. iron strap hinges, dov. bracket feet, yel. pine secondary wood, old ref., repl. pulls, lacking orig. lock, 31" x 49" x 22". **$1,900**

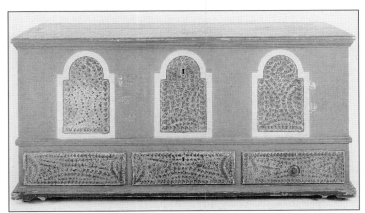

A-PA Nov. 2001   Pook & Pook, Inc.

Dower Chest, PA, dec. pine, ca 1800, w/ lift lid over case w/ blue sponged panels, trimmed in white, red sponged ground, 3 drawers w/ blue sponged surfaces, back of lock signed "W. Clewell", lacks feet, 48" w, 24" H. **$4,250**

A-PA Apr. 2001   York Town Auction, Inc.

Dutch Cupboard, Lancaster Co., PA. w/ orig. painted decor. **$12,000**

A-PA May 2001   Horst Auction Center

Chippendale Dutch Cupboard, late 18th C., Lancaster Co., PA, dovetailed const., w/ candle drawers, hand wrought iron rat tail hinges, repairs to molding, refinished & interior repainted, 66" W, 22½" D, 86½" H. **$24,000**

A-PA Sept. 2001   Pook & Pook Inc.

Chippendale Dutch Cupboard, PA, cherry, ca. 1790, 2 parts, feet rest., 84" H, 51½" W. **$8,500**

A-PA Nov. 2001   Conestoga Auction Company

Dutch Cupboard, PA, Chippendale, w/ grain paint, minor restor. to the orig. ogee bracket feet, 85" H, 67" W, 23" D. **$27,500**

A-PA Sept. 2001   Pook & Pook Inc.

Pennsylvania Chippendale Wall Cupboard, walnut, ca. 1780, two sections, 87" H, 64" W. **$12,000**

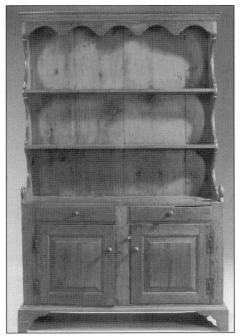

A-SC Sept. 2001   Charlton Hall
                                        Galleries, Inc.

Stepback Cupboard, Am. pine, ca.
1850, 75" H, 45" W, 17" D. **$1,100**

A-SC March 2001   Charlton Hall
                                        Galleries, Inc.

Stepback Cupboard, Am., pine, ca.
1870, 83" H, 50½" W, 23" D. **$1,700**

A-MA Feb. 2001   Skinner, Inc.

Stepback Cupboard, PA or Ohio, ca.
1830-40, w/ all-over old red paint, brass
pulls old, imper., 88" H, 50" W. **$18,400**

A-NH Aug. 2001
                            Northeast Auctions

Chippendale Stepback Cupboard, PA pine, two sections, 75"
H, 54" W. **$5,000**

A-OH Feb. 2001   Garth's Auctions, Inc.

Dutch Cupboard, OH, two sections, pine, poplar & walnut w/
original brown grain decor. Wear to paint. 50½" W, 20" D,
89¼" H. **$3,575**

A-PA Nov. 2001   Conestoga Auction Company

Corner Cupboard, tiger maple, w/ shaped bracket feet, 79" H, 45" W. **$4,510**

A-SC Dec. 2001   Charlton Hall Galleries, Inc.

Corner Cabinet, Am. walnut, early 20th C., w/ scalloped bottom rail & bracket feet, 78¾" H, 40" W, 19" D. **$1,400**

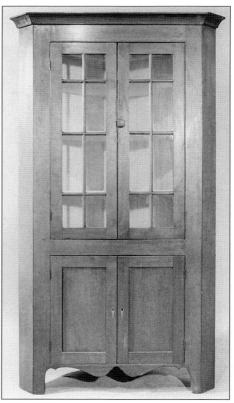

A-OH Feb. 2001   Garth's Auctions, Inc.

Corner Cupboard, cherry & poplar w/ old red wash, eight panes of glass in each door & repl. wooden pull, restor. to cornice, 42" W, 81¼" H. **$4,070**

A-PA Nov. 2001   Conestoga Auction Company

Corner Cupboard, PA., architectural w/ interior serpentine shelves, reeded stiles, softwood, 92½" H, 56" face. **$3,630**

A-PA May 2001   Horst Auction Center

Architectural Corner Cupboard, reworked early 19th C. PA, cherry, one-pc, refinished, 54" W, 32½" D, 92" H. **$5,000**

A-PA Nov. 2001   Pook & Pook, Inc.

Corner Cupboard, PA, painted cherry, ca. 1830, w/ orig. red paint, 48½" W, 90" H. **$9,000**

A-NY Nov. 2000   Hesse Galleries

Corner Cupboard, two sections, w/ interior shelves. 83¾" H. **$3,850**

A-OH Jan. 2001   Garth's Auctions, Inc.

Corner Cupboard, refinished cherry w/ three int. shelves, 40½" W, 78½" H. **$1,650**

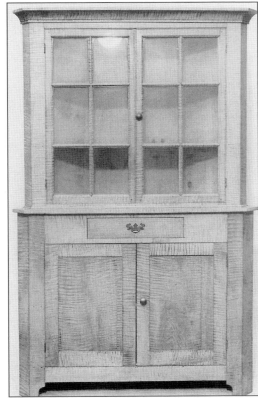

A-OH Aug. 2001   Garth's Auctions, Inc.

Corner Cupboard, two-piece tiger maple, good curl w/ mellow golden finish, pine secondary wood, 20th C., 46" W, 75¼" H. **$1,980**

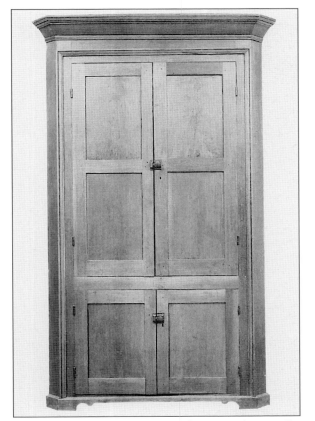

A-PA Nov. 2001   Conestoga Auction Company

Corner Cupboard, PA, w/ blind door, walnut, 89" H, 54" face. **$3,850**

A-PA Nov. 2001   **Conestoga Auction Company**

Corner Cupboard, PA, two sections, green painted surface, 86" H, 43" face. **$4,400**

A-NC July 2001   **Robert S. Brunk Auction Services, Inc.**

Corner Cupboard, NC, 19th C., lg. drawer flanked by two figured walnut panels, yel. pine secondary wood, old ref., losses to cornice, 54¼" W, 89¼" H. **$8,500**

A-PA Apr. 2001   **Pook & Pook, Inc.**

Corner Cupboard, PA, walnut, ca. 1795, molded cornice over keystone & rosette fascia, glazed door w/ H-hinges enclosing 2 scalloped shelves, straight bracket feet, 49½" W, 89" H. **$2,900**

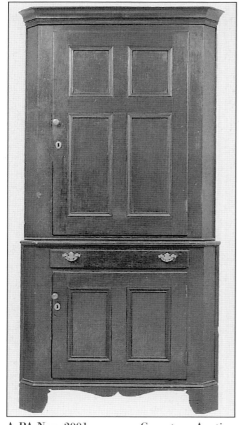

A-OH Apr. 2001   **Garth's Auctions, Inc.**

Hepplewhite Cupboard, two sections, Canadian, refinished pine w/ earlier red paint, glued splits in feet, case 48" W, cornice 52½" W, 78½" H. **$935**

A-Feb. 2001   **Skinner, Inc.**

Corner Cupboard, New England, pine, ca. 18th C., old refinish w/ old red interior on shelves, one side of cornice is replm., 88" H, 50" W, 20" D. **$4,830**

A-NC July 2001   **Robert S. Brunk Auction Services, Inc.**

Corner Cupboard, NC, walnut, reeded medial molding above doors, w/ chamfered figured walnut panels, scalloped shelves, orig. H brass hinges, old ref., flaws & losses, 90½" x 51". **$19,000**

A-MA Feb. 2001   Skinner, Inc.

Cupboard, pine & cherry, probably New England, early 19th C. Int. includes 21 scratchbeaded drawers & 7 compartments over 3 shelves, early red paint & surface imperfections, 59" H, 27¾" W, 11¼" D. **$4,370**

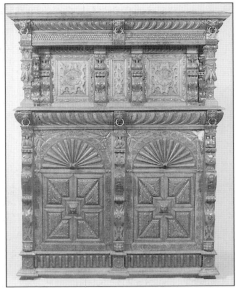

A-SC Dec. 2001   Charlton Hall
                                        Galleries, Inc.

Continental Cabinet on Cabinet, carved oak, third quarter 19th C., some reprs. & restor., some missing molding, 84¼" H, 64" W, 23" D. **$1,800**

A-IA Apr. 2001 Gene Harris Auction Center

Oak Kitchen Cupboard w/ leaded glass panes, ca. 1910. **$425**

A-IA June 2001   Jackson's International
                                  Auctioneers

Oak China Closet w/ curved glass on sides & door. Orig. finish, 48" W, 7½" H. **$3,680**

A-SC June 2001   Charlton Hall
                                        Galleries, Inc.

Stained Glass Cabinet, Eng. oak, ca. 1890, 88½" H, 43" W, 21" D. **$650**

A-NC July 2001   Robert S. Brunk Auction Services, Inc.

Jelly Cupboard, GA, yel. pine, nailed drawer above two paneled doors, cut nails, later blue paint, losses, separations & reprs., 49" x 41" x 18". **$800**

A-NC July 2001   Robert S. Brunk Auction Services, Inc.

Pie Safe, TN, mid 19th C., walnut, mortise & tenon constr., w/ poplar backboards, ref., rust, 56½" x 58½". **$3,200**

A-NC July 2001   Robert S. Brunk Auction Services, Inc.

Pie Safe, TN, w/ twelve tin panels, cherry, dov. drawer, back w/ tongue-and-groove boards, ref., some replm., 60½" x 46½" x 17". **$1,400**

A-OH Aug. 2001   Garth's Auctions, Inc.

Southern Pie Safe, cherry w/ old dk. varnish, poplar & yel. pine secondary wood. attrib. to Washington County, VA, the orig. Rich Brothers punched tins, dk. red over earlier gr. paint on all tins, turned legs, two dov. drawers at top, 51" W, 46½" H. **$3,300**

A-NC July 2001   Robert S. Brunk Auction Services, Inc.

Sideboard, TN, 19th C., cherry, dov. drawers, chamfered panels, wooden pulls, inlaid kite escut., tongue-and-groove poplar backboards w/ orig. cut nails, ref., minor finish flaws, some stains, 43" x 63" x 20". **$3,900**

A-SC March 2001   Charlton Hall Galleries, Inc.

Sideboard, walnut, Piedmont, SC, ca. 1795-1810, body fitted & flanked by two wine drawers; raised on six tapered legs, 40½" H, 65⅝" L. **$7,500**

A-NH Mar. 2001   Northeast Auctions

Hepplewhite Sideboard, Am., inlaid mahogany, N.Y. or N.J., serpentine front & ovolu corners, conforming case of drawers & cupboard doors, sq. tapered legs w/ flame birch inlaid panels, 71" L, 41" H. **$15,000**

A-SC June 2001   Charlton Hall Galleries, Inc.

Victorian Sideboard, carved walnut w/ marble-top, ca. 1870, 81" H, 51" W, 23" D. **$2,600**

A-NC July 2001   Robert S. Brunk Auction Services, Inc.

Sideboard, VA, ca. 1795-1805, inlaid mah., top w/ lt. wood string inlay at corners, center legs diamond shaped w/ string inlay, white pine & poplar secondary woods, orig. pulls, surface stains & flaws, veneer losses, 39¼" x 74" x 31½". **$31,000**

A-PA May 2001   Horst Auctioneers

Spice Chest, walnut, 18th C. Chester Co., PA w/ a dart board in maple and red cedar inlay on door, solid sides, interior fittings include a single full length drawer across at top and bottom, w/ two drawers in the second & fourth tier, & three drawers in center tier. Dovetailed construction, 14¼" W, 10" D, 16" H. **$139,000**

A-MA Feb. 2001   Skinner, Inc.

Pine Paneled Wall Cupboard, New England, early 19th C. w/ all-over yellow & brown paint, orig. hdw. w/ imperf., 29¼" H, 28" W. **$12,500**

A-PA Apr. 2001   Pook & Pook, Inc.

Hanging Cupboard, PA, walnut, ca. 1730, wrt. iron butterfly hinges, door flanked by two secret compartments, automatically locking when door is locked, 26" W, 39" H. **$1,900**

A-PA Nov. 2001   Pook & Pook, Inc.

Hanging Wall Cupboard, PA, ca. 1800, inlaid walnut w/ molded cornice, line inlaid door, single drawer & shelf, scrolled sides, 15½" W, 28¼" H. **$6,750**

A-PA May 2001   Horst Auction Center

Chimney Cupboard, late 19th C., PA, refinished. 27" W, 16" D, 66" H. **$500**

A-NH Aug. 2001   Northeast Auctions

Apothecary Chest, New England, green painted case w/ 24" graduated grain painted drawers on bracket base, 54" H, 30" W, 17" D. **$7,000**

A-SC Dec. 2001 — Charlton Hall Galleries, Inc.

Left

Victorian Dresser & Mirror, Am., ca. 1865, marble-top serpentine front, marble has minor hairline cracks & chip on edge, 89" H, 84½" W, 25½" D. **$1,000**

A-SC Sept. 2001 — Charlton Hall Galleries, Inc.

Right

Victorian Dresser & Mirror, Am., mah., ca. 1865 w/ white & gray veined marble top, serpentine front, 90" H, 49" W, 23" D. **$900**

A-IA Apr. 2001 — Gene Harris Auction Center

Victorian Chest of Drawers w/ mirror, ash. **$200**
Victorian Dresser w/ mirror, ash w/ walnut trim. **$200**

A-IA Apr. 2001 — Gene Harris Auction Center

Left

Victorian 4 pc. Bedroom Set, walnut, inc. bed, wardrobe, dresser & commode. **$6,500**

A-IA Apr. 2001 Gene Harris Auction Center

Oak Hall Tree w/ beveled mirror & lift seat. **$1,300**

A-IA Apr. 2001 Gene Harris Auction Center

Drop-Front Writing Desk, cherry w/ hand carved details, brass trim. **$1,250**

A-IA June 2001 Jackson's International Auctioneers

Spool Cabinet / Countertop Desk w/ pencil tray & ink well. Clark's Mile End Spool Cotton logo on drawer fronts, 29" L, 22" W, 14" H. **$603**

A-PA May 2001 Horst Auction Center

Wardrobe, PA, late 19th C., w/ grain painted decor., interior fitted w/ heavy round dowel for clothes & cast iron hook, 29½" wide, 78¼" H. **$250**

A-NY Nov. 2000 Hesse Galleries

Left
Sheraton Bow-Front Chest, in figured wood, decor. w/ carved flower pots. 41" W x 46" H. **$1,870**

A-SC June 2001 Charlton Hall Galleries, Inc.

Partner's Desk, George II style, walnut w/ serpentine shaped top & gilt tolled leather writing surface, 31" H, 66" W, 42" D. **$4,600**

A-PA Nov. 2001 Conestoga Auction Company

Desk, Chippendale, curly applewood, ca. 1770-1790, mid-Atlantic states, 42½" H, 45" W, 23½" D. **$3,520**

A-NH May, 2001   Northeast Auctions

Slant-Lid Desk, New England, tiger maple w/ fitted interior, shaped apron & bracket feet, 36" W., 42" H. **$6,500**

A-IA Apr. 2001   Gene Harris Auction Center

Secretary & Bookcase, quarter sawed oak w/ beveled mirror, 69" H, 47" W. **$1,600**

A-PA Sept. 2001   Pook & Pook Inc.

Chippendale Slant Front Desk, ca. 1790, Delaware Valley, ca. 1790, walnut w/ fitted interior, 43" H, 41" W. **$3,300**

A-NC July 2001   Robert S. Brunk Auction Services, Inc.

Sugar Desk, 19th C., cherry, hinged slant front w/ 3 int. dov. drawers w/ two compartments, dov. back panel w/ carved rosettes, orig. iron lock, old ref., reprs., separation in slant front, 43" x 45¾" x 24" . **$19,000**

A-OH Nov. 2001   Garth's Auctions, Inc.
Hepplewhite Secretary, mah. w/ mah. inlay, rest., 57" H, 35" W. **$2,530**

A-NH Nov. 2001   Northeast Auctions
Chippendale Blockfront Desk, New England, mahogany w/ fitted interior, 46" H, 44" W. **$35,000**

A-NH Mar. 2001   Northeast Auctions
Sheraton Secretary, NH, cherry, bird's eye maple & mahogany veneer, upper case w/ crossbanded hinged fall-front door, compartmented int. w/ drawers & cubbyholes. 40½" W, 50" H. **$4,250**

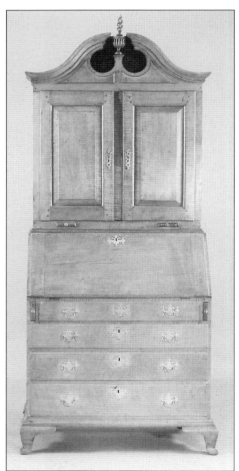

A-NH Mar. 2001   Northeast Auctions
Chippendale Slant-Lid Secretary, RI, tiger maple, two parts, 91" H, case width 37". **$70,000**

A-NC July 2001   Robert S. Brunk Auction Services, Inc.
Chest / Bookcase, NC, ca. 1790-1820, white pine secondary wood, orig. brass hinges, replm. & ref., 97¾" x 36¼" x 18¾". **$18,000**

A-NH Mar. 2001   Northeast Auctions
Secretary, MA, mahogany carved blockfront, int. w/ carved shells & compartments, all above candleslides, lower w/ thumb-molded lid w/ fan carving, stepped int. w/ fan carved prospect door & flanking document drawers, ball & claw feet, fitted w/ brass carrying handles, 41" W, 95" H. **$27,500**

A-SC Dec. 2001   Charlton Hall
Galleries, Inc.

Victorian Davenport Desk, Eng., walnut,
last quarter 19th C., w/ fitted interior,
leather inset top, side bank of four short
drawers, 34" H, 21" W, 21½" D. **$1,100**

A-PA Oct. 2001   York Town Auction, Inc.

Mahogany Secretary, ca. 1790, attrib. to
John Shaw, untouched condition. **$21,000**

A-NH Mar. 2001   Northeast Auctions

Chippendale Secretary, Am. walnut, two
part, interior w/ pigeonholes & drawers,
43¾" W, 83½" H. **$8,000**

A-PA Apr. 2001   Pook & Pook, Inc.

Writing Desk, New England, birch & maple, ca. 1800, upper
section opens to fitted int., base has fall front surface, tall straight
bracket feet, 29½" W, 48¾" H. **$2,900**

A-NH Aug. 2001   Northeast Auctions

Chippendale Secretary, NH, figured maple & birch, two parts,
66½" H, case width 42". **$10,500**

A-PA Nov. 2001   Conestoga Auction Company

Desk, Chippendale, ca. 1760-1790, cherry, w/ complex locks for secret compartments, 43½" H, 40½ " W, 23½" D. **$3,300**

A-OH Feb. 2001   Garth's Auctions, Inc.

Hepplewhite Slant Lid Desk, tiger maple, pine & poplar secondary woods, dovetailed case w/ walnut beading, orig. emb. beehive brasses. ten int. dov. drawers also w/ line inlay, sm. brass pulls, 11 pigeon holes w/ scalloped trim across tops, slight edge damage, one glue block missing, sm. feet pad added, 39½" W, 20" D, 43" H. **$12,100**

A-PA Nov. 2001   Conestoga Auction Company

Desk w/ slant lid, mahogany, transitional w/ interior drawers & compartments, original brass pulls & escutcheons, 43" H, 42½" W. **$2,860**

A-PA Sept. 2001   Pook & Pook Inc.

Chippendale Slant Front Desk, PA, walnut, ca. 1775, w/ interior fittings, old rest. to feet, 48" H, 38" W. **$2,000**

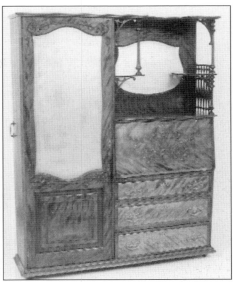

A-IA June 2001   Jackson's International Auctioneers

Victorian Cylinder Secretary, oak w/ orig. red felt writing surface, 36" W, 84" H. **$862**

A-IA Dec. 2001   Jackson's International Auctioneers

Oak Secretary Bookcase, ca. 1900, 65" W, 83" H. **$3,450**

A-IA June 2001   Jackson's International Auctioneers

Secretary / Wardrobe Combination, mahogany, 53" W, 71" H. **$805**

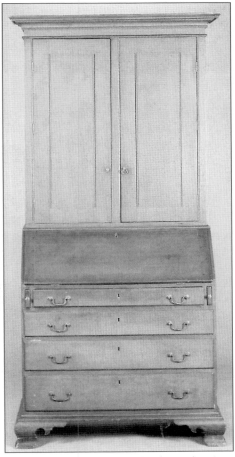

A-SC June 2001   Charlton Hall Galleries, Inc.

Secretaire/bookcase, Am. Fed., mah. 19th C., 79" H, 36½" W. **$4,400**

A-NC July 2001   Robert S. Brunk Auction Services, Inc.

Secretary, NC, walnut, ca. 1790-1810, cove on back for chair rail, ogee bracket feet w/ rounded returns, old ref., lt. wear on brass hinges, repl. & restor., finish flaws, 93" x 43½" x 23½". **$44,000**

A-NH Aug. 2001   Northeast Auctions

Chippendale Secretary, CT, cherry, two parts, fitted interior, 83" H, 36" W, 18" D. **$16,500**

A-NH Mar. 2001   Northeast Auctions

Hepplewhite Mirror, inlaid mahogany & giltwood w/ églomisé panel, giltwood swan's neck crest centering a raised floral urn over a frieze w/ inlaid shell medallion, shaped apron w/ elaborate scrolling, 56½" x 21½". **$2,500**

A-NH Mar. 2001   Northeast Auctions

Chippendale Mirror, mahogany & giltwood, swan's neck crest w/ giltwood scrolls w/ foliate terminals centering a phoenix over a frieze w/ applied oval beading, shaped apron, 65" x 28½". **$2,750**

A-NH Mar. 2001   Northeast Auctions

Chippendale Mirror, mahogany w/ giltwood, shaped & carved crest w/ giltwood foliate scrolls, stylized eagle above frame, mirror plate centered within flower & fruit pendants over an apron w/ incised leafage, 52½" x 24¾". **$3,000**

A-MA Mar. 2001   Skinner, Inc.

Chippendale Looking Glass, mah. & mah. veneer, Eng., late 18th C., gilt ho-ho bird above molded & parcel gilt mirror surrounds scrolling & inlaid pendant, rest., 21" W., 42" H. **$1,150**

Chippendale Looking Glass, mah. & mah. veneer inlaid, PA, early 19th C., pinecone-form ears over mirror glass in beaded frame inlaid w/ contrasting stringing above scrolling pendant, repl. glass, old ref., reprs., 19½" W., 39½" H. **$632**

Chippendale Looking Glass, mah. veneer & giltwood, ca. 1780, carved & gilt ho-ho bird above mirror glass, molded frame w/ incised gilt liner over scrolling pendant, mirror glass repl., regilding, imper., 22" W, 41" H. **$920**

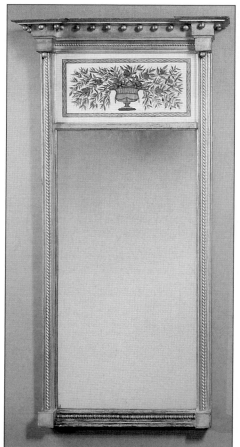

A-Apr. 2001   William Doyle Galleries

Federal Gilt-wood Looking Glass, labeled B. Cermenati, Portsmouth, 1812, 53½" H, 27" W. **$3,450**

A-NH Mar. 2001   Northeast Auctions

Shaving Mirror, Federal, mah. w/ mirror on ogee feet, 26″ H. **$1,750**

A-PA Feb. 2001   Pook & Pook, Inc.

Girondole Giltwood Mirror, ca 1790, Am. or Eng. 55″ L, 29″ W. **$8,000**

A-PA Sept. 2001   Pook & Pook Inc.

Chippendale Mirror, mah., ca. 1780, w/ elaborate scrolled crest & ears surrounding a gilded spread wing phoeniz, 39¼″ x 21″. **$1,600**

Chippendale Stool, mah. w/ upholstered top, resting on carved cabriole legs w/ ball & claw feet, 20″ H, 24″ W, 20″ D. **$250**
Queen Anne Stool, walnut w/ upholstered slip seat, resting on cabriole legs w/ pad feet, 17″ H, 22″ W, 17″ D. **$200**
Queen Anne Stool, walnut w/ upholstered top, early 20th C., resting on cabriole legs w/ pad feet, 19″ H, 26″ W, 17″ D. **$250**

A-SC June 2001   Charlton Hall Galleries, Inc.

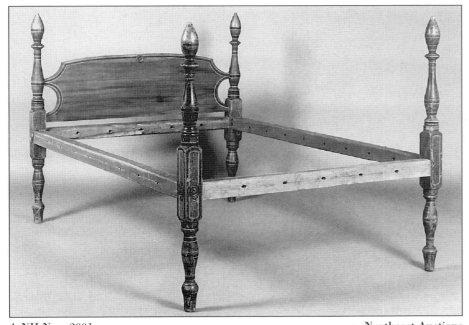

A-NH Nov. 2001   Northeast Auctions

Bedstead, Federal w/ grain painted decor. in deep red w/ green & yellow banded borders. 49½″ H, 54″ W. **$4,500**

A-IA June 2001   Jackson's International Auctioneers

Victorian Bed, walnut w/ applied carving, 56″ W, headboard 80″ H. **$517**

A-SC Dec. 2001   Charlton Hall
Galleries, Inc.

Regency Cellaret, mah., first quarter 19th C., w/ metal lined int. & brass handles, 32⅜" L, 24¾" W, 23" H. **$1,400**

A-IA June 2001   Jackson's International
Auctioneers

Grand Piano, Conover, walnut w/ Feb. 1876 to 1885 patent date. **$3,335**

A-MA Mar. 2001   Skinner, Inc.

Canterbury, Georgian mah. & mah. veneer, ca. 1780, ring-turned balusters joined by sq. rails on turned spindles, base w/ single drawer, casters, pulls orig., old ref., minor imper., 20" W, 14½" D, 21¼" H. **$2,185**

A-NH Mar. 2001   Northeast Auctions

Rococo Etagere, N.Y., elaborately carved rosewood by J. & J. Meeks, upper section arched cove molded & pierced dec. below elaborate carved crests, tripartite mirror backplate behind shelves, w/ foliate carved dec. overall, 72" W, 9½' H. **$58,000**

A-IA Apr. 2001   Gene Harris Auction Center

Drop Front Desk, mahogany, ca. mid-19th C., w/ incised & carved decor. 65½" H, 29¼" W. **$1,500**

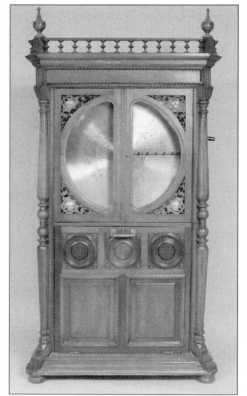

A-IA Dec. 2001   Jackson's International
Auctioneers

Mahogany Cased Regina Music Box, ca. 1898, in two sections for playing 27" discs w/ storage. orig. condition. 87" high. **$21,850**

A-PA Sept. 2001   Pook & Pook Inc.

Hepplewhite Banquet Table, 3-part, Am., ca. 1800, legs w/ stylized tulip inlay over 3 lower bellflowers & terminating in spade feet, 28½" H, 102" open. **$6,250**

A-SC Dec. 2001   Charlton Hall Galleries, Inc.

Gateleg Drop-leaf Breakfast Table, Am., mah., ca. 1800, 28¾" H, 48" W, 62¾" L. (open). **$450**

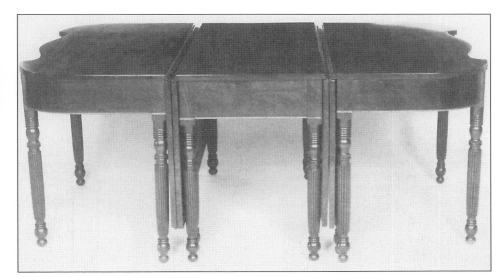

A-NH Aug. 2001   Northeast Auctions

Dining Table, New England, Sheraton, 3-part, mah., length 154" open. **$3,000**

A-NH Aug. 2001   Northeast Auctions

Dining Table, Regency, 3-pedestal, mah., molded legs w/ brass ferules on rollers & one additional leaf, 29" H, 50" W, 114" open. **$2,750**

A-NC July 2001   Robert S. Brunk Auction Services, Inc.

Chippendale Tea Table, NC, ca. 1770-1785, mah. w/ white pine secondary wood, carved open work in arch of ea. leg, egg & claw feet, some carving appears to be later, 8¾" x 33¼" x 32 7/8". **$15,000**

A-NH Aug. 2001   Northeast Auctions

Table, NY Classical, mah., w/ D-form hinged leaves, 28½" H, 40" L, depth closed 22". **$2,750**

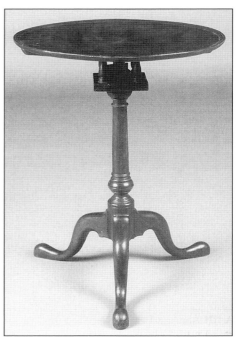

A-NH Nov. 2001   Northeast Auctions

Candlestand, Q.A., mah. w/ tilt top & birdcage, circular top has molded edge, 20" diam., 28" H. **$9,000**

A-NH May, 2001   Northeast Auctions

Dining Table, Am. Sheraton, mah. two-part w/ two additional leaves, 29" H., 41" W., length open 68". **$4,500**

A-Apr. 2001   William Doyle Galleries

Q.A. Tilt-top Candlestand, MA, Salem area, mah., w/ snake feet, top 22" x 15", 28" H. **$10,000**

Card Table, MA, mah. w/ bird's eye maple panels, 29" H, 36" W, 17" D. **$4,250**

Card Table, mah. & mah. veneer inlay, PA or Balt., ca. 1790, string inlaid edges w/ concave center & diamond-shaped inlaid dies, tapering feet w/ banded cuffs, ref., reprs., 35¾" W, 28" H. **$5,750**

Card Table, MA, Sheraton, inlaid mah. & flame birch w/ hinged top, 29" H. **$5,500**

Sheraton Card Table, MA, tiger maple veneer, rect. hinged top w/ bowed front & sides, outset corners above conforming apron, turned & reeded legs, 18½" x 36" top, 29½" H. **$7,750**

FURNITURE

A-SC March 2001   Charlton Hall Galleries, Inc.

Pembroke Table, Fed. mah., Charleston, SC, ca. 1810 w/ inlay, some veneer missing, 29" H., 22½" W. (closed). **$19,000**

A-NC July 2001   Robert S. Brunk Auction Services, Inc.

Pembroke Table, 19th C., Am., cherry, dov. drawer, top reset, old ref., 27" x 20" (opens to 40") x 32½". **$3,000**

A-NH Mar. 2001   Northeast Auctions

Chippendale Card Table, N.Y., mahogany, rect. hinged top above a frieze w/ long drawer, cabriole legs, ball & claw feet, 32" x 14¾" x 27½" H. **$6,000**

A-NH Mar. 2001   Northeast Auctions

Sheraton Card Table, New England, bird's eye maple & mahogany, folding top w/ shaped sides, turned & reeded leg tapering to feet, 36" W, 29½" H. **$1,600**

A-IA June 2001   Jackson's Antiques & Fine Art

Victorian Walnut Table w/ marble top w/ turned center post, carved skirt, 30" L, 21" W, 30" H. **$402**

A-MA Feb. 2001   Skinner, Inc.

Federal Candlestand, probably NH, ca. 1810, w/ exaggerated legs terminating in human feet, minor imper., old brown paint, 27" H, 15½" W, 16½" D. **$10,925**

A-NC July 2001   Robert S. Brunk Auction Services, Inc.

Stand, 19th C. style, inlaid birch & bird's eye maple, two dov. drawers, rebuilt, 29" x 18½" x 17". **$750**
Table, walnut, mortise-and-tenon constr., top w/ ovolo corners, dov. drawer, yel. pine & poplar secondary woods, top boards may be repl., old ref., 29¾" x 33½" x 23". **$550**
Stand, NC, walnut, dov. case & drawer, turned maple pedestal base, finish flaws & losses, minor reprs., 27¾" x 18¾" x 18¼". **$1,800**

A-PA May 2001   Horst Auction Center

Sheraton Table, cherry, w/ drop leaf, dovetailed drawers, 15½" W, 23" D, 26½" H. **$700**

A-NH Aug. 2001   Northeast Auctions

Hutch Table, NY, maple w/ trestle base w/ heart cut-outs, scrubbed top, box seat, base w/ remnants of red, 42" D. **$19,000**

A-PA Nov. 2001   Pook & Pook, Inc.

Tavern Table, Q.A., PA, walnut, ca. 1765, w/ rect. batten top over frame w/ 2 drawers, splayed turned legs, pad feet, old patch to top, 52" L, 35" D, 30½" H. **$5,000**

A-NH Mar. 2001   Northeast Auctions

Drop Leaf Table, MA, Sheraton, mahogany two-drawer, w/ turned & reeded legs, 18½" W, 28½" H. **$2,000**

Work Table, Salem, mahogany, attrib. to Samuel Field McIntire, outset corners, two short drawers, flowerhead carving on star-punched ground on rope-turned legs, 23" x 20" x 28" H. **$2,400**

A-MA Feb. 2001   Skinner, Inc.

Harvest Table, New England, early 19th C., pine w/ scrubbed top, imperf., 20½" H, 102½" L, 18" D. **$11,500**

A-NC July 2001   Robert S. Brunk Auction Services, Inc.

Tea Table, 18th C., cherry, two-board top, pad feet, mortise-and-tenon constr., traces orig. ora./red paint, various old stains on top, 26½" x 36¼" x 27½". **$10,500**

A-NH Aug. 2001   Northeast Auctions

Tea Table, New England, w/ black paint on raked cylindrical legs & off-center pad feet, 25" H, top 22" x 33". **$7,250**

A-CA June 2001   Butterfields

Q.A. Maple & Pine Tavern Table, painted base w/ molded box stretchers raised on baluster-turned feet, 22" H., 24" W., 19" D. **$10,575**

A-OH Aug. 2001   Garth's Auctions, Inc.

Stand, two drawer of tiger maple, golden varnished w/ pine secondary wood, well-turned tapered legs w/ raised ring cuffs, nailed drawers have turned pulls. **$468**

A-PA Nov. 2001   Conestoga Auction Company

Left

Work Table, walnut, Lancaster Co., PA, early 1800s, 30" H, 55½" W, 20" D. **$2,640**

A-NH Mar. 2001   Northeast Auctions

Huntboard, Federal, Moore County North Carolina, overall height 48 ", 51" L. **$11,000**

A-MA Feb. 2001   Skinner, Inc.

Pine Table, New England, late 18th C., w/ scrubbed pine top, single hinged leaf overhang & drawer w/ orig. pull, old dark brown paint, imperf., 29" H, 42½" W. **$6,325**

A-IA Apr. 2001 Gene Harris Auction Center
Oak Library Table, heavily carved w/
griffins at ends. 29½" H, 62" L & 38" W.
$2,500

A-IA Apr. 2001 Gene Harris Auction Center
Victorian Table, walnut w/ square top.
$650

A-IA Apr. 2001 Gene Harris Auction Center
Victorian Drop Leaf Table, walnut. **$250**

A-SC Dec. 2001   Charlton Hall Galleries, Inc.
Hepplewhite Bow-front Sideboard, mah., mid 19th C., w/
inlaid top, resting on tapering bellflower inlaid legs, 41" H, 62"
W, 21½" D. **$4,600**

A-PA Oct.2001   York Town Auction, Inc.
New England Ladder Back Side Chair, w/ rush seat. **$300**
New England Dressing Table, maple w/ decor. **$4,250**

A-Apr. 2001   William Doyle Galleries
Bowfront Server, Sheraton, MA, mah., 38½" L, 17¼" H. **$23,000**

A-PA May 2001   Horst Auction Center
Left to Right
Arrow Back Chair (half) w/ plank seat & remnants of orig. green
paint. **$250**
Table, Am. Empire, mahogany w/ mahogany veneer, top 16½"
x 20" X 29" H. **$275**
Arrow Back Rocker, ca. 1850, w/ reddish-brown paint, yellow
striping & green banding, wear. **$50**

A-MA May 2001   **Craftsman**
                               Auctions
Roycroft Bedroom Set, w/ bed,
dresser, vanity, chair, blanket
stand & waste basket. From
Roycroft Inn, ca. 1906. All
pieces marked w/ Roycroft Inn
registration numbers. **$15,000**

A-NJ May 2001   Craftsman

Limbert Sideboard w/ plate-rail & good orig. finish, branded mark, 38½" x 60" x 22½" **$4,500**

A-MA May, 2001   Craftsman

Stickley Brothers Sideboard, in untouched original finish, 45" x 72" x 24". **$5,500**

A-NJ May 2001   Craftsman

L. & J.G. Stickley China Cabinet w/ hammered copper pulls, orig. finish, co-joined mark, 62" x 44" x 16¼" **$8,000**

A-NJ May 2001   Craftsman

L. & J.G. Stickley Two-door Bookcase, w/ gallery top, cleaned orig. finish, 56" x 39½" x 12¾". **$5,000**

A-MA May, 2001   Craftsman

Roycroft Waste Basket, mah., fine refinish, w/ carved orb. 16" x 13½". **$1,750**

A-MA May, 2001   Craftsman

Gustav Stickley Blanket Box, w/ iron hardware & dov. sides, enhanced finish, brand & paper label, 17¼" x 36" x 22". **$4,000**

A-NJ May 2001   Craftsman

Stickley Bros. Teacart w/ removable glass-topped tray lined w/ embroidered fabric, orig. finish, branded, 30¾" x 34" x 19" **$1,300**

A-NJ May 2001   Craftsman

L. & J.G. Stickley Table, gate-leg dropleaf, orig. finish, branded, 30" x 42" x 42" (open) **$2,500**

A-NJ Jan 2001   Craftsman

L. & J. G. Stickley Hat Box Dresser, w/ backsplash & wooden pulls, ref. 49¾" x 36" x 28". **$3,500**

A-NJ Jan 2001   Craftsman

Gustav Stickley Table, hex. w/ orig. tacked-on leather top, orig. finish, sm. chip to inside of leg, leather in excellent condition, mid-period & first paper label, 30" x 55" diam. **$20,000**

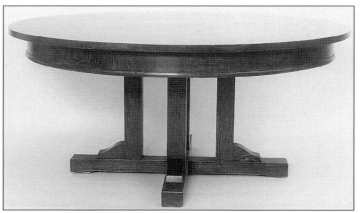

A-MA March, 2001   Craftsman

Roycroft Dining Table, round w/ carved orb, orig. finish w/ overcoat, top enhanced, 28½" x 60". **$6,325**

A-MA May, 2001   Craftsman

Stickley Brothers Sideboard, untouched orig. finish. Quaint tag, 45" x 72" x 25". **$6,500**

A-MA May, 2001   Craftsman

Roycroft Bookcase, w/ Dard Hunter design leaded glass doors, orig. finish w/ lt. overcoat, carved orb, 49¼" x 52" x 17¼". **$10,500**

A-NJ May 2001   Craftsman

Bookcase, Arts & Crafts, Eng., w/ inlaid tulips in pewter, ebony & fruitwood, leaded glass panels w/ treen tear-shaped inserts, orig. finish, 52½" x 46" x 12½". **$2,300**

A-MA May, 2001   Craftsman

Gustav Stickley Bookcase, w/ mitered mullions, orig. finish, very good color, early box sig., 56" x 49" x 12". **$9,000**

FURNITURE

A-MA March, 2001   Craftsman

Left

Old Hickory Rocker, w/ spindled sides, orig. finish, slightly weathered & loose, branded, 36" x 25" x 20". **$460**

A-MA May, 2001   Craftsman

Right

Gustav Stickley Willow Chair, w/ orig. finish, unsigned, 32" x 31" x 27". **$3,600**

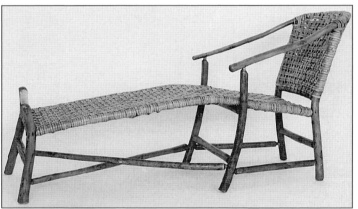

A-MA March, 2001   Craftsman

Porch Swing, child's sized w/ orig. finish, some bark separation & reed brittleness, arms loose, 16" x 30" x 17". **$230**

A-MA March, 2001   Craftsman

Old Hickory Lounge Chair, w/ orig. finish, minor water damage at feet, branded, 33" x 54" x 22". **$1,955**

A-NJ May 2001   Craftsman

Gustav Stickley Arm Chairs & Ottoman, wicker, loose cushions w/ minor breaks in caning & some unravelling at feet, unmkd., largest 41½" x 30¼" x 21" **$4,500**

Charles Stickley Settle, restoration to one post, fine refinish, repl. leather branded, 39" x 84" x 32". **$4,750**

Gustav Stickley Morris Chair, w/ bow arms, untouched orig. finish, some loss, replaced leather, 37" x 30" x 36". **$11,000**

Gustav Stickley Morris Chair, w/ newly upholstered loose cushions, ref., unmkd. 40" x 28" x 34" **$5,000**

Gustav Stickley Dining Side Chairs, rabbit-ear w/ new tacked-on leather seats, reprs. to legs, unmkd. **$4,750**

L. & J.G. Stickley Even-arm Settle w/ drop-in spring seat, orig. finish, reupholstered seat, unmkd. 34" x 76½" x 31" **$5,500**

L. & J.G. Stickley Morris Chair, in orig. finish, signed "Handcraft". **$23,000**

GLASS

Agata Glass was patented by Joseph Locke of the New England Glass Company of Cambridge, Massachusetts, in 1877. The application of a metallic stain left a mottled design characteristic of agata, hence the name.

Amber Glass is the name of any glassware having a yellowish-brown color. It became popular during the last quarter of the 19th century.

Amberina Glass was patented by the New England Glass Company in 1833. It is generally recognized as a clear yellow glass shading to a deep red or fuchsia at the top. When the colors are opposite, it is known as reverse amberina. It was machine-pressed into molds, free blown, cut and pattern molded. Almost every glass factory here and in Europe produced this ware, however, few pieces were ever marked.

Amethyst Glass – The term identifies any glassware made in the proper dark purple shade. It became popular after the Civil War.

Art Glass is a general term given to various types of ornamental glass made to be decorative rather than functional. It dates primarily from the late Victorian period to the present day and, during the span of time, glassmakers have achieved fantastic effects of shape, color, pattern, texture and decoration.

Aventurine Glass The Venetians are credited with the discovery of aventurine during the 1860s. It was produced by various mixes of copper in yellow glass. When the finished pieces were broken, ground or crushed, they were used as decorative material by glassblowers. Therefore, a piece of aventurine glass consists of many tiny glittering particles on the body of the object, suggestive of sprinkled gold crumbs or dust. Other colors in aventurine are known to exist.

Baccarat Glass was first made in France in 1756, by La Compagnie des Cristelleries de Baccarat—until the firm went bankrupt. Production began for the second time during the 1820s and the firm is still in operation, producing fine glassware and paperweights. Baccarat is famous for its earlier paperweights made during the last half of the 19th century.

Bohemian Glass is named for its country of origin. It is ornate, overlay, or flashed glassware, popular during the Victorian era.

Bristol Glass is a lightweight opaque glass, often having a light bluish tint, and decorated with enamels. The ware is a product of Bristol, England—a glass center since the 1700s.

Burmese – Fredrick Shirley developed this shaded art glass at the now-famous old Mt. Washington Glass Company in New Bedford, Massachusetts, and patented his discovery under the name of "Burmese" on December 15, 1885. The ware was also made in England by Thomas Webb & Sons. Burmese is a hand-blown glass with the exception of a few pieces that were pattern molded. The latter are either ribbed, hobnail or diamond quilted in design. This ware is found in two textures or finishes: the original glazed or shiny finish, and the dull, velvety, satin finish. It is a homogeneous single-layered glass that was never lined, cased, or plated. Although its color varies slightly, it always shades from a delicate yellow at the base to salmon-pink at the top. The blending of colors is so gradual that it is difficult to determine where a color ends and the other begins.

Cambridge glasswares were produced by the Cambridge Glass Company in Ohio, from 1901 until the firm closed in 1954.

Cameo Glass can by defined as any glass in which the surface has been cut away to leave a design in relief. Cutting is accomplished by the use of hand-cutting tools, wheel cutting and hydrofluoric acid. This ware can be clear or colored glass of a single layer, or glass with multiple layers of clear or colored glass.

Although cameo glass has been produced for centuries, the majority available today dates from the late 1800s. It has been produced in England, France and other parts of Europe, as well as the United States. The most famous of the French masters of cameo wares was Emile Gallé.

Carnival Glass was an inexpensive, pressed iridescent glassware made from about 1900 through the 1920s. It was made in quantities by Northwood Glass Company, Fenton Art Glass Company and others, to compete with the expensive art glass of the peroid. It was

originally called "taffeta" glass during the 1920s, when carnivals gave examples as premiums or prizes.

Chocolate Glass, sometimes mistakenly called caramel slag because of its streaked appearance, was made by the Indiana Tumbler & Goblet Company of Greentown, IN, from 1900 to 1903. It was also made by the National Glass Company factories, and later by Fenton from 1907 to 1915.

Consolidated Lamp & Glass Co. of Coraopolis, PA, was founded in 1894 and closed in 1967. The company made lamps, art glass and tablewares. Items made after 1925 are of the greatest interest to collectors.

Coralene – The term coralene denotes a type of decoration rather than a kind of glass—consisting of many tiny beads, either of colored or transparent glass—decorating the surface. The most popular design used resembled coral or seaweed, hence the name.

Crackle Glass – This type of art glass was an invention of the Venetians, which spread rapidly to other countries. It is made by plunging red-hot glass into cold water, then reheating and reblowing it, thus producing an unusual outer surface which appears to be covered with a multitude of tiny fractures, but is perfectly smooth to the touch.

Cranberry Glass – The term "cranberry glass" refers to color only, not to a particular type of glass. It is undoubtedly the most familiar colored glass known to collectors. This ware was blown or molded, and often decorated with enamels.

Crown Milano glass was made by Frederick Shirley at the Mt. Washington Glass Company, New Bedford, Massachusetts, from 1886-1888. It is ivory in color with a satin finish, and was embellished with floral sprays, scrolls and gold enamel.

Crown Tuscan glass has a pink-opaque body. It was originally produced in 1936 by A.J. Bennett, president of the Cambridge Glass Company of Cambridge, Ohio. The line was discontinued in 1954. Occasionally referred to as Royal Crown Tuscan, this ware was named for a scenic area in

Italy, and it has been said that its color was taken from the flash-colored sky at sunrise. When trans-illuminated, examples do have all of the blaze of a sunrise—a characteristic that is even applied to new examples of the ware reproduced by Mrs. Elizabeth Degenhart of Crystal Art Glass, and Harold D. Bennett, Guernsey Glass Company of Cambridge, Ohio.

Custard Glass was manufactured in the United States for a period of about 30 years (1885-1915). Although Harry Northwood was the first and largest manufacturer of custard glass, it was also produced by the Heisey Glass Company, Diamond Glass Company, Fenton Art Glass Company and a number of others.

The name custard glass is derived from its "custard yellow" color which may shade light yellow to ivory to light green-glass that is opaque to opalescent. Most pieces have fiery opalescence when held to the light. Both the color and glow of this ware came from the use of uranium salts in the glass. It is generally a heavy type pressed glass made in a variety of different patterns.

Cut Overlay – The term identifies pieces of glassware usually having a milk-white exterior that have been cased with cranberry, blue or amber glass. Other examples are deep blue, amber or cranberry on crystal glass, and the majority of pieces have been decorated with dainty flowers. Although Bohemian glass manufacturers produced some very choice pieces during the 19th century, fine examples were also made in America, as well as in France and England.

Daum Nancy is the mark found on pieces of French cameo glass made by August and Jean Daum after 1875.

Durand Art Glass was made by Victor Durand from 1879 to 1935 at the Durand Art Glass Works in Vineland, New Jersey. The glass resembles Tiffany in quality. Drawn white feather designs and thinly drawn glass threading (quite brittle) applied around the main body of the ware, are striking examples of Durand creations on an iridescent surface.

Findlay or Onyx art glass was manufactured about 1890 for only a short time by the Dalzell Gilmore Leighton Company of Findlay, Ohio.

Flashed Wares were popular during the late 19th century. They were made by partially coating the inner surface of an object with a thin plating of glass of another, more dominant color—usually red. These pieces can readily be identified by holding the object to the light and examining the rim, as it will show more than one layer of glass. Many pieces of "rubina crystal" (cranberry to clear), "blue amberina" (blue to amber), and "rubina verde" (cranberry to green), were manufactured in this way.

Francisware is a hobnail glassware with frosted or clear glass hobs and stained amber rims and tops. It was produced during the late 1880s by Hobbs, Brockunier and Company.

Fry Glass was made by the H.C. Fry Company, Rochester, Pennsylvania, from 1901, when the firm was organized, until 1934, when operations ceased. The firm specialized in the manufacturing of cut glassware. The production of their famous "foval" glass did not begin until the 1920s. The firm also produced a variety of glass specialties, oven wares and etched glass.

Gallé glass was made in Nancy, France, by Emile Gallé at the Gallé Factory, founded in 1874. The firm produced both enameled and cameo glass, pottery, furniture and other art nouveau items. After Gallé's death in 1904, the factory continued operating until 1935.

Greentown glass was made in Greentown, Indiana, by the Indiana Tumbler and Goblet Company from 1894 until 1903. The firm produced a variety of pressed glasswares in addition to milk and chocolate glass.

Gunderson Peachblow is a more recent type art glass produced in 1952 by the Gunderson-Pairpoint Glass Works of New Bedford, Massachusetts, successors to the Mt. Washington Glass Company. Gunderson pieces have a soft satin finish shading from white at the base to a deep rose at the top.

Hobnail – The term "hobnail" identifies any glassware having "bumps" – flattened, rounded or pointed – over the outer surface of the glass. A variety of patterns exists. Many of the fine early examples were produced by Hobbs, Brockunier and Company, Wheeling,

West Virginia, and the New England Glass Company.

Holly Amber, originally known as "golden agate," is a pressed glass pattern which features holly berries and leaves over its glossy surface. Its color shades from golden brown tones to opalescent streaks. This ware was produced by the Indiana Tumbler and Goblet Company for only 6 months, from January 1 to June 13, 1903. Examples are rare and expensive.

Imperial Glass – The Imperial Glass Company of Bellaire, Ohio, was organized in 1901 by a group of prominent citizens of Wheeling, West Virginia. A variey of fine art glass, in addition to carnival glass, was produced by the firm. The two trademarks which identified the ware were issued in June 1914. One consisted of the firm's name, "Imperial," by double-pointed arrows.

Latticino is the name given to articles of glass in which a network of tiny milk-white lines appear, crisscrossing between two walls of glass. It is a type of filigree glassware developed during the 16th century by the Venetians.

Legras Glass – Cameo, acid cut and enameled glasswares were made by August J.F. Legras at Saint-Denis, France, from 1864-1914.

Loetz Glass was made in Austria just before the turn of the century. As Loetz worked in the Tiffany factory before returning to Austria, much of his glass is similar in appearance to Tiffany wares. Loetz glass is often marked "Loetz" or "Loetz-Austria."

Lutz Glass was made by Nicholas Lutz, a Frenchman, who worked at the Boston and Sandwich Glass Company from 1870 to 1888, when it closed. He also produced fine glass at the Mt. Washington Glass Company. Lutz is noted for two different types of glass—striped and threaded wares. Other glass houses also produced similar glass, and these wares were known as Lutz-type.

Mary Gregory was an artist for the Boston and Sandwich Glass Company during the last quarter of the 19th century. She decorated glassware with white enamel figures of young children engaged in playing, collecting butterflies, etc., in white on transparent glass, both clear and colored. Today the term "Mary Gregory" glass applies to any glassware that remotely resembles her work.

Mercury Glass is a double-walled glass that dates from the 1850s to about 1910. It was made in England as well as the United States during this period. Its interior, usually in the form of vases, is lined with flashing mercury, giving the items an all over silvery appearance. The entrance hole in the base of each piece was sealed over. Many pieces were decorated.

Milk Glass is an opaque pressed glassware usually of milk-white color, although green, amethyst, black, and shades of blue were made. Milk glass was produced in quantity in the United States during the 1880s, in a variety of patterns.

Millefiori – This decorative glassware is considered to be a specialty of the Venetians. It is sometimes called "glass of a thousand flowers," and has been made for centuries. Very thin colored glass rods are arranged in bundles, then fused together with heat. When the piece of glass is sliced across, it has a design like that of many small flowers. These tiny wafer-thin slices are then embedded in larger masses of glass, enlarged and shaped.

Moser Glass was made by Ludwig Moser at Karlsbad. The ware is considered to be another type of art nouveau glass, as it was produced during its heyday– during the early 1900s. Principal colors included amethyst, cranberry, green and blue, with fancy enameled decoration.

Mother-of-Pearl, often abbreviated in descriptions as M.O.P., is a glass composed of two or more layers, with a pattern showing through to the other surface. The pattern, caused by internal air traps, is created by expanding the inside layer of molten glass into molds with varying design. When another layer of glass is applied, this brings out the design. The final layer of glass is then acid dipped, and the result is mother-of-pearl satin ware. Patterns are numerous. The most frequently found are the diamond quilted, raindrop and herringbone. This ware can be one solid color, a single color shading light to dark,

two colors blended or a variety of colors which include the rainbow effect. In addition, many pieces are decorated with colorful enamels, coralene beading, and other applied glass decorations.

Nailsea Glass was first produced in England from 1788 to 1873. The characteristics that identify this ware are the "pulled" loopings and swirls of colored glass over the body of the object.

New England Peachblow was patented in 1886 by the New England Glass Company. It is a single-layered glass shading from opaque white at the base to deep rose-red or raspberry at the top. Some pieces have a glossy surface, but most were given an acid bath to produce a soft, matte finish.

New Martinsville Peachblow Glass was produced from 1901-1907 at New Martinsville, Pennsylvania.

Opalescent Glass – The term refers to glasswares which have a milky white effect in the glass, usually on a colored ground. There are three basic types of this ware. Presently, the most popular includes pressed glass patterns found in table settings. Here the opalescence appears at the top rim, the base, or a combination of both. On blown or mold-blown glass, the pattern itself consists of this milky effect–such as Spanish lace. Another example is the opalescent points on some pieces of hobnail glass. These wares are lighter weight. The third group includes opalescent novelties, primarily of the pressed variety.

Peking Glass is a type of Chinese cameo glass produced from the 1700s, well into the 19th century.

Phoenix Glass – The firm was established in Beaver County, Pennsylvania, during the late 1800s, and produced a variety of commercial glasswares. During the 1930s the factory made a desirable sculptured gift-type glassware which has become very collectible in recent years. Vases, lamps, bowls, ginger jars, candlesticks, etc., were made until the 1950s in various colors with a satin finish.

Pigeon Blood is a bright reddish-orange glassware dating from the early 1900s.

Pomona Glass was invented in 1884 by Joseph Locke at the New England Glass Company.

Pressed Glass was the inexpensive glassware produced in quantity to fill the increasing demand for tablewares when Americans moved away from the simple table utensils of pioneer times. During the 1820s, ingenious Yankees invented and perfected machinery for successfully pressing glass. About 1865, manufacturers began to color their products. Literally hundreds of different patterns were produced.

Quezal is a very fine quality blown iridescent glassware produced by Martin Bach, in his factory in Brooklyn, New York, from 1901-1920. Named after the Central American bird, quezal glassware has an iridescent finish, featuring contrasting colored glass threads. Green, white and gold colors are most often found.

Rosaline Glass is a product of the Steuben Glass Works of Corning, New York. The firm was founded by Frederick Carter and T.C. Hawkes, Sr. Rosaline is a rose-colored jade glass or colored alabaster. The firm is now owned by the Corning Glass Company, which is presently producing fine glass of exceptional qualtiy.

Royal Flemish Art Glass was made by the Mt. Washington Glass Works during the 1880s. It has an acid finish which may consist of one or more colors, decorated with raised gold enameled lines separating into sections. Fanciful painted enamel designs also decorate this ware. Royal Flemish glass is marked "RF," with the letter "R" reversed and backed to the letter "F," within a four-sided orange-red diamond mark.

Rubina Glass is a transparent blown glassware that shades from clear to red. One of the first to produce this crystal during the late 1800s was Hobbs, Brockunier and Company of Wheeling, West Virginia.

Rubina Verde is a blown art glass made by Hobbs, Brockunier and Company, during the late 1800s. It is a transparent glassware that shades from red to yellow-green.

Sabino Glass originated in Paris, France, in the 1920s. The company was founded by Marius-Ernest Sabino, and was noted for art deco figures, vases, nudes and animals in clear, opalescent and colored glass.

Sandwich Glass – One of the most interesting and enduring pages from America's past is Sandwich glass produced by the famous Boston and Sandwich Glass Company at Sandwich, Massachusetts. The firm began operations in 1825, and the glass flourished until 1888, when the factory closed. Despite the popularity of Sandwich Glass, little is known about its founder, Deming Jarvis. The Sandwich Glass house turned out hundreds of designs in both plain and figured patterns in colors and crystal, so that no one type could be considered entirely typical—but the best known is the "lacy" glass produced there. The variety and multitude of designs and patterns produced by the company over the years is a tribute to its greatness.

Silver Deposit Glass was made during the late 19th and early 20th centuries. Silver was deposited on the glass surface by a chemical process so that a pattern appeared against a clear or colored ground. This ware is sometimes referred to as "silver overlay."

Slag Glass was originally known as "mosaic" and "marble glass" because of its streaked appearance. Production in the United States began about 1880. The largest producer of this ware was Challinor, Taylor and Company.

Spanish Lace is a Victorian glass pattern that is easily identified by its distinct opalescent flower and leaf pattern. It belongs to the shaded opalescent glass family.

Steuben – The Steuben Glass Works was founded in 1904, by Frederick Carter, an Englishman, and T.G. Hawkes, Sr., at Corning, New York. In 1918, the firm was purchased by the Corning Glass Company. However, Steuben remained with the firm, designing a bounty of fine art glass of exceptional quality.

Stevens & Williams of Stourbridge, England, made many fine art glass pieces covering the full range of late Victorian ware between the 1830s and 1930s. Many forms were decorated with applied glass flowers, leaves and fruit. After World War I, the firm

began producing lead crystal and new glass colors.

Stiegel-Type Glass – Henry William Stiegel founded America's first flint glass factory during the 1760s at Manheim, Pennsylvania. Stiegel glass is flint or crystal glass; it is thin and clear, and has a bell-like ring when tapped. The ware is quite brittle and fragile. Designs were painted free-hand on the glass–birds, animals and architectural motifs, surrounded by leaves and flowers. The engraved glass resulted from craftsmen etching the glass surface with a copper wheel, then cutting the desired patterns.

It is extremely difficult to identify, with certainty, a piece of original Stiegel glass. Part of the problem resulted from the lack of an identifying mark on the products. Additionally, many of the craftsmen moved to other areas after the Stiegel plant closed—producing a similar glass product. Therefore, when one is uncertain about the origin of this type of ware, it is referred to as "Stiegel type" glass.

Tiffany Glass was made by Louis Comfort Tiffany, one of America's outstanding glass designers of the art nouveau period, from about 1870 to the 1930s. Tiffany's designs included a variety of lamps, bronze work, silver, pottery and stained glass windows. Practically all items made were marked "L.C. Tiffany" or "L.C.T." in addition to the word "Favrile".

Tortoiseshell Glass – As its name indicates, this type of glassware resembles the color of tortoiseshell, and has deep, rich brown tones combined with amber and cream colored shades. Tortoiseshell glass was originally produced in 1880 by Francis Poh, a German chemist. It was also made in the United States by the Sandwich Glass Works and other glass houses during the late 1800s.

Val St. Lambert Cristalleries – The firm is located in Belgium, and was founded in 1825. It is still in operation.

Vasa Murrhina glassware was produced in quantity at the Vasa Murrhina Art Glass Company of Sandwich, Massachusetts, during the late 1800s. John C. Devoy, assignor to the firm, registered a patent on July 1, 1884, for the process of decorating glassware with particles of mica flakes coated with

copper, gold, nickel or silver, sandwiched between an inner layer of clear or transparent colored glass. The ware was also produced by other American glass firms and in England.

Vaseline Glass – The term "vaseline" refers to color only, as it resembles the greenish-yellow color typical of the oily petroleum jelly known as Vaseline. This ware has been produced in a variety of patterns both here and in Europe–from the late 1800s. It has been made in both clear and opaque yellow, vaseline combined with clear glass, and occasionally the two colors are combined in one piece.

Verlys Glass is a type of art glass produced in France after 1931. The Heisey Glass Company, Newark, Ohio, produced identical glass for a short time, after having obtained the rights and formula from the French factory. French produced ware can be identified from the American product by the signature. The French is mold marked, whereas the American glass is etched script signed.

Wavecrest Glass is an opaque white glassware made from the late 1890s by French factories and the Pairpoint Manufacturing Company at New Bedford, Massachusetts. Items were decorated by the C.F. Monroe Company of Meriden, Connecticut, with painted pastel enamels. The name wavecrest was used after 1898 with the initials for the company "C.F.M. Co." Operations ceased during World War II.

Webb Glass was made by Thomas Webb & Sons of Stourbridge, England, during the late Victorian period. The firm produced a variety of different types of art and cameo glass.

Wheeling Peachblow – With its simple lines and delicate shadings, Wheeling Peachblow was produced soon after 1883, by J.H. Hobbs, Brockunier and Company at Wheeling, West Virginia. It is a two-layered glass, lined or cased inside with an opaque, milk-white type of plated glassware. The outer layer shades from a bright yellow at the base to a mahogany red at the top. The majority of pieces produced are in the glossy finish.

A-OH Apr 2001

First Row

Daum Nancy Cameo Stick Vase, dec. w/ burgundy & gr. long stemmed flowers, the background at base is dark mottled blue extending upward to mottled yel. & pink, sgn. Daum Nancy w/ cross of Lorraine, 19¾" H. **$550**

Wavecrest Vase, dec. w/ white shasta daisies on mauve ground outlined w/ rose tracery, sgn. w/ red Wavecrest mark, 11½" H. **$2,000**

Federzeichnung MOP Vase, w/ air trapped opal octopus dec. on br. satin w/ overall gold tracery, 13" H. **$1,600**

Steuben Blue Aurene Vase, w/ 3" white leaf & vine dec., sgn. Steuben Aurene, 10" H. **$4,500**

Royal Flemish Tankard Vase, earthtone colors & dec. w/ a medallion shield w/ gold dec., 12" H. **$1,550**

Tiffany Vase, irid. gold w/ gr. heart & fine dec., sgn. Tiffany Inc. Favrile, 8¾" H. **$3,000**

Daum Nancy Cameo Vase w/ gr. stalks of wild flowers against a mottled peach & ora. ground, sgn. Daum Nancy w/ Cross of Lorraine, 6½" H. **$2,300**

Steuben Fan Vase, blue, sgn. Aurene, 7½" H. **$1,000**

Tiffany Vase, tomato red w/ mustard yel. int., sgn. L.C. Tiffany, 7¾" H. **$4,000**

Webb Cameo Peachblow Vase, Eng., peachblow w/ multiple stems of flowers, buds & leaves on peach to deep pink ground, 9¼" H. **$3,000**

Second Row

Daum Nancy Vase w/ embossed silver base & handles, dec. w/ cascading gr. ivy against a Martele gr. & opal. ground, sgn. w/ Cross of Lorraine, 10" H. **$2,750**

Muller Fres French Cameo Vase dec. w/ dark pines against a mottled blue & amber sky, known as "Broken Pine", sgn. Muller Fres Luneville, 9½" H. **$1,500**

Galle Cameo Vase, Fr., w/ forest gr. trees on shaded lt. gr. to pink frosted ground, sgn., 9½" H. **$1,500**

Burmese Jack in Pulpit Vase, Mt. Washington, footed trumpet shape dec. w/ enameled wild flowers & trailing vines, 14" H. **$1,450**

Wheeling Peachblow Stick Vase w/ rarely seen amber rigaree band around collar, 8¼" H. **$900**

Steuben Gold Aurene Basket w/ applied gold handle, sgn. 8" H. **$1,500**

Wedgwood Stick Vase w/ blue luster w/ multi. colored hummingbirds on exterior, ora. int. 7½" H. **$1,250**

Tiffany Favrile Vase, Mt. Washington, shades from soft blue to soft pink w/ berry pontil, 6¾" H. **$4,600**

Peachblow Vase, Mt. Washington, shades from soft blue to soft pink w/ berry pontil, 6¾" H. **$4,600**

Wavecrest Dresser Box dec. w/ red & blue flower sprays & br. leafy stems against an opal ground, 6¼" H. **$900**

Wheeling Peachblow Morgan Vase by Hobbs Brockunier, on orig. amber glass griffin w/ chips, 10¼" H. **$900**

Burmese Stick Vase by Thomas Webb & sons w/ circular Webb mark, dec. w/ multi. floral sprays on leafy stems, 9¾" H. **$950**

Third Row

Wavecrest Glove Box, hinged, w/ soft blue background dec. w/ enameled daisies, sgn. w/ Wavecrest mark, 10" L. x 5½" H. **$1,800**

Wheeling Peachblow Pitcher, w/ applied amber reeded handle, 4½" H. **$2,000**

Steuben Vase, gr. jade acid cutback in the Matsu patt., 8" H. **$1,400**

Burmese Brides Bowl, Mt. Washington, dec. w/ white & peach flowers on soft yel. to rose ruffled top, bowl 9" W, 4¾" H. **$2,000**

Gallé Came Vase w/ amber flower pods on dark amber blown out leaves & vines, sgn. in cameo Gallé, 7¼" H. **$6,000**

Pickle Caster, Mt. Washington Albertine, white to mauve body dec. w/ raised enameled flowers, 4" H. orig. Pairpoint silver plate holder w/ lid & tongs, 8" H. **$2,200**

Royal Flemish Vase w/ earthen colored body dec. w/ raised gold foliage, 3 medallions, neck dec. w/ fleur-de-lis against a wine ground, 13" H. **$2,900**

Fourth Row

Steuben Gold Aurene Vase w/ gr. heart & vine dec. on irid. gold ground, sgn. Aurene, 5" H. **$3,400**

French Cameo Vase sgn. Devez w/ lavender boats sailing at sunset, 6¾" H. **$850**

Tiffany Mini Flower Form Vase, sgn. LC Tiffany-Favrile w/ orig. label, 7" H. **$1,400**

Gallé French Cameo Vase w/ blue growing morning glories set against frosted yel. sky, sgn., 6" H. **$1,200**

Loetz Paperweight Vase, gr. & silver pulled feathers on an ora. ground cased in crystal, 4½" H. **$2,700**

Quezal Trifold Lily Vase, gold irid. , sgn., 5¾" H. **$950**

Durand Vase, iridescent blue King Tut patt. on gr. ground, gold int., 5¾" H. **$950**

Daum Nancy Pillow Vase w/ fall colored trees over grayish hillside, sgn. in enamel w/ cross of Lorraine, 4¼" H. **$2,300**

Opaque Tumbler w/ mottled blue mineral satin dec., by New England Glass Co., 3¾" H. **$400**

Fifth Row

Peachblow Creamer, Mt. Washington, shading from soft blue to pink w/ applied blue handle, 4" H. **$800**

Webb Cameo Vase, Eng., w/ trumpet flowering vine against a soft blue ground, 4" H. **$1,350**

Agata Vase, New England Glass Co., shades from soft pink to rose ruffled top w/ dec., 4¾" H. **$1,150**

Alexandrite Cream Pitcher, shades from amber to fuschia to blue w/ honeycomb patt., amber handle, 2½" H. **$1,800**

MOP Vase by Stevens & Williams, Eng., cranberry w/ random air trapped yel. design, 4¾" H. **$1,050**

Sugar Shaker, Mt. Washington, dec. w/ colored flowers on ribbed body, 4" H. **$5,000**

Cologne Bottle, Stevens & Williams intaglio cut, amber w/ silver cap, 5" H. **$2,550**

Cameo Vase, Eng., Prussian blue w/ stemmed flowers, 4½" H. **$950**

A-IA Dec. 2001   Jackson's International Auctioneers

Cameo Vase, ca. 1921, gray glass w/ custard glass mottling overlaid in deep burgundy. Sgn. "A DeLatte Nancy". 10½" H **$1,380**

Richard Cameo Vase, ca. 1910, gray glass w/ internal lime shading overlaid w/ light amethyst & hunter green. 14½" H **$920**

Cameo Vase, ca. 1910, gray glass w/ internal white mottling overlaid w/ turquoise & amethyst colored glass. Sgn. "Muller Freres Luneville". 7¼" H **$1,150**

First Row
Bohemian Vases, pr., ca. 1930, cranberry glass overlaid w/ white opaque, 12" H. **$546**
French Art Glass Vase, ca. 1920, gray glass w/ yellow, orange & purple mottled, 8" H. **$172**
Castor Set, mid 20th C., silver & cut glass, 15" H. **$172**

Second Row
French Art Glass Perfume, ca. 1920, orange satin glass w/ cobalt stopper, 6" H. **$86.25**
Czech Art Glass Vase, ca. 1925, red glass w/ purple design under a crystal finish, 7¾" H. **$92**
Victorian Slag Celery Vase, late 19th C., purple w/ white marbling, 8" H. **$92**
Victorian Mantle Urns, pr. ruby flashed, gray satin decorated w/ anchor & laurel wreath, 16½" H. **$126**
English Cameo Brides Basket, ca. 1910, white opaque glass overlaid w/ pink, 9½" diam. **$747**

Third Row
Victorian GWTW Style Lamp, ca. 1880, red satin glass w/ embossed poppy design. Later electric, 23" H. **$488**
Victorian Glass Pitcher, green w/ white, blue & pink florals, 10½" H. **$46**
Cast Brass Glass Vigil Lamp, w/ ruby red glass, 7" H. **$80**
Bohemian Glass Vase, ca. 1890, ruby flashed & cut glass, 9½" H. **$57**
Victorian Dresser Box, translucent white glass, 2½" H. **$34**
Bladder Flask, ca. 1900, cranberry glass, 9½" H. **$92**
Moser Decorated Tumbler, ca. 1920, amber glass w/ enameled & applied jewel panels, 3¾" H. **$57**
Victorian Glass Handled Vase, blue shading to white, 12" H. **$115**
Glass and Pewter Ewer, ca. 1900, cranberry glass, 8" H. **$57**
Bohemian Amethyst Covered Jar, ca. 1910, 14" H. **$86.25**

Victorian Syrup Jar, "Findley Onyx" in opalescent glass w/ silvered florals, 7" H. **$488**
Victorian Glass Pitcher, green glass w/ embossed & gilt leaves, 9½" H. **$23**

Fourth Row
Victorian Cracker Jar, w/ embossed scrolled acanthus design & silvered lid. Embossed "O.S.M.C.O.", Oneida NY", 8" H. **$172**
Victorian Brides Bowl, glass & silvered in white opaque w/ red shaded rim, 10" H. **$143**
Finger Lamp, ca. 1890, custard glass, 6" H. **$172**
Czech Art Glass Table Lamp, ca. 1920, black base amethyst, shade in opalescent brown & yellow tortoise shell. No wiring, 10" H. **$143**
Victorian Brides Basket, pink glass bowl in silvered frame, 9" diam. **$143**
Trophy Pitcher, ca. 1905, cranberry glass & sterling overlay. Inscribed "Magnolia Lawn Tennis Assc. 1905 Singles First Won by R.C. Seaver", 7" H. **$1,035**
Victorian Amberina Night Lamp, applied amber petal feet, 6" H. **$287**
Victorian Amberina Vase, w/ amber petal feet, 12" H. **$373**
Victorian Biscuit Jar, white opaque glass, 7" H. **$80**

Fifth Row
Bohemian Dresser Tray, ca. 1900, flashed & cut glass, 12" x 9¾". **$115**
Glass Whimseys, pr., 18th C., decor. rosettes on baluster pedestal bases, 7" H. **$690**
Ruby Glass Covered Sugar Bowl & Pickle Caster, in silver frame. **$316**
Czech Whimsical Figure of Santa Claus, ca. 1960, sculpted red, white & black, 9½" H. **$115**
Biscuit Jar, Pairpoint glass in translucent white w/ blown out melon ribs. Sgn. "Pairpoint", 7" H. **$546**
Crown Milano Rose Bowl, white satin w/ enameled florals. 5" diam. **$488**
Bohemian Glass Bowl, ca. 1890, flashed ruby & cut glass, 11½" diam. **$207**

A-ME May 2001   James D. Julia, Inc.

First Row
Brides Bowl, cranberry & white spatter glass w/ applied clear edge around ruffled rim. Silver plated holder is signed Derby Silver Co. Bowl 4½" H x 11" diam., overall 11½" H w/ handle. **$115**
Brides Bowl, satin glass shaded apricot & pink exterior w/ enamel white & purple wisteria decor. Lemon yellow interior, 5½" H x 10" diam. **$920**
Mt. Washington Colonial Ware Biscuit Jar, decor w/ dancing man & woman surrounded by gold scrolls, 6" H x 7" diam **$402**

Second Row
Bride's Bowl, M.O.P. satin glass w/ diamond quilted shading from apricot to white. Silver plated holder signed "Rockford", 8¼" diam x 11" H in holder. **$287**
English Bride's Bowl, yellow & pink swirl base w/ swirl ribbing & applied clear rigaree around bowl. Silver plated holder signed "Wilcox", 8" diam. **$230**
Bride's Bowl, Victorian, pink cased w/ enameled flowers. Bowl 9½" diam. x 10" H in holder. Silver plated holder signed "Brooklyn Silverplate Co." **$230**
Libbey Amberina Bowl, signed, fuchsia to amber w/ rolled rim, 9½" diam. **$345**

A-NJ May 2001   Craftsman

Tiffany Favrile Glass Bowl, w/ gold blue-gr. & deep violet irid., sgn. L.C. Tiffany/Favrile, 3" x 13½" diam. **$2,100**

Top Row

Wavecrest Glass Vase, ca. 1890, opaque glass w/ rose blossoms on green variegated ground. Silvered rim & base, missing handles, 11" H. **$460**

Enameled Vase, white opaque glass w/ flowers, 12" H. **$46**

Victorian Bristol Enameled Vase, pr., in pale butterscotch w/ enameled florals, 14½" H. **$161**

Enameled Vase, pr., white opaque w/ apple blossoms on orange wash ground, 10½" H. **$69**

Mary Gregory Style Vase, cranberry glass shading to clear, enameled in white, 12¼" H. **$144**

Second Row

Spatter Pitcher, white, pink & yellow mottle w/ clear handl,. 8" H. **$69**

Cruet, cranberry w/ clear handle, 5" H. **$23**

Victorian Glass Bottle, white opaque w/ enameled spider mums, 9" H. **$63**

Ewer, blue shading to white w/ applied handles, 9½" H. **$58**

Peachblow Vase, pink & white glass decor. w/ enameled florals & applied ruby & crystal beads, 12" H. **$127**

Jack in the Pulpit Vase, pale green w/ mottled green & cranberry, 8¾" H. **$46**

Vase, blue opalescent w/ applied green feet & enameled florals, 12" H. **$104**

Italian Vase, satin glass w/ applied flowers, 8¼" H. **$35**

Glass Bowl, Thumbprint patt., sapphire glass w/ amber tripod legs, 8" H. **$58**

Victorian Glass Vase, blue shaded top, applied handles & enameled butterfly & floral decor., 7½" H. **$52**

Ewer, pale blue shading to white w/ applied amber rim & thorn handle, glossy finish, 11½" H. **$138**

Mary Gregory Vase, cobalt w/ enameled figure, 8" H. **$86**

Third Row

Victorian Vase, pr., white opaque w/ amber & pink overlay florals, some minor losses, 7½" H. **$46**

Glass Ewer, pink glass w/ silver flecks under paperweight finish w/ applied fruit, 7½" H. **$115**

Victorian Vase, cranberry shading to white w/ enameled birds & strawberries, 5½" H. **$46**

Larkin Soap Glass Bottle, ca. 1900, green glass embossed "Larkin Soap Co. Buffalo" w/ orig. paper label "Lavender Ammonia Salt", 3½" H. **$35**

Brides Basket, cased glass w/ shaded cranberry interior & applied amber rim., silvered metal frame, 12½" H. **$230**

Victorian Double Vase, pr., applied flowers & green coil, 7½" H. **$127**

Ewer, cased white glass w/ pink int. & applied amber decor, 10" H. **$201**

Ewer, satin alabaster w/ applied blue opaque handle, enameled w/ bird & cherry blossoms, 10½" H. **$92**

Victorian Vase, cranberry w/ opalescent ribs & yellow applied rigaree color, 6" H. **$58**

Victorian Vase, frosty white w/ shaded cranberry, 10½" H. **$46**

Fourth Row

Glass Compote, ca. 1925, in crystal w/ finely gilt florals & ribbon bow,. 8¼" H. **$35**

Lampshade, amber w/ hobnail patt., 9" diam. **$259**

Glass Cane, clear w/ spiraling colors of blue, red & white, 62" L. **$230**

Brides Bowl, satin glass shading from cranberry to white w/ enameled scrolls & florals, minor flake, 11" diam. **$127**

Porcelain Master Salt, in a reticulated basket w/ bracket feet & cranberry glass insert, 5" L. **$230**

Pickle Caster, w/ yellow button & daisy insert in silvered frame, 11" H. **$288**

Rose Bowl, w/ blown shell design & enameled florals, 4¼" diam. **$92**

Burmese Rose Bowl, satin glass, 4" diam. **$35**

Fifth Row

Glass Ewer, yellow w/ amber int. & clear applied florals, 9" H. **$46**

Victorian Basket, cranberry rim & white opalescent flowers on clear ground, 9½" L. **$92**

Mary Gregory Vase, sapphire blue w/ white enamel scene, 8" H. **$69**

Glass Tumbler, pink w/ draped patt. 3½" H. **$23**

Alabaster Vase, w/ pink int. & enameled florals, 6" H. **$46**

Italian Glass Ewer, green shading to white w/ applied handle & enameled florals, 9" H. **$58**

Victorian Peachblow Rose Bowl, satin finish, 4¾" diam. **$46**

Victorian Glass Ewer, enameled bird & florals, applied thorn handle, 10" H. **$69**

Fenton Carnival Glass Goblets, set of four, blue "Orange Tree" patt., 5¼" H. **$259**

A-MA Mar. 2001

Skinner, Inc.

Paperweights

Millefiori, two, concentric rings of various red, white & blue floral canes, 3½" diam., 3" H. **$460**

Fruit, MA, ca. 1860, cluster of fruit in red, yel. & gr. in a latticinio basket, imper. 2¾" diam., 1⅞" H. **$546**

Sailboat, late 19th C., enameled white ship silhouette w/ red flag, blue water, 3 facets, 3¾" diam., 4" H. **$3,450**

Fruit, MA, ca. 1860, cluster fruit in white basket, 2⅝" diam., 2" H. **$200**

Pansy, attrib. to Baccarat, Fr., yel. purple & red pansy & bud, bright gr. leafy stem, star-cut base, imper., 3" diam., 2¼" H. **$345**

Red Dahlia, MA., ca. 1870, red petal flower w/ white cone center, gr. leafy stem set on white latticinio ground, surface scratches, 3⅛" diam., 2" H. **$460**

A-OH Mar. 2001   Garth's Auctions, Inc.

Brown Vase, w/ opalescent int., quatrefoil ruffled rim, Federzeichnung design, w/ patent mark on bottom, 6½" H. **$2,090**
Diamond Quilted MOP Vase, satin glass, yellow shading to brown, ivory int, 6" H. **$192**
Daum Nancy Cameo Vase, pale blue opal., w/ enameled landscape, 5¾" H. **$1,485**
Agata Vase, by N. Eng. Glass Co., ivory shading to pink, 6" H. **$1,045**
Cameo Vase, sgn. "LeGras" w/ wooded landscape, 5¾" H. **$1,045**

A-VA Sept. 2001 Green Valley Auctions, Inc.
Goblet, opaque black, 6" H. **$2,600**

A-IA Dec. 2001   Jackson's International Auctioneers

Daum Nancy Cameo Vase, ca. 1900, gray glass internally decorated w/ rose & yellow & enameled in shades of charcoal & brown, 3½" H. **$920**
Pate de Verre Tray, ca. 1920, in mottled yellow & amber translucent glass. Beetle in black & brown. Incised "A. Walter Nancy" & "Berge S.C." 5", diam. **$1,035**
Cameo Vase, ca. 1910, gray glass w/

internal yellow mottling & vitrified red, yellow & blue. Sgn. "Daum Nancy", 5¼" H. **$1,725**
Cameo Spice Dish, ca. 1900, gray glass internally decorated w/ yellow & peach. Sgn. "Daum Nancy", 2¼" diam. **$1,725**
Cameo Vase, ca. 1900, gray glass internally decorated w/ mottled colors of yellow, amber, blue & green. Sgn. "Muller Fres Luneville", 7¼" H. **$1,495.**
Cameo Vase, ca. 1910, opalescent &

green cut w/ design of berries in shades of green & red. Sgn. "Daum Nancy", 3¾" H. **$1,035**
Pate de Verre Paperweight, ca. 1920, translucent jade glass w/ black & forest green mottling. Inscribed "A. Walter Nancy" & "Berge SC". 3" L. **$1,150**
Cameo Glass Vase, ca. 1910, rose tinted glass w/ opalescent mottling. Inscribed "Lamartine", 3½" H. **$632**

A-OH Mar. 2001   Garth's Auctions, Inc.

Cut Overlay Glass Cologne Bottle, dark amber cut to yellow w/ flowering branches, w/ repousse scrollwork, 5" H. **$1,265**
Cameo Vase, sgn. "Gallé" w/ acid etched four petal flowers in lavender/ blue/ green, outlined in white on pale peach ground, 6⅜" H. **$825**

Scenic Oval Cameo Vase, sgn. "LeGras" w/ enameled landscape of trees, shepherd & flock, shades of green/ blue & black on sunset ground, 4¼" H. **$440**
Trumpet Vase, sgn. "Quezal" w/ deep irid. gold w/ pin, yellow & pale blue, 5½" H. **$825**

Round Vase, Smith Bros. w/ red lion mark & trademark, dark ivory gound w/ handpainted daisies, 3⅝" H. **$165**

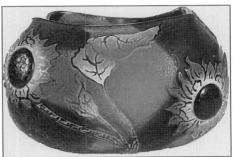

A-KS Aug. 2001   Woody Auction

Cameo Bowl, cranberry & dark green acid cut, sgn. Daum Nancy. 10" x 9" x 6½" **$9,000**

A-IA Dec. 2001   Jackson's International Auctioneers

French Cameo Vase, ca. 1900, gray glass w/cut design in burgundy, 12" H. **$431**
Cameo Vase, ca. 1920, gray glass w/ opalescent lining overlaid in chocolate brown. sgn. "Richard", 6" H. **$287**
French Vase, ca. 1900, gray glass w/ scene on shaded amber ground & white frothy base, 16¼" H. **$575**
Cameo Vase, ca. 1920, gray glass w/ yellow tint overlaid in blue & magenta. sgn. "DeVez", 4¼" H. **$316**
Cameo Vase, ca. 1920, citrine glass overlaid w/ magenta & green, sgn. "Michel-Paris", 6" H. **$747**
Glass Atomizer, ca. 1920, gray glass w/ scene in browns, sgn. "Auzies", 9" H. **$143**
Legras Cameo Vase, ca. 1910, opalescent glass w/ green, pink & brown, sgn. "Legras", 6" H. **$402**
French Stoppered Bottle, ca. 1920, gray glass w/ polychrome scene, 5½" H. **$287**
Cameo Night Lamp, ca. 1920, gray glass w/ design in shades of burgundy, sgn. "Legras", 6" H. **$345**
Gallé Vase, ca. 1910, gray glass w/ yellow tint overlaid w/ lime green, sgn. "Gallé", 5¾" H. **$316**
Cameo Vase, ca. 1910, gray glass w/ scene in brown shades on custard ground, sgn. "Chouvenin", 7" H. **$230**
Glass Vase, 20th C., gray glass w/ yellow lining overlaid in brown. Engraved "Daum Nancy", 5½" H. **$287**

A-KS Aug. 2001   Woody Auction

Cameo Vase, Stevens & Williams, gourdshaped, cranberry w/ white. 13½" H. **$1,900**

A-IA June 2001　　　　　　　　　　　　　Jackson's International Auctioneers

Tiffany Favrile Glass

Top Row
Vase, ca. 1908, amethyst glass w/ gold iridescent finish. Inscribed "L.C. Tiffany-Favrile". 4" H. **$1,725**
Vase, ca. 1902, pale green w/ pale amber rim & iridized int. Inscribed "L.C.T." 6" H. **$6,900**
Vase, ca. 1916, opalescent glass w/ iridized int., pulled green feather decor. 5" H. **$3,000**
Center Row
Vase, ca. 1907, pale green glass w/ iridized int., incised "L.C.T.", 3½" H. **$1,725**
Bowl, ca. 1912, in blue iridized glass, docorated w/ pale green leaves & vines on silvery blue finish. Inscribed "L.C. Tiffany-Favrile". 4¾" Diam. **$3,335**
Miniature Vase, ca. 1900, amber glass w/ iridized finish. Paper label, inscribed "L.C.T.", 1¾" H. **$575**

Miniature Vase, ca. 1913, pale yellow w/ iridized finish. Inscribed "L.C. Tiffany-Favrile",. 1½" H. **$575**
Miniature Vase, ca. 1905, pale yellow w/ iridized finish. Partial paper label, inscribed "L.C.T.", 1¾" H. **$575**
Bottom Row
Miniature Vase, ca. 1900, amethyst glass w/ iridized finish. Inscribed "L.C.T.", 5" H. **$690**
Spice Dish, ca. 1902, pale green w/ iridized finsih. Inscribed "L.C.T.". **$288**
Shade, ca. 1899-1920, gray glass, w/ golden yellow rim, 4½" H. **$230**
Tiffany Favrile Glass Vase, ca. 1899-1920, green glass w/ pulled crimson feather decor., 6" H. **$1,121**

A-KS Jan. 2001　　　　　　　**Woody Auction**
Carnival Glass Ice Cream Bowl, Northwood's Peacock At Urn patt., stippled blue. **$2,750**

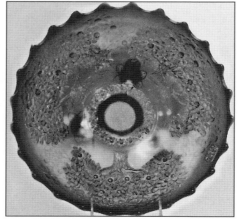

A-KS Jan. 2001　　　　　　　**Woody Auction**
Carnival Glass Footed Bowl, Fenton, Orange Tree patt., dark green. **$6,500**

A-KS Jan. 2001　　　　　　　**Woody Auction**
Carnival Glass Plate, Fenton, Orange Tree patt., irid. blue. **$575**

A-KS Aug. 2001   Woody Auction

Burmese Epergne & Fairy Lamps, Clarke's fairy fames & crystal arms attached to decorated bowl. One dome signed "Clarke". 10" H. **$6,000**

A-KS Aug. 2001   Woody Auction

Two-Handled Crown Milano Squatty Vase, gold enameled decor. 5½" H **$1,000**

A-KS Aug. 2001   Woody Auction

Moser Vase, pr., cranberry, 15" H. **$4,100**

A-VA Sept. 2000 Green Valley Auctions, Inc.

Punch Bowl, Thumbprint patt., 12" H, 14" diam. **$5,250**

A-MA Mar. 2001   Skinner, Inc.

Blown Glass Whimsey Bellows
Three vessels (one illustrated), late 19th C., decanter w/ transparent pink w/ white applied rigaree, Prince of Wales feathers, prunts, handles & circular foot, second & third are colorless flasks w/ white & transparent pink marby & applied colorless rigaree, prunts & handles, 16" H, 12½" H, & 10½" H. **$747**
Colored Bottle, late 19th C., white w/ red & blue loop designs, applied colorless rim, quilled neck, prunt, rigaree, handles & circular base, imper., 11¾" H. **$460**
Colored Bottle, late 19th C., cobalt blue w/ white marby, applied colorless rigaree, prunt, leaf, handles & circular base, imper., 11¼" H. **$345**
Colored Bottle, late 19th C., transparent ruby w/ white marby & applied ruby quilling at neck & colorless rigaree, prunt handles & circular base, imper., 9¾" H. **$258**
Colored Bottle, late 19th C., colorless w/ translucent red & opaque white loop designs, 12¼" H. **$200**
Colored Bottle, late 19th C., colorless w/ chartreuse, white & pink loop designs, imper., 14½" H. **$300**

A-OH Apr. 2001   Garth's Auctions, Inc.

Compote, brilliant amethyst ribbon, hexagonal base w/ rayed bottom, sawtooth edge, straw marks, 8¼" diam., 8½" H. **$22,000**

A-OH Apr 2001

Early Auction Company

First Row

Heisey Parfaits, Colonial patt., six w/ "H" inside diamond mark, one chipped, 6¾" H. **$125**

Adventure Bud Vase, amethyst ground w/ bold flecks, together w/ pink vase, 5½" H. (not illus.) **$70**

Purple Slag Compote, w/ sphinx design, 4" H, together w/ milk pitcher w/ impr. Dutch scene, 6½" H. (not illus.) **$95**

Martinsville Muranese Bowl, alt. opal. pink & vertical bands, mauve irid. int. 4" H x 8¼" W. **$95**

Perfumes, two Baccarat Amberina, in rose swirl patt., 6½" H. (one illus.) **$15**

Heisey Wines, four, Colonial patt., w/ "H" inside diamond mark, 6½" H. (one illus.) **$45**

Wine w/ triple stem, irid., 5¾" H. **$175**

Second Row

Findley Onyx Syrup, w/ opal body & silver inclusions, 7" H. **$425**

French Cameo Vase, cranberry cut against frosted ground, sgn. Baccarat 1915, 6" H. **$225**

Amberina Tumbler, Thumbprint patt., 6" H, together w/ sq. top bowl, 2½" H, 5¼" L. **$225**

Hawkes Green Etched Fan Vase, sgn., 7½" H. **$100**

Third Row

Mary Gergory Vase, blk. amethyst w/ white figure of girl, 9½" H., & an amber tumbler w/ blue coralene dec., 3¾" H. (not illus.) **$160**

Rubina Rose Bowl, vertical ribbed w/ crimped top, 4½" H. **$50**

Amberina Water Pitcher, Thumbprint patt., 7¾" H. **$160**

Aventurine Vase, w/ blue body & int. pink & white diagonal particles & overall gold flecks, set on three pronged feet, 6¾" H. **$185**

Amberina Pitcher, D.Q. w/ applied handle, 6¾" H. **$600**

Fourth Row

Pomona Water Pitcher, w/ red & blue flowers on gr. stems & applied twist rope handle & collar, 7½" H. **$225**

Tiffany Goblet w/ twist stem, sgn. LCT, 7¼" H. **$400**

Bowl, ruffled top, amber body w/ crimson white & br. tortoise shell dec., 6" H, 10" W. **$70**

Steuben Aurene Goblet, sgn. 4¼" H., together w/ Steuben Verre de Sole sherbet, 3¼" H. (not illus.) **$290**

Lutz Finger Bowl, w/ underplate, (not illus.) w/ pink & irid. gold bordered white dec. 3¼" H. **$175**

Pink Slag Salt, 4¼" H, together w/ white glass vase dec. w/ gold coralene, 5" H. **$575**

Quezal Gold Iridescent Shade, together w/ a sgn. Steuben 4½" H. lamp shade. **$200**

A-OH Jan. 2001

Garth's Auctions

Peachblow Vase, N.E. Glass Co., white shading to pink, 4⅝" H. **$495**

St. Louis Cameo Bowl, orange/ pink iris, chartreuse gr. ground, w/ stamped label, 2¼" H. **$302**

Quezal Shade, gold irid. w/ silvery pink & blue highlights, rim flakes, 5¾" H. **$110**

Cameo Vase w/ aqua ground & white branches & bamboo decor., 2 int. broken blisters, 2⅞" H. **$577**

Burmese Vase, yel. to pink, 4" H. **$110**

A-OH Apr 2001   Early Auction Company

First Row

Crown Milano Creamer w/ yel. air trap dec. on sunset ora./red ground, 2¾" H. **$450**

Quezal Stick Vase, blue base to blue/gr. top, sgn. in silver, 6¼" H. **$1,000**

Steuben Goblets, set of five, cranberry w/ clear crystal stems, 8" H. (one illus.) **$250**

Loetz Covered Compote, irid. blue w/ blue oil spot foot & bowl, 8½" H. **$650**

Steuben Stump Vase w/ 3 prongs, jade gr. on alabaster foot, 6¼" H. **$700**

Steuben Fan Vase, footed, light blue w/ controlled bubbles & threaded rim, 8¼" H. **$150**

Second Row

Moser Footed Tumbler, amber w/ blue foot & dec. w/ multi. colored flowers w/ heart shaped leaves, 4¼" H. **$500**

Webb Peachblow Vase, glossy finish floral dec., 5" H. **$170**

Slag Glass, 3 pcs. consisting of 5" pitcher (illus.), covered compote 8½" H., and a sugar w/ swan dec. **$90**

Gunderson Burmese Goblet, shades from cream to pink w/ glossy finish, 6¼" H. **$150**

Blue Jade Creamer, together w/ Rosaline covered dresser jar, 3" H. **$225**

Amberina Lemonades, vertical ribbed w/ applied amber handles (one illus.) 5" H. **$175**

Steuben Goblets, one Fr. blue, sgn., 7" H; an amethyst footed goblet w/ crystal stem 6" H., illus.; and an amethyst w/ blue stem, sgn. w/ Steuben Fleur-de-lis, 5¾" H. **$450**

Third Row

Yellow Jade Bowl, attrib. to Stevens & Williams, w/ an alabaster foot, 3¼" H. **$85**

French Blue Water Pitcher, D.Q. design, 10¾" H. **$500**

Pink Slag Sauce Dish, Inverted Fan patt., 2½" H., Est. $150-225 n/s

Rindskopf Stick Vase, Bohemian, red base color w/ striated white & blue pulled feathers, 6" H. **$100**

Peloton Vase w/ tri fold ruffled rim, dec. w/ striations of blue, red & yel. on glossy white ground, 6¾" H. **$125**

Fourth Row

Stevens & Williams Trumpet Vases, (one illus.), w/ alabaster foot extended up to an apricot fold over rim, 11¾" H. **$200**

Rosaline Dresser Jar, 3" H, together w/ a blue jade creamer **$170**

Cut Velvet Stick Vase, ribbed, deep pink & white, 6¼" H. **$175**

Steuben Goblet, amethyst w/ blue stem, 5¾" H. **$150**

Amberina Bowl, Daisy & Button patt. w/ scalloped rim, 4" H., 10" L. **$350**

Royal Doulton Stoneware Pitcher, light br., to dk. br. w/ raised hunting scene, 9½" H. **$200**

Steuben Goblet, cobalt blue, 6" H. **$150**

Steuben Topaz Candlesticks (one illus.) in Honeycomb patt., & sgn. w/ Steuben Fleur-de-lis, 12" H. **$700**

A-KS Jan. 2001   Woody Auction

Carnival Glass Plate, Fenton's Peacock at Urn patt., electric blue **$1,800**

GLASS

A-ME May 2001   James D. Julia, Inc.

Cameo Vase, sgn. Webb, sapphire blue background w/ white columbine leaves, 8" H. **$2,700**
Cameo Vase, Webb, unsign. w/ soft blue ground & white floral designs, a butterfly cameo on reverse side, 7" H. **$1,080**

A-KS Aug. 2001   Woody Auction

English Cameo Stick Vase, cranberry w/ white, artist sgn. J. Millward, 11¾" H. **$3,000**

A-ME May 2001   James D. Julia, Inc.

First Row
Mt. Washington Crown Milano Biscuit Jar, w/ gold chrysanthemum decor & orig. silver plated cover w/ butterfly finial, 8½" H x 7" W. **$1,495**
French Cameo Biscuit Jar, w/ decor of pink & white enameled flowers. Signed on base "VS", 6" H x 6" diam. **$1,550**
Moser Persian Vase, cranberry w/ three-handles & slight iridescent surface, 16" H x 12" diam. **$2,012**
Mt. Washington Royal Flemish Vase, decor. of peacock w/ jewels (three missing), sgn., 13" H. **$5,750**
Royal Flemish Cracker Jar, thistle decor & sgn., Pairpoint, 11" H overall. **$920**

Second Row
Mt. Washington Crown Milano Cracker Jar, painted Burmese background w/ acorn & oak leaf design, sgn., 9" H x 7" diam. **$431**
Jewelry Box, w/ lily decor on pink Kelva background. Pink satin lining. Signed Kelva. 5¾" Sq. **$632**
Mt. Washington Royal Flemish Oil Lamp Font, 4½" H. **$1,500**
Mt. Washington Crown Milano Sweetmeat, w/ thistle decor on diamond quilted patt., sgn., 5" H x 4¼" diam. **$402**
Jewelry Box, w/ pink floral decor. Signed Nakara. Metal feet modified, 4¼" H x 4½" W **$345**

A-KS Aug. 2001   Woody Auction

English Cameo Stick Vase, cranberry w/ white, artist sgn. J. Millward, 11¾" H. **$1,000**

A-OH Jan. 2001   Garth's Auctions

Cameo Vase, sgn. 'A Delatte, Nancy' w/ acid etched pine cones & branches in purple/ black on orange ground, minor imper, 3⅛" H. **$275**
Agata Bowl, N.E. Glass Co., pink shaded to dark pink, minor imper. 2⅜" H. **$1,265**
Wheeling Peach Blow Vase, w/ dark butterscotch shading to deep red, white int. 8¼" H. **$550**
Findlay Onyx Spooner w/ silver colored flowers, rim flakes, 4" H. **$437**
Steuben Calcite Bowl sgn. "F. Carder Aurene" w/ irid. white ext., gold int., 2½" H. **$275**

A-IA Dec. 2001   Jackson's International
                    Auctioneers & Appraisers

Daum Nancy Cameo Glass
Covered Box, ca. 1910, decor. w/ flowers & leaves w/ splashes of blue & amethyst, amber & green, sgn. "Daum Nancy" w/ Croix de Lorraine, 5" diam. **$2,300**

A-IA Dec. 2001   Jackson's International
                    Auctioneers & Appraisers

Daum Nancy Cameo Glass
Vase, ca. 1910, sgn., shades from yellow to amber w/ bleeding hearts & green vine decor., 7¼" H. **$1,380**

A-ME May 2001   James D. Julia, Inc.

First Row
Mt. Washington Burmese Glass Jack-In-The-Pulpit Vases, pr., matte finish, 16" H. **$1,550**
Crown Milano Ewer, w/ applied handle, decor includes landscape scene w/ sheep & shepherd. Signed, 10" H. **$4,887**
Crown Milano Biscuit Jar, decor of dandelions on painted Burnese background & silver plated hardware, 7" H x 4¾" diam. **$575**
Mt. Washington Crown Milano Lamp Base, decor. w/ blue & white asters on branches & green, brown leaves on painted Burnese background. Orig. Crown Milano paper label, 14¼" H **$575**

Mt. Washington Crown Milano Vase, w/ heavy enameled gold & silver azalea blossoms, 13½" H. **$2,472**
Second Row
Fairy Lamp, pyramid size Burmese fairy shades mounted in signed "CLARK ET AL" shade cup, 4⅜" H x 8" W. **$1,380**
Webb Burmese Epergne, five arms w/ miniature vases w/ all over floral decor, 9½" H. **$1,265**
Triple Rosebowls, peachblow pink satin glass, 3¼" H x 8½" L. **$150**
Fairy Lamp, w/ Burmese shade mounted in matching shade cup, signed "S. CLARK TRADEMARK FAIRY PYRAMID", 4" H. **$690**

A-IA Dec. 2001   Jackson's International
                    Auctioneers & Appraisers

Daum Nancy Cameo Glass
Vase, ca. 1900, light blue to green ground decor. w/ orange leaves & brown trees, 9¼" H. **$2,990**

A-OH Jan. 2001   Garth's Auctions, Inc.

Durand Vase, gold irid. w/ pink highlights, sgn. 6" H. **$550**
Cameo Vase, Eng., cranberry ground w/ white bands & branches, rim imper., 6½" H. **$522**
Fairy Lamp, w/ satin finish, deep pink shading to white, possibly Gunderson, glass holder mkd. Clark's, 6" H. **$165**
Cameo Vase, Mt. Washington, cut in low relief, purple w/ lt. blue inter., 6½" H. **$550**
Durand Vase, sgn. w/ silvery blue shading and magenta highlights, scratches on shoulder, 4⅞" H. **$522**

A-IA Dec. 2001   Jackson's International
Auctioneers & Appraisers

Devez Cameo Scenic Vase, ca. 1910, burgundy & cobalt glass cut w/ mountain lake & village scene, sgn. 12" H. **$1,495**

A-IA Dec. 2001   Jackson's International Auctioneers

Gallé Cameo Vase, ca. 1910, in gray glass overlaid w/ green & brown, 5¼" H. **$460**
Cameo Vase, ca. 1900, gray glass internally decorated w/ opalescent & peach mottling. Sgn. "Daum Nancy", 4¾" H. **$1,035**
Cameo Vase, ca. 1910, gray glass w/ pink tint overlaid in green & purple. Sgn. "Gallé", 6" H. **$632**
Cameo Vase, ca. 1900, amethyst colored glass w/ design heightened in gilt. Sgn. "Daum Nancy", 4½" H. **$517**
Cameo Vase, ca. 1910, gray glass w/ peach tint overlaid in opalescent, lime & forest green. Sgn. "Legras". Minor burst bubble, 5½" H. **$402**
Cameo Vase, ca. 1910, light blue translucent glass overlaid in lavender. Sgn. "Richard", 9½" H. **$431**
Wheel Carved Cameo Vase, ca. 1900, gray glass internally decorated w/ splashes of pink & yellow. Engraved "Daum Nancy", 5" H. **$2,127**
Cameo Vase, ca. 1910, citrine colored glass overlaid w/ maroon & blue. Sgn. "DeVez", 5¾" H. **$747**

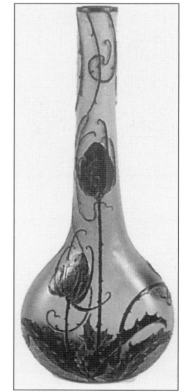

A-KS Aug. 2001   Woody Auction

French Cameo Cut Vase, lavender background, sgn. Mont Joye, 19" H. **$3,000**

A-ME May 2001   James D. Julia, Inc.

Gallé French Cameo Glass Vase, apricot to pale peach colored background w/ bright purple & green cameo design, sgn., 20" H x 9" diam. **$4,600**

Daum French Cameo Glass Vase, brilliant yellow, orange & pink background w/ cameo carved floral design, sgn., 24" H. **$4,025**

French Cameo Glass Vase, sgn. Daum, pink & yellow striped background w/ cameo enameled decor. of orange & purple, sgn., 9" H. **$8,050**

Gallé Cameo Vase, green fern decor w/ poppies on shaded salmon background, 14" H **$4,650**

A-OH Jan. 2001   Garth's Auctions, Inc.

Row 1, Left to Right

Scenic Cameo Glass Vase, sgn. "Daum Nancy", w/ grey ground, 3⅜" H. **$7,760**

Wheeling Peachblow Morgan Vase, yel. to cranberry, minor grinding, 8" H. **$1,155**

Loetz Glass Bowl w/ orange silvery blue striated irid. bands, 4½" H. **$412**

Wheeling Peachblow Morgan Vase, yellow to cranberry, flakes, 7½" H. **$495**

Cameo Glass Vase w/ sheel cut waterlilies in green on orange ground, sgn. "Muller Croismare pres Nancy" w/ butterfly, 4¼" H. **$770**

Row 2, Left to Right

Burmese Glass Biscuit Jar w/ decor. Pairpoint silverplate rim, 7¼" H. **$605**

Scenic Cameo Vase sgn. "DeVez" w/ etched decor. br. & yel. , 7⅞" H. **$880**

Vase, sgn. "Loetz Austria" w/ irid. gr. ground, 6⅝" H. **$1,045**

Vase, sgn. "Kew Blas" w/ gold/ pink/ gr. irid. feathered design, 7⅞" H, **$990**

Coralene Biscuit Jar w/ cranberry/ yel. seaweed, bead loss, 6⅞" H. **$302**

A-OH Jan. 2001   Garth's Auctions, Inc.

Cameo Vase, sgn. "Gallé". Acid etched lilies in purple & dark gr. on white ground, 12" H. **$1,375**

A-OH Nov. 2001   Garth's Auctions, Inc.

A-OH Feb. 2001   Garth's Auctions, Inc.

First row

Figural Bitters Bottle, deep amber Indian maiden w/ shield mkd. "Brown's Celebrated Indian Herb Bitters", "Pat. 1867", filled chip, 10½" H. **$99**

Bitters Bottle, amber, "Wm. Radam's Microbe Killer", w/ shield shaped label, sickness, 10¼" H. **$143**

Sandwich Glass Oil Lamp, apple gr. w/ paneled base & block variant font, int. residue, 8¾" H. plus collar **$250**

Bitters Bottle, deep golden amber w/ molded bark & a canoe, "H.H. Warner & Co" & "Tippecanoe", 9" H. **$88**

Ink Bottle, deep cobalt, mold blown, gothic arch patt., mkd. "Carter" at base 9¾" H. **$121**

Second row

Glass Oil Lamp, clear pressed, base w/ flakes & bruise, 8¼" H. plus brass collar & burning fluid burner **$154**

Oil Lamp, clear, pressed waterfall base w/ biscuit corners & blown font, brass collar, flakes w/ damage, 6" H. overall. **$115**

Bottles, two, grass gr. "Pine Tree Tar Cordial, Phila". "Patent 1859", 7¾" H., & slightly opaque cornflower blue bottle "John Ryan 1866 Savannah, GA", 7⅜" H. **$286**

Finger Lamps, pressed glass, two, Waffle & Thumbprint patt. w/ pewter burning fluid burner & snuffer cap, 5" H. and a lyre patt. w/ brass collar, 4" H. **$302**

Pressed Glass Oil Lamp, clear, baluster stem & font w/ bull's-eye & elongated thumbprint, base flaked, pewter collar & whale oil burner, 8¼" H. **$330**

Glass Kugels, three, two sm. have good gold color & brass hangers, 2½", 2¾" diam, third is lime gr. w/ a tin hanger, 3⅝" diam., all w/ minor wear **$55**

Glass Kugels, two, deep blue cobalt w/ copper hanger, one sapphire w/ brass hanger, some wear, 3⅝" diam. **$66**

Glass Kugels, three, light gold w/ brass hanger, wear & some flaking, 2⅝" diam., silver w/ brass hanger, some wear, 2¼" diam., & deep gold w/ copper hanger, some wear & tiny pot stone, 2½" diam. **$100**

Second Row

Glass Kugel, cobalt, copper hanger, minor wear, 4½" diam. **$55**

Glass Kugel, light teal gr. w/ copper hanger, some wear & blister, 4½" diam. **$99**

Glass Kugels, two, lime gr., wear, 4¾" diam., & lt. gold, wear, flaking & sm. bruise, 5½" diam., both have copper hangers. **$55**

Glass Kugels, two, red (shown), wear, 2¾" diam., & deep gold, blisters w/ minor flaking, 2¾" diam., both have brass hangers. **$99**

Glass Kugels, four, two lt. gold, 3¼" diam., 3¾" diam., deep gold 2⅝" diam., & one w/ little coloring or silvering left, 2¼" diam., 3 have minor wear, brass hangers & one repl. tin hanger. **$28**

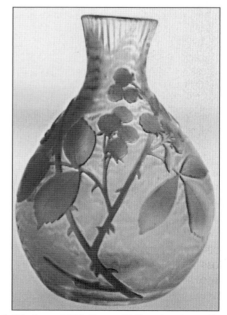

A-VA Sept. 2001 Green Valley Auctions, Inc.

Cameo Vase, w/ stripes of orange, purple & lt. green, acid-cut, by C. Dorflinger & Sons, 5" H. **$1,200**

A-MA Mar. 2001   Skinner, Inc.

Witch Balls, two similar, free-blown glass, MA, clear balls w/ four white loops on columnar stand, 8" diam. 16" H. & 7" diam. 15" H. **$2,070**
Bellows Bottle, parti-colored blown glass, MA, ca. 1885, applied lip over alt. red & white loop within colorless glass bellows form body, applied clear rigaree & bellows handles on applied clear round foot, lacks stopper, 5" W., 14½" H. **$373**
"Latticinio" Fluid Lamp, pink, white & clear free-blown glass, MA., ca. 1870-80, font w/ pink ribbons & fine white & clear threads joined by clear wafer to white & clear threaded baluster-form standard, minor inclusion, 5¼" diam., 10¼" H. **$3,220**
Witch Balls, pr. free-blown glass w/ stands, MA, ca. 1850-70, clear w/ four white loopings on baluster & ball-form stands, one stand w/ loss at base, 8" diam., 15¼" H. **$1,150**
Vase blown glass, red & opalescent white, ca. 1860-80, flared scalloped rim & applied base w/ knop & round foot, minor wear. **$1,955**

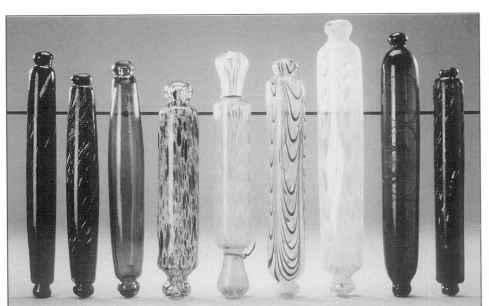

A-MA Mar. 2001   Skinner, Inc.

Glass Whimsey Rolling Pins, six, blown glass, Eng., 19th C., 1st amber w/ white speckles, 15⅛" L; 2nd blk. w/ white speckles, 14" L; 3rd pale translucent gr., 14½" L; 4th colorless white w/ blue & red speckles, 13¼" L; 5th pale aqua w/ white loops, 15" L; 6th diminutive translucent aqua, (not shown) 6¼" L. **$1,265**
Glass Whimsey Rolling Pins, four, blown glass, Eng. & possibly Eastern U.S., 19th C., 1st colorless w/ white & amethyst loop designs, 14¾" L; 2nd colorless w/ white loop designs, 17" L; 3rd blue w/ transfer-printed dec. & verses, 16" L; 4th dk. amber w/ white speckles, imper., 14" L. **$1,955**

A-VA Sept. 2000 Green Valley Auctions, Inc.

Westward Ho
Covered Compote, 9" diam., 16" H **$1350**
Covered Compote, 8" diam., 14½" H **$800**
Covered Compote, 7" diam., 12½" H **$350**
Covered Compote, 6" diam, 11½" H **$125**

A-VA Sept. 2000 Green Valley Auctions, Inc.

Spoon Holder, cut Spiked Argus patt., 7¼" H. **$90**
Vase, heavy lead glass, 10½" H, 6¼" diam. rim. **$130**

A-VA Sept. 2000 Green Valley Auctions, Inc.

Covered Compote, Thumbprint patt., 8" diam. rim, 14½" H. **$4,200**
Open Compote, Thumbprint patt., 10⅜" diam, rim, 8¾" H. **$600**

A-MA Mar. 2001   Skinner, Inc.

Pressed Glass Vases

First Row

Amethyst Vase, Bigler patt., poss. Boston & Sandwich Glass Company, Sandwich, MA, ca. 1840-60 w/ minor imper., 3" sq. base, 11¼" H. **$2,185**

Vaseline Vases, four-printie, possibly Sandwich w/ imper., 4½" base, 11½" H. **$1,035**

Paneled Tulip, blue-gr., Boston & Sandwich Glass Co., ca. 1845-65, octagonal base, 4½" diam., imper., 9½" H. **$4,025**

Bull's Eye & Ellipse patt., emerald gr., possibly N. Eng., 19th C., w/ base chips & other imper., 3¼" diam. **$1,035**

Amethyst Vase, possibly Sandwich, mid-19th C., sq. base, imper., 3¾" diam., 11½" H. **$2,185**

Amethyst Vase, Loop patt., MA, mid-19th C., w/ imper., base 3" diam., 10" H. **$2,070**

Second Row

Bull's-Eye & Ellipse patt., two similar emerald gr., 19th C., w/ hexogon bases, minor imper., 3¾" diam., 8¾" H.; 8¾" diam., 9" H. **$4,025**

Bull's-Eye & Ellipse patt., vaseline w/ minor imper., 3¼" diam., 7½" H. **$230**

Amethyst Vase, Twisted Loop patt., MA, ca. 1840-60, w/ circular faceted base, minor imper., 4" diam., 10" H. **$3,220**

Emerald Green Vases, Tulip patt., pr. w/ octagonal bases, minor imper., 4¼" diam., 10" H. **$9,200**

Three-Printie Block Vase, possibly N. Eng., 19th C., imper., 9¾" H. **$1,265**

Sapphire Blue Vases, similar, ca. 1850-80 w/ imper., 3¾" diam., 11⅛" H.; 3¾" diam., 11⅜" H. **$3,680**

Amethyst Vase, Tulip patt., MA, ca. 1845-65, w/ minor imper., 4⅜" diam., 10" H. **$4,600**

A-MA Mar. 2001   Skinner, Inc.

Cologne, emerald gr., blown molded, ca. 1840-70, faceted stopper, chips, minor roughness, 7¼" H. **$460**

Cologne, Amberina blown molded, ca. 1840-70, faceted stopper, minor imper. 7⅞" H. **$633**

Cologne, blue-gr. blown molded, elongated loop patt., ca. 1840-70, faceted stopper, rim chips, minor wear, 7¾" H. **$862**

Cologne, lt. gr. blown molded, ca. 1840-70, w/ faceted hex. stopper, chips, 6½" H. **$257**

Bar Bottle, canary blown molded "no ring", ca. 1855-70, w/ heavy bar rim over shaped neck, minor wear, lacks stopper, 10" H. **$517**

Cologne, amethyst blown molded, ca. 1840-70, w/ faceted hexogon stopper, several minor chips, 6¾" H. **$632**

Cologne, opaque pale blue blown molded, 2nd half 19th C., shaped faceted hexogon stopper over petal-form rim, white & gold enamel scrolling leaf vine design, shedding surface, 6" H, 4" diam. **$316**

Cologne, gr. canary blown molded, elongated Loop patt., MA, ca. 1840-70, paneled octagonal body w/ petals at the base, minor imper., 6¾" H. **$431**

Cologne, deep blue gr. blown molded elongated Loop patt. 1840-70, w/ faceted stopper, rim chip & crack, 7¾" H. **$460**

A-IA Sept. 2001   Jackson's International Auctioneers

Milk Glass

1144 Dish, w/ Robin on the Nest cover, one eye missing, 6" L. **$11**

1145 Dish, w/ fox cover, open lace base, chips, 8" L, 6½" h. **$62**

1146 Swan Cover, w/ open lace border, 9" L, 6" H. **$62**

1147 Hen On The Nest, w/ brown eyes, open tail, eggs protruding, 6½" H. **$34**

1148 Dish, w/ reclining cat, glass eyes, Pat. Aug. 1899, 6½" H. **$56**

1149 Dish, w/ hand holding a small bird w/ blue eyes & ring on finger, Pat. Aug. 1899, 8" L. **$22**

1150 Covered Dish, w/ camel having 2 humps, 5½" H. **$22**

1151 Covered Dishes, pair w/ chicks emerging from egg & pheasant on nest, chipped, 6" L. **$22**

1152 Dish, w/ cover, blue & white duck, missing eyes, 10" L. **$45**

1153 Covered Dish, form of pheasant, 6" L. **$17**

1154 Hen On The Nest, w/ red eyes & basket base, 8" L. **$39**

1155 Covered Dish in Form of Lamb, 5½" L. **$11**

1156 Swan Centerpiece, in form of frog, w/ pink acid finish, flakes, 9" L. **$34**

1157 Covered Dish, blue & white dog on blue base, small chip on lid, 5" L. **$11**

1158 Admiral Dewey, covered dish, cannon on drum, 4" diam. **$17**

1159 Covered Dish, w/ cannon on drum, 4" diam. **$45**

1160 Blue & White Covered Dish, lion, 5½" L. **$45**

1161 Covered Dish, swan w/ basket weave base, 9" L. **$45**

1162 Covered Dish, w/ Uncle Sam sitting on a gun boat, chips on base, 7" L. **$28**

1163 Dish, w/ cannon on drum. **$11**

1164 Covered Dish, w/ chick & egg in basket, paint worn. **$34**

1165 Sugar & Creamer, in leaf pattern & covered dish w/ cat. **$34**

1166 War Souvenir, Spanish-American w/ hen guarding eggs, 6" L. **$28**

1167 Hens on Nest, one mkd. "Vallerysthal", and one mkd. "Westmoreland", 2½" L. **$56**

1168 Covered Dish, w/ reclining lion, 5½" L. **$17**

1169 Robin on Nest, w/ acid finish mkd. "Westmoreland." **$6**

1169A Glass Hens on Nest, 7 blue & white w/ amethyst & white heads, two all amethyst. **$213**

A-VA Sept. 2001 Green Valley Auctions, Inc.

Jar, blue opalescent, 10½" H. **$230**
Jar, cranberry, 10" H. **$1,000**
Jar, blue to clear, 11¼" H. **$700**

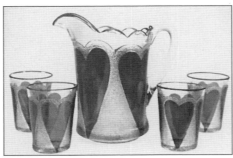

A-VA Sept. 2001 Green Valley Auctions, Inc.

Water Set, ruby stained, pitcher 8¾" H, tumblers 4⅛" H. **$3,200**

A-VA Sept. 2000   Green Valley Auctions, Inc.

Flint Goblets
Scarab, patt. **$130**
Tackle Block, patt. **$40**
Inverted Prisms & Concave Diamond Band, patt. 5⅜" H. **$110**
Waffle & Thumbprint, patt. 6¼" H. **$70.00**

A-VA Sept. 2000   Green Valley Auctions, Inc.

Non-Flint Tableware
Cheese Dish, Frosted Lion patt., 6" H, 7¾" diam. **$675**
Marmalade Jar, Frosted Lion patt., 6¾" H, 3½" diam. **$50**
Egg Cup, Frosted Lion patt., 3½" H, 2¾" diam. **$80**

A-VA Sept. 2000   Green Valley Auctions, Inc.

Flint Goblets
Panelled Fern, patt. **$45**   Panelled Ovals, patt. **$45**
Panelled Finetooth, patt. **$120**   Powder & Shot, patt. **$50**
    Prism & Crescent, patt. **$130**

A-VA Sept. 2000   Green Valley Auctions, Inc.

Open Compote, Sawtooth patt., 8" dia., 6" H. **$100**
Creamer & Covered Sugar, Smocking patt., 5⅛ H & 7⅝" H. **$240**
Covered Sugars, Smocking variant, pr., 4¼" & 6" H. **$20**

A-VA Sept. 2000   Green Valley Auctions, Inc.

Non-Flint Tableware
Covered Compote, Snail patt., 13" H, 8" diam. **$170**
Covered Compote, Snail patt., 11½" H, 7" diam. **$90**
Cracker Jar, Snail patt., 8¾" H, 4¼" diam. rim. **$350**

A-VA Sept. 2000   Green Valley Auctions, Inc.

Non-Flint Tableware
Covered Compote, Frosted Eagle patt., 10¾" H, 7" diam. **$35**
Covered Sugar Bowl, Frosted Flower Band patt., 9" H, 4¼" diam. **$110**
Covered Dish, Frosted Pheasant patt., 8½" x 6" oval, 7½" H. **$60**

A-MA Mar. 2001   Skinner, Inc.

Flasks

Blown Molded, Washington-Taylor portrait, med. gr. double collared, mouth-pontil scar, quart, attrib. to Dyotteville Glass Works, PA, ca. 1860-80. **$172**

Blown Molded, Washington-Taylor portrait, sapphire blue, sheared mouth-pontil scar, pint, attrib. to Dyotteville Glass Works, PA, ca. 1840-60, minor edge roughness. **$4,887**

Blown Molded, "Success to the Railroad", golden amber, sheared mouth-pontil scar, pint, Lancaster, N.Y. Glass Works, ca. 1849. **$4,312**

Blown Molded, "Genl Taylor", monument portrait, med. amethyst, sheared mouth-pontil scar, pint, Baltimore Glass Works, MD, ca. 1830-50. **$16,100**

Blown Molded, "Lockport Glass Works", N.Y., Washington portrait, med. gr. double collared mouth-iron pontil mark, quart, ca. 1845-60. **$4,025**

A-IA Dec. 2001   Jackson's International Auctioneers

U.S. Coin Glass

Lidded Syrup, w/ Seated Liberty quarter coins, 7" H. **$1,092**

Low Bowl, w/ Seated Liberty quarter coins, 6¼" D. **$690**

Compote, w/ Seated Liberty quarter coins on bowl & ten-cent coins on pedestal, 7¼" H. **$747**

Finger Lamp, w/ Seated Liberty twenty-cent coins on foot, 5" H. **$1,092**

Footed Sauce Dish, w/ Seated Liberty quarter dollar coin on bowl, 4" D. **$230**

Compote, w/ Seated Liberty quarter on bowl & one dime on pedestal, 6½" H. **$661**

Toothpick Holder, w/ Morgan Head one-dollar coin, roughness, 3" H. **$575**

Berry Dish, w/ Seated Liberty quarter dollar coins, 3½" D. **$230**

Stoppered Cruit ,w/ Seated Liberty quarter coin on base & one dime on stopper, 5½" H. **$1,150**

Compote, w/ Seated Liberty quarter on rim and one dime on base, 5½" H. **$747**

Goblet, w/ Seated Liberty dime on bowl, 6¼" H. **$488**

Bread Plate, w/ Seated Liberty and Morgan Head half dollar & one dollar coins on rim & base, 7" W, 10" L. **$1,150**

KITCHEN COLLECTIBLES

A-Pa Mar. 2001   Conestoga Auction Company

Woodenware

First Row, Left to Right

Foot Stool w/ dark blue & yellow geometric & star design, repr. to top, 9″ diam., 5½″ H. **$935**

Burlwood Butter Bowl, 19th C., mint, 17″ diam. **$2,420**

Candle Box, walnut, 19th C. w/ double sliding beveled lids & dov. const., 7″ W, 14″ L, 6″ H. **$275**

Second Row, Left to Right

Pastry Mold, maple, 19th C, w/ carved bird & floral designs, 11 ¼ L. **$412**

Butter Print w/ tapered handle, maple, 19th C., w/ carved tulip design, 4½″ diam. **$467**

Butter Print w/ double carved tulip, 3¼″ W, 4¼″ L. **$1,540**

Butter Print w/ carved sheaf of wheat design, 4¼″ diam. **$137**

A-NY Nov. 2000   Hesse Galleries

Lehn Wooden Cups, one w/ orig. paint decor., marbleized brown, 3⅛″ H. Second w/ three strawberries motif, 2¾″ H. **$715**

A-NY Nov. 2000   Hesse Galleries

Lehn Staved Wooden Box, w/ cover, orig. paint through out. 8½″ H. **$517**

A-MA Oct. 2001   Skinner, Inc.

Shaker Dipper, carved, N.Y. or N. Eng., mid-19th C., w/ finely shaped handle, 4¼″ diam., 6¼″ L, 2¾″ H. **$747**

Bowl, lg. wooden turned w/ blue paint, Am. 19th C., wear 19⅝″ diam., 7″ H. **$1,610**

Hanging Candle Box, Eng., mid-19th C., raised panel lid w/ hanging hole, containing early candles, dipped rushes & wax tapers, minor imper., 19½″ x 5¾″ x 4¼″. **$373**

Mirror, Q.A., 18th C., w/ walnut & walnut burl veneers, imper., 10⅜″ W., 16⅛″ H, sold w/ WALL SCRUB BOX, pine. **$373**

Knives, four carved wood & steel, Am., 19th C., wear, 11¼″, 10¼″, 9½″, 8⅜″. **$800**

Covered Bowl, mustard & br. grain-painted wood turned, PA, early 19th C., repair, 10″ diam., 8¾″ H. **$3,335**

Knife, carved, painted wood, steel & whalebone, Am., 19th C., red painted handle dec., heart-shaped whalebone inlay & sm. photo w/ carved ropetwist frame, wear, 9¼″ L. **$1,035**

Preening Greenwing Teal Bird, carved & painted, orig. br., tan, white & gr. paint, glass eyes, sm. chips, wear, 10¼″ L, 4½″ W, 4½″ H. **$488**

A-PA Nov. 2001   Conestoga Auction Company

Woodenware

Mixing bowl w/ orig. blue painted surface, 6½″ H, 19″ D. **$1,815**

Turned Wood Bowl w/ orig. red painted surface, 8″ H, 22″ D. **$3,300**

Mixing Bowl w/ orig. green painted surface, 10½″ H, 28″ D. **$4,675**

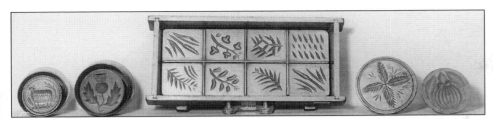

A-OH Feb. 2001   Garth's Auctions, Inc.

Cased Butter Print, unusual, sheep w/ rope twist border, refinished w/ two filled-in age cracks 2¾" diam. **$412**

Cased Butter Print, carved pomegranate, case is impr. "Patd. Apr. 17, 1866", 3¾" diam. **$110**

Cased Wooden Mold, unusual grid of stylized leaves, grass & acorns in a dov. frame secured w/ brass tacks, two feet attached w/ copper screws & white porcelain knob, 12⅛" x 5¼", 3⅜" H. **$121**

Butter Presses, two, pomegranate w/ natural finish, screw-in handle, 2⅞" diam, & four leaves w/ lightly ref. surface, inset handle may not be orig., 3½" diam. **$55**

Cased Butter Print, stylized cow, rope twist border, dk. patina, 4⅞" diam. **$220**
Cased Butter Print, acorn & leaf w/ rope twist border, dk. patina, 4⅝" diam. **$137**
Cased Butter Print, cow standing at fence w/ rope twist border, scrubbed finish, 4¼" diam. **$220**

A-IA Aug. 2001   Gene Harris Antique
                           Auction Center, Inc.

Toy Ice Cream Freezer, Wonder, missing one band. **$225**
Toy Ice Cream Freezer, Dana. **$325**
Toy Ice Cream Freezer, White Mountain Junior. **$450**
Toy Ice Cream Freezer, Wonder. **$450**
Toy Ice Cream Freezer, Dana. **$225**
Toy Ice Cream Freezer, Gem. **$225**
Ice Cream Individual Serving Container, Red Wing, w/ tin spoon, Dayton, OH. **$30**

A-PA Nov. 2001   Conestoga Auction Company

Baskets
First row

Covered Market Basket, oak & willow, lid is attached to handle of basket, 9" x 3". **$71**

Arschbacke Basket, painted dark green w/ red handle, oak splint, 13" x 12½". **$1,650**

Arschbacke Basket, oak const. w/ wire nails, wear & breaks, 10" x 10". **$71**

Second row

Arschbacke Basket, oak splint w/ nails securing rim to handle, orig., 11" x 12". **$330**

Arschbacke Basket, oak, lightly dyed, wear & fading, 10¼" x 9½". **$27**

Market Basket, oak splint w/ wire nails, red wash, surface wear & bottom breaks, 12" x 11". **$110**

Market Basket w/ double wrapped thick handle, oak splint, 12" x 8". **$192.50**

Third row

Berry Basket, oak splint, 6" x 5". **$71**

Miniature Arschbacke Basket, oak splint w/ chip carved handle, 5" x 4½". **$2,420**

Rye Straw Table Basket w/ open rim & simple foot, 12" x 4". **$165**

Minature Arschbacke Basket, oak splint w/ strap handle, 4" x 4". **$220**

Miniature Arschbacke Buttocks Basket, oak splint, 2" x 2". **$165**

Arschbacke Basket w/ controlled weave, minor breaks, 6" x 5" x 5". **$522**

Berry Basket, oak splint w/ chip carved handle, few breaks, 4" x 4½". **$1,760**

A-OH Feb. 2001   Garth's Auctions, Inc.

Coffee Mill, cast iron w/ decor., signed "Lane Brothers, Poughkeepsie, N.Y., The Swift Mill", #16 on base, w/ orig. red & blk. w/ decals around hopper, cast decals, handle missing & soldered reprs., molded oak base, honest overall wear, 36" H. **$1,210**

A-OH Apr. 2001   Garth's Auctions, Inc.

Tobacco Box, Dutch Brass, engr. scenes of couple & cherub on ea. side, Dutch script, resoldered hinge, 2½" x 4¾" L., 1" H. **$110**
Tobacco Box, Dutch, copper body w/ brass lid, engr. floral designs scenes of the three wise men on lid & base, Dutch script, 2" x 7" L., 3/8" H. **$440**
Butter Paddle, tiger maple w/ good patina, age crack & old edge chips in bowl, simple hooked handle, 8" L. **$165**
Burl Butter Paddle, dk. patina, simple hooked handle, 9¾" L. **$715**
Lollipop Butter Print, soft worn finish, carved heart leaves & chip carved stars, hole through handle, 6½" L. **$1,375**
Butter Print, primitive carved eagle w/ rayed starbursts, dk. patina w/ worn surface, lg. one pc. handle, 4⅜" diam. **$330**

Butter Print, PA, vibrant & deeply carved tulip w/ buds, age cracks 7 inset handle missing **$1,485**
Butter Print, PA, nicely carved tulip, good patina, age cracks, 5" diam. **$605**

A-OH Nov. 2001   Garth's Auctions, Inc.

Coffee Grinder, dovetailed w/ canted sides, iron top w/ brass hopper, mkd. "P.O. Wein No. 0", dents, 5¾" H, plus arm. **$220**
Treenware Containers, eight, shades of red stain, two shaped like rolling pins, 8¼" L. the rest are urn shaped, cylindrical or ovoid bucket w/ string handle, button finials in ivory, wear, 2" to 4¼" H. **$495**

A-OH Feb. 2001   Garth's Auctions, Inc.

First Row
Lollypop Butter Print, tiger maple w/ leaf design & chip carved edge, good patina w/ lightly scrubbed surface, age crack 8¾" L. **$330**
Butter Print, styled eagle w/ shield & laurel leaves, 3¾" diam. **$192**
Butter Print, deeply carved cow, scrubbed finish w/ age cracks, 4⅜" diam. **$165**
Butter Print, stylized eagle, good patina, prominent turning rings, 3" diam. **$275**
Butter Paddle, tiger maple, hooked handle, wear from use & short age crack, 9⅝" L. **$110**

Second Row
Butter Print, well-carved cow, dk. patina & signs of use, screw in handle missing, ring hanger added, 3¼" diam. **$192**
Butter Print, acorns & leaves, soft slightly shiny finish, short age crack, 3⅝" diam. **$110**
Butter Print, stylized tulip & rayed edge. dk. patina, inset handle missing, 4½" diam. **$137**
Butter Print, Prince of Wales feather crest, varnished w/ dk. br. paint or thick stain on back, age cracks, screw in handle, 3¼" diam. **$110**

A-NH Aug. 2001   Northeast Auctions
Cast Iron Coffee Grinder w/ eagle finial, mkd., Enterprise Mfg. Co., 39" H. **$3,500**

A-MA Feb. 2001   Skinner, Inc.

Baskets
Row 1, Left to Right
Splint Creel, painted forest green, Am., early 19th C., w/ carved wooden wire-hinged top, 8½" H. **$920**
Vertical Shaped Wooden Basket, Am. late 19th C., slats joined by twisted wire banding, painted surface, 18" H, 12½" D. **$862**
Native American Splint Basket, 19th C., old patina w/ red & orange banding, minor imperf. **$200**
Row 2, Left to Right
Native American Splint Basket, 19th C., old patina w/ black-painted fern design, 4" H, **$345**

Seven Woven Splint Baskets, 19th/20th C., comprising of 2 melon-form, 2 egg, two-handled basket, small w/ blue paint shown, and basket w/ green paint shown at far right. **$2,875**
Miniature, Am., 19th C., w/ loop handles & old taupe paint, 3" H. **$1,150**
Orange Painted Basket, Am., late 19th C., w/ fixed handle, 6" H. **$57**
Miniature Painted Bushel Basket, Am., 19th C., w/ old cream-white paint over red, 3¼" H. **$747**

A-NH Nov. 2001   Northeast Auctions

Four Nantucket Nesting Baskets, cylindrical w/ swing handle, 7½"-11½". **$4,200**
Scrimshaw Tooth w/ memorial scene & red sealing wax highlights, 5½" L. **$3,500**
Nantucket Open Basket w/ inset heart shaped handle, 4½" H overall, 11" diam. **$2,500**

Nantucket One Egg Basket w/ swing handle, 4" diam. **$2,500**
Miniature Bust Portrait by Abraham Parsell, of ship's captain, in brass frame inset in black painted frame, 2¼" x 1½". **$1,500**
Nantucket Oval Open Basket w/ twin d-form handles, 5¼" H, 10" L. **$650**

KITCHEN COLLECTIBLES

A-CA June 2001   Butterfields

Burled Maple Bowl, late 18th, early 19th C., cylindrical form w/ molded rim & base, 19½" diam., 7" H. **$3,818**

Burl Wood Bowls, three, one of tapering cylindrical form, two globular in form, greatest height 5". **$2,643**

A-CA June 2001   Butterfields

Peaseware Lidded Bowls, consisting of seven globular-form, two w/ floral painted decor. & one globular-form open salt. **$2,937**

A-NY Nov. 2000   Hesse Galleries

Butter Print, one w/ flower pot & plant, flat back, 3½" diam. Second w/ single flower, stem back, 3½" diam. **$632**

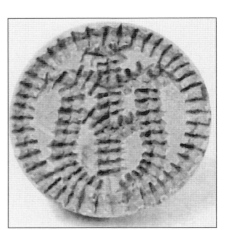

A-NY Nov. 2000   Hesse Galleries

Butter Print, tulip, knob back. 3¹⁄₁₆" diam. **$231**

A-MA Feb. 2001   Skinner, Inc.

Woodenware

Carved Burl Bowl, Am., 19th C., w/ banded rim, old surface, 4¼" H, 12" diam. **$632**

Carved Wood Scoop, Am., 19th C., 9½" L. **$20**

Alaska Wood Bowl, ca. 1886 w/ double molded rim, 2" H, 8½" W, & 17" L. **$1,150**

Shallow Burlwood Bowl & Scoop, 18th C., old surface, shrinkage crack to front of scoop, bowl 10½" diam., scoop 7½" L. **$2,070**

Carved Wood Canoe Cup, 19th C., w/ elongated bowl w/ carved beaver, 2¼" H, 5½" L. **$517**

Carved Footed & Handled Burl Bowl, 18th C., 8" H, 18" L, 14½" W. **$5,750**

A-NY Nov. 2000   Hesse Galleries

Butter Print, eagle & star, knob back. 3⅝" diam. **$863**

A-ME May 2001   James D. Julia, Inc.

GWTW Lamp, white milk glass w/ painted multicolored decor, green & gold background. Ball shade is replacement, 31" H. **$632**

Overlay Lamps, pr., foreign made in white cut to clear w/ gold decor. Some wear to gold decor, 25" H. **$1,667**

GWTW Lamp, white milk glass w/ rose & green decor on pink & green, 27" H. **$460**

Banquet Lamp, white milk glass w/ heavy pink & gold decor. Mounted on cast brass foot, 22" H. **$287**

Dragon Tea Caddy Lamp, cast metal rectangular base, 10" ruby glass shade w/ acid etched decor, 21" H. **$1,265**

Table Lamp, w/ floral decor. porcelain base in shades of dark blue w/ gold highlights, 31" H. **$575**

A-ME May 2001   James D. Julia, Inc.

GWTW Lamp, white milk glass w/ fruit decor. on green, pink & blue background. Ball shade is a repainted replacement, 27" H. **$517**

Miller Banquet Lamp, white metal, brass & marbled lamp body w/ reverse frosted 8½" shade w/ gold griffin decor, 29" H. **$460**

GWTW Lamp, white milk glass w/ milti colored decor. on blue, pink & green ground, 28" H. **$690**

A-ME May 2001   James D. Julia, Inc.

GWTW Lamp, Bradley & Hubbard w/ copperized metal font, griffin handles, pale green cased glass shade, 23" H. **$517**

GWTW Lamp, white milk glass w/ rose decor. on green & yellow ground. Shade is repainted replacement, 26" H. **$460**

GWTW Lamp, copper plated metal base w/ winged griffin handles & 1/2" reverse frosted clear glass shade w/ gold decor., 21" H. **$287**

LIGHTING

A-VA Sept. 2001 Green Valley Auctions, Inc.

Kerosene Lamp, lt. yellow green, small flake under foot, 4¾" H. **$45.00**

Kerosene Lamp, md. green, tiny flakes on base, 4¾" H. **$80.00**

Kerosene Lamp, smoke foot, lt. olive green, 4¾" H. **$190.00**

Kerosene Lamp, 4¾" H. **$175.00**

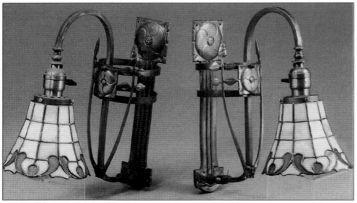

A-NJ May 2001   Craftsman

Wall Sconces, Arts & Crafts, brass, Eng., w/ Am. leaded-glass period shades, unmarked, 14½"H, shades 6" diam. **$2,200**

A-NJ Jan 2001   Craftsman

Tiffany Desk Lamp, w/ acid-etched bronze base & harp. Favrile glass shade w/ feathered patt. in a gold irid. finish, base stamped TIFFANY STUDIOS NY, shade etched L.C.T. Favrile, 13½" x 7" diam. **$4,500**

A-MA Mar. 2001   Skinner, Inc.

Pressed Glass Pattern Lamps
Bigler, pr., turquoise, MA., ca. 1840-60, octagonal concave paneled standards, 3" diam., 9¾" H. **$4,600**
Three-Printie Block, vaseline, 19th C., on knop & paneled hex. base, minor imper., 8" H. **$373**
Bigler, deep amethyst, MA., ca. 1840-60, octagonal concave paneled standard & sq. base, imper., 3" diam., 9½" H. **$2,185**
Bigler, amethyst, MA., ca. 1840-60, octagonal concave paneled standard & sq. base, minor imper., 3" diam., 9½" H. **$2,185**

Waisted Loop, yel. canary, MA, ca. 1840-60, pressed monument base, minor chips, 3½" diam., 10½" H. **$2,990**
Cobalt Blue, mid-19th C., arched faceted font on hex. tiered standard & base, minor imper., 4¼" W, 9¼" H. **$3,105**
Two Similar Waisted, 19th C., on hex. standards & tiered hexogon bases, minor imper., 8" H. & 8½" H. **$805**
Acanthus Leaf, blue & clambroth, MA., mid-19th C., font w/ six leaves on standard, 12 beads on vasiform standard w/four leaves on tiered beaded sq. base, sand finish, imper., 4" diam., 10¼" H. **$1,150**

A-ME May 2001   James D. Julia, Inc.

Hanging Lamp, red brass parker frame w/ raspberry shading to white M.O.P. satin glass. Herringbone patt. w/ matching colored font. Thirty-two crystal prisms, 14" diam. **$1,437**

Hanging Chandelier, cast iron w/ three-arms, acid etched, floral decor. on shades. One shade is cranberry, one opalescent blue & third opalescent pink. **$805**

A-IA Dec. 2001   Jackson's International Auctioneers

Table Lamp, w/ carmel slag glass shade w/ enameled grape design. Bronze bamboo patt. base, unmarked. Attrib. to Handel, 23" H. **$1,610**

A-SC June 2001   Charlton Hall Galleries, Inc.

Art Glass Lamp, 20th C., w/ bell shaped shade on baluster shaped stem, dec. w/ swirling feather design in amber & blue, 20" H. **$850**

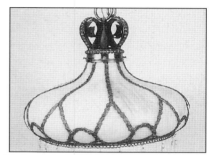

A-IA Sept. 2001   Gene Harris Antique Auction Center, Inc.

Yellow Slag Glass Hanging Shade sgn. Handel, 17" W. **$1,100**

A-MA Mar. 2001   Skinner, Inc.

Glass Fluid Lamps
Gilt-metal & Cut Double Overlay, MA, 19th C., frosted cut glass shade over foliate ring, standard embellished w/ foliage & an eagle centering image of George Washington, marble base, wear & minor imper., 6" diam., 28½" H. **$2,415**

Gilt-metal & Cut Overlay, MA, 19th C., frosted cut glass shade over scrolling foliate ring, overlay white cut to clear standard, marble base, minor wear & imper., 6" diam., 28½" H. **$1,265**

Gilt-metal & Cut Overlay Quatrefoil, MA, ca. 1860-80, frosted & cut colorless glass shade over slash & quatrefoil font, punty standard & gilt-metal & marble base, 6¼" diam., 33¼" H. **$10,350**

Cut Double Overlay, 19th C., w/ frosted & cut glass shade & glass chimney over foliate brass rings, blue cut to white cut to clear standard, marble base, 5½" diam., 30½" H. **$4,600**

A-IA Apr. 2001   Gene Harris Auction Center

Victorian Hanging Lamp w/ cranberry hobnail shade, brass fittings. **$1,900**

A-CA June 2001　　　　Butterfields

Tiffany Favrile Glass Shade on an unmkd. patinated bronze standard. The domical shade is composed of mottled amber & green glass, w/ stamped mark, shade 16½" diam., 22½" H. **$8,812**

A-CA June 2001　　　　Butterfields

Tiffany Floor Lamp, composing of radiating graduated rectangular & diamond-shaped tiles in mottled & striated amber, white & butterscotch. The border includes textured amber, brown & white rectangular glass on a textured gilt-bronze cylindrical standard, over a circular base on ball feet. Shade sgn. "Tiffany Studios New York", base w/ impressed mark, 6'6" H. **$63,375**

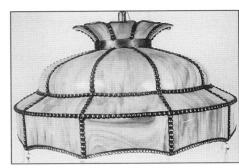

A-IA Sept. 2001　　　Gene Harris Antique Auction Center, Inc.

Hanging Pink Slag Glass Shade, 24" diam. **$300**

A-IA Sept. 2001　　　Gene Harris Antique Auction Center, Inc.

Hanging Leaded Glass Shade w/ floral & grape design, 23½" diam. **$700**

A-CA June 2001　　　　Butterfields

Tiffany Patinated Bronze Lamp, w/ an associated Tiffany leaded glass Dragon fly shade, w/ radiating pendant dragonflies amid shaped green glass tiles. Base mkd. "Tiffany Studios/ New York & T.G. & D. Co.", shade 14" diam., 19½" H. **$40,625**

A-CA June 2001　　　　Butterfields

Tiffany Bronze & Favrile Glass Six-Light Chandelier, w/ lilly-form iridescent gold glass shades w/ green-brown patina, shades sgn. "L.C.T.", 18" H. **$9,987**

A-IA Sept. 2001　　　Gene Harris Antique Auction Center, Inc.

Cut Glass Parlor Lamp sgn. Pairpoint, 18½" H. **$500**

A-NJ May 2001   Craftsman
Heintz Boudoir Lamp, Sterling-on-Bronze, w/ overlay of day lilies on the bulbous base. Cut-out shade w/ orig. pleated fabric liner, few scratches, 11" x 11½" **$2,700**

A-MA May, 2001   Craftsman
Handel Desk Lamp, orig. patina, fabric label, 12" H. **$1,200**

A-MA May, 2001   Craftsman
Handel Desk Lamp, orig. patina, fabric label, 12" H. **$1,200**

A-MA Mar. 2001   Skinner, Inc.

Glass Fluid Lamps
Cut Double Overlay, MA, ca. 1860-80, cobalt blue cut to white cut clear glass font, brass connector on marble base w/ gilt-metal trim, minor imper., 16¼" H. **$9,775**
Cut Overlay, ca. 1860-80, transparent turquoise blue cut to clear glass font, brass connector on marble base w/ gilt-metal trim, minor wear, 16⅛" H. **$4,025**
Cut Double Overlay, pr., MA, ca. 1860-80, cobalt blue cut to white cut to clear glass on font, flared fluted columnar brass standard, marble bases w/ brass trim, minor imper. 11¾" H. **$4,025**
Cut Double Overlay, MA, ca. 1860-80, cranberry cut to white, cut to clear glass on font, flared fluted columnar brass standard, marble base w/ brass trim, minor wear, 12½" H. **$2,070**

Cut Overlay, MA, ca. 1860-80, transparent amethyst glass cut to clear on font, flared fluted columnar standard, marble base w/ brass trim, minor wear, 10⅝" H. **$2,530**
Cut Double Overlay, 1860-80, cranberry cut to white cut to clear glass on font, flared fluted columnar brass standard, marble base w/ brass trim, imper., 13½" H. **$1,955**
Cut Overlay, MA, ca. 1860-80, white cut to transparent gr. w/ gilt outlines on glass font, suspended leaves on brass connector joins standard on marble base w/ gilt-metal trim, minor imper., 16¼" H. **$6,900**
Cut Double Overlay, MA, ca. 1860-80, cobalt blue cut to white to clear glass font, brass connector joins standard on marble base w/ gilt-metal trim, minor imper., 16½" H. **$12,650**

A-ME May 2001　　　　James D. Julia, Inc.

First Row

Overlay Lamp, white cut to cranberry w/ Moorish windows. Chipping to the overlay glass, 13½" H. **$575**

Overlay Lamp, white cut to clear. w/ manf. defect in one cut circle caused by a burst bubble. Normal wear to marble edges, 11" H. **$390**

Overlay Lamp, cranberry cut to clear. Minor wear to base & font, 12½" H. **$977**

Second Row

Overlay Lamp, cobalt blue cut to clear, 18½" H. **$1,092**

Table Lamp, cut crystal font on brass stem & double step marble base, 11¾" H. **$180**

Overlay Lamp, green cut to clear. Some chipping to marble base, 20¼" H **$603**

Overlay Lamp, white cut to cranberry w/ Moorish windows, 13" H. **$575**

Overlay Lamp, ruby cut to clear w/ pearl top flanged chimney. Some missing overlay glass, 13" H. **$480**

Overlay Lamp, white cut to cranberry w/ Moorish windows, chip on foot, 13" H. **$270**

A-ME May 2001　　　　James D. Julia, Inc.

GWTW Larkin Lamp, yellow background w/ multi-colored rose decor, 28½" H. **$1,495**

GWTW Lamp, brass font w/ copper colored handles. White milk glass 8½" shade w/ green, brown & gold background, 20" H. **$287**

GWTW Lamp, white milk glass w/ multi-colored decor on pink & blue ground, 22" H. **$460**

GWTW Lamp, copper plated metal font w/ silver & brass winged griffin handles. 8" frosted crystal shade, 22½" H. **$201**

Banquet Lamp, Bradley & Hubbard, brass plated base, lamp signed B & H, 30" H. **$575**

A-VA Sept. 2000 Green Valley Auctions, Inc.

Oil Lamp, Acanthus Leaf patt., 11½" H. **$60**

Oil Lamp, Argus patt., 8½" H. **$110**

Oil Lamp, Baby Thumbprint patt., 3½" H. **$320**

Oil Lamp, Bellflower patt., 7¼" H. **$80**

A-VA Sept. 2000 Green Valley Auctions, Inc.

Oil Lamp, blown conical font, 9" H. **$150**

Oil Lamp, blown conical font, 9" H. **$160**

Oil Lamp, blown conical font, 6⅞" H. **$140**

Oil Lamp, blown conical font, 6¾" H. **$150**

Oil Lamp, blown conical font, 6½" H. **$280**

A-VA Sept. 2001 Green Valley Auctions, Inc.
Peg Lamps, pr., cased red to pink satin, brass saucer base candlesticks, 5½" shade, 16" H, overall. **$1,800.00**

A-VA Sept. 2001 Green Valley Auctions, Inc.
Kerosene Lamp, rose to white to clear, 13" H. **$1,550.00**
Kerosene Lamp, cranberry to clear, 8½" H, to burner. **$475.00**
Kerosene Lamp, fiery opalescent cut to clear, 8½" H. **$250.00**

A-VA Sept. 2000 Green Valley Auctions, Inc.
Kerosene Lamp, Cathedral patt., 12½" H. **$180**
Kerosene Lamp, Cathedral patt., 12½" H. **$180**
Kerosene Lamp, Chicago patt., 9⅞" H. **$130**

A-VA Sept. 2000 Green Valley Auctions, Inc.
Kerosene Lamp, Greek Key patt., 8¾" H. **$400**
Kerosene Lamp, Hobbs Snowflake patt., 7½" H. **$190**
Kerosene Lamp, Hobnail patt., 15¼" H. **$180**
Kerosene Lamp, Hobnail patt., 4¾" H. **$310**

A-ME May 2001   James D. Julia, Inc.

First Row
Whale Oil Finger Lamps, pr., cobalt blue glass w/ single tube whale oil burners & pewter collars. One lamp has ¼" crack in body where handle is attached, 3½" H. **$1,380**
Whale Oil Finger Lamps, pr., teal green glass w/ single tube whale oil burners. Both lamps damaged, 3¼" H. **$575**

Second Row
Whale Oil Finger Lamps, pr., in amethyst glass. Both cracked body, 3¼" H. **$345**
Whale Oil Finger Lamp, sky blue glass, 3¼" H. **$690**
Whale Oil Finger Lamp, white opalescent, 3¼" H. **$1,495**

Third Row
Whale Oil Finger Lamp, green glass, 3¼" H **$620**
Whale Oil Finger Lamp, cobalt blue glass. ¼" chip on handle base, 3¼" H. **$690**
Minature Whale Oil Finger Lamp, dark amethyst glass, 3¼" H. **$6,037**
Vaseline Candleholder, light green, edge roughness. **$115**

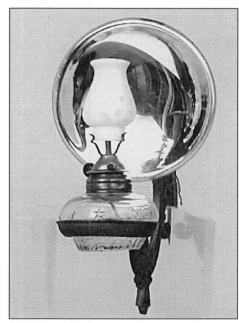

A-ME May 2001   James D. Julia, Inc.
Minature Wall Bracket Lamp, w clear glass font & white milk glass chimney shade, mkd. "Nightwatch". **$460**

A-ME May 2001   James D. Julia, Inc.

First Row

Shades, pr., cream & green pulled feathers on gold iridescent background, sgn., 5" H x 5¼" diam. **$345**

Shades, pr., green & gold iridescent w/ gold interior, 5" H. **$517**

Steuben Shade, set of 8, sgn., ribbed gold Aurene, 5" H. **$1,265**

Quezal Shade, sgn., snake skin, blue-green & gold iridescence w/ gold interior, 5" H 4" diam. **$660**

Second Row

Steuben Shade, sgn., gold ribbed, 5¼" H. Small chips on fitter. **$250**

Quezal Shade, pr., red iridescence w/ blue highlight, 5½" H. **$575**

Steuben Shade, sgn., pulled feather in green on gold iridescent, 3½" H. **$431**

Steuben Shade, pr., sgn., gold Aurene, 4½" H x 4¾" diam. **$287**

Tiffany Shade, pr. (pictured most right in second & third rows), sgn., w/ gold iridescence, 5" H. **$1,495**

Third Row

Shades, set of three, gold Aurene ribbed, sgn., 4¼" H x 4¾" diam. **$278**

Quezal Shade, pr., sgn., decor. of gold pulled feather on cream background, 5½" H. **$776**

Quezal Shade, pr., sgn., cylindrical of gold iridescent background w/ cream pulled feather design, 5" H. **$546**

A-VA Sept. 2000 Green Valley Auctions, Inc.

Miniature Lamp, blue milk glass, 7¾" H. **$280**

Miniature Lamp, milk glass, 8¼" H. **$70**

A-VA Sept. 2000 Green Valley Auctions, Inc.

Kerosene Lamp, Applesauce patt., 12¾" H. **$600**

Atterbury Cottage Lamp, 11" H. **$110**

Kerosene Lamp, w/ball base, 5¾" H. **$170**

Kerosene Lamp, barrel shape, 9¼" H. **$220**

A-ME May 2001   James D. Julia, Inc.

First Row

Table Lamp, caramel & white slag w/ border of pink & green. Shade 18" diam, 24" H overall. **$690**

Hanging Chandelier, leaded glass varigated slag w/ mottled green, white, caramel & lavender, 22" diam. **$1,400**

Table Lamp, w/ brown slag & leaded blue slag inserts. Shade 19" diam, 22" H overall. **$345**

Second Row

Table Lamp, Phoenix reverse painted, sky shades from salmon to light yellow, landscape includes reds, yellows, gray, browns. Shade 18" diam, 23" H overall. **$1,525**

Hanging Chandelier, leaded, decor. all over with variegated pink roses, 29" diam. **$1,150**

Table Lamp, Phoenix reverse painted, w/ panoramic forest scene w/ leafy trees. Shade 18" diam, 23" H overall. **$1,420**

A-OH Nov. 2001   Garth's Auctions, Inc.

Punched Tin Lantern, sq. w/ pointed top, tin candle socket & ring handle, door has chained latch, 11⅜" H. **$825**

Lantern, tin w/ three beveled edge glass panes, mkd. "Duntafil Patent", 9¾" H. **$412**

Punched Tin Revere Lanterns, one illus. has shiny surface, 11" H., plus ring, second has minor damage & resoldered hinges, 12½" H. plus ring **$715**

Footwarmer, w/ punched tin heart designs, mortised wooden frame w/ turned posts & wire bale handle, latch repl., 5¾" H. **$192**

Lamp, w/ glass font, brass burner & tin frame w/ reflector, & an eight-tube tin candlemold w/ strap handle, 10¼" not illus. **$275**

A-NY Apr. 2001   Hesse Galleries

Demilune Lantern, pierced tin, w/ two candle sockets, 19½" H. **$220**

A-NY Apr. 2001   Hesse Galleries

Lamps, pr., brass, for camphene or whale oil burners; burners not included, 8⅝" H. **$110**

A-PA Oct. 2001   Conestoga Auction Company

Tin & Iron Ware

Row 1, Left to Right

Miniature Four Tube Candle Mold w/ splayed top & platform base, 3" x 3". **$412**

Candle Mold, small size w/ five tubes on platform base & handle, 4½" H. **$440**

Miniature Candle Sconces, pr., by Schutty, Lititz, PA, ca. 1900, 3½" H. **$1,100**

Row 2, Left to Right

Fat Lamp w/ scalloped saucer base & applied handle, 2" H, 4½" D. **$71**

Child's ABC Mug w/ embossed design, 2½" H & ABC plate 2¼" D. **$247**

Betty Lamp, stamped "P.D. 1852" (Peter Derr, Berks Co., PA) w/ shaped brass reservoir & copper base, wrt. iron arm & hanging spike w/ brass chain wick pick, 5½" H. **$3,960**

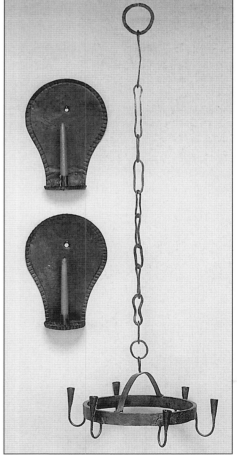

A-CA June 2001   Butterfields

Tin Wall Sconces, pr., 19th C., w/ crimped border & drip pan, 13½" H. **$822**

Wrought Iron Six-Light Chandelier, Am. or Cont., late 18th or early 19th C., 27" diam., 8" H. **$1,116**

LIGHTING

Miner's Dagger Sticks, three wrought iron candleholders, two at 8¼" H & one 10" H. **$187**

Bristol Glass Spring Candle Lamps, pr., 20" H. **$220**

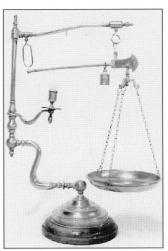

Balance Scale w/ Integral Candle Socket, brass w/ wooden base. Candlestick arm rotates to locate light, 22¾" H. **$286**

Lacemaker's Lamp, free blown, orig. tin & cork burner, 8⅜" H. **$396**
Lacemaker's Lamp, French, light amethyst, cut glass font, 10¾" H. **$192**

Bristol Glass Spring Candle Lamps, pr., 19" H. **$247**

Sandwich Whale Oil Lamp, ca. 1835, cobalt blue w/ deep purple tones, 9½" H. **$742**

Flemish Spout Lamp, brass, (also known as barber's lamp), 13⅞" H. **$77**

Student Lamp, ca. 1875, brass w/ yellow satin glass shade, 21¼" H. **$495**

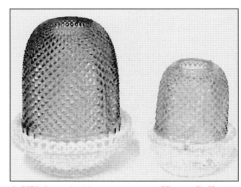

Clark's Fairy Pyramid Lamp, two, first w/ green font, 5" H, second with amber, 3¾" H, clear bases. **$58**

A-NY Apr. 2001   Hesse Galleries
Rush Light Holder, w/ penny feet, 9" H.
$165

A-NY Apr. 2001   Hesse Galleries
Chamberstick & Lamp Combination, tin,
7¾" H. **$115**

A-NY Apr. 2001   Hesse Galleries
Milk Glass Lamp, D.P. patt. w/ Victor
burner, excluding chimney, 11½" H. **$115**

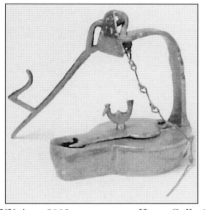

A-NY Apr. 2001   Hesse Galleries
Betty Lamp, brass, imprinted 1840, wick
tube missing, 9½" H. **$93**

A-NY Apr. 2001   Hesse Galleries
Camphene Lamp, w/ orig. brass collar &
two prong pewter burner, 13⅛" H. **$539**

A-NY Apr. 2001   Hesse Galleries
Peg Lamp, cranberry w/ brass candle-
stick, marked "HS" on thumb wheel, 14⅞"
H. **$225**

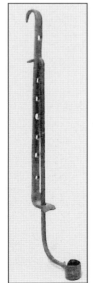

A-NY Apr. 2001   Hesse Galleries
Loom Light, 18th C., adjustable wrought
iron, 16½" H. **$280**

A-NY Apr. 2001   Hesse Galleries
Canting Lamp, tin, w/ reflector back.
Chamberlaine Patent, traces of paint
remain, 12" H. **$1,375**

A-NY Apr. 2001   Hesse Galleries
Wax Jack, Sheffield silverplate w/
extinguisher, 5¼" H. **$187**

A-NY Apr. 2001   Hesse Galleries

Trunnion Lamp, brass, w/ double spout, 10" H. **$55**

A-NY Apr. 2001   Hesse Galleries

Whale Oil Lamp, tin, marked "Patented May 6th 1856, Samuel Davis", 7¼" H. **$742**

A-NY Apr. 2001   Hesse Galleries

Whale Oil Lamp, pr., w/ tumbler base, sandwich glass w/ brass collar, one w/ pewter, 12¼" H. **$935**

A-NY Apr. 2001   Hesse Galleries

Oil Lamp, brass & amethyst glass, marked "Rundbrenner" on thumb wheel. Mounted on base, 11¼" H. **$93**

A-NY Apr. 2001   Hesse Galleries

Kerosene Lamp, brass, ca. 1870s, w/ flashed cranberry chimney, P & A Hornet burner, 10¼" H. **$110**

A-NY Apr. 2001   Hesse Galleries

Trunnion Lamp, brass, w/ double spout, 10" H. **$55**

A-NY Apr. 2001   Hesse Galleries

Peg Lamp, cranberry glass & brass candle-stick, brass collar & burner, marked "R.S. Merrill's Patent, July 10, '66", 11⅞" H. **$170**

A-NY Apr. 2001   Hesse Galleries

Camphene Burning Lamp, pewter w/ brass burner screws in, imprinted with 5 on bottom, 10" H. **$44**

A-NY Apr. 2001   Hesse Galleries

Configurated Glass Hand Lamps, two amber colored w/ applied handles, 3¼" H. **$176**

A-SC June 2001   Charlton Hall Galleries, Inc.

First Row
Sterling Four Light Candelabra, Mexican, pr., mid 20th C., 10½" H, 11" diam. **$1,000**
Sterling Silver Coffee Service, 3-piece, by Fisher, Colton & Kinson, VT, ca. 1877, coffeepot 9" H, all mkd. **$600**
Gorham Silver Center Bowl, RI, ca. 1941, 12" diam., 3" H. **$300**
Second Row
Sterling Silver Tray, Fuchs & Beiderhase, NY, ca. 1891-1896, 10¾" sq. **$450**
Silver-Plated Bowl, crystal center, Art Deco, mid 20th C., 7¾" H, 14¼" W, 9" D. **$350**
Sterling Silver Center Bowl, Tiffany & Co., ca. 1943, w/ two floral form handles, 2½" H, 11¼" W. **$1,200**
Sterling Silver Cake Stand, three-tier, by Black, Starr & Frost, ca. 1900, 16" H, 11" diam. **$1,100**
Third Row
Silver-Plated Serving Tray, double handled, first half of 20th C., 18" W, 29" L. **$225**
Silver-Plated Serving Tray, w/ handles, 20th C., 17½" W, 27" L. **$275**

A-SC June 2001   Carlton Hall Galleries, Inc.
Sterling Silver Paul Revere Bowl, 20th C., Tiffany & Co., 3⅞" H, 7¾" diam. **$450**

A-SC June 2001   Carlton Hall Galleries, Inc.
Cream Pitcher, sterling silver mounted cut-crystal, by Black, Starr & Frost, NY, ca. 1876, 7" H. **$350**

A-SC March 2001   Charlton Hall Galleries, Inc.
Sterling Silver Coffee & Tea Service, five-piece, Watson Company, ca. 1915, approx. 64 troy oz, 10½" H. **$2,600**

A-NY Apr. 2001   Hesse Galleries
Chamberstick w/ Snuffer, Sheffield silverplate, crown imprinted on handle, 5¾" H. **$137**

A-SC Dec. 2001   Charlton Hall Galleries, Inc.

Tiffany Studios Desk Set, nine pc., gilt bronze & MOP ca. 1920, "Abalone" patt. **$4,800**

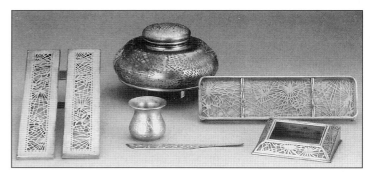

A-CA June 2001   Butterfields

Desk Set, Tiffany gilt bronze, 7 pc. set, in the etch metal & glass pine needle pattern, comprising of inkwell, pen tray, two blotter ends, letter opener, small frame & small vase, some fitted w/ striated white & butterscotch glass panels, each mkd. "Tiffany Studios/ New York", ca. 1898-1928. **$2,350**

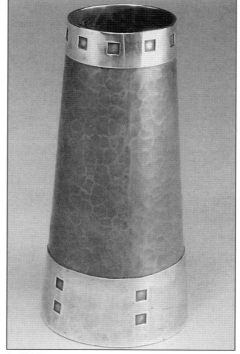

A-NJ May 2001   Craftsman

Brass Coffee Set, four-piece, hand hammered, polished brass, riveted spouts & boar's tusks handles, monogrammed mkd. Jarvie, 9" x 7". **$2,000**

A-NJ May 2001   Craftsman

Circular Tray, Roycroft, hammered copper w/ riveted handles & orig. reddish patina, stamped orb & cross mark, 18" diam. **$600**

A-NJ Jan 2001   Craftsman

Gustav Stickley Coal Scuttle, hammered copper, riveted arrow motif iron handles, orig. patina, impressed circular stamp, "Gustav Stickley, The Craftsman Workshops", 24" x 15". **$9,500**

A-NJ Jan 2001   Craftsman

Roycroft Vase, hvy. gauge hammered copper, by Dard Hunter w/ cut-out silver band overlay to rim & base, orig. patina, Orb & Cross mark, 7" x 3½". **$9,000**

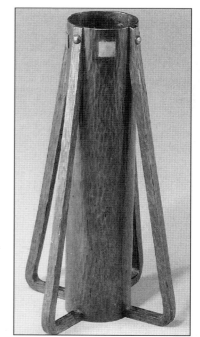

A-NJ Jan 2001   Craftsman

Roycroft Vase, "Egyptian" hammered copper w/ four buttresses & applied German silver squares orig. patina, Orb & Cross mark, 7⅞". **$4,500**

A-NY Nov. 2000　　　　Hesse Galleries
Toleware Bread Tray, 12¾" L. **$990**

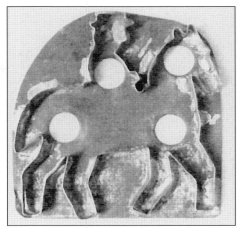

A-NY Nov. 2000　　　　Hesse Galleries
Cookie Cutter, tin horse & rider. 5½" H.
$472

A-NY Nov. 2000　　　　Hesse Galleries
Cookie Cutter, tin raindeer. 6¼" H. **$374**

A-PA Oct. 2001　　　　Conestoga Auction Company

Tin Cookie Cutters
Row 1, Left to Right
Pig Form w/ folded edge & handle, 3" x 5". **$60**
Spread Wing Eagle Form w/ punched decor. around finger hole, 4½" x 4½". **$247**
Love Birds, shield & bell form w/ folded edge & handle, 3½" H, 5½" W. **$253**
Squirrel Form w/ scalloped tail & punched decor., 4" H, 5" W. **$192**
Row 2, Left to Right
Rabbit Form w/ punched decor. 2½" H, 4½ W. **$104**
Man on Horseback w/ folded edge handle, some rust, 7½" H, 5½" W. **$357**
Tomahawk Form w/ folded edge handle, 6¼" H, 4½" W. **$71**
Bird & Rodent Forms, bird 3" H, rodent 2½" H. **$33**
Row 3, Left to Right
Goose Form w/ minor rust, 5½" H, 5¼" W. **$38**
Stag Form w/ minor losses, 5½" H, 4½" W. **$121**
Horse Form, 4" H, 4¼" W. **$38**
Leaf & Heart Forms w/ folded rim handles, heart 3½" H, leaf 5½" H. **$44**

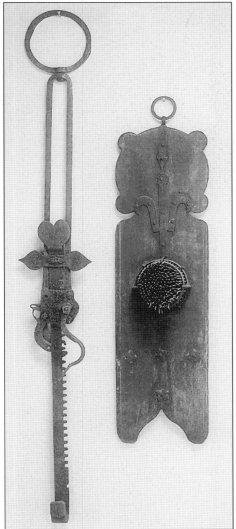

A-CA June 2001　　　　Butterfields
Wrought Iron Trammel, 18th C., w/
heart-shaped adjustable gear & crank, 5'
L., 9" W. **$646**
Wrought Iron & Wood Hatchel, Am. 18th
C., backboard centering a banded group
of teeth hung on a strap, metal hook, 41"
L, 11" W. **$881**

A-NY Nov. 2000   Hesse Galleries

Coffeepot, pewter, marked "F. Porter, Westbrook, No. 1". 10¾" H. **$357**

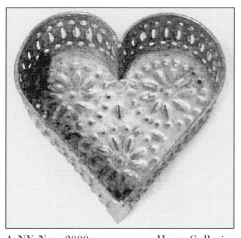

A-NY Nov. 2000   Hesse Galleries

Cheese Mold, heart form footed pierced tin. 6" H. **$440**

A-NY Nov. 2000   Hesse Galleries

Toleware Syrup Pitcher, 4" H. **$990**

A-NY Nov. 2000   Hesse Galleries

Coffeepot, pewter, marked "Boardman & Co.". 10" H. **$370**

A-NY Nov. 2000   Hesse Galleries

Coffeepot, pewter, marked "F. Porter, Westbrook, No. 1". 11½" H **$495**

A-NY Nov. 2000   Hesse Galleries

Toleware Covered Sugar, 3¾" H. **$4,400**

A-NY Nov. 2000   Hesse Galleries

Bedroom Stove, cast iron, "Laurel" "No. 2 Patented 1856". 27½" H. **$77**

A-NY Nov. 2000   Hesse Galleries

Coffeepot, pewter, marked "Boardman & Hart, New York". 11" H **$192**

A-NY Nov. 2000   Hesse Galleries

Toleware Coffeepot, near mint condition. 10½" H. **$11,000**

A-NH Nov. 2001

Northeast Auctions

Pewter

First Row

Tankards, Eng. & continental incl. two tapered Eng. examples, one mkd. Townsend & Compton, London; two Ger. lidded tankards w/ incised dec., mkd. ADK, 1794; one w/ man & woman w/ maker's touch; and a sm. tankard w/ banding, tallest 10" H, (four illus.) **$2,500**

Deep Dishes, Am., two, one by Thomas Danforth, and second by Samuel Kilbourne of Baltimore, both 13" diam. **$2,200**

Porringers, 6 of graduated sizes, w/ handles, old Eng. designs, diam. of largest 5½", smallest 2". **$1,200**

Second Row

Charger & Coffeepot, Eng., charger w/ multiple reeded edge; the domed coffeepot w/ pear shaped body, serpent-form spout & wooden handle, 11" H. (first illus.) **$1,300**

Teapot, by Samuel Simpson of CT; water pitcher by Rufus Dunham of ME; & a domed pear-shaped coffeepot 10½" H. (part illus.) **$650**

Measures, Eng. & Scottish, lidded, one mkd. SBD, tallest 5½". **$950**

Chargers, three w/ ribbed edges & a domed-top flagon, one charger by Thomas Danforth, 13½" diam; one by Townsend & Compton, London 14¾"; & a 13¾" example by Christopher Baldwin of Wigan, together w/ a flagon 13" H. **$2,400**

Candlesticks, pr. w/ removable bobeche & mkd. J. Weekes of NY; second pair by F. Porter of Westbrook, ME, and a sm. single candlestick mkd. Flagg & Homan, Cincinnati, OH, (part illus.) **$1,500**

Pitcher & Two Teapots, Am., one w/ wooden handle mkd. R. Gleason, pitcher 10" H. (part illus.) **$750**

Oil Lamps, collection of six incl. two similar mkd. Morey & Ober, Boston; one mkd. F. Porter, Westbrook; a sm. pr. w/ barrel-form fonts & a tall example w/ bulbous font on spiral standard, tallest 10". (part illus.) **$900**

Third Row

Footed Measures, 6 pear-shaped, dec. w/ banding & ranging in size from one quart to ¼ gill, together w/ similar ½ gill, height of tallest 6", (six illus.) **$800**

Porringers, 5 of graduated size & a two-handled porringer, one w/ touch of

Samuel Hamlin, one w/ cast initials S.G. another w/ initials G.I., diam. of largest 6¼", smallest 3". **$1,600**

Plates, eight w/ touch marks of Thomas Danforth III & Parks Boyd; Samuel Kilbourne & George Lightnes; William Billings; Samuel Danforth; William Danforth & Ashbil Griswold. **$3,100**

Britianna Candlesticks, w/ turned candlecups on baluster turned & banded standards w/ stepped circular bases, 10" H, together w/ single pewter chamber candlestick by Henry Hopper, NY. **$1,700**

Plates, Am. & Eng., 8¼" diam. w/ makers' marks incl. Badger, Boardman, Calder, Melville, Bassett & two mkd. London. **$2,400**

Plates, Am., 8" w/ makers' marks incl. Blakeslee Barnes, Richard Austin, Joseph & Thomas Danforth, Jacob Whitmore, Samuel Pierce & Nathaniel Austin. **$2,700**

Basins, three of grad. size w/ inverted rims, one w/ touch of Boardman & Co.; one stamped TD & SB for Boardman, & one mkd. London. Diam. of largest 9¼", together w/ four pewter beakers, (part. illus.) **$700**

A-OH Jan. 2001   Garth's Auctions, Inc.

First Row

Pewter Teapot, tooled lines on body & lid, touch mark for Rufus Dunham, ME, ca. 1837-1861, minor marks & edge damage, 6½" H. **$247**

Pewter Plates, three, all have "Love" & lovebirds touch marks, two have additional "London" mark, attrib. to PA, two are 7¾" diam., one is 8½" diam. **$715**

A-OH Jan. 2001   Garth's Auctions, Inc.

First Row

Pewter Plate, touch mark used by both Samuel Hamlin & his son, CT & RI, early 1800s, repr. & some wear, 11½" diam. **$363**

Pewter Plate, touch mark for William Calder, RI, ca. 1817-1856, lt. overall pitting, 11⅜" diam. **$357**

Pewter Teapot, touch mark for William Calder, RI, ca. 1817-1856, dent & handle repr. 7½" H. **$165**

Pewter Plate, partial "London" & Crown marks w/ "WW" polished, wear, 12¼" diam. **$302**

Second Row

Pewter Plates, two, partial eagle mark, (pictured), repr. some damage, 9" diam., & touch mark for "Grunewald", damage 9" diam. **$137**

Pewter Mugs & Measures, three, unmkd. pr. of "pints" w/ bulbous bodies & scroll handles, damage & repr. 5" H, straight sided w/ scroll ear handle, 5⅞" H. **$467**

Pewter Plates, two, one has touch mark "Love" PA, (pictured), 8⅜" diam., and one William Calder, RI, ca. 1817-1856, some pitting, 10⅜" diam. **$385**

Pewter Teapot, urn shaped, finial has worn wooden wafer, eagle touch mark "Boardman & Co. N.Y." & "X", minor damage & lid out of shape, 7⅛" H. **$220**

Second Row

Pewter Plate, partial "London" touch mark used by John Skinner, MA, ca. 1760-1790, 8½" diam. **$302**

Pewter Beakers, two, tooled lines, stepped bases, not exact pr., both have "X" & "TD & SB" touch marks for Thomas Danforth & Sherman Boardman, CT, ca. 1805-1850, one has some pitting w/ silver coating, 5⅛" H. **$880**

Pewter Teapot, cone shaped lid, touch mark "H.B. Ward", CT, ca. 1840, scrolled handle has worn blk. paint & damage, finial repl., 8½" H. **$220**

Pewter Chalices, pr., touch mark "Leonard, Reed & Barton, MA, ca. 1835-1840, polished, 7" H. **$385**

Pewter Basin, faint eagle touch mark for Gershom Jones, RI, ca. 1774-1809, some pitting & scratches, sm. repr. 7¾" diam., 1¾" H. **$220**

A-OH Jan. 2001   Garth's Auctions, Inc.

Pewter Porringers

Pierced Flowered Handle, touch mark for Samuel Hamlin, Jr., RI, ca. 1801-1856, minor dents, 5⅜" diam. **$550**

Pierced Crown Handle, cast touch mark "IG", N. Eng., 4¼" diam. **$220**

Taster Size, unmkd. but pierced handle type attrib. to Lee or Isaac C. Lewis, damage, 2⅛" diam. **$330**

A-OH Jan. 2001   Garth's Auctions, Inc.

Pewter Porringers

Pierced Crown Handle, cast touch mark "IG", N. Eng., minor dent, 4¼" diam. **$330**

Pierced Floral Handle, touch mark "TD & SB", dent, 5¼" diam. **$660**

A-OH Jan. 2001   Garth's Auctions, Inc.

Pewter Teapot, tooled lines, touch mark for James H. Putnam, MA, ca. 1830-1835, repr. hinge & possibly base, 8¾" H. **$192**

Pewter Plate, partial eagle touch mark for Samuel Danforth w/ "Hartford", CT, ca. 1795-1816, minor wear & dents, 7⅞" diam. **$357**

Pewter Creamers, two, unmkd. lidded w/ thumb catch & scrolled handle, 6¼" H. One w/ scrolled handle, 5¼" H., both have some battering & pitting. **$137**

Pewter Plate, eagle touch mark for Tomas Danforth III, Stepney or Rocky Hill, CT & PA, ca. 1777-1818, minor wear & battering, 7⅞" diam. **$385**

A-OH Jan. 2001   Garth's Auctions, Inc.

First Row

Pewter Plate, touch marks for Frederick Bassett, N.Y. & CT, ca. 1761-1800, minor wear & dents, 8½" diam. **$825**

Pewter Plate, eagle touch mark for Thomas Danforth Boardman, CT, ca. 1805-1850, 8½" diam. **$495**

Pewter Basin, eagle touch mark for Blakslee Barns, PA, 1812-1817, also rect. mark "B. Barns, Philada.", minor scratches & dent, 11⅛" diam., 1⅛" H. **$467**

Pewter Plate, touch mark for Samuel Kilbourn, CT, ca. 1794-1813 & Baltimore MD, ca. 1814-1839, repr., 8⅝" diam. **$137**

Pewter Plate, eagle touch mark for Thomas Danforth Boardman, CT, ca. 1805-1850, knife scratches, 7¾" diam. **$357**

Second Row

Pewter Plate, touch marks for Nathaniel Austin, MA, ca. 1763-1800, shallow dents & pitting, 9½" diam. **$275**

Pewter Plate, touch mark for Richard Austin, MA, 1792-1817, slight pitting & wear, 7¾" diam. **$165**

Pewter Teapot, flared foot & neck w/ scrolled handle & tooled lines on body & lid, touch mark "W. Humiston Troy, NY, ca. 1840-1860, damage 7¾" H. **$275**

Pewter Plate, touch marks for Blakslee Barns, 1812-1817, also mkd. "B. Barns, Philada.", minor wear w/ small dents, 7¾" diam. **$275**

Pewter Plate, eagle touch marks for George Lightner, MA, ca. 1806-1815, minor dents, 7⅞" diam. **$412**

METALS

Railroad Ware

First row

Coffeepot, ca. 19th C., silver plate, "Dixie" engraved, ornate embossed handle & lid, insulated zinc lining & copper bottom, lid detached, some damage & losses, 11" H. **$58**

Elgin, Joliet & Eastern RR Presentation Bowls (pr.), stainless steel w/ enameled "Chicago Outer Belt" logo, 12" diam. **$23**

Pullman Water Bottle, by Stanley, impressed "Pullman" on front, 11" H. **$35** Ice Bucket, Poole Silver Co., silverplate, glass lined, 9" H. **$23**

Second row

Chicago & Eastern Illinois RR Silver Plate Coffeepot, "Reed & Barton 086-H, C&E.I.RY.Co" on base, 10 oz. size, 7" H. **$265**

Union Pacific System Silvered Oval Trays (set of 10), U.P. System logo stamped on front, backstamped "Reed & Barton 1322-12, U.P. System", worn condition, 12" L. **$127**

Pullman Thermos Bottles (pr.), "Stanley Vacuum", minor damage on 1, 11" H. **$69**

Union Pacific System Silvered Oval Trays (set of 10), U.P. system logo stamped on front, backstamped "International Silver Co. C.S.72", worn condition, 11" L. **$127**

Third row

Silvered Cream & Sugar, ca. 19th C., embossed w/ chased designs, RR initials indistinguishable, no lid on sugar, 5" H. **$12**

Missouri Pacific & Iron Mountain Silvered Tea Pot, engraved on front "M.P.I.Mt.RY", back stamped "Missouri Pacific & Iron Mountain R. Wallace 03295". 10 oz. size, 4½" H. **$230**

Louisville & Nashville Divided Trays (set of 4), embossed "L&N" logo on front, backstamped "International Silver L&N", 12" L. **$316**

North Shore Line RR Silver Lidded Creamer & Lakawana RR Silvered Ice Cream Cup Holder, creamer backstamped "Wallace 0333, 6 oz. North Shore Line", cup holder embossed Lakawana logo on front, backstamped "Reed & Barton 6124-S, DL&WRR". 5½" L. **$403**

Nashville, Chattanooga & St. Louis Silvered Coffee Server applied embossed "N.C.&St.L" logo on front, gooseneck spout with long wood handle, backstamped "Reed & Barton 482-32 oz, N.C.&St.L". **$518**

Union Pacific RR Silvered Plate Covers (set of 7), 3 side stamped w/ winged locomotive, ea. backstamped "International Silver-05085, U.P.R.R.", 11" diam. **$138**

Union Pacific Silvered Coffeepot, 32 oz., side stamped "The Challenger" figural wing finial on lid, backstamped "International Silver 05085, 32 oz, U.P.R.R." **$115**

Railroad Hollowware (2 pcs.), I.S. Silver "Commodore Perry", 3 handled tooth pick & a side stamped "Soo Line" tea pot. **$58**

Fourth row

New York Central Silvered Cocoa Pot, impressed "NYC" on lid, worn condition, 5½" H. **$35**

Silvered Underplates (pr.), 1 North Shore & 1 South Shore, by R. Wallace, 6" diam. **$138**

Shrimp Bowl, 2 piece footed glass, silvered collar, attributed to Louisville & Nashville Railroad, 5" diam. **$17**

Silvered Cocoa Pots (pr.), "Chicago & Alton, A Seaboard Coast Line", 10 oz. size, worn condition. **$92**

Silvered Railroad Teapots (pr.), one faintly stamped "Soo Line", 7½" L. **$127**

West Point Route Silvered Low Bowl, ornate embossed rim w/ side stamped "West Point Route" by Reed & Barton, 7" diam. **$316**

Chicago Great Western Railway Silvered Sauce Tureen, two handles w/ lid, backstamped "C.G.W.R.R.-Reed & Barton", 8" L. **$127**

New York Central Silvered Sugar Bowl, impressed "NYC" on hinged lid, 3¾" H. **$46**

Silvered Bowls (pr.), 1 stamped inside "Florida East Coast Railway-Flager System-the Over Sea RR", 1 backstamped "North Shore Line", 4½" diam. **$259**

Erie Railroad Silvered Coffeepot, 8 oz. size, side stamped w/ "Erie" logo, backstamped "Gorham", 5" H. **$345**

Silvered Cocoa Pots (pr.), for "A.C.L.R.R. & "Great Northern", both worn, 6" H. **$58**

Silvered Corn Rests (3 pr.) 1 pr. marked "C&N.W.RY", second pair marked "PRR". 1 of 3rd pair marked "N.Y.C. Diner", 3" L. **$115**

Fifth row

Silvered Railroad Ware (8 pc. set), worn w/ some damage. **$92**

Atlantic Coast Line, (3 pc. set), porcelain soup bowls, ca. 1955, grey band interior, backstamped "Sterling-Atlantic Coast Line", 7" diam. **$12**

Hall China Condiment Jars (pr.), green glaze, applicator lids, embossed "horse radish" & "mustard", w/ "Northwestern" egg cup, 4" H. **$35**

RR China Creamers (pr.), unmarked Kansas City Southern w/ red transfer florals in Roxbury patt. & a "Sterling" w/ green floral band (minor flake)., **$35**

Syracuse China (8 pc. set), salmon on white w/ floral patt., 2-10" oval platters, four 5½" plates & 3 egg cups. **$115**

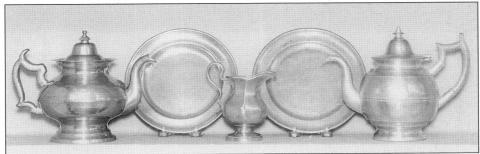

A-OH Jan. 2001   Garth's Auctions, Inc.

Pewter Teapot, tooled lines & petal wafer finial, touch mark for James H. Putnam, MA, ca. 1830-1835, minor wear & blk. paint handle wear, 7½" H. **$330**

Pewter Teapot, tooled lines & worn wooden wafer finial, touch mark for Roswell Gleason, MA, ca. 1822-1871, lt. pitting on all surfaces except lid, 7½" H. **$440**

Pewter Plate, partial touch marks for Joseph Danforth, CT, ca. 1780-1788, minor wear & pitting, 7⅞" diam. **$440**

Pewter Plate, partial touch marks for Thomas Danforth II, CT, ca. 1775-1782, some wear & pitting, 8" diam. **$220**

Pewter Teapot, tooled lines, touch mark for Eben Smith, MA, ca. 1813-1856, overall surface wear, 7⅞" H. **$247**

Cast-Iron

First row

Standing Scottie Door Stop, cast iron, 8¾" W, 11" H. **$161**

Elephant Door Stop, cast iron, orig. paint, may have held light, 9" H, 11" L. **$150**

Fox Terrier Door Stop, Hubley, cast iron, 8½" H. **$115**

Persian Cat Door Stop, cast iron, overpainted, 6½" W, 8½" H. **$104**

Second row

Boston Terrier Door Stop, cast iron, major paint loss, 9" L, 9" H,. **$35**

French Bull Dog, cast iron, worn paint, 7½" W, 6¾" H. **$173**

Ship Door Stop, cast iron, worn paint, 11" W, 12" H. **$92**

Boston Terrier Door Stop, cast iron, overpainted, 10" W, 10" H. **$104**

Third row

Frog on Mushroom Door Stop, cast iron, worn orig. paint, w/ frog door stop in orig. green paint, 6"H. **$259**

Hubley Fox Terrier Door Stop, cast iron, overpainted, 8½" H. **$46**

London Royal Coach, cast iron, worn electroplate finish, 12½" L, 7½" H, 2½" W. **$69**

Lion Door Stop, cast iron, old gold paint, 7". **$58**

Fourth row

Boston Terrier Door Stop, original paint, 9" H, 7" L. **$173**

Lion Door Stop, cast iron, old gold paint, 6½". **$46**

Double Scottie Door Stop, cast iron, old black paint, 8¾" L, 6¼" H. **$173**

Boston Terrier Door Stop, cast iron, old worn paint, 9" W, 7" H. **$104**

Railroad Paperweight, cast iron w/ bulldog, "Lima Locomotive Works, Inc.", Grey-Iron Commercial Castings. **$138**

German Shepherd Door Stops (pr.), w/ wedge under door. **$104**

Fifth row

Rooster Door Stops (pr.), bronzed, one w/ minor damage, mounted on wooden bases, 5" H. **$104**

Bulldog Door Stop, cast iron, partially overpainted, 5½" H, 8½" L. **$138**

Dog Nutcracker, cast iron, L.A. Althoff Chicago, overpainted, 5¾" H, 11" L. **$35**

Dog Nutcracker, cast iron, 12" L, 5¼" H. **$6**

Alligator Match Safe, cast iron, marked "Union Iron Works Decator, Ill.", original paint, 8½" L. **$127**

Sixth row

Boston Terrier Paperweights (pr.), cast iron, original paint, 3¼" H. **$150**

Dutch Woman Door Stop, cast iron, original paint, 2½" W, 4" H. **$58**

Teddy Roosevelt Desk Paperweight, cast metal over plaster, bottom loose, 5" H. **$12**

Dog Nutcracker, cast iron, 8½" L. **$6**

Alligator Match Safe, cast iron, marked "Union Iron Works Decator, Ill.", original paint, 8½" L. **$127**

Scottie Dog Paperweights (set of 4), cast iron, 3 w/ advertising, 1 overpainted, 1¾" H. **$104**

A-MA Feb. 2001   Skinner, Inc.

Cast-Iron & Aluminum

Washboard, Am., mid-19th C. 21½" H. **$1,150**

Musical Note Andirons made by Tennessee Chrom. Plate Co., ca. 1925, 17½" H. **$1,725**

Palm Frond Andirons, early 20th C., 22" H. **$2,185**

Cat Andirons, Midwestern U.S., early 20th C., 13½" H. **$2,530**

Cast Aluminum Washboard w/ molded wavy line scrubbing area, mkd. J. Fyla & X. Bez. on reverse, 15" H. **$634**

A-OH Jan. 2001   Garth's Auctions, Inc.

Pewter Teapot, partial touch marks for William Savage, CT, late 1830s, blk. paint on handle, lt. overall pitting, 10" H. **$440**

Pewter Bellied Measures, assem. set of five, Eng., one mkd. "Yates", wear & dents, 1¾" to 3¾" H. **$247**

Pewter Teapot, touch mark for "E. Wells", spout & handle have wear, minor dents, 7⅞" H. **$137**

METALS

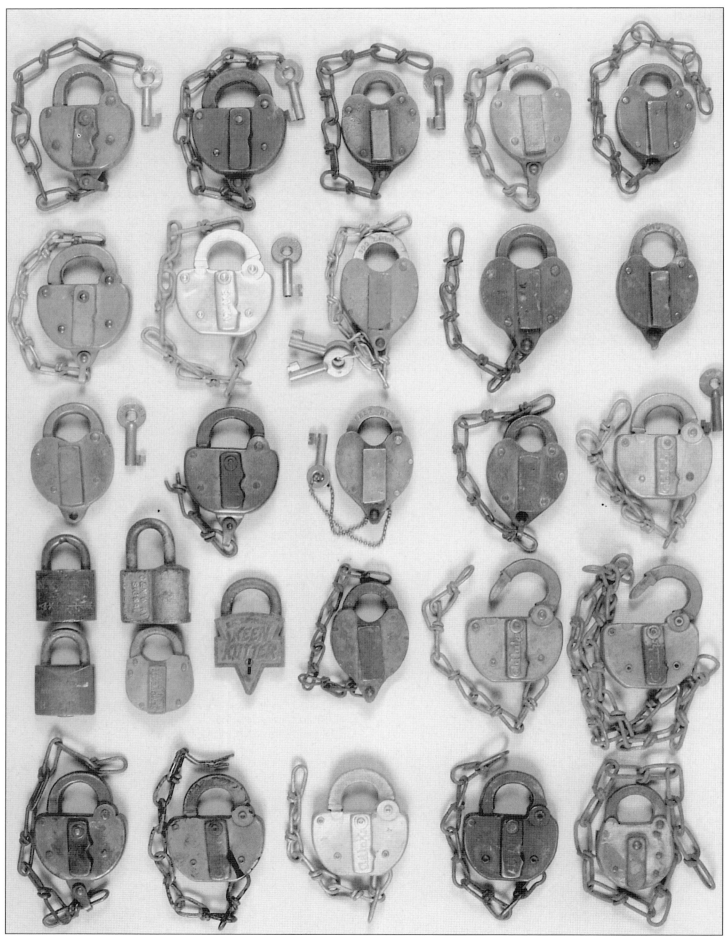

Locks

First row

Soo Line Steel Lock, MSTP & SSM RY stamped on shackle w/ key. **$17**

Soo Line Steel Lock, MSTP & SSM R stamped on shackle w/ key. **$17**

Brass Lock, no name w/ key, MO PAC II stamped on key. **$12**

Brass RR Lock, "NN RR" stamped on shackle. **$23**

Brass RR Lock, heart-shaped, letters illegible. **$12**

Second row

Soo Line Steel Lock, "Soo SW" stamped on shackle. **$17**

Steel Railroad Lock, "A C RLY" stamped on back. **$58**

Soo Line Brass Lock, "Soo Line" stamped on shackle w/ two keys labeled Soo Line. **$35**

Illinois Central Brass Lock, heart-shaped, "ICR CO" stamped on shackle. **$35**

Brass Railroad Lock, heart-shaped, "NNG-CO" stamped on shackle. **$12**

Third row

Rock Island Lines Brass Lock, "RI & P RY" stamped on shackle, w/ key labeled "RI & P RY". **$104**

Steel Railroad Lock, "GB & W" stamped on shackle. **$58**

Belt Line Brass Lock, heart-shaped, "BELT RY" stamped on shackle, Hansl Mfg. Co. **$40**

Brass Lock, MO RR markings. **$12**

Pennsylvania Line Railroad Steel Lock, "P RR" stamped on back w/ key. **$17**

Fourth row

Locks (4 pcs.), 3 steel, 1 steel, Soo Lines, B&O RR, NYC RR & C & NW RY stamped on fronts. **$29**

Brass Keen Kutter Lock, embossed raised Keen Kutter, red. **$86**

Chicago, Minneapolis St. Paul Brass Lock, heart-shaped, CMSTP&P RR stamped on shackle. **$29**

Steel Lock, CN&L stamped on back. **$6**

Steel Lock, P&N stamped on back. **$12**

Fifth row

Soo Line Steel Lock MSTP&SSM RR stamped on shackle. **$17**

Steel Lock AC&HB stamped on back. **$57**

Gulf Mobil Steel Lock GM RY stamped on back. **$46**

Steel Lock AB&C RR stamped on back. **$69**

Seaboard Airlines Steel Lock stamped on shackle. **$6**

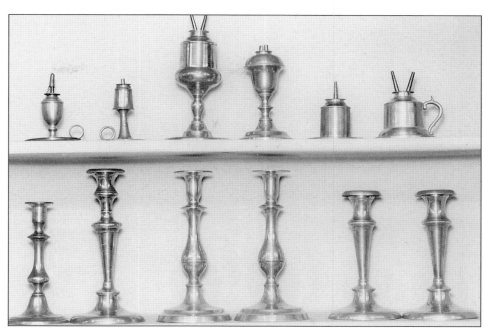

A-OH Jan. 2001   Garth's Auctions, Inc.

First Row

Pewter Finger Lamps, two, saucer bases & ring handles, touch mark for James H. Putnam, MA, ca. 1830-1835, mismatched burning fluid burner w/ snuffer cap, lt. pitting, overall 4⅛" H. and one unmkd. w/ mismatched whale oil burner, overall 4½" H. **$275**

Pewter Lamp, touch mark for Roswell Gleason, MA, ca. 1822-1871, whale oil burner, minor dents & sm. split, 6½" H. **$412**

Pewter Lamp, saucer base, baluster stem & acorn font, touch mark for Martin Hyde N.Y. City, ca. 1850, burning fluid burner, minor dent & repr. on base, polished or silver coated w/ lt. wear or pitting, 8½" H. **$220**

Pewter Lamp, saucer base & cylindrical font, touch mark for Capen & Molineux, N.Y. City & MA, ca. 1844-1854, burning fluid burner, lt. pitting, 4" H. **$110**

Pewter Finger Lamp, scrolled ear handle cylindrical font, touch mark for Capen & Molineux, N.Y. City & MA, ca. 1844-1854, polished, burning fluid burner may be mismatch, 4½ H. **$110**

Second Row

Pewter Candlesticks, two, largest has touch mark for Henry Hopper, N.Y. City, ca, 1842-1847, polished, sm. repr., lt. pitting & bobeche has battered rim, 10" H. and one w/ baluster stem & push up, wear & scratches, 8" H. **$412**

Pewter Candlesticks, pr., similar, unmkd Homan & Co., OH, ca. 1842-1854, scratches & one has minor damage on lower stem, polished, 9¾" H. **$385**

Pewter Lamp, pr. conical stems w/ flared sockets, touch marks for Ostrander & Norris, N.Y. City 1848-1850, polished w/ some pitting & possible repr., bobeche slightly dented, 8½" H. **$687**

A-OH Jan. 2001   Garth's Auctions, Inc.

Candlesticks, two brass, both w/ octagonal stepped bases, drilled sockets, one has splits, repr. & damaged socket, 7" H, one has damage at drilled hole, 7⅛" H. **$220**

Candlesticks, two brass w/ push ups, shorter one has saucer base, 4½" H, 7½" H. **$275**

Pottery Grease Lamp, found in N.Y., deep saucer base & long spout, grainy tan glaze, minor flake, 7" H. **$165**

Candlesticks, two brass, both w/ octagonal bases, drilled sockets, baluster stem slightly crooked, 6½" H, other has repr. at stem & base, also crooked, 6⅞" H. **$192**

A-OH Jan. 2001   Garth's Auctions, Inc.

Pewter Porringers
Pierced "Old English" Handle, mkd. "TD & SB", 4" diam. **$715**
Pierced Floral Handle, touch mark for William Calder, RI, ca. 1817-1856, 5" diam. **$660**
Unmarked Handle, type attrib. to PA, 5½" diam. **$660**

A-OH Jan. 2001   Garth's Auctions, Inc.

Pewter Porringers
Pierced Crown Handle, unmkd., minor split & dent, 4½" diam. **$55**
Pierced "Old English" Handle, unmkd. 3¾" diam. **$330**

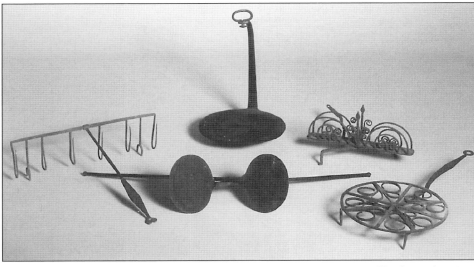

A-NH Aug. 2001   Northeast Auctions

Ironware, Left to Right
Fish or Bird Broiler w/ brand on handle, 23½" H, 19" W. **$1,300**
Wafer-Iron w/ monogram & dated Dec. 17, 1785, w/ 7" oval pans extending to scissor handles, 27½" L. **$500**
Single-Arm Griddle w/ half bail, 17"H, 11½" D. **$900**
Swivel Toaster, painted red w/ twisted graduated arches, 14" x 14". **$500**
Rotating Broiler w/ double scrolled motifs, 22½" L, 12¼" D. **$900**

A-MA Feb. 2001   Skinner, Inc.

Row 1
Iron Lock w/ key & figural lock plate, 19th C., w/ male & female silhouettes, minor surface corrosion, 11" H, 8½" W. **$632**
Incised Iron Cleaver w/ brass & wood handle, ca. 1880, surface rust & nicks on blade, 7" H, 12¼" L. **$1,840**
Iron & Brass Figural Cleaver, 20th C., shaped blade w/ eagle's head & handle terminating in brass boot w/ stand, surface corrosion, 4½" H, 11½" L. **$431**
Row 2
Iron & Wood Figural Tobacco Cutter, 19th C., surface rust, 9½" L. **$920**
Iron Figural Flint Striker, late 18th/ early 19th C., in form of a child kneeling on a scrolling sled, minor surface corrosion, with stand 3½" H. **$1,265**
Figural Iron Chopper on Wood Board, Am. 19th C., old red paint, wear at blade. 8" H, 15" L. **$449**

A-OH Nov. 2001   Garth's Auctions, Inc.

Wrought Iron Hanging Utensil Rack, w/ stepped crest, scrolled rods & 5 hooks, 21¼" L, 13" H. **$495**
Wrought Iron Utensils, 2 skimmers w/ brass bowls & fork w/ scrollwork **$165**
Wrought Iron Spit, w/ heart handle & twisted detail, 26" L, & two spatulas (one illus.) **$247**

A-PA Mar. 2001   **Conestoga Auction Company**

Toleware
Apple Tray w/ rolled rounded ends, crystallized center w/ polychrome fruit, flower & foliate decor. 7½" W, 12½" L, 2½" H. **$2,200**
Coffeepot, PA 19th C. w/ three bands of polychrome fruit, floral & foliate decor. on black ground, 8½" H. **$2,750**
Tole Trinket Box w/ rose, bud & foliate decor. on hinged lid, 6½ W, 2½ H. **$2,200**

A-PA Sept. 2001   **Pook & Pook Inc.**

Rush Light, wrought iron w/ candle holder, ca. 1800, w/ swivel hook, 23" L. **$600**
Ram's Horn Hinges, ca. 1800 w/ remnants of white paint. **$950**
Wrought Iron Skimmer, PA, w/ incised scroll & punched decor., together w/ two brass & iron ladles, a brass skimmer and later ladle. **$500**
Wrought Iron Hasp, PA, ca. 1800, in tulip form w/ cut out heart decor. **$450**
Weathervane, wrought iron directional, ca. 1800, in form of arrow & tulip, 26" L. **$1,200**
Massive Wrought Iron Barn Door Thumb Latch (attached to board), ca. 1800, 24" L. **$1,200**
Cast Iron Door Stops, an elephant w/ orig. paint, together w/ smaller elephant, conestoga wagon, chicken & painted door stop. **$850**
Kitchen Implements, 18th & 19th C., iron form w/ heart terminal, brass iron taster & ladle w/ rattail terminal, & an English food chopper mkd. J. Wiss & Sons. **$1,700**
Wrought Iron Tulip Thumb Latch, PA, ca. 1800, together w/ a pierced thumb pull. **$325**
Tulip Thumb Latch, PA, ca. 1800 w/ old red surface, 13" L, together w/ smaller latch 9" L. **$1,900**
Lantern, tin & glass, 19th C w/ reflector & oil lamp, 25" H, 15" W, together w/ another tin & glass lantern. **$1,000**
Cast Iron Rose Finials, late 19th C., pair. **$200**
Flesh Fork, wrought iron, NY, 19th/20th C, tines from a heart & another on handle, 36" L. **$425**

A-NH Aug. 2001   **Northeast Auctions**

Theorem, Am. watercolor of fruit on marble slab table, 14" x 16" sight. **$2,700**

A-NH Nov. 2001   **Northeast Auctions**

Theorem, w/ wicker basket of colorful flowers and green leaves in orig. mah. frame, 15½" x 20¼", sight. **$5,000**

A-PA Feb. 2001   **Pook & Pook, Inc.**

Sampler, by Frances Burley, ca. 1840, silk on silk depicting flowers, bird houses, trees, animals and central player within floral border, 15½' x 11½". **$950**

A-PA Nov. 2001   **Conestoga Auction Company**

Theorem, sgn. D.Y. Ellinger, w/ brightly colored rooster in orig. red & black decor. frame, 17½" x 17" overall. **$3,025**

A-NY Nov. 2000   **Hesse Galleries**

Hattie K. Brunner Painting, "Auction with Hattie" 8½" x 6½". **$2,860**

A-PA Feb. 2001   **Pook & Pook, Inc.**

Fraktur, dated 1785 for Anna Margretha Rappin, Lancaster, PA, w/ central script surrounded by printed bird & floral motif, on paper, hand colored, 13½" x 16½". **$3,100**

A-PA Nov. 2001   **Conestoga Auction Company**

Theorem, sgn. D. Ellinger, depicting a Canton bowl filled w/ fruit with a bee and bird in an orig. grain decor. frame, 17½" x 22¼". **$5,500**

A-NY Nov. 2000   **Hesse Galleries**

Hattie K. Brunner Painting, "Winter", rural landscape w/ covered bridge. 14½" x 10½". **$2,090**

A-PA Feb. 2001   **Pook & Pook, Inc.**

House Blessing, (haus segen), Isaac Palm, Lancaster, PA, w/ central heart enclosing script, 13" x 16½". **$2,500**

A-PA Sept. 2001   Pook & Pook, Inc.

Painting, British, 19th C., oil on canvas of the Grand National Steeplechase 1885, sgn. "E.B. Herberte, 1885", 30" x 50". **$17,000**

A-IA Aug. 2001   Gene Harris Antique Auction Center, Inc.

Litho Print, "Modern Woodmen of America", copyright 1897 by Jacob Lauffer. In orig. grain painted frame, 38" x 23¼". **$500**

A-NH Mar. 2001   Northeast Auctions

Painting by Eric Sloan (1910-1985), "Sun and Barn Wood", oil on masonite, 29" x 38". **$19,000**

A-SC Dec. 2001   Charlton Hall Galleries, Inc.

Oil on Academy Board, William Aiken Walker, Am., SC, ca. 1838-1921, "Old Joseph With His Cotton Pickings", signed, 8" H, 4" W. **$7,500**

A-SC Dec. 2001   Charlton Hall Galleries, Inc.

Oil on Academy Board, William Aiken Walker, Am., SC, ca. 1838-1921, "Josephine With Her Cotton Pickings", signed, 8" H, 4" W. **$7,500**

A-CA June 2001   Butterfields

Mourning Picture, Am., silk & chenille embroidered, dated 1803. The forested landscape includes a church & a town w/ a waterfall, all within a gilt & ebonized frame, 16" x 14". **$4,700**

PAINTINGS & PICTURES

A-SC March 2001   Charlton Hall
    Galleries, Inc.

Portrait Miniature, French School, 18th
C., young woman, unsigned, 2 1/16" H,
1 5/8" W. **$550**

A-SC March 2001   Charlton Hall
    Galleries, Inc.

Portrait Miniature, Richard Cosway R.A.,
late 18-early 19th C., lady, unsigned,
3 1/4"H., 2 3/4" W. **$1,100**

A-SC March 2001   Charlton Hall
    Galleries, Inc.

Portrait Miniature, French School, 18-19th
C., gentleman, unsigned, 2 11/16" diam.
$900

A-SC March 2001   Charlton Hall
    Galleries, Inc.

Portrait Miniature, French School, 18th
C., young man, unsigned, 3 1/8" diam.
$2,100

A-SC March 2001   Charlton Hall
    Galleries, Inc.

Portrait Miniature, French School, 18th
C., of lady, unsigned, 2 1/4" x 1 3/4". **$300**

A-SC March 2001   Charlton Hall
    Galleries, Inc.

Portrait Miniature, Charles Fraser,
Charleston SC, ca. 1782-1860,
unsigned, 3 1/8" H, 2 3/4" H. **$850**

A-MA Feb. 2001   Skinner, Inc.

Miniature Portrait on Ivory, Am. School,
ca. 1800, unsigned bust in orig. gilded
copper case, 2 1/2" W, 3" H. **$2,875**

A-NH Mar. 2001   Northeast Auctions

Vermont Portraits framed together. Amaziah Richmond & Hannah Richmond by Thomas
Ware, ca. 1823, oil on canvas, 27" x 24". **$19,000**

ABC Plates – Alphabet plates were made especially for children as teaching aids. They date from the late 1700s and were made of various material including porcelain, pottery, glass, pewter, tin and ironstone.

Amphora Art Pottery was made at the Amphora Porcelain Works in the TeplitzTum area of Bohemia during the late 19th and early 20th centuries. Numerous potteries were located there.

Anna Pottery – The Anna Pottery was established in Anna, IL, in 1859 by Cornwall and Wallace Kirkpatrick, and closed in 1894. The company produced utilitarian wares, gift wares and pig-shaped bottles and jugs with special inscriptions, which are the most collectible pieces.

Battersea Enamels – The name "Battersea" is a general term for those metal objects decorated with enamels, such as pill, patch, and snuff boxes, doorknobs, and such. The process of fusing enamel onto metal–usually copper–began about 1750 in the Battersea District of London. Today the name has become a generic term for similar objects–mistakenly called "Battersea".

Belleek porcelain was first made at Fermanagh, Ireland, in 1857. Today this ware is still being made in buildings within walking distance of the original clay pits, according to the skills and traditions of the original artisans. Irish Belleek is famous for its thinness and delicacy. Similar wares were also produced in other European countries, as well as in the United States.

Bennington Pottery – The first pottery works in Bennington, Vermont, was established by Captain John Norton in 1793, and for 101 years it was owned and operated by succeeding generations of Nortons. Today the term "Bennington" is synonymous with the finest in American ceramics because the town was the home of several pottery operations during the last century–each producing under different labels. Today items produced at Bennington are now conveniently, if inaccurately, dubbed "Bennington." One of the popular types of pottery produced there is known as "Rockingham." The term denotes the rich, solid brown glazed pottery from which many household items were made. The ware was first produced by the Marquis of Rockingham in Swinton, England–hence the name.

Beswick – An earthenware produced in Staffordshire, England, by John Beswick in 1936. The company is now a part of Royal Doulton Tableware, Ltd.

Bisque – The term applies to pieces of porcelain or pottery which have been fired but left in an unglazed state.

Bloor Derby – "Derby" porcelain dates from about 1755 when William Duesbury began the production of porcelain at Derby. In 1769 he purchased the famous Chelsea Works and operated both factories. During the Chelsea-Derby period, some of the finest examples of English porcelains were made. Because of their fine quality, in 1773 King George III gave Duesbury the patent to mark his porcelain wares "Crown Derby." Duesbury died in 1796. In 1810 the factory was purchased by Robert Bloor, a senior clerk. Bloor revived the Imari styles which had been so popular. After his death in 1845, former workmen continued to produce fine porcelains using the traditional Derby patterns. The firm was reorganized in 1876, and in 1878 a new factory was built. In 1890, Queen Victoria appointed the company "Manufacturers to Her Majesty" with the right to be known as Royal Crown Derby.

Buffalo Pottery – The Buffalo Pottery of Buffalo, New York, was organized in 1901. The firm was an adjunct of the Larkin Soap Company, which was established to produce china and pottery premiums for that company. Of the many different types produced, the Buffalo Pottery is most famous for its "Deldare" line, which was developed in 1905.

Canary Luster earthenware dates to the early 1800s, and was produced by potters in the Staffordshire District of England. The body of this ware is a golden yellow and decorated with transfer printing, usually in black.

Canton porcelain is a blue-and-white decorated ware produced near Canton, China, from the late 1700s through the last century. Its hand-decorated Chinese scenes have historical as well as mythological significance.

Capo-di-Monte, originally a soft paste porcelain, is Italian in origin. The first ware was made during the 1700s near Naples. Although numerous marks were used, the most familiar to us is the crown over the letter N. Mythological subjects, executed in either high or low relief and tinted in bright colors on a light ground, were a favorite decoration. The earlier wares had a peculiar grayish color as compared to the whiter bodies of later examples.

Carlsbad porcelain was made by several factories in the area from the 1800s and exported to the United States. When Carlsbad became a part of Czechoslovakia after World War I, wares were frequently marked "Karlsbad." Items marked "Victoria" were made for Lazarus & Rosenfeldt, importers.

Castleford earthenware was produced in England from the late 1700s until around 1820. Its molded decoration is similar to Prattware.

Celedon – Chinese porcelain having a velvet-textured greenish-gray glaze. Japanese and other oriental factories also made celedon glazed wares.

Chelsea – An early soft paste porcelain manufactured at Chelsea in London from around 1745 to 1769. Chelsea is considered to be one of the most famous of English porcelain factories.

Chelsea Keramic Art Works – The firm was established in 1872, in Chelsea, MA, by members of the Robertson family. The firm used the mark CKAW. The company closed in 1889, but was reorganized in 1891, as the Chelsea Pottery U.S. In 1895, the factory became the Dedham Pottery of Dedham, MA, and closed in 1943.

Chinese Export Porcelain was made in quantity in China during the 1700s and early 1800s. The term identifies a variety of porcelain wares made for export to Europe and the United States. Since many thought the product to be of joint Chinese and English manufacture, it has also been known as "Oriental" or "Chinese Lowestoft."

As much of this ware was made to order for the American and European market, it was frequently adorned with seals of states or the coat of arms of individuals, in addition to eagles, sailing scenes, flowers, religious and mythological scenes.

Clarice Cliff Pottery – Clarice Cliff (1889-1972) was a designer who worked at A.J. Wilkinson, Ltd.'s Royal Staffordshire Pottery at Burslem, England. Cliff's earthenwares were bright and colorful art deco designs which included squares, circles, bands, conical shapes and simple landscapes incorporated with the designs. Cliff used several different printed marks, each of which incorporated a facsimile of her signature–and generally the name of the pattern.

Clews Pottery – (see also, Historical Staffordshire) was made by George Clews & Co., of Brownhill Pottery, Tunstall, England, from 1806-1861.

Clifton Pottery – William Long founded the Clifton Pottery in Clifton, NJ, in 1905.

Pottery was simply marked CLIFTON. Long worked until 1908, producing a line called Crystal Patina. The Chesapeake Pottery Company made majolica marked Clifton Ware, which oftentimes confuses collectors.

Coalport porcelain has been made by the Coalport Porcelain Works in England since 1795. The ware is still being produced at Stoke-on-Trent.

Coors Pottery – Coors ware was made in Golden, CO, by the Coors Beverage Co. from the turn of the century until the pottery was destroyed by fire in the 1930s.

Copeland-Spode – The firm was founded by Josiah Spode in 1770 in Staffordshire, England. From 1847, W.T. Copeland & Sons, Ltd., succeeded Spode, using the designation "Late Spode" to its wares. The firm is still in operation.

Copper Luster – See Lusterwares.

Cordey – Boleslaw Cybis was one of the founders of the Cordey China Company, Trenton, NJ. Production began in 1942. In 1969, the company was purchased by the Lightron Corporation, and operated as the Schiller Cordey Company. Around 1950, Cybis began producing fine porcelain figurines.

Cowan Pottery – Guy Cowan produced art pottery in Rocky River, OH, from 1913 to 1931. He used a stylized mark with the word COWAN on most pieces. Also, Cowan mass-produced a line marked LAKEWARE.

Crown Ducal – English porcelain made by A.G. Richardson & Co., Ltd. since 1916.

Cup Plates were used where cups were handleless and saucers were deep. During the early 1800s, it was very fashionable to drink from a saucer. Thus, a variety of fancy small plates were produced for the cup to rest in. The lacy Sandwich examples are very collectible.

Davenport pottery and porcelain was made at the Davenport Factory in Longport, Staffordshire, England, from 1793 until 1887 when the pottery closed. Most of the wares produced there– porcelains, creamwares, ironstone, earthenwares and other products– were marked.

Dedham (Chelsea Art Works) – The firm was founded in 1872, at Chelsea, Massachusetts, by James Robertson & Sons, and closed in 1889. In 1891, the pottery was reopened under the name of The Chelsea Pottery, U.S. The first and most popular blue underglaze decoration for the desirable "Cracque Ware" was

the rabbit motif–designed by Joseph L. Smith. In 1893, construction was started on the new pottery in Dedham, Massachusetts, and production began in 1895. The name of the pottery was then changed to "Dedham Pottery," to eliminate the confusion with the English Chelsea Ware. The famed crackleware finish became synonymous with the name. Because of its popularity, more than 50 patterns of tableware were made.

Delft – Holland is famous for its fine examples of tin-glazed pottery dating from the 16th century. Although blue and white is the most popular color, other colors were also made. The majority of the ware found today is from the late Victorian period and when the name Holland appears with the Delft factory mark, this indicates that the item was made after 1891.

Dorchester Pottery was established by George Henderson in Dorchester, a part of Boston, Massachusetts, in 1895. Production included stonewares, industrial wares, and later, some decorated tablewares. The pottery is still in production.

Doulton – The pottery was established in Lambeth in 1815 by John Doulton and John Watts. When Watts retired in 1845, the firm became known as Doulton & Company. In 1901, King Edward VII conferred a double honor on the company by presentation of the Royal Warrant, authorizing their chairman to use the word "Royal" in describing products. A variety of wares were made over the years for the American market. The firm is still in production.

Dresden – The term identifies any china produced in the town of Dresden, Germany. The most famous factory in Dresden is the Meissen factory. During the 18th century, English and Americans used the name "Dresden china" for wares produced at Meissen which has led to much confusion. The city of Dresden which was the capital of Saxony, was better known in 18th century Europe than Meissen. Therefore, Dresden became a generic term for all porcelains produced and decorated in the city of Dresden and surrounding districts, including Meissen. By the mid-19th century, about thirty factories in the city of Dresden were producing and decorating porcelains in the style of Meissen. Therefore, do not make the mistake of thinking all pieces marked Dresden were made at the Meissen factory. Meissen pieces generally have crossed swords marks and are listed under Meissen.

Flowing Blue ironstone is a highly glazed dinnerware made at Staffordshire by a variety of potters. It became popular about 1825. Items were printed with Oriental patterns and the color flowed from the design over the white body, so that the finished product appeared smeared. Although purple and brown colors were also made, the deep cobalt blue shades were the most popular. Later wares were less blurred, having more white ground.

Frankoma – The Frank Pottery was founded in 1933, by John Frank, Sapulpa, OK. The company produced decorative wares from 1936-38. Early wares were made from a light cream-colored clay, but in 1956 changed to a red brick clay. This along with the glazes helps to determine the period of production.

Fulper – The Fulper mark was used by the American Pottery Company of Flemington, NJ. Fulper art pottery was produced from approximately 1910 to 1930.

Gallé – Emile Gallé was a designer who made glass, pottery, furniture and other Art Nouveau items. He founded his factory in France in 1874. Ceramic pieces were marked with the initials E.G. impressed, Em. Gallé Faiencerie de Nancy, or a version of his signature.

Gaudy Dutch is the most spectacular of the gaudy wares. It was made for the Pennsylvania Dutch market from about 1785 until the 1820s. This soft paste tableware is lightweight and frail in appearance. Its rich cobalt blue decoration was applied to the biscuit, glazed and fired–then other colors were applied over the first glaze–and the object was fired again. No luster is included in its decoration.

Gaudy Ironstone was made in Staffordshire from the early 1850s until around 1865. This ware is heavier than Gaudy Welsh or Gaudy Dutch, as its texture is a mixture of pottery and porcelain clay.

Gaudy Welsh, produced in England from about 1830, resembles Gaudy Dutch in decoration, but the workmanship is not as fine and its texture is more comparable to that of spatterware. Luster is usually included with the decoration.

Gouda Pottery – Gouda and the surrounding areas of Holland have been one of the principal Dutch pottery centers since the 17th century. The Zenith pottery and the Zuid-Hooandsche pottery, produced the brightly colored wares marked GOUDA from 1880 to about 1940. Many pieces of Gouda featured art nouveau or art deco designs.

Grueby – Grueby Faience Company, Boston, MA, was founded in 1897 by William H. Grueby. The company produced hand thrown art pottery in natural shapes, hand molded and hand tooled. A variety of colored glazes, singly or in combinations were used, with green being the most prominent color. The company closed in 1908.

Haeger – The Haeger Potteries, Inc., Dundee, IL, began making art wares in 1914. Their early pieces were marked with HAEGER written over the letter "H." Around 1938, the mark changed to ROYAL HAEGER.

Hampshire – In 1871, James S. Taft founded the Hampshire Pottery Company in Keene, NH. The company produced redware, stoneware, and majolica decorated wares in 1879. In 1883, the company introduced a line of colored glazed wares, including a Royal Worcester-type pink, blue, green, olive and reddish-brown. Pottery was marked with the printed mark or the impressed name HAMPSHIRE POTTERY or J.S.T. & CO., KEENE, N.H.

Harker – The Harker Pottery Company of East Liverpool, OH, was founded in 1840. The company made a variety of different types of pottery including yellowware from native clays. Whiteware and Rockingham-type brown-glazed pottery were also produced in quantities.

Historical Staffordshire – The term refers to a particular blue-on-white, transfer-printed earthenware produced in quantity during the early 1800s by many potters in the Staffordshire District. The central decoration was usually an American city scene or landscape, frequently showing some mode of transportation in the foreground. Other designs included portraits and patriotic emblems. Each potter had a characteristic border, which is helpful to identify a particular ware, as many pieces are unmarked. Later transfer-printed wares were made in sepia, pink, green and black, but the early cobalt blue examples are the most desirable.

Hull – In 1905, Addis E. Hull purchased the Acme Pottery Company in Crooksville, OH. In 1917, Hull began producing art pottery, stoneware and novelties, including the Little Red Riding Hood line. Most pieces had a matte finish with shades of pink and blue or brown predominating. After a flood and fire in 1950, the factory was reopened in 1952 as the Hull Pottery Company. Pre-1950

vases are marked Hull USA or HULL ART USA. Post-1950 pieces are simply marked HULL in large script or block letters. Paper labels were also used.

Hummel – Hummel items are the original creations of Berta Hummel, born in 1909 in Germany. Hummel collectibles are made by W. Goebel Porzellanfabrik of Oeslau, Germany, now Rodenthal, West Germany. They were first made in 1934. All authentic Hummels bear both the signature, M.I. Hummel, and a Goebel trademark. However, various trademarks were used to identify the year of production.

Ironstone is a heavy, durable, utilitarian ware made from the slag of iron furnaces, ground and mixed with clay. Charles Mason of Lane Delft, Staffordshire, patented the formula in 1823. Much of the early ware was decorated in imitation of Imari, in addition to transfer-printed blue ware, flowing blues and browns. During the mid-19th century, the plain white enlivened only by embossed designs became fashionable. Literally hundreds of patterns were made for export.

Jackfield Pottery – is English in origin. It was first produced during the 17th century; however, most items available today date from the last century. It is a red-bodied pottery, often decorated with scrolls and flowers in relief, then covered with a black glaze.

Jasperware – is a very hard, unglazed porcelain with a colored ground, varying from blues and greens to lavender, red, yellow or black. White designs were generally applied in relief to these wares, and often reflect a classical motif. Jasperware was first produced by Wedgwood's Etruria Works in 1775. Many other English potters produced jasperware, including Copeland, Spode and Adams.

Jugtown Pottery – This North Carolina pottery has been made since the 18th century. In 1915 Jacques Busbee organized what was to become the Jugtown Pottery in 1921. Production was discontinued in 1958.

King's Rose is a decorated creamware produced in the Staffordshire district of England during the 1820-1840 period. The rose decorations are usually in red, green, yellow and pink. This ware is often referred to as "Queen's Rose."

Leeds Pottery was established by Charles Green in 1758 at Leeds, Yorkshire, England. Early wares are unmarked. From 1775, the impressed mark "Leeds Pottery"

was used. After 1880, the name "Hartley, Greens & Co." was added, and the impressed or incised letters "LP" were also used to identify the ware.

Limoges – The name identifies fine porcelain wares produced by many factories at Limoges, France, since the mid-1800s. A variety of different marks identify wares made there including Haviland china.

Liverpool Pottery – The term applies to wares produced by many potters located in Liverpool, England, from the early 1700s, for American trade. Their print-decorated pitchers–referred to as "jugs" in England–have been especially popular. These featured patriotic emblems, prominent men, ships, etc., and can be easily identified, as nearly all are melon-shaped with a very pointed lip, strap handle and graceful curved body.

Lonhuda – In 1892, William Long, Alfred Day, and W.W. Hunter organized the Lonhuda Pottery Company of Steubenville, OH. The firm produced underglaze slip-decorated pottery until 1896, when production ceased. Although the company used a variety of marks, the earliest included the letters LPCP.

Lotus Ware – This thin, Belleek-like porcelain was made by the Knowles, Taylor & Knowles Company of Easter Liverpool, OH, from 1890 to 1900.

Lusterware – John Hancock of Hanley, England, invented this type of decoration on earthenwares during the early 1800s. The copper, bronze, ruby, gold, purple, yellow, pink and mottled pink luster finishes were made from gold painted on the glazed objects, then fired. The latter type is often referred to as "Sunderland Luster." Its pinkish tones vary in color and pattern. The silver lusters were made from platinum.

Maastricht Ware – Petrus Regout founded the De Sphinx pottery in 1835 at Maastricht, Holland. The company specialized in transfer painted earthenwares.

Majolica – The word "majolica" is a general term for any pottery glazed with an opaque tin enamel that conceals the color of the clay body. It has been produced by many countries for centuries. Majolica took its name from the Spanish island of Jamorca, where figuline (a potter's clay) is found. This ware frequently depicted elements in nature: birds, flowers, leaves and fish. English manufacturers marked their wares, and most can be identified through the English Registry mark, and/or the potter-designer's mark, while most continental pieces had an incised number.

Although many American potteries produced majolica between 1850 and 1900, only a few chose to identify their wares. Among these were the firm of Griffen, Smith & Hill, George Morely, Edwin Bennett, Chesapeake Pottery Company, and the new Milford-Wannoppe Pottery Company.

Marblehead – This hand thrown pottery had its beginning in 1905 as a therapeutic program by Dr. J. Hall for the patients of a Marblehead, MA, sanitarium. Later, production was moved to another site and the factory continued under the management of A.E. Baggs until it closed in 1936. The most desirable pieces found today are decorated with conventionalized designs.

Matt-Morgan – By 1883, Matt Morgan, an English artist, was producing art pottery in Cincinnati, OH, that resembled Moorish wares. Incised designs and colors were applied to raised panels, and then shiny or matte glazes were applied. The firm lasted only a few years.

McCoy Pottery – The J.W. McCoy Pottery was established in 1899. Production of art pottery began after 1926, when the name was changed to Brush McCoy.

Meissen – The history of Meissen porcelain began in Germany in 1710 in the Albrechtsburg fortress of Meissen. The company was first directed by Johann Boettger, who developed the first truly white porcelain in Europe. The crossed swords mark of the Meissen factory was adopted in 1723.

Mettlach, Germany, located in the Zoar Basin, was the location of the famous Villeroy & Boch factories from 1836 until 1921, when the factory was destroyed by fire. Steins (dating from about 1842) and other stonewares with bas relief decorations were their specialty.

Minton – Thomas Minton established his pottery in 1793 at Stoke-on-Trent, Hanley, England. During the early years, Minton concentrated on blue transfer painted earthenwares, plain bone china, and cream colored earthenware. During the first quarter of the 19th century, a large selection of figures and ornamental wares were produced in addition to their tableware lines. In 1968, Minton became a member of the Royal Doulton Tableware group, and retains its reputation for fine quality hand painted and gilted tablewares.

Mochaware – This banded creamware was first produced in England during the late 1700s. The early ware was lightweight and thin, having colorful bands of bright colors decorating a body that is cream colored to very light brown. After 1840, the ware became heavier in body and the color was often quite light – almost white. Mochaware can easily be identified by its colorful banded decorations – on and between the bands – including feathery ferns, lacy trees, seaweeds, squiggly designs and lowly earthworms.

Moorcroft – William Moorcroft established the Moorcroft Pottery, in Burslem, England, in 1913. The majority of the art pottery wares were hand thrown. The company initially used an impressed mark, MOORCROFT, BURSLEM, with a signature mark, W. MOORCROFT, following. Walker, William's son, continued the business after his father's death in 1945, producing the same style wares. Contemporary pieces are marked simply MOORCROFT with export pieces also marked MADE IN ENGLAND.

Newcomb – William and Ellsworth Woodward founded Newcomb Pottery at Sophie Newcomb College, New Orleans, LA, in 1896. Students decorated the high quality art pottery pieces with a variety of designs that have a decidedly southern flavor. Production continued through the 1940s. Marks include the letters "NC" and often have the incised initials of the artist as well. Most pieces have a matte glaze.

Niloak Pottery with its prominent swirled, marbelized designs, is a 20th century pottery first produced at Benton, Arkansas, in 1911, by the Niloak Pottery Company. Production ceased in 1946.

Nippon porcelain has been produced in quantity for the American market since the late 19th century. After 1891, when it became obligatory to include the country of origin on all imports, the Japanese tradesmark "Nippon" was used. Numerous other marks appear on this ware, identifying the manufacturer, artist or importer. The handpainted Nippon examples are extremely popular today and prices are on the rise.

Norse Pottery was founded in 1903 in Edgerton, WI. The company moved to Rockford, IL, in 1904, where they produced a black pottery which resembled early bronze items. The firm closed in 1913.

Ohr Pottery was produced by George E. Ohr in Biloxi, Mississippi, around 1883. Today Ohr is recognized as one of the leading potters in the American Art Pottery movement. Early work was often signed with an impressed stamp in block letters–G.E. OHR BILOXI. Later pieces were often marked G.E. Ohr in flowing script. Ohr closed the pottery in 1906, storing more than 6,000 pieces as a legacy to his family. These pieces remained in storage until 1972.

Old Ivory dinnerware was made in Silesia, Germany, during the late 1800s. It derives its name from the background color of the china. Marked pieces usually have a pattern number on the base, and the word "Silesia" with a crown.

Ott & Brewer – The company operated the Etruria Pottery in Trenton, NJ, from 1863 to 1893. A variety of marks were used which incorporated the initials O & B.

Owens – The Owens Pottery began production in Zanesville, OH, in 1891. The first art pottery was made after 1896, and pieces were usually marked OWENS. Production of art pottery was discontinued about 1907.

Paul Revere Pottery – This pottery was made at several locations in and around Boston, MA, between 1906 and 1942. The company was operated as a settlement house program for girls. Many pieces were signed S.E.G. for Saturday Evening Girls. The young artists concentrated on children's dishes and tiles.

Peters & Reed Pottery Company of Zanesville, Ohio, was founded by John D. Peters and Adam Reed about the turn of the century. Their wares, although seldom marked, can be identified by the characteristic red or yellow clay body touched with green. This pottery was best known for its matte glaze pieces–especially one type, called Moss Aztec, combined a red earthenware body with a green glaze. The company changed hands in 1920 and was renamed the Zane Pottery Company. Examples marked "Zaneware" are often identical to earlier pieces.

Pewabic – Mary Chase Perry Stratton founded the Pewabic Pottery in 1903 in Detroit, MI. Many types of art pottery were produced here, including pieces with matte green glaze and an iridescent crystaline glaze. Operations ceased after the death of Mary Stratton in 1961, but the company was reactivated by Michigan State University in 1968.

Pisgah Forest Pottery – The pottery was founded near Mt. Pisgah in North Carolina in 1914, by Walter B. Stephen. The pottery remains in operation.

Quimper – Tin-glazed hand-painted pottery has been produced in Quimper, France, dating back to the 17th century. It is named for a French town where numerous potteries were located. The popular peasant design first appeared during the 1860s, and many variations exist. Florals and geometrics were equally as popular. The HR and HR QUIMPER marks are found on Henriot pieces prior to 1922.

Redware is one of the most popular forms of country pottery. It has a soft, porous body and its color varies from reddish-brown tones to deep wine to light orange. It was produced in mostly utilitarian forms by potters in small factories, or by potters working on their farms, to fill their everyday needs. The most desirable examples are the slip-decorated pieces, or the rare and expensive "sgraffito" examples which have scratched or incised line decoration. Slip decoration was made by tracing the design on the redware shape, with a clay having a creamy consistency in contrasting colors. When dried, the design was slightly raised above the surface.

Red Wing Art Pottery and Stoneware – The name includes several potteries located in Red Wing, MN. David Hallem established his pottery in 1868, producing stoneware items with a red wing stamped under the glaze as its mark. The Minnesota Stoneware Co. began production in 1883. The North Star Stoneware company began production in 1892, and used a raised star and the words Red Wing as it mark. The two latter firms merged in 1892, producing stoneware until 1920, when the company introduced a pottery line. In 1936, the name was changed to Red Wing Potteries. The plant closed in 1967.

Ridgway – Throughout the 19th century the Ridgway family, through partnerships, held positions of importance in Shelton and Hanley, Staffordshire, England. Their wares have been made since 1808, and their transfer-design dinner sets are the most widely known product. Many pieces are unmarked, but later marks include the initials of the many partnerships.

Riviera – This dinnerware was made by the Homer Laughlin Company of Newell, WV, from 1938 to 1950.

Rockingham – See Bennington Pottery.

Rookwood Pottery – The Rookwood Pottery began production at Cincinnati, Ohio, in 1880 under the direction of Maria Longworth Nichols Storer, and operated until 1960. The name was derived from the family estate, "Rookwood," because of the "rooks" or "crows" which inhabited the wooded areas. All pieces of this art pottery are marked, usually bearing the famous flame.

Rorstrand Faience – The firm was founded in 1726 near Stockholm, Sweden. Items dating from the early 1900s and having an art noveau influence are very expensive and much in demand.

Rose Medallion ware dates from the 18th century. It was decorated and exported from Canton, China, in quantity. The name generally applied to those pieces having medallions with figures of people, alternating with panels of flowers, birds and butterflies. When all the medallions are filled with flowers, the ware is identified as Rose Canton.

Rose Tapestry – See Royal Bayreuth.

Roseville Pottery – The Roseville Pottery was organized in 1890 in Roseville, Ohio. The firm produced utilitarian stoneware in the plant formerly owned by the Owens Pottery of Roseville, also producers of stoneware, and the Linden Avenue Plant at Zanesville, Ohio, originally built by the Clark Stoneware Company. In 1900, an art line of pottery was created to compete with Owens and Weller lines. The new ware was named "Rozanne," and it was produced at the Zanesville location. Following its success, other prestige lines were created. The Azurine line was introduced about 1902.

Royal Bayreuth manufactory began in Tettau in 1794 at the first porcelain factory in Bavaria. Wares made there were on the same par with Meissen. Fire destroyed the original factory during the 1800s. Many of the wares available today were made at the new factory which began production in 1897. These include Rose Tapestry, Sunbonnet Baby novelties and the Devil and Card items. The Royal Bayreuth blue mark has the 1794 founding date incorporated with the mark.

Royal Bonn – The trade name identifies a variety of porcelain items made during the 19th century by the Bonn China Manufactory, established in 1755 by Elmer August. Most of the ware found today is from the Victorian period.

Royal Crown Derby – The company was established in 1875, in Derby, England, and has no connection with the earlier Derby factories which operated in the late 18th and early 19th centuries. Derby porcelain produced from 1878 to 1890 carries the standard crown printed mark.

From 1891 forward, the mark carries the "Royal Crown Derby" wording, and during the 20th century, "Made in England" and "English Bone China" were added to the mark. Today the company is a part of Royal Doulton Tableware, Ltd.

Royal Doulton wares have been made from 1901, when King Edward VII conferred a double honor on the Doulton Pottery by the presentation of the Royal Warrant, authorizing their chairman to use the word "Royal" in describing products. A variety of wares has been produced for the American market. The firm is still in production.

Royal Dux was produced in Bohemia during the late 1800s. Large quantities of this decorative porcelain ware were exported to the United States. Royal Dux figurines are especially popular.

Royal Rudolstadt – This hard paste ware was first made in Rudolstadt, Thuringen, East Germany, by Ernst Bohne in 1882. The ware was never labeled "Royal Rudolstadt" originally, but the word "Royal" was added later as part of an import mark. This porcelain was imported by Lewis Straus and Sons of New York.

Royal Worcester – The Worcester factory was established in 1751 in England. This is a tastefully decorated porcelain noted for its creamy white lusterless surface. Serious collectors prefer items from the Dr. Wall (the activator of the concern) period of production which extended from the time the factory was established to 1785.

Roycroft Pottery was made by the Roycrofter community of East Aurora, New York, during the late 19th and early 20th centuries. The firm was founded by Elbert Hubbard. Products produced included pottery, furniture, metalware, jewelry and leatherwork.

R.S. Germany porcelain with a variety of marks was produced at the Tillowitz, Germany, factory of Reinhold Schlegelmilch from about 1869 to 1956.

R.S. Prussia porcelain was produced during the mid-1800s by Erdman Schlegelmilch in Suhl. His brother, Reinhold, founded a factory in 1869, in Tillowitz in lower Silesia. Both made fine quality porcelain, using both satin and high gloss finishes with comparable decoration. Additionally, both brothers used the same R.S. mark in the same colors, the initials in memory of their father, Rudolph Schlegelmilch. It has not been determined when production at the two factories ceased.

Ruskin is a British art pottery. The pottery, located at West Smethwick, Birmingham, England, was started by William H. Taylor. His name was used as the mark until around 1899. The firm discontinued producing new pieces of pottery in 1933, but continued to glaze and market their remaining wares until 1935. Ruskin pottery is noted for its exceptionally fine glazes.

Sarreguemines ware is the name of a porcelain factory in Sarreguemines, Lorraine, France, that made ceramics from about 1775. The factory was regarded as one of the most prominent manufacturers of French faience. Their transfer printed wares and majolica were made during the nineteenth century.

Satsuma is a Japanese pottery having a distinctive creamy crackled glaze decorated with bright enamels and often with Japanese figures. The majority of the ware available today includes the mass-produced wares dating from the 1850s. Their quality does not compare to the fine early examples.

Sewer Tile – Sewer tile figures were made by workers at sewer tile and pipe factories during the late nineteeth and early twentieth centuries. Vases and figurines with added decorations are now considered folk art by collectors.

Shawnee Pottery – The Shawnee Pottery Company was founded in 1937 in Zanesville, OH. The plant closed in 1961.

Shearwater Pottery – was founded by G.W. Anderson, along with his wife and their three sons. Local Ocean Springs, MS, clays were used to produce their wares during the 1930s, and the company is still in business.

Sleepy Eye – The Sleepy Eye Milling Company, Sleepy Eye, MN, used the image of the 19th century Indian chief for advertising purposes from 1883 to 1921. The company offered a variety of premiums.

Spatterware is soft paste tableware, laboriously decorated with hand-drawn flowers, birds, buildings, trees, etc., with "spatter" decoration chiefly as a background. It was produced in considerable quantity from the early 1800s to around 1850.

To achieve this type of decoration, small bits of sponge were cut into different shapes–leaves, hearts, rosettes, vines, geometrical patterns, etc.–and mounted on the end of a short stick for convenience in dipping into the pigment.

Spongeware, as it is known, is a decorative white earthenware. Color–usually blue, blue/green, brown/tan/blue, or blue/brown–was applied to the white clay base. Because the color was often applied with a color-soaked sponge, the term "spongeware" became common for this ware. A variety of utilitarian items were produced–pitchers, cookie jars, bean pots, water coolers, etc. Marked examples are rare.

Staffordshire is a district in England where a variety of pottery and porcelain wares has been produced by many factories in the area.

Stickspatter – The term identifies a type of decoration that combines hand-painting and transfer-painted decoration. "Spattering" was done with either a sponge or brush containing a moderate supply of pigment. Stickspatter was developed from the traditional Staffordshire spatterware, as the earlier ware was time consuming and expensive to produce. Although most of this ware was made in England from the 1850s to the late 1800s, it was also produced in Holland, France and elsewhere.

Tea Leaf is a lightweight stone china decorated with copper or gold "tea leaf" sprigs. It was first made by Anthony Shaw of Longport, England, during the 1850s. By the late 1800s, other potters in Staffordshire were producing the popular ware for export to the United States. As a result, there is a noticeable diversity in decoration.

Teco Pottery is an art pottery line made by the Terra Cotta Tile works of Terra Cotta, Illinois. The firm was organized in 1881, by William D. Gates. The Teco line was first made in 1885, but not sold commercially until 1902, and was discontinued during the 1920s.

UHL Pottery – This pottery was made in Evansville, IN, in 1854. In 1908, the pottery was moved to Huntingburg, IN, where their stoneware and glazed pottery was made until the mid-1940s.

Union Porcelain Works – The company first marked their wares with an eagle's head holding the letter "S" in its beak around 1876; the letters "U.P.W." were sometimes added.

Van Briggle Pottery was established at Colorado Springs, Colorado, in 1900, by Artus Van Briggle and his wife, Anna.

Most of the ware was marked. The first mark included two joined "A's," representing their first two initials. The firm is still in operation.

Villeroy & Boch – The pottery was founded in 1841, at Mettlach, Germany. The firm produced many types of pottery including the famous Mettlach steins. Although most of their wares were made in the city of Mettlach, they also had factories in other locations. Fortunately for collectors, there is a dating code impressed on the bottom of most pieces that makes it possible to determine the age of the piece.

Volkmar pottery was made by Charles Volkmar, New York, from 1879 to around 1911. Volkmar had been a painter, therefore many of his artistic designs often look like oil paintings drawn on pottery.

Walrath – Frederich Walrath worked in Rochester, NY, New York City, and at the Newcomb Pottery in New Orleans, LA. He signed his pottery items "Walrath Pottery." He died in 1920.

Warwick china was made in Sheeling, WV, in a pottery from 1887 to 1951. The most familiar Warwick pieces have a shaded brown background. Many pieces were made with hand painted or decal decorations. The word ILGA is sometimes included with the Warwick mark.

Wedgwood Pottery was established by Josiah Wedgwood in 1759, in England. A tremendous variety of fine wares has been produced through the years including basalt, lusterwares, creamware, jasperware, bisque, agate, Queen's Ware and others. The system of marks used by the firm clearly indicates when each piece was made.

Weller Pottery – Samuel A. Weller established the Weller pottery in 1872, in Fultonham, Ohio. In 1888, the pottery was moved to Piece Street in Putnam, Ohio–now a part of Zanesville, Ohio. The production of art pottery began in 1893, and by late 1897 several prestige lines were being produced, including Samantha and Dickensware. Other later types included Weller's Louwelsa, Aurora, Turada and the rare Sicardo which is the most sought after and most expensive today. The firm closed in 1948.

Wheatley – Thomas J. Wheatley worked with the founders of the art pottery movement in Cincinnati, Ohio. He established the Wheatley Pottery in 1880, which was purchased by the Cambridge Tile Manufacturing Company in 1927.

A-IA June 2001   Jackson's Auctioneers & Appraisers

Flow Blue China, partial set, floral patt. by Thomas Hughes & Son, England, five piece place setting for eight, approx. 100 pieces, minor chips & cracks. **$1,092**

A-SC June 2001   Charlton Hall
                                  Galleries, Inc.

Royal Worcester Porcelain
Vase, ca. 1887 w/ fancy rim & vibrantly colored insets w/ butterflies, gilt & branches, 9" H. **$425**

A-PA Mar. 2001   Conestoga Auction Company

Copper Luster
Row 1, Left to Right
Pitcher, w/ dolphin handle & polychrome floral sprays on blue band, 7½" H. **$247**
Tumbler, w/ copper luster floral & foliate decor. on blue band, 3½" H. **$38**
Pitcher, w/ green floral decor. on yellow/orange ground, 7½" H. **$302**
Tumbler, w/ horizontal rib & blue stripe decor., pink luster interior band, 3½" H. **$49**
Pitcher, w/ dolphin handle & polychrome basket of flowers decor. on blue band, 7½" H. **$275**

Row 2, Left to Right
Goblet, w/ beaded edge, fruit, floral & foliate sprays on blue band, 3½" H. **$71**
Cream Pitcher, w/ polychrome sheep herder scene on blue band, 4¼" H. **$104**
Cream Pitcher, r w/ Dolphin Handle & dog head spout, decor. w/ flowers on blue band, 4½" H. **$440**
Cream Pitcher, w/ polychrome basket of flowers on blue band, 4½" H. **$176**
Cream Pitcher, decor. w/ polychrome basket of flowers on yellow band, 4" H. **$121**

A-SC June 2001   Charlton Hall
                                  Galleries, Inc.

Royal Worcester Porcelain
Vase, ca. 1897 w/ classical decor., sgn. N. Davis, 12½" H. **$1,120**

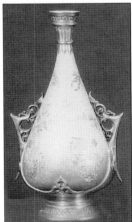

A-SC June 2001   Charlton Hall
                                  Galleries, Inc.

Royal Worcester Porcelain
Vase, ca. 1888 w/ gilt rim, floral & vine decor. on powder blue ground, 18¼" H. **$1,000**

Buffalo Pottery

Top Row

Deldare Vase, sgn. "GHS", Buffalo Pottery stamp, 7" H. **$402**

Deldare Pitcher, artist sgn. "E. Van Horn", Buffalo Pottery stamp 1908, 9" H. **$575**

Deldare Vase, artist sgn. "N. Foster", Buffalo Pottery stamp 1908, 8" H. **$977**

Deldare Dresser Tray, artist sgn. "W. Foster", Buffalo Pottery stamp 1909, 12" x 9". **$402**

Deldare Pitcher, artist sgn. "Stiner", Buffalo Pottery stamp 1908, 8" H. **$632**

Deldare Pitcher, artist sgn. "P. Hall", Buffalo Pottery stamp 1908, 7" H. **$374**

Deldare Pitcher, artist sgn., Buffalo Pottery stamp 1908, 6" H. **$287**

Second Row

Deldare Plates, pr., artist sgn., ca. Buffalo Pottery stamp 1909, 9½" & 10" diam. **$316**

Deldare Relish Dish, artist sgn. "H. Bell", Buffalo Pottery stamp 1908, 12" x 6½". **$374**

Deldare Fern Bowl, artist sgn. "A. Wade", Buffalo Pottery stamp 1909, 8" diam. **$402**

Deldare Plate, three, artist sgn, Buffalo Pottery stamp 1908, 6¼", 7¼" & 8½" diam. **$201**

Third Row

Deldare Flat Rim Soup Bowl, artist sgn. "N. Sheehan", Buffalo Pottery stamp 1908, 8¾" diam. **$230**

Deldare Six-sided Open Sugar, artist sgn. "J.G.", Buffalo Pottery stamp 1908, 4" diam., 3" H. **$230**

Deldare Relish Dish, artist sgn. "E. Dowlman", Buffalo Pottery stamp 1908, 12" x 6½". **$402**

Deldare Chop Plate, artist sgn. "W. Foster" Buffalo Pottery stamp 1908, 13¾" diam. **$460**

Deldare Tea Set, artist sgn. & Buffalo Pottery stamp, teapot 5½" H, sugar 4" H, creamer 2½" H. **$805**

Deldare Mug, artist sgn. "A.S.", Buffalo Pottery stamp 1908, 4½" H. **$144**

Deldare Mug, artist sgn. "E. Dowlman", Buffalo Pottery stamp 1909, 3½" H. **$172**

Fourth Row

Deldare Tea Tile, artist sgn. "A. Wade", Buffalo Pottery stamp 1908, 6¼" H. **$115**

Deldare Cereal Bowl, artist sgn. "Fardy", Buffalo Pottery stamp 1924, 5¼" diam., 2½" H. **$201**

Deldare Cereal Bowl, artist sgn. "G. Beatty", Buffalo Pottery stamp 1924, 5½" diam., 2½" H. **$172**

Deldare Flat Rim Soup Bowl, artist sgn. "W.F.", Buffalo Pottery stamp 1908, 6¼" diam., 2" H. **$172**

Deldare Coffee Cup & Saucer, pr. cups, one saucer, artist sgn., Buffalo Pottery stamp 1909, hairline on one cup. **$86**

Deldare Powder Jar w/ Lid, Buffalo Pottery stamp 1908, 2½" H, 4¼" diam. **$345**

Buffalo Pottery "Cinderella" Jar, many colors, Brown Buffalo & Eagle logo 1906, 6" H. **$115**

Buffalo Pottery Jar, multicolor hand decor., logo 1906, 6" H. **$374**

Buffalo "Holland" Jar, hand decor. on white, logo 1907, 6¼" H. **$287**

Buffalo Pottery Jar, richly decor., logo 1906 & 1907, 8¼" H. **$575**

Fifth Row

Buffalo Pottery Spittoon, green on white, ca. 1905-1910, 8" diam, 5" H. **$92**

Buffalo Pottery China Teapot, white w/ silver decor., pewter lid w/ tea ball, ca. 1915, 7" H. **$92**

Buffalo Pottery Dutch Jar, vivid hand decor., logo 1907, 6½" H. **$195**

Buffalo Pottery "Blue Willow" Vase, decor. in reds, browns & cobalt blue w/ gold. logo 1908, 7" H. **$374**

Buffalo Pottery Plate, colorful hand decor., ca. 1907, 10" diam. **$144**

Sixth Row

Buffalo Pottery "Campbell Kids" Feeding Dish, ca. 1913-1918, 7½" diam. **$69**

Buffalo Pottery "Campbell Kids" Feeding Plate, signed, 7½" diam. **$115**

Buffalo Pottery "Campbell Kids" Feeding Dish, marked Buffalo Pottery, 7½" diam. **$103**

Buffalo Pottery "Gaudy Willow", vibrant colors w/ coin gold. Two 5" diam. sauces, one 7½" diam. bowl, one 8¼" diam. plate, & two 9" plates, logo "Semi-Vitreous Buffalo Pottery 1911". **$230**

A-SC March 2001   Charlton Hall Galleries, Inc.

Royal Worcester Porcelain

First Row

Ewer, ca. 1887, w/ floral & gilt dec., 17¼" H. **$1,800**

Vase & Cover, ca. 1894, w/ floral & gilt dec., 7⅛" H., 5½" diam. **$600**

Pitcher, ca. 1889, w/ floral & gilt dec., 6" H. **$425**

Vase, ca. 1891, w/ floral & gilt dec., 10¾" H. **$1,400**

Second Row

Pitcher, ca. 1889, w/ floral & gilt dec., 8⅞" H. **$850**

Ewer, ca. 1893, decorated w/ floral & gilt dec., 7¾" H. **$200**

Pitcher, ca. 1890, gilt twig handle w/ floral dec., 5½" H. **$200**

Compote, ca. 1888, dec. in floral design w/ gilt dec., 3½" H, 10" W, 7¾" diam. **$550**

Vase, ca. 1883, w/ floral & gilt dec., 5 1/16" H. **$400**

Pitcher, ca. 1889, w/ floral & gilt dec., 7¾" H. **$800**

Porcelain

863 Nippon Low Bowl, hand painted w/ open roses, footed, w/ blue maple leaf mark, 10" diam. **$56**

864 Chocolate Pot, Japanese, ca. 1890, w/ hand painted mums & gilt trim, 9" H. **$22**

865 Scenic Bowl, German, "Richmond Castle" w/ cobalt & gold decor., 11" diam. **$37**

866 Chocolate Pot, decor. w/ large roses, 11" H. **$44**

867 Belleek Vase by Willets, decor. w/ large red roses & sgn. Pearce, 8" H. **$157**

868 Coffeepot, decor. w/ red, pink & yellow roses on Rosenthal blank, 8" H. **$45**

869 Wine Cooler, w/ hand painted floral decor., mkd. "Made In Germany", 6½" H. **$101**

870 Cake Plate w/ handles, 10" diam., & dish w/ satin finish, chips, 8½" L. **$22**

871 Bread Tray mkd. "Bavaria", w/ raised gilt decor. including acorns & oak leaves, 12½" L. **$28**

872 French Urn, w/ classical scene & gilt highlights, 6" diam. **$17**

873 Chelsea Plate, mkd. & decor. w/ multicolored birds, 9½" diam. **$67**

874 Dresden Desk Set, mkd. w/ floral & gilt decor. includes stamp box, ink well, pen holder & desk pad corners, minor repairs. **$112**

875 Tray, gilt decorated w/ turquoise bands & mkd. "T. Goode & Co., London, Minton's China". **$34**

876 Art Deco Plate, w/ gold & incised decor. of a nude in foliage, mkd. "Thomas Sevres Bavaria". **$56**

877 Leaf Form Dish, w/ molded floral & gilt decor., 9" L. **$11**

878 Pickard Table Setting, 3 pcs., w/ rose & daisy decor; a Rosenthal creamer & sugar on an R.S. Prussia tray, 12" L. **$67**

879 Covered Urns, pair, ca. 1870, w/ Imari decor., mkd. "Davenport, Longport, Staffordshire", one lid repaired, 8½" H. **$450**

880 Pickard Vase, mkd., ca. 1905, decor. w/ large roses, chips, 14½" H. **$168**

881 French Pomade Jars, set of three w/ floral decor., 2½" - 3½" H. **$112**

882 R.S. Prussia Cracker Jar, sugar & creamer w/ red mark, decor. w/ roses. **$392**

883 Pitcher, w/ underplate & mkd. "Royal Munich", floral decor., 6" H. **$112**

884 Stamp Dispenser, 2 pcs., w/ hand painted roses & filt, 2½" H. **$11**

885 R.S. Germany Hair Receiver & Nappy, w/ relief molded strawberries, **$39**

886 Royal Vienna Celery Tray w/ 4 young beauties, sgn. "Kaufman", 13" L. **$123**

887 Dresser, 5 pcs., w/ hand painted floral decor. w/ two covered boxes, pin tray, ring tree & cup. **$101**

888 Nippon Plaque, hand painted w/ pierced foot rim for hanging, w/ green M wreath mkd. **$101**

889 Willets Belleek Vase, decor., w/ colorful mums, mkd. 7" diam. **$168**

890 Celery Tray, mkd. "T & V Limoges", decor. w/ poppies, fern & gilt, 14" L. **$56**

891 Bread Plate, possibly Leeds, hand painted decor., w/ open basket weave edge, minor hairlines, 12" diam. **$134**

892 R.S. Germany Syrup, w/ yellow iris decor., 5" H. **$34**

893 Limoges Pin Tray, decor. w/ blue & white chariot scene, mkd., 4" H. **$11**

894 R.S. Germany Toothpick Holder, footed, w/ red mark, 2" H. **$90**

895 R.S. Germany Cake Plate, w/ handles & decor. w/ tulips, 11" diam. **$56**

896 Nippon Child's Service, incl. hand painted cup & saucer, bowl & plate. **$112**

897 Hand Painted Covered Jar, hair receiver, bowl & pin tray. **$101**

898 Lenox Ramekins, set of 8, decor. w/ floral swags, sterling frames. **$252**

899 Cup & Saucer w/ floral decor., mkd. "Austria". **$22**

900 Nippon Tray, hand painted w/ pumpkins, leaves & gilt, & small bowl. **$112**

A-SC Sept. 2001   Charlton Hall Galleries, Inc.

Meissen Tea & Coffee Service, porcelain, thirty pieces, 20th C., consisting of coffeepot, teapot, covered sugar, creamer, two serving plates, 12 cups w/ saucers. **$750**

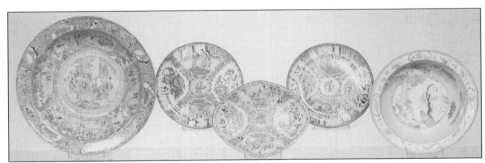

A-SC June 2001   Charlton Hall Galleries, Inc.

Rose Medallion Punch Bowl, ca. 1865, dec. w/ butterflies, birds, flowers & fruit, int. w/ garden scenes, 5½' H, 14½" diam. **$475**

Rose Medallion Plates, pr., ca. 1840, w/ four alternating panels depicting birds, flowers & figures, 9½" diam. **$100**

Rose Medallion Bowl, ca. 1860, dec. w/ panels of figures & butterflies, 1¾" H, 10" L. **$180**

Chinese Porcelain Bowl, 19th C., w/ dec. floral border & landscapes, centering a woman in a garden, 4" H, 11" diam. **$140**

Porcelain

First Row

Royal Rudolstadt Porcelain Ewer, late 19th C., gilt heightened florals on peach ground. Mkd. "KW Rudolstadt Germany", 12¾" H. **$150**

Austrian Majolica Ewer, late 19th C., multi colored green, blue & yellow, 13" H. **$100**

Paris Porcelain Vase, pr., mid 19th C., hand painted, cobalt blue & gilt leaves. Some repair, 14½" H. **$287**

German Vase, late 19th C., w/ hand painted florals trimmed in gilt, 14" H. **$23**

Nippon Handled Vase, w/ paneled scenic design. Green "M in wreath" mark, 12" H. **$345**

Second Row

Meissen Porcelain Figure, ca. 1840, blue, 9" H. **$345**

Porcelain Candelabra, pr., early 20th C., mkd. "Dresden Germany", 12½" H. **$201**

Dresden Floral Urn, mid 20th C., mkd. "Made in Germany Von Schierholz", 10½" H. **$115**

Austrian Portrait Vase, early 20th C., iridized glaze in purples, greens & golds, 4½" H. **$201**

R.S. Poland Vase, ca. 1920, decor. of yellow roses on satin ground. Mkd. "R.S. Poland", 7" H. **$92**

German Jasperware Cheese Keeper, ca. 1900, pale green w/ applied white figures, 11" diam. & 10" H. **$201**

Royal Bonn Artist Portrait Vase, ca. 1900, purple to blue shaded ground. Artist sgn. "E. Vock" mkd. "Royal Bonn Germany" 12". **$460**

R.S. Prussia Footed Teapot, ca. 1900, w/ white & pink poppy decor., repair to spout, red RSP mark, 8" L. **$172**

Dresden Figural Compotes, pr., mid 19th C., minor losses, 12" H. **$258**

German Bisque Figure, ca. 1890, w/ polychrome & raised gilt decor., 10¼" H. **$69**

Third Row

Capo-di-Monte Cabinet Plates, pr., ca. 1900, 9¼" diam. **$143**

Royal Bayreuth Rose Tapestry Hatpin Holder, base sgn. "Royal Bayreuth", 4½" H. **$287**

Oriental Satsuma Vase, pr., ca. 1900, 12" H. **$201**

Austrian Portrait Vase, ca. 1920, iridized purple, blue & gold ground, 10" H. **$316**

R.S. Suhl Two-Handled Portrait Bowl, ca. 1910, red R.S. Suhl & Beehive mark, 4" H. **$316**

Sévres Bolted Urns, pr., ca. 1850, colorful floral cartouche on a cobalt ground, 7½" H. **$800**

R.S. Tillowitz Vase, ca. 1910, mkd., 9" H. **$287**

Fourth Row

Dresden Porcelain Urn, ca. 1870, applied floral swags w/ matching lid, repairs, 15½" H. **$690**

R.S. Prussia Muffineer, ca. 1900, w/ pink roses. Red mark, 4¾" H. **$143**

Dresden Cabinet Vase, ca 1880, mkd. in blue w/ Crown RC & Dresden, 4½" H. **$632**

Vase, pr. ca. 1910, mkd. "R.S. Poland" 4½" H, second w/ scenic cottage mkd. "R.S. Germany", 4¼" H. **$230**

German Bisque Bust, ca. 1890, 13" H. **$575**

Dresden Figural Compote, mid 20th C., 12" H. **$402**

Meissen Figural Lamp, late 19th C., 10¼" H. **$747**

R.S. Prussia Vase, ca. 1900, yellow pansies, red mark, 8" H. **$230**

Bisque Figure, late 19th C., mkd. "R.S. Germany Rudolstadt", 18" H. **$316**

Fifth Row

Berry Set, six piece, ca. 1900, red roses on pale green. Mkd. "R.S. Prussia", 9¼" diam & 5¾" diam. **$402**

R.S. Prussia Toothpick Holder & Shakers, 3 pieces w/ 2 shakers, one repaired. **$69**

Bowl, ca. 1920, mkd. "R.S. Suhl", 8" L. **$201**

German Porcelain Figural Plaque, ca. 1900, w/ heavy relief, 14" H. **$86**

Footed Hair Receiver & Ring Tree, 2 piece, ca. 1910, mkd. "R.S. Poland". **$115**

Royal Bayreuth Plate, ca. 1910, Rose Tapestry patt., mkd. 7½" diam. **$138**

Royal Vienna Portrait Plates, pr., ca. 1920, blue beehive mark. 9½" diam. **$258**

Nappy, ca. 1910, heart shaped w/ apple blossom decor. Mkd. "R.S. Poland", 6" L. **$86**

Scuttelmug, ca. 1910, red roses decor., mkd. "R.S. Prussia", 3½" H. **$69**

A-SC June 2001   Charlton Hall Galleries, Inc.

First Row

Porcelain Cornucopia Vases, Old Paris style, pr., 9" H, 8" W. **$600**

Earthenware Blackamoor Spill Vases, Italian, pr., 20th C., ea. in the form of a blk. man holding a cornucopia, 12¾" H. **$450**

Rose Medallion Charger, ca. 1920, w/ scenic panels, 12" diam. **$250**

A-SC June 2001   Charlton Hall Galleries, Inc.

Covered Cake Dish, Wedgwood Jasperware, ca. 1900, w/ applied border of leaves, two flower heads & fitted w/ single handle. The sides w/ applied motifs of classical Greek figures. Fitted in underplate w/ conforming design, 7" H, 11¼" diam. **$650**

Famille Rose Charger, ca. 1820, w/ scrolling floral border, 12½" diam. **$200**

901 902 903 904 905 915 906 907
909 911 917
908 910 913 914 916 918
912
919 921 923 929 931
920 922 924 925 926 927 928 930 932
933 935 938 942 944
934 936 941 945
937 939 940
946 948 951
947 950 952 952

Nippon Porcelain

901 Hand Painted Bowl, w/ pierced handles, rose decor., gilt & blue mkd., 9½" L. **$22**

902 Wine Jug, w/ hand painted windmill scene, moriage handles, hairline, blue mk, 10" H. **$112**

903 Scenic Plaque, w/ hand painted garden scene, pierced for hanging, green mkd., 10¼" diam. **$112**

904 Vase, decor. w/ large flowers & gilt, mkd. "Royal Nippon", 19" H. **$123**

905 Scenic Plaque, decor. w/ hand painted windmill, rim pierced for hanging, green mkd., 10¼" diam. **$112**

906 Vase, w/ hand painted purple iris, green mkd., 9" H. **$448**

907 Cake Plate, w/ hand painted roses & gilt trim, mkd. "Royal Kinran", w/ crown, 11" L. **$156**

908 Candlesticks, decor. w/ cherry blossoms, green leaf mkd., 4½" H. **$123**

909 Mug, decor. w/ oriental landscape in raised enamel, green mkd., 5" H. **$67**

910 Humidor, decor. w/ hand painted tree lined shore, green mkd., 5½" H. **$224**

911 Milk Set, w/ floral decor., rim outlined in gold, 3 pcs., "M" in wreath mkd., 6" H. **$101**

912 Mug, decor. w/ hand painted landscape & raised enameling, green mkd., 5½" H. **$112**

913 Cake Plate, decor. w/ hand painted house in meadow, blue mkd., 10½" diam. **$56**

914 Plaque, decor. w/ ivy covered trees, pierced for hanging, 9½" diam. **$179**

915 Pitcher, melon rib form w/ scissor handle & decor. w/ roses, green leaf mkd. **$213**

916 Humidor, square form w/ four scenic panels of sailboats, green leaf mkd., 4½" H. **$308**

917 Humidor, melon form w/ mountain cottage scene, green leaf mark, 5½" H. **$588**

918 Muffineer & Mug, both w/ scenic decor. & green mkd., 4½" H. **$112**

919 Bowl, w/ hand painted cottage, gilt handles, green mkd., 9½" L. **$34**

920 Covered Syrup, decorated w/ hand painted flowers & enameled decor. on red/ white ground, blue leaf mark, 4½" H. **$45**

921 Scenic Vase, w/ hand painted meadow & enameling, green wreath mkd., 6" H. **$67**

922 Basket w/ coralene decor. of flowers & gilt, US Patent mkd., 4½" diam. **$202**

923 Plaque, decor. w/ hand painted horse race, pierced for hanging, green mkd., 6½" L. **$392**

924 Creamer & Sugar, decor. w/ scenic panels, green wreath mkd. **$224**

925 Vase, decor. w/ hand painted roses, leaves & fruit, w/ blue mkd., 14½" H. **$1,344**

926 Rose Bowl, decor., w/ hand painted apple blossoms, blue leaf mkd., 5½" diam. **$67**

927 Covered Pitcher, w/ hand painted flowers on pearlized ground, "T & T" mkd., 8½" H. **$56**

928 Miniature Tazza, hand painted w/ roses on a stippled gilt ground, Kinran crown mkd., 5" H. **$34**

929 Fernery, four footed square form, w/ hand painted scenic panels & gold enameling, green wreath mkd., 7" L. **$1,190**

930 Covered Biscuit Jar, decor w/ roses under a cobalt rim, repair to lid, blue leaf mark, 8" H. **$190**

931 Nut Bowl, w/ handles, painted w/ walnuts & leafage, green wreath mkd. **$101**

932 Scenic Ash Receiver, embossed mold w/ windmill scene, green wreath mark, 5" L. **$101**

933 Nut Tray, molded in relief, hand painted w/ nuts, green wreath mark, 8" L. **$78**

934 Nut Dish, decor. w/ peanuts, molded in relief peanut shell, footed w/ green "M" wreath mk, 8¼" L. **$67**

935 Handled Basket, w/ painted house in meadow, enameled handle, green leaf mkd., 7½" L. **$45**

936 Berry Server & Underplate, decor. in gilt scrolls & roses, bottom perforated for drainage, blue Royal Crown mkd., 7½" diam. **$112**

937 Cigar Receiver, hand painted w/ enameled playing cards motif on heart shaped form, 4½" L. **$448**

938 Scenic Plates, pair w/ hand painted house in meadow & saw tooth enameled rim, 8½" & 9½" diam. **$78**

939 Match Receiver, w/ open panels for strike card, hand painted, green wreath mkd., 2½" H. **$45**

940 Footed Bowl, w/ bird of paradise decor., 3 paw feet, green wreath mkd., 7" diam. **$17**

941 Jam Server, 3 pcs., hand painted w/ floral & gilt decor. green wreath mkd., 4½" H. **$45**

942 Handled Vase, hand painted w/ cartoon scenic cottage, footed, green wreath mkd., 5½" H. **$101**

943 Sauce Set, 4 pc. decor. w/ hand painted landscapes, orig. underplate, lid & ladle, green wreath mkd., 3½" H. **$146**

944 Nut Bowl, w/ hand painted decor., 3 handles, raised enameling, green wreath mkd., 7" diam. **$45**

945 Tray, w/ hand painted cottage, green wreath mkd., 7½" L. **$101**

946 Tea Strainer, 2 pc., cobalt blue decor. w/ roses, 6" L. **$67**

947 Scenic Plaque, decor. w/ painted riverside cottage & sailboat, rim pierced for hanging, green wreath mkd., 7½" diam. **$112**

948 Tea Service, 18 pcs., w/ luster decor., teapot, creamer, sugar, 3 cups, 6 saucers & 6 plates, green wreath mkd. **$67**

950 Nut Service, 7 pcs. w/ hand painted peanut shells & leafage in moriage, green wreath mkd. **$67**

951 Nippon Set, incomplete, consisting of creamer, sugar, 5 cups & saucers, hand painted w/ sailboat scene. **$78**

952 Nippon Spoon Rest & Nut Bowl, hand painted w/ relief mold, 8" & 6" L. **$34**

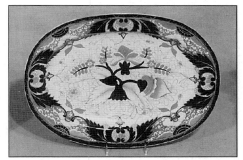

A-SC June 2001   Charlton Hall Galleries, Inc.

Worcester Porcelain Platter, Chamberlain's, ca. 1811-1820, in the Imari palette, 13¾" H, 18¾" W. **$425**

A-SC June 2001   Charlton Hall Galleries, Inc.

Rose Medallion Vase, late 19th C., w/ lion form handles, dec. w/ scenic panels, 13¾" H. **$200**

Pottery

Top Row

Serving Pitcher, cobalt blue on mottled brown, German, 14" H. **$400**

Majolica Compote, greens, browns & blues, int. pink, marked "JBD", 19" H, 14" L. **$805**

Royal Doulton Jardiniére, Greek Key design in black, 8½" diam., 7" H. **$460**

Roseville "Snowberry" Basket, shades rose to pink. **$253**

Majolica Tobacco Humidor, decor. in relief, 6" H, 5" diam. **$69**

Second Row

Mettlach Beer Stein, one liter, 10½" H. **$632**

Van Briggle Pottery Lamp, matte maroon base, orig. shade, 22" H. **$316**

Majolica Spill Vase, blue & orange, 10" H. **$69**

Third Row

Hull "Water Lily" Handled Basket, pink & green. **$259**

Mettlach Wall Plaque, "Rheinstein", 17½" diam. **$1,035**

Roseville Art Pottery, three pieces, "Water Lily" vase, rose color, "Gardenia" bowl, shades of brown to yellow, & "Foxglove" candlestick, green. **$115**

Mettlach Wall Plaque, "Stolzenfels", 17½" diam. **$1,035**

Hull "Wild Flower" Pitcher, yellow & pink. **$230**

Fourth Row

Cookie Jar, two piece, white w/ yellow, red, blue decor. **$402**

Majolica Pitcher, marked "FGS", 10" H. **$115**

Roseville "Peony" Bud Vase, 4½" H. **$80**

Hull "Water Lily" Jardiniére, rose & tan, 8½" H. **$103**

Roseville Jardiniéres, pr., one dark blue in "bushberry" patt., one turquoise in "white rose" patt. 3" H. **$92**

Majolica Pitcher, grey, red & brown, 11" H. **$138**

Roseville "Cosmos" Urn, marked, 4" H. **$103**

Majolica Pitcher, embossed "FGS", 7" H. **$172**

Roseville "Topeo" Vase, blue & green, 6½" H. **$172**

Fifth Row

"Longwy" Apothecary Jar w/ Lid, blue background, 11½" H. **$201**

"Longwy" Footed Fruit Standard, very colorful, 5" H, 9¼" diam. **$345**

Sewer Pipe Spaniel, glossy brown, 9½" H. **$230**

Sewer Pipe Spaniel, flat brown w/ black highlights, 2 minor chips, 9½" H. **$201**

Roseville "Fuchsia" Jardiniére, brown & green. **$230**

Roseville "Pine Cone" Vase, blue, paper label, 9½" H. **$575**

Weller Ovoid Vase, matte finish, crackling, 7" H. **$230**

Moorcroft Ovoid Vase, outlines in relief, 8½" H. **$632**

Fulper Flat Bowl, green & black matte, 5" diam., 1½" H. **$92**

A-SC June 2001   Charlton Hall Galleries, Inc.

Earthenware Stein, German, early 20th C., w medieval figures standing in archways, metal cover. **$140**

A-SC March 2001   Charlton Hall Galleries, Inc.

Figural Grouping, Ger., porcelain, Greiner & Halzapfel, ca. 1910, man & woman in 18th C. costume playing flute, 7¾" H. **$200**

Figural Compote, porcelain, Carl Thieme, ca. 1900, flanked w/ figures of a man & woman resting on pedestal base, & dec. w/ painted & applied flowers, mkd. w/ blue cross swords & T, 10½" diam., 15" H. **$700**

Figural Grouping, Meissen, early 20th C., man & woman in 18th C. dress, dec. w/ applied flowers; mkd. w/ blue swords under glaze w/ hash mark, 8¾" H, 10½" W **$425**

Stein w/ cover, porcelain, Capo-di-Monte, ca. 1890, dec. w/ raised figures in a classical design, finial repr., 14" H. **$300**

A-NH Aug. 2001   Northeast Auctions

Transfer Decorated Liverpool Earthenware

Row 1

Pitcher, Farmer's Arms decor., agricultural trophies & verse, 9" H. **$2,750**

Jug, Success To America Whose Militia w/ American ship under spout, 8¼" H. **$5,500**

George Washington Pitcher, possibly Herculaneum w/ blue enamel decor., 5½" H, **$7,500**

Creamware Rum Bowl w/ nautical black transfers, 9" diam. **$900**

Bowl w/ black transfer interior decor. of British ship & vignette of Sailor's Farewell on exterior, 6½" diam. **$1,750**

Jug w/ Memento Mori & Masonic transfer decor. & Masonic symbols, Wasington in Masonic apron beneath spout, 8" H. **$1,750**

Jug w/ black transfer decor. Recto : Hope with an anchor, 9½" H, **$300**

Row 2, Left to Right

Liverpool Plates, five w/ black transfers of sailing ships, some w/ polychrome decor., 9" diam. **$4,000**

Pitcher, Peace, Plenty & Independence w/ eagle beneath spout, reverse w/ George Washington & Liberty w/ map, 9" H. **$3,000**

Jug, Commodore Preble, w/ black transfer w/ vignette of Preble & angel, American eagle & Herculaneum Pottery, Liverpool, 8" H. **$2,000**

Historical Jug, Washington His Country's Father w/ nation's crest, sgn. Ric'd Hall & Son, 6" H. **$750**

Jug, mulberry transfer-printed Sailor's Farewell w/ poem, under spout, vignette of mother & children, 9" H. **$1,250**

A-NH Mar, 2001   Northeast Auctions

Chinese Export Plates

Four Armorial Famille Rose Plates, w/ gilt spearhead borders & crest of King, ca. 1748, 9¼" diam., two illus. **$2,750**

Yongzheng Soup Plate, w/ polychrome decor. & vignettes, coat-of-arms of Chapman, ca. 1735. **$2,000**

A-NH Mar, 2001   Northeast Auctions

Chinese Armorial Plates

Two Famille Rose Armorial Soup Plates, w/ borders of floral vignettes, birds and crest, dated 1768 in Roman numerals, 8½" diam. **$1,600**

Famille Rose Armorial Plate, w/ central coat-of -arms of Clerke, ca. 1765, 9" diam. **$1,100**

Famille Rose Soup Plate, w/ coat-of-arms of Elton, ca. 1760, 8¼" diam. **$500**

A-IN Mar. 2001   Majolica Auctions

Majolica

Cheese Keeper, Wedgwood urn & floral design w/ oriental taste, rim repair to stand, minor rim imperfection to cover. **$750**

Cheese Keeper, Holdcraft, mottled design w/ swags of musical instruments, putti & other items in relief, repair, 9" H, **$1,000**

Cheese Keeper, Victoria Pottery Co., albino floral, ribbon & bow design, rim repair to undertray, 8" H. **$300**

A-IN Mar. 2001　　　　　Majolica Auctions

Majolica

Oyster Plate, 9 wells, Minton light green, 10" diam. **$550**
Oyster Plate, 6 wells w/ large cracker well, Minton turquoise & brown, 9¾" diam. **$950**
Oyster Plate, 6 wells w/ cracker well, brown & green w/ daisy patt., repair, 10" diam. **$1,000**
Oyster Plate, Victoria Pottery Co., (VPC), unsigned, turquoise wells & red center, 9¾" diam. **$500**
Oyster Plate, Wedgwood ocean patt., minor rim repair, 9" diam. **$500**
Oyster Plate, 6 wells, Minton mottled patt., 9" diam. **$750**
Oyster Plate, 6 wells, Minton mottled patt., 9" diam. **$750**
Oyster Plate, Minton mottled patt., 9" diam. **$700**
Oyster Plate, 6 wells, Minton turquoise, 9" diam. **$550**
Oyster Plate, 6 wells, Minton turquoise. **$500**
Oyster Plate, 6 wells, Minton turquoise, 9" diam. **$500**
Oyster Plate, alt. pink & white wells, 9¼" diam. **$400**

A-IN Mar. 2001　　　　　Majolica Auctions

Majolica

Oyster Plate, 6 wells, George Jones patt., turquoise, raised center shell, 7¾" diam. **$1,700**
Oyster Plate, 5 wells, George Jones patt., turquoise, raised center shell, 7½" diam. **$1,300**
Oyster Plate, 6 wells, George Jones patt., turquoise, raised center well, 8½" diam. **$1,400**

A-IN Mar. 2001　　　　　Majolica Auctions

Majolica

Sardine Box, George Jones & Sons, shell covered patt., repair to bottom rim of box. **$2,600**

A-IN Mar. 2001　　　　　Majolica Auctions

Majolica

Calla Lily Cachepot, George Jones, minor hairline, 7½" H., 8½" diam. **$850**

A-IN Mar. 2001　　　　　Majolica Auctions

Majolica

Pitcher, George Jones, pink acanthus leaves & wheat patt. w/ yellow rope rim & base, mint, 7¼" H. **$5,000**

A-IN Mar. 2001　　　　　　　　　　Majolica Auctions

Majolica

First row

Platter, Etruscan Shell & Seaweed patt., rim nicks, 13½″ diam. **$450**

Plate, Etruscan Shell & Seaweed patt., 9¼″ diam. **$276**

Plate, set, Etruscan Shell & Seaweed patt., minor rim wear, 6-8″ diam. **$750**

Platter, Etruscan Shell & Seaweed patt., rim nicks. **$550**

Waste Bowl, Etruscan Shell & Seaweed patt. **$150**

Salt & Pepper Shakers, pr., Etruscan Coral patt., minor base nick. **$400**

Cups & Saucers, set, Etruscan Shell & Seaweed patt., various condition. **$300**

Mustache Cup and Saucer, Etruscan Shell & Seaweed patt. **$250**

Second row

Salad Bowl, Etruscan Shell & Seaweed patt., minor base nick. **$300**

Humidor, Etruscan Shell & Seaweed patt., one shell reattached. **$600**

Spittoon, Etruscan Shell & Seaweed patt. rim repair. **$400**

Butter Dish, covered, Etruscan Shell & Seaweed patt., minor glaze imperfection in bottom of base. **$500**

Bowl, Etruscan Shell & Seaweed patt., minor rim wear, 8½″ diam. **$150**

Third row

Sauce Dishes, set of 4, Etruscan Shell & Seaweed shape. **$525**

Cup & Saucer, Etruscan Cauliflower patt. **$100**

Tea Set, 3 pieces, Etruscan Cauliflower patt. **$400**

Waste Bowl, Etruscan Cauliflower patt. **$225**

Fourth row

Cake Stand, Etruscan Cauliflower patt., minor rim nick, 9″ diam., **$150**

Cake Stand, Etruscan Cauliflower patt., minor glaze imperfection. **$150**

Cake Stand, Etruscan Cauliflower patt., 8¾″ diam. **$170**

Waste Bowl, Etruscan Cauliflower patt. **$100**

Cup & Saucer, Etruscan Cauliflower patt. **$150**

Plate, Etruscan Cauliflower patt., 8″ diam. **$100**

Plate, Etruscan Cauliflower patt., minor rim chips to back, 9″ diam., **$125**

A-IA Sept. 2001　　　　　　Gene Harris Auction Center

Tea Leaf Tureen w/ underplate & ladle, Meakin. **$170**

Tea Leaf Salt & Pepper Shakers, **$30**

A-IN Mar. 2001　　　　　　　　　　Majolica Auctions

French Choicey Majolica Rooster Figure, signed Louis Carrier Belleuse, minor repair, 21″ H. **$3,250**

A-IN Mar. 2001　　　　　　　　　　Majolica Auctions

Majolica

George Jones Picket Fence Cheese Keeper, turquoise, minor rim nick to base, 7″ H. **$2,750**

A-IN Mar. 2001　　　　　　　　　　Majolica Auctions

Majolica

Cheese Keeper, George Jones, wheat, daisy & picket fence, turquoise, repair to handle & top of cover, 10″ H. **$7,000**

A-OH Mar. 2001   Garth's Auctions, Inc.

Majolica
First Row

Plates, three leaf shaped, yel., gr. & pink, 10" L., aqua, yel. gr. & burgundy, 8¾" L., gr. br. (not pic.), 8¾" L. **$137**

Plate, lg. leaf shaped, pink, gr. & yel. w/ br. branch handle, mkd. for Griffen, Smith & Co., enamel chip 11¾" H. **$192**

Plates, three, gr. & white, & two w/ yel., ink & gr., (one not pic.), mkd. for Griffen, Smith & Co., minor wear, touched up flakes, 9" L. **$165**

Second Row

Plates, two, gr., lighter has leaves on textured ground, 8¼" diam., darker has grape vines & strawberries, unglazed spots, 9⅛" diam. **$55**

Creamer & Teapot, in Seaweed & Shell patt., shades of pink, gr. & br., mkd. for Griffen, Smith & Co., creamer has darker colors & has two hairlines, 3⅝", 5½" H. **$577**

Pitcher, Seaweed & Shell patt. in shades of pink, gr. & br. w/ blue, mkd. for Griffen, Smith & Co., 5¾" H. **$385**

A-OH Mar. 2001   Garth's Auctions, Inc.

Majolica
First Row

Plate, lt. aqua ground w/ white pebbled surface & a flying stork in white, yel. & blue, imp. "JH", wear, 8½" diam. **$110**

Plate, goldenrod ground w/ blue daisy-like flowers w/ green leaves, indented rim, 8¼" diam. **$82**

Platter, asparagus & artichokes w/ leaves in white, burgundy & shades of gr. 10½" x 13¼". **$357**

Plates, molded borders, similar color w/ blue rims, lt. blue grounds & shades of pink, gr. & br., pink roses, 8⅛" diam., 2nd has long billed, crested bird w/ additional yel. color, ink stamp, 8¼" dia. **$247**

Second Row

Plates, two lg., one w/ leaf border w/ shaggy dog in center, gr., yel. & br. on an ivory ground, 11¼" diam., bl. berry branch in green, purple, br., pink, & yel. on ivory basket weave ground, 10½" diam. **$192**

Pitcher, in form of pineapple, yel. & br. w/ a gr. neck & handle, enamel wear, 9" H. **$165**

Serving Tray, dk. blue ground w/ white water lily & gr. leaves, br. branches form two handles, one w/ glued chip, 8" x 11¼". **$165**

A-OH Jan. 2001   Garth's Auctions, Inc.

English Enameled Boxes
First row

Oval Box, molded pale blue base w/ white lid, w/ red & blue floral ribbons w/ blk. verse "Have communion w/ few speak evil of none", int. lid mirror, hairlines & wear, 1⅝" L. **$330**

Oval Box, molded aqua base, white lid w/ blue & red edging & yel. birds "Love & Live Happy", int. lid cracked mirror, base has damage, 1½" L. **$330**

Box, yel. w/ white foliage, white reserved on lid & front have polychrome birds, repr., 1⅞" L. **$137**

Rectangular Box, deep cobalt base, white lid has beaded oval w/ pale tan & gilt lovebirds on plinth, cobalt oval w/ gilt "A Token of Esteem", int. lid has mirror, base repr., 1½" L. **$137**

Oval Box, gr. base & white lid, lid has yel. & gr. beading w/ br. squiggled line & "In Remembrance of Friendship", int. has cracked mirror, hairlines & filled in chips, 1¾" L. **$110**

Second row

Oval Box, molded pink base, white lid has polychrome flowers w/ bird & "A Trifle from Penzance", int. lid has mirror, 1¾" L. **$357**

Oval Box, molded lt. blue base, white lid has woman in blue dress w/ bird "May the Heart of my Love Prove as true as the Dove", int. lid has worn mirror, hairlines & some damage, 1⅞" L. **$137**

Oval Box, molded pale pink base, white lid w/ steamer ship "A Present from Chepstow", hairlines & base has repr., 1⅝" L. **$110**

Oval Box, pale aqua base & white lid w/ yel. bird on a blue urn, "The Gift of a Friend", int. lid has worn mirror, lid damaged, 1¾" L. **$110**

Oval Boxes, two, one molded teal gr. base w/ verse "May he who loves sincerely…", 1⅞" L. and one w/ dk. blue base, white lid has couple & lovebirds "Love & Live Happy", 1¾" L, both have damage & one has cracked mirror **$110**

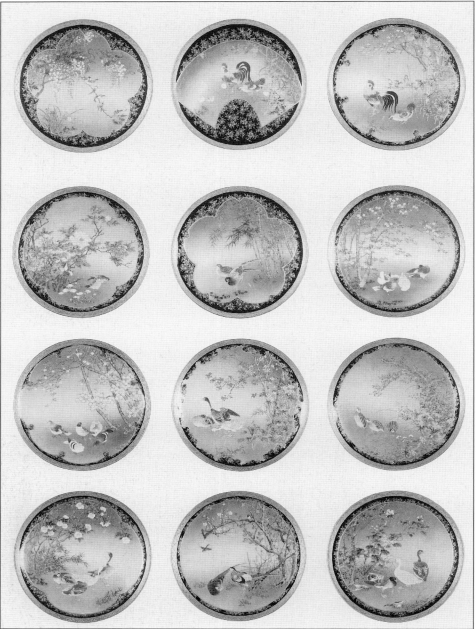

A-SC March 2001   **Charlton Hall Galleries, Inc.**

Earthenware Cabinet Plates, set of twelve, Satsuma, sgn. Kinkozan zo, late 19th C., dec. w/ gilt border, painted flowers, birds & fowl in wooded landscapes, mkd. w/ impr. Painted mark on underside, 8½" diam. **$23,000**

A-NJ May 2001   **Craftsman**

Rookwood Vase, by William Hentschel, ca. 1914, w/ inverted water lilies under waves in red, gr. & amber, flame mark, 8½" H. **$1,400**

A-NJ May 2001   **Craftsman**

Chelsea Pottery Vase, porcelain crackleware by Hugh Robertson w/ white flowers on indigo ground, rest., sgn., 5½" x 4¼" **$850**

A-PA Oct. 2001   **Conestoga Auction Company**

Leeds Pottery
Charger, w/ yellow urn & polychrome flowers & blue feather edge, 13¼" diam. **$715**
Handleless Cup & Saucer, child's size w/ green & brown design. **$154**
Charger, w/ blue landscape decor. & blue scalloped edge decor., 12½" diam. **$495**

A-PA Nov. 2001   Conestoga Auction Company

Flow Blue
First row
Covered Tureen w/ under plate, Peking patt., hairline on underplate, 7" H. **$220**
Platter, Sgn. E. Challinor (chip & reprs.), Pelew patt., 9½" x 13". **$192**
Butter Tub, Floral patt. w/ attached saucer base & pierced open handle lid, 3½" H, 7½" D. **$275**
Second row
Coffeepot, Temple patt., reprs., 8½" H. **$1,375**

Soup Tureen, Peking patt., hairline on rim of base & chip on lid, 11" H. **$850**
Coffeepot, Temple patt., reprs. to spout, 9½" H. **$907**
Third row
Coffeepot, Chapoo patt. w/ spout repr. & chip on lid, 11" H. **$3,520**
Dome Cheese Dish, Persianna patt., w/ pedestal base, 12" H. **$1,925**
Coffeepot w/ floral & foliate design w/ chip on spout & finial repair, 9" H. **$522**

A-IN Mar. 2001   Majolica Auctions
Game Dish, Wedgwood Love Birds patt., 11½" diam. **$1,300**

A-NJ May 2001   Craftsman
Royal Doulton Lambeth Vases, pr., handpainted in the Art Nouveau style by Margaret Walker, w/ stamped mark, 8¼" x 4½". **$1,300**

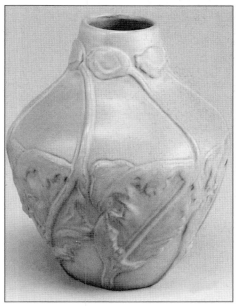

A-NJ May 2001   Craftsman
Van Briggle Vase, ca. 1905, embossed w/ poppy pods & leaves under matte turquoise glaze, br. clay showing through, 10" H. **$3,500**

Game Dish, Love Birds patt., minor hairline to base, 13" diam. **$1,500**
Game Dish, rabbit finial, dead game w/ drapes of grapes & vine, yellow rope border, includes insert, 10" diam. **$800**

A-SC June 2001   Charlton Hall Galleries, Inc.

A-IA Aug. 2001   Gene Harris Antique Auction Center, Inc.

Pottery Cat, 19th C., glazed yellow w/ green & brown streaking. 10½" H **$5,250**

Snuff Boxes

First Row

Snuff Box, Fr. enamel, ca. 1830, dec. w/ 2 hands supporting hearts & motto " Be Happy", over conforming body in rose, 1⅛" H, 2" W, 1½" D. **$325**

Battersea Snuff Box, ca. 1875, Eng. enamel, cartouche-form shaped lid dec. w/ floral spray, 1⅛" H, 2⅝" W, 2" D. **$650**

French Enamel Bonbonniére, ca. 1800, dec. w/ scenic landscape in rose, 1⅛" H, 2⅛" W, 1½" D. **$550**

Second Row

Sévres Porcelain Oval Snuff Box, late 18th-early 19th C., bombé shaped body dec., w/ cartouches of cherub & trophies on cobalt ground, 1½" H, 2½" W, 1¾" D. **$475**

French Porcelain Oval Snuff Box, ca. 1860, dec. w/ floral sprays jewel-work, 1½" H, 3" W, 2⅛" D. **$300**

English Battersea, enamel bonbonniére, ca. 1825, dec. w/ 2 pigeons, a bundle of wheat, & motto "Peach & Plenty", 1¼" H, 2" W, 1½" D. **$600**

Third Row

French Faience Snuff Box, early 19th C., dec. w/ pastoral landscape, mkd. on underside w/ cross, 1½" H, 2½" W, 1¾" D. **$275**

French Stained Ivory Snuff Box, ca. 1760, dec. w/ scrolling foliate scene w/ cherub & motto, underside dec. w/ squirrel, nuts & insects, ¾" H, 3¼" W, 2¾" D. **$800**

English Battersea, enamel bonbonniére, ca. 1780, dec. w/ 2 white doves perched on an urn, int. w/ mirrored lid, 1½" H, 1½" D. **$500**

Fourth Row

English Battersea, enamel snuff box, ca. 1760, w/ transfer dec. depicting figures in country landscape w/ metal mounts, 1⅛" H, 2½" W, 1½" D. **$300**

English Battersea, enamel bonbonniére, ca. 1780, dec. w/ memorial scene over a shaped pink base, 1" H, 2½" W, 1½" D. **$500**

A-IN Mar. 2001   Majolica Auctions

Garden Seat, Minton cobalt Passion Flower patt., repair to feet & flower points. **$5,250**

A-ME May 2001   James D. Julia, Inc.

Weller Pottery Jardiniére, marked w/ water staining to interior, 32" H. **$1,035**

Goldscheider Vase, terra cotta featuring full-relief Victorian maid, 28" H. **$2,185**

Weller Jardiniére and Base, w/ abstract floral design on mottled brown & green background, 29" H. **$575**

A-PA Oct. 2001   Conestoga Auction Company

Leeds Pottery
Cream Pitcher, "Pineapple" patt., w/ embossed designs, 4½" H. **$825**

Bowl, w/ blue, green & tan floral & foliate decor. w/ chain link & floral border, 5" H, 11¼" D. **$880**
Cream Pitcher, w/ blue & yellow floral bud & leaf decor., hairline to spout, 4½" H. **$132**

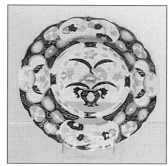

A-SC June 2001   Charlton Hall
                                  Galleries, Inc.

Ironstone Soup Bowls, pr., Mason's, ca. 1849, w/ scalloped rim, dec. in the Imari palette, 10¼" diam. **$275**

A-PA June 2001   Pook & Pook, Inc.

Dresden White Porcelain Parrots perched on tree stumps, ca. 1900, 18" H. **$650**

A-PA Nov. 2001   Conestoga Auction Company

Rockingham Glazed Pottery
First row
Seated Spaniel w/ shaped base, chips on base, 10½" H. **$330**
Pie Plate w/ flared edge, 11" D. **$82**
Toby Character Pitcher w/ edge wear on top, 9¼" H. **$110**
Second row
Book Form Flask w/ chips, 6½" H. **$192**
Toby Character Cream Pitcher w/ chips, 6½" H. **$38**
Mug w/ panel ribbed sides, reprs. 3½" H. **$11**
Soap Dish, covered w/ canted corners, no liner, 5½" L, 3½" H. **$220**

Covered Sugar w/ chip on inside lid, 5¼" H. **$60**
Third row
Vegetable Bowl w/ flared edge, 6½" H. **$33**
Inkwell w/ embossed face & flower decor., chips on base, 4½" D. **$77**
Inkwell, shoe form w/ chip at receptacle, 4½" H. **$93**
Soap Dish, footed. **$49**
Mug w/ applied ear handle & molded base. **$55**
Still Bank, cottage building, w/ chip, 2½" H. **$176**

A-PA June 2001   Pook & Pook, Inc.

Dresden Porcelain Rooster, ca. 1900, standing over basket of fruit, 25" H, minor losses. **$1,500**

A-PA Mar. 2001   Conestoga Auction Company

A-NY Nov. 2000   Hesse Galleries
Redware Jar, Berks Co., tulip decor. 6¾"
H. **$4,730**

Rockingham Glazed Pottery
Row 1, Left to Right
Teapot, "Rebekah at the Well" patt.,
embossed design, 8" H. **$104**
Pie Plate, w/ flared edge, 10¼" D. **$110**
Pitcher, w/ embossed star & tulip design,
sm. vertical hairline, 8" H. **$71**
Row 2, Left to Right
Salt Box, w/ hanging hole & embossed
peacock & fountain design, 6" H. **$192**
Covered Sugar Bowl, w/ pedestal base,
5½" H. **$220**

Mug, w/ applied ear handle & molded
base, 4" H. **$104**
Plate, square form w/ shell & scroll
design, splayed edge, 8½" D. **$55**
Row 3, Left to Right
Bowls, two graduated oval vegetable
bowls w/ flared edges, 11¼" x 12".
$275
Straining Plate, w/ perforated bottom &
rolled edge, 9½" D. **$110**
Soap Dish, ribbed patt., 2½" H, 4½" L.
$49

A-NY Nov. 2000   Hesse Galleries
Redware Jar, Berks Co., slip decor. 7¼"
H. **$687**

P-PA Nov. 2001   Conestoga Auction Company
Blue Decorated Staffordshire
Foot Bath depicting boating scenes w/ open handles, 21" L,
8½" H. **$825**

P-PA Nov. 2001   Conestoga Auction Company
Blue Decorated Staffordshire
Water Pitcher, "Rebecca, at the Well" patt., 8½" H. **$1,155**
Plate depicting boating scene w/ cottage & castle in
background, 9¾" D. **$66**

A-NH Aug. 2001   Northeast Auctions

Pink Sunderland Luster (unless noted)
Row 1
Newcastle Pink Luster w/ black transfer of Cast Iron Bridge, 8½" H. **$1,000**
Two Frog Mugs w/ black transfer decor. first w/ Sailor's Farewell, second at right, w/ Cast Iron Bridge, both 5" H. **$1,000**
Pitcher w/ black transfer decor. of Landlord Caution by Dawson's Low Ford Pottery, 8¼" H. **$800**
Pitcher w/ black transfer poem, To A Friend. **$3,700**
Bowl w/ black transfer decor. of Cast Iron Bridge & Sailor's Farewell, 9½" H. **$600**
Pitcher w/ black transfer decor. of Masonic motif, 9¼" H. **$900**
Pitcher w/ black transfer incl. red, yellow & green highlights, small ship vignette & poem. Faith, Hope & Charity under spout, 8¼" H. **$2,200**
Pitcher w/ black transfer of Cast Iron Bridge & Friendship poem under spout, 9½" H. **$1,600**
Row 2, Left to Right
Large Pitcher w/ black transfer of Sailor's Farewell & Cast Iron Bridge under spout, by Garrison Pottery, 9¼" H. **$1,300**
Small Jug w/ black transfer, highlighted in red & green, decor. w/ ship, 6" H. **$850**

Large Pitcher w/ black transfer & polychrome decor., The Mariner's Arms, 8½" H. **$1,000**
Newcastle Pitcher w/ black transfer decor. of Sailor's Farewell, 7¼" H. **$950**
Large English Creamware Pitcher w/ black transfer decor. & pink luster bands, w/ polychrome decor., Masonic symbols & Vignettes, sgn. Thos. Baddeley Hanley, 9½" H. **$1,900**
Large Newcastle Pitcher w/ black transfer decor, sailor's poem & ship under spout, 9½" H. **$1,300**
Large Pitcher w/ black transfer decor. & Sailor's Farewell, 9½" H. **$1,000**
Newcastle Pitcher w/ black transfer decor. of Mariner's Arms & poem under spout, & polychrome highlights, 6½" H. **$1,900**
Large Pitcher w/ black transfer decor. by Garrison Pottery, w/ poem to Friendship & Cast Iron Bridge under spout, 9½" H. **$900**
Row 3, Left to Right
Pink Luster Pitcher w/ black tranfer-printed decor. & polychrome highlights, Sailor's Farewell & poem under spout, 9½" H. **$2,000**

Pitcher w/ black transfer-printed decor. of Cast Iron Bridge, "God Speed the Plow", & handwritten name T. Webb & poem under spout, by Dixon Austin & Co., Sunderland, 1813, 7¼" H. **$900**
Newcastle Pitcher w/ black transfer & polychrome highlights, poem & Cast Iron Bridge, made by Tyneside Pottery, 7½" H. **$1,200**
Orange Sunderland Luster Pitcher w/ black transfer vignettes w/ polychrome decor., The Mariner's Arms under spout, 9½" H. **$3,200**
Newcastle Pitcher w/ black transfer & polychrome highlights, vignette w/ I'll drink to the girl that I love dearly, 7½" H. **$1,400**
Pitcher w/ black transfer & polychrome highlights, sailing vignette & motto Success to Fishermen, 7½" H. **$900**
Pitcher w/ black transfer & polychrome highlights, floral painted neck, view of Cast Iron Bridge & God Speed the Plow, inscrip. under spout, Sep. 12th, 1833. **$2,000**
Large Pitcher w/ black transfer of British ship & poem 'Bless British Isles', schooner & poem w/ depiction of Mariner's Compass & ships, 9½" H. **$1,200**

A-NH Mar, 2001   Northeast Auctions

Chinese Amorial Plates
Octagonal Plate, w/ polychrome floral vignette, coat-of-arms of the Anglo-Prussian Society & lion crest at top, ca. 1760, 8½" diam. **$1,200**
Famille Rose Plate, w/ floral border & coat-of-arms of Lindsay, ca. 1755, 8½" diam. **$650**
Famille Rose Plate, w/ coat-of-arms of Meares, surmounted by a mermaid, ca. 1765, 8½" diam. **$1,200**

A-PA Oct. 2001   Conestoga Auction Company

Ironstone China – Green Wheat Pattern

Row 1

Waste Bowl, 3½" H, 5½" D, **$192**
Cream Pitcher, sgn. Elsmore & Forster, 6¼" H. **$275**
Coffeepot, sgn. Elsmore & Forster, 9½" H. **$577**
Sugar Bowl, sgn. Elsmore & Forster, 8" H. **$357**

Row 2

Cup & Saucer, sgn. Elsmore & Forster. **$192**
Handleless Cup & Saucer, sgn. Elsmore & Forster. **$330**
Gravy Boat, 5½" H. **$247**
Mug, 3½" H. **$308**

A-PA Oct. 2001   Conestoga Auction Company

Spatterware

Row 1

Plate, "School House" patt., w/ blue house, red border, 8¼" D. **$3,190**
Coffeepot, "Tulip" patt. w/ bold yellow, red tulip & green leaves, chips on inside rim, 9" H. **$18,700**
Handleless Cup & Saucer, "Christmas Balls" patt., red & yellow design, chip on base of cup. **$1,045**

Row 2

Handleless Cup & Saucer, "Morning Glory" patt., w/ blue flower & yellow border. **$1,870**
Sugar Bowl, w/ bold red & blue, paneled sides, reprs. **$1,375**
Handleless Cup & Saucer, "Thistle" patt., w/ red flower, green leaves, red & yellow border. **$2,530**

Row 3

Toddy Plate, "Acorn" patt., purple, brown acorns, 6¼" D. **$1,870**
Handleless Cup & Saucer, "Drape" patt., w/ yellow, blue cornflower & green leaves. **$9,075**
Handleless Cup & Saucer, "Fish" patt., red w/ brown, red & green fish. **$27,500**

Row 4

Dinner Plate, "Rose" patt., w/ red & blue border, chip repr. on edge, **$467**
Soup Plate, "Dahlia" patt. w/ red around border, 10¼" D. **$1,650**
Dinner Plate, "Peafowl" patt. w/ blue, red, yellow & green peafowl. **$577**

A-PA Oct. 2001   Conestoga Auction Company

Historical Blue Staffordshire China
Row 1
Handleless Cup & Saucer, "Landing of General Lafayette" patt., sgn. Clews. **$522**
Covered Sugar Bowl, "Lafayette at the Tomb of Franklin" patt., unmkd. but made by T. Mayer, tiny sliver broken off underside of lid & glued back, 6½" H. **$660**
Sauce Boat & Underplate, "States" patt., sgn. Clews, sauce boat, 5" H x 7¾" L, underplate 6¼" x 8¼". **$1,760**
Cup Plate, "Castle Garden Battery, New York" patt., sgn. Wood, 3⅝" D. **$247**
Row 2
Plate, "Winter View of Pittsfield, Mass", sgn. Clews, 8" D. **$357**
Small PLatter, "East View of La Grange, The Residence of the Marquis Lafayette" patt., sgn. Wood, 7¾" x 9¾". **$385**
Wilkes Design Plate, "Playing at Draught's", sgn. Clews, 7¾" D. **$165**
Plate, "Commodore MacDonough's Victory" patt., sgn Wood, 7¾" D. **$357**

A-PA Mar. 2001   Conestoga Auction Company

Historical Blue Staffordshire
Handleless Cup & Saucer, decor. w/ fishing scene. **$154**

A-PA Mar. 2001   Conestoga Auction Company

Historical Blue Staffordshire
Toddy Plate, "Regent Park, London", 6" diam. **$121**

A-PA Mar. 2001   Conestoga Auction Company

Historical Blue Staffordshire
Handleless Cup & Saucer, depic. man playing lyre. **$165**

A-PA Oct. 2001   Conestoga Auction Company

Spatterware
Row 1
Miniature Platter, blue & green "Rainbow" patt., 3½" x 4¼". **$880**
Leeds Small Cannister, brown & blue "Rainbow" patt., sponge decorated w/ green incised, decor., 3" H. **$1,485**
Handleless Cup & Saucer, yellow "thistle" patt., red flower, green leaves, tiny chip on base rim of cup. **$2,090**

Child's Size Handleless Cup & Saucer, brown & green "Rainbow" patt., several pin nips on edge of cup. **$880**
Row 2
Handleless Cup & Saucer, red, blue & green "Criss-Cross" patt., sm. chip on base rim of saucer. **$3520**
Handleless Cup & Saucer, yellow. **$550**
Handleless Cup & Saucer, red & blue "Bull's Eye" patt.. **$605**

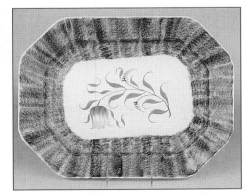

A-PA Oct. 2001   Conestoga Auction Company

Spatterware Platter, "Tulip" patt. w/ purple & blue rainbow spatter, rim chip repair 14" x 18". **$8,250**

POTTERY / PORCELAIN

A-PA Oct. 2001   Conestoga Auction Company

Canary Yellow Luster Ware

Row 1

Toothpick Holder, bear form on platform base, 3¼" h. **$1,155**

Child's Mug, w/ black transfer depicting teacher & child, 2½" H. **$880**

Milk Pitcher, w/ silver luster floral & foliate design, spout repr., 5½" H. **$357**

Spill Vase, w/ floral & leaf decor., brown & rust bands, tiny hairlines around base, 5¼" H. **$385**

Waste Bowl, w/ maroon decor. of mother & child, glazing wear on base, 5¼" diam. 2½" H. **$247**

Child's Mug, w/ black transfer verse encircled within an acorn & leaf wreath, 2¼" H. **$687**

Row 2

Handleless Cup & Saucer, w/ rust flowers & blue leaves. **$797**

Handleless Cup & Saucer, pr., 1 illus. w/ rust transfer decor., mkd. "Sewell", chip on base of one cup. **$440**

Handleless Cup & Saucer, pr., 1 illus., w/ rust transfer decor. **$412**

Cup & Saucer, w/ rust flowers & green leaves, repairs on saucer/ hairline on cup. **$880**

A-PA Oct. 2001   Conestoga Auction Company

Early Adams Rose Pattern

Row 1

Plates, pair (1 illus), mkd. Adams, 6" diam. **$192**

Coffeepot, wear chips, mkd. Adams, **$4,950**

Plates, pr. (1 illus.), w/ impressed Adams mark, 5" diam. **$522**

Milk Pitcher, w/ shell form spout, 8" H. **$935**

Row 2

Plates, set of four, (1 illus.) 3 mkd. Adams, 9½" diam. **$467**

Platter, mkd. Adams, 9" x 11". **$687**

Plates, set of four, (1 illus.) mkd. Adams, 8½" diam. **$357**

A-PA Mar. 2001   Conestoga Auction Company

Historical Blue Staffordshire

Plate, w/ trans. decor. "Barrington Hall" by Clews, 8¾" diam. **$154**

Plate, w/ trans. decor. "Landing of General Lafayette" by Clews, 10" diam. **$385**

A-PA Oct. 2001   Conestoga Auction Company

Leeds Pottery

Plate, w/ blue feather scalloped edge w/ polychrome basket of flowers, 9½" D. **$715**

Plate, w/ sprig center, blue & yellow flower border, 6¼" D. **$137**

Plate, w/ green, yellow & blue peafowl center & blue feather edge, chip repair, 9½" D. **$467**

A-PA Oct. 2001   Conestoga Auction Company

Spatterware Paneled Pitcher, blue w/ double sided decor. of gray fort w/ green trees in foreground, 12" H. **$2,200**

Spatterware Foot Tub, w/ open handles, blue sponge decor. w/ red, yellow & green floral decor., 13" diam., 19" W, 8½" H. **$4,400**

A-PA Mar. 2001   Conestoga Auction Company

Historical Blue Staffordshire

Plate, w/ trans. decor. "St. Peters Rome" by Wood & Sons, 10" diam. **$192**

Soup Plate, w/ hunt scene by Woods & Sons, edge chip, 10" diam. **$632**

A-PA Oct. 2001   Conestoga Auction Company

Spatterware

Row 1

Handleless Cup & Saucer, w/ blue, yellow & red peafowl, brown border. **$2,860**

Paneled Plate, "Acorn" patt., w/ yellow acorns, red border, 8¼" diam. **$3,850**

Cup Plate, "Morning Glory" patt., w/ blue flower & green leaves, chip on edge, 5¼" diam., **$1,870**

Row 2

Teapot, "Thistle" patt., w/ red & yellow rainbow, red thistle & green leaves, wear chips & married lid. 5½" H. **$4,000**

Teapot, miniature w/ rainbow, chip repair to lid, 4" H. **$715**

Sugar Bowl, "Rooster" patt., w/ red, chip & repairs, 4½" H. **$1,210**

Milk Pitcher, w/ rainbow, minor glazing wear around spout, 7½" H. **$12,000**

Row 3

Handleless Cup, "School House" patt., w/ red & green spatter. **$4,125**

Squirrel Eating a Nut, w/ purple, yellow & green decor., 3½" H. **$1,210**

Cream Pitcher, "Dahlia" patt., w/ red & blue flower w/ green sprigs, purple ground, 4½" H. **$8,800**

Handleless Cup & Saucer, w/ blue, red & green guinea hen, red ground, saucer has repr. **$440**

Row 4

Plate, "Star" patt. w/ blue sunburst border, 9½" diam. **$577**

Plate, blue & green rainbow w/ central "Bull's Eye" design, 9½" diam. **$110**

Plate, "Peafowl" patt., w/ incised feather edge, blue, yellow & red peafowl, 9¼" diam. **$577**

POTTERY / PORCELAIN

A-PA Oct. 2001   Conestoga Auction Company

Historical Blue Staffordshire

Plate, "Landing of Lafayette" patt., sgn. Clews, chip repair on edge, 10" D. **$137**

Plate, "States" patt., w/ central view of a three-story building & observatory, unmkd. but made by Clews, 10½" D. **$330**

Pattern (level) Plate, "Baltimore & Ohio Railroad", sgn. Wood, 10" D. **$880**

Teapot, w/ brown confetti design & embossed berry & leaf bands. **$2,530**

Row 2

Screw Lid Salve Box, w/ brown, tan & opaque white comb decor., sgn. "G.C." on outside of lid & dated 1785 on inside. Repairs. 3¼" diam., 1¼" H. **$2,310**

Bowl, w/ blue, brown & opaque white earthworm decor. on brown band flanked by dark brown stripes, 6¼" diam., 3" H. **$1,320**

Bowl, w/ flared edge, green geometric band above opaque white zigzag lines on dark brown ground, 10¼" diam., 5" H. **$3,410**

Cream Pitcher, French, w/ blue, opaque white & black cat's eye decor. on tan ground sgn. "L.M. & CIE., Depose", (2 minor chips on upper rim), 5½" H. **$1,760**

Master Salt, w/ brown, tan & opaque white cat's eye decor. on blue ground flanked by dark brown stripes, 6¼" diam., 3" H. **$1,320**

A-PA Oct. 2001   Conestoga Auction Company

Mocha Ware

Row 1

Mug, w/ dark brown/ orange/ tan & opaque white swirl decor., 6" H. **$5,775**

Pepper Pot, w/ brown, tan & opaque zigzag earthworm decor. on gray/green ground and dark brown bands, edge wear, 4½" H. **$1,980**

Pitcher, w/ tan & blue bands decor. w/ opaque & brown zigzag & looping decor., 8¼" H. **$11,540**

Spill Vase, w/ polychrome sanded decor., edge chips, 4½" H. **$247**

A-PA Oct. 2001   Conestoga Auction Company

Spatterware

Row 1

Basket of Strawberries Form Window Stop, rare red and black rainbow, repairs, 4¾" H. **$440**

Paneled Pitcher, red and green rainbow w/ embossed shell design under spout, 6½" H. **$1,925**

Blue "Fort" Pattern Paneled Plate, brown, gray & red fort w/ green foreground & trees, tiny chip on edge and 2" hairline in body, 7½" D. **$192**

Figurine, elephant form with blue, red, yel., black and green, two base rim chips, 4" H. **$3,080**

Row 2

Handleless Cup and Saucer, red "tulip" patt. with purple, yellow & green **$770**

Covered Sugar Bowl, blue "rose" patt., red flower with green leaves, lid repaired, 7½" H. **$440**

Handleless Cup & Saucer, green "Peafowl" patt. with blue, yellow & red. **$715**

Row 3

Paneled Plate, blue "Acorn" patt. w/ brown, teal & green, 8¼" D. **$880**

Paneled Plate, red & green "Rainbow" patt., 9¼" D. **$302**

A-OH Feb. 2001   Garth's Auctions, Inc.

First Row

Softpaste Creamer, molded bumps w/ pink, purple & yel. enamel & molded face in flesh tones & br., br. rim stripe, rim flake, 4½" H. **$220**

Gaudy Welsh Creamers, two, octagonal w/ sunflower design in blue, ora. & gr. w/ copper luster, molded snake handles in gr. & rust, marked "Allertons, Est. 1831, Made in Eng.", 4½"H & 5¾" H. **$137**

Gaudy Welsh Creamer, "Cambrian Rose" design in blue, ora. & gr. w/ copper luster, scrolled handle & diamond quilted spout, gr. has wear 5¼" H. **$275**

Gaudy Welsh Creamer, flower basket design in blue, ora. & copper luster, molded branch handle & satyr mask spout, tooled lines on base & beaded rim, stains & hairlines, 5" H. **$110**

Second Row

Bennington Parian Pitcher, "Cascade Patt.", molded waterfall over rocky cliff w/ tree branch handle, glazed int., relief "Bennington" lozenge mark, 9⅜" H. **$550**

Bowl & Pitcher, blue & white stick spatter bowl, stain & crow's foot in bottom 1" diam., 2½" H; mocha pitcher, blue stripes 7 blue & blue-grey bands w/ molded leaf handle ends, flake on spout, cracks, 6½" H. **$192**

Staffordshire Plate, dk. blue "America" & "Independence", states border w/ acorn leaf, scalloped rim, impressed "Clews", cracked, 10½" diam. **$110**

A-OH Nov. 2001   Garth's Auctions, Inc.

Spatterware

First row

Teapot, rainbow, red & blue, flakes, hairline & glued finial, 9¼" H. **$550**

Creamer, blue, "Fort" patt., grey & br. w/ gr. spatter trees, stains, 4" H. **$247**

Plate, rainbow, red, blue & yel. border, rim chips, 8¾" diam. **$1,320**

Handleless Cup & Saucer, blue, "Dahlia" patt., red, blue & gr., hairlines. **$220**

Teapot, blue, peafowl in gr. ochre & pink, few flakes, finial restr., 8⅝" H. **$990**

Second row

Plate, deep yel. w/ red & gr. thistle center, chip & lt. staining, 8⅜" diam. **$1,540**

Plates, two, strong purple w/ tulip centers in red, blue & gr., paint retouched, 8⅜" diam. **$385**

Pitcher, deep yel., red & gr. tulip on both sides, molded fan under spout, few flakes, int. stains, spout rest., 6⅜" H. **$4,675**

Plate, blue, molded feather edge w/ a red, yel. & blue peafowl center, old paper labels w/ some history, 8½" diam. **$687**

Plates, two, red, peafowl design, gr. red & blue tail (illus.), wear & sm. rim flakes, 9½" diam., one in gr., yel. & blue, 8½" diam. **$715**

A-OH Apr. 2001   Garth's Auctions, Inc.

First Row

Sewer Tile Dogs, two, both molded, smaller one has sm. holes for eyes & nose, lt. br. glaze 7 edge chips, 4½" H., dk. br. slightly metallic glaze, 5¾" H. **$220**

Sewer Tile Dog, hand modeled w/ tooled fur & facial features, matte glaze w/ metallic speckles, traces of white paint, 7½" H. **$110**

A-MA Mar. 2001   Skinner, Inc

Earthenware

First Row

Creamware Jug, barrel-form, ca. 1800, banded in ochre & br. w/ gr. glazed band of reeding & two undec. rouletted bands, 3 bands of ochre are dec. w/ "seaweed" motifs, 6½" H. **$3,737**

Pearlware Bowl, London shape, ca. 1830, banded in taupe & blk. w/ earthworm dec., on taupe field in blk., white & ochre, gr. glazed rouletted rim, 6¼" diam. **$546**

Creamware Jug, barrel-form, ca. 1820 w/ alt. slip bands of blk. & br. dec. w/ combed blue, blk. & white cat's eyes on br. bands & white wavy trailed lines on the blk. bands, bordered by gr. glazed rouletted bands, extruded handle w/ gr. glazed foliate terminals, 7" H. **$8,625**

Creamware Pint Mug, ca. 1795, w/ chestnut br. slip field banded in blk. w/ blk. mocha "trees", flared foot & foliate terminals, 4½" H. **$977**

Pearlware Pint Jug, ca. 1820, w/ make-do tinsmith's repl. handle, two cobalt glazed rouletted bands, bracketing in ora. field w/ combed blk. bands, 4¾" H. **$1,955**

Second Row

Creamware Bowl, hemispherical, ca. 1800, banded in ora. & blue w/ blk. slip-filled rouletted bands, 7¼" diam. **$805**

Creamware Cup & Saucer, ca. 1780, dipped in brick red slip, int. of both cup & saucer remain undec., intertwined handle is red, foliate terminals cream-colored, saucer 5⅛" diam. **$257**

Hemispherical Bowl, Fr. ca., 1810, banded in buff w/ blk. borders, well-delineated mocha "trees" on buff field, 7½" diam. **$747**

Pearlware Jug, baluster-form, ca. 1830, w/ looping earthworm dec. in white, rust, blue & blk. w/ blk. slip-filled rouletted bands, number "24" impr. at base of extruded handle to indicate "potter's dozen" size, 4⅞" H. **$5,175**

Pearlware Bowl, hemispherical, ca. 1790, engine-turned through br. slip to create geometric patt. below a gr. glazed reeded rim, 6" diam. **$862**

A-OH Jan. 2001   Garth's Auctions, Inc.

Plate, soft paste, pink border w/ bright strawberries & pink roses in center, scratch & two sm. chips, 8¼" diam. **$467**

A-NC July 2001   Robert S. Brunk Auction Services, Inc.

Spatterware Pitcher, red, blue, gr. & red peafowl dec., spout crack, minor discoloration, 11" H. **$1,000**

Spatterware Plate, paneled blue, rose & gr. leaf dec., old paper label verse indicating purchase in 1851, discoloration, 8¼" diam. **$375**

Stoneware Teapot, red & gr. spongeware dec., red flower w/ gr. leaves, spout chip, minor flaws, 9" H. **$475**

A-NC July 2001   Robert S. Brunk Auction Services, Inc.

Spatterware, handleless cup & saucer, blue, gr. & red peafowl design, mkd. "Y". **$600**

Pearlware Plate, gr. shell-edged plate, yel., blue & br. peafowl in tree w/ gr. spongeware foliage, base w/ circular impr. mark, 8" diam. **$650**

Spatterware, cup & saucer, red, rose design w/ gr. leaves, 6" saucer, cup 2½" x 4". **$400**

A-OH Apr. 2001   Garth's Auctions, Inc.

Spatterware

First Row

Plate, blue spatterware, peafowl in red, yel. & gr. w/ long tail into border, yel. w/ sm. burst bubbles, rim flakes, 9½" diam. **$770**

Cups & Saucers, two spatterware handleless, red rims w/ peafowl in gr. yel. & blue. **$165**

Pitcher, rainbow spatterware in blue & reddish purple, paneled sides, molded spout, slight wear, repr., 7⅝" H. **$1,705**

Cup & Saucer, mini. yel. spatterware, red & gr. tulip, hairlines & flake. **$1,760**

Plate, red spatterware, peafowl in dk. blue, gr. & dk. br. w/ a long tail, short hairline & in-the-making chip, 8⅝" diam. **$715**

Second Row

Plate, rainbow spatterware, lt. red, blue & yel. border, rim flake, 8½" diam. **$3,300**

Creamer, blue spatterware, paneled, peafowl in red, gr. & blue, squiggly branches, minor flake, 5⅝" H. **$770**

Pitcher, purple spatterware, paneled, acorns in yel. & teal gr. w/ gr. & dk. br. leaves, br. & yel. has bubbles, stains & rim repr., good color, 8½" H. **$3,630**

Creamer, stick spatter, floral designs w/ purple on rim, handle & base & a band of red flowers w/ gr. & blue leaves, hairline, 4" H. **$165**

Plate, blue spatterware, white shield in middle w/ blue stripes & red stars, back mkd. "Pekin China, T & - Boothe", 9¼" diam. **$1,155**

A-OH Apr. 2001   Garth's Auctions, Inc.

First Row

Canton Platters, two, octagonal w/ lt. blue pictured, rim flakes, 1" x 7½", other is oval w/ a mottled blue, rim flakes, 12" x 9¼". **$550**

Canton Dish, leaf shaped, rim flakes, 7⅜" x 5¼". **$100**

Canton Covered Vegetable, diamond shaped w/ scalloped edges, fruit finial & ora. peel glaze, unglazed bottom 9½" W, 3¼" H. **$220**

Canton Covered Vegetable, w/ molded finial & two boar's head handle, lid is undersized, 6½" W, 4⅝" D, 4½" H, plus octagonal tray, ora. peel glaze, roughness & rim chip, 9⅝" x 7¼". **$220**

Second Row

Nanking Strainer Insert, river scene w/ man walking on bridge, ora. peel glaze, 11⅞" x 8¾". **$350**

Canton Covered Vegetable, diamond shaped w/ scalloped edges, fruit finial, minor rim flakes, 10½" w, 8½" D, 4" H. **$110**

Canton Platter, octagonal, bottom is unglazed, 12¼" x 9⅜". **$330**

A-OH Apr. 2001   Garth's Auctions, Inc.

Soup Bowl, soft paste, flower & strawberry border in red, gr. pink & yel w/ basket of strawberries & roses in center, 8¼" diam. **$880**

A-OH Apr. 2001   Garth's Auctions, Inc.

Sewer Tile Pig, well-dressed w/ pants, vest & bow tie, molded w/ a reddish br. glaze, few wear spots, 7⅞" H. **$302**

A-NH May 2001   **Northeast Auctions**

Staffordshire Pearlware With Blue Transfer Decoration

Row 1, Left to Right

Platter from the Zoological series w/ elephants, 18¼" L. **$3,600**

Serving bowls (l to r), two from the Quadruped series w/ lion cartouche, one marked Hall, 12" diam. (left), second at right of tureen, 11" L. **$1,800**

Soup Tureen from the Quadruped series w/ camel cartouche, w/ elaborate scrolled handles, together with undertray & ladle, tureen 14" L. **$4,250**

Platter from the Zoological series w/ elephants. **$1,500**

Row 2, Left to Right

Footed Serving Bowls (l to r) two from the Quadruped series, sq. shaped, each depicting rescue at sea w/ dogs, 10" L. **$3,400**

Dinner Plates (8), decor. w/ lion from the Quadruped series by Hall, 10" D. **$1,500**

Sauce Tureens, covered (3), w/ ladies & undertrays from the Quadruped series. Tureens w/ rabbit & fox, ladies w/ hyena, undertrays w/ wolf & rooster, most marked Hall, trays 8" L, 2 illus. **$4,000**

Platter decor. w/ moose & hunters, from Quadruped series by Hall, 15½" L. **$1,700**

Gravy Boats from Quadruped series w/ fox cartouche, 7" L, 2 illus. **$2,000**

Dinner Plates (8) from Quadruped series, mkd. Hall, 10" diam. **$1,600**

Row 3 Left to Right

Dinner Plates (8) from the Quadruped series, 2 mkd. Hall. **$1,500**

Dinner Plates, 5-10" w/ lion cartouche: 2- 6¼" plates w/ dog, mkd. Hall: & 2 cup plates w/ hyena, part illus. **$1,200**

Dinner Plates (8) from the Quadruped series by Hall, 10" diam. **$1,600**

Cup Plates (10) from the Quadruped series w/ hyena decor. **$1,300**

Dinner Plates (8) w/ lion decor. from the Quadruped series, 10" diam. **$1,700**

A-IA June 2001   **Jackson's Auctioneers & Appraisers**

Haviland China, partial set, "Ranson" patt. decor. w/ small roses, on cream ground, mkd. "Haviland France" in green & "Decor. by Haviland & Co., Limoges" in red, approx. 80 pcs. incl. 10 six-piece place settings plus serving pcs., minor flaws. **$402**

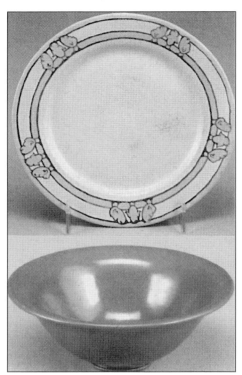

A-MA May 2001   Craftsman

Saturday Evening Girls Plate, decor. w/ a band of yellow chicks on white ground, dated 1911; & a bowl dated 1922, w/ simi-matte teal glaze. **$700**

A-SC June 2001   **Charlton Hall Galleries, Inc.**

Earthenware Stein, German, early 20th C., figural w/ hunting scene, lid has repairs. **$100**

A-PA Oct. 2001   Conestoga Auction Company

Historical Blue Staffordshire
Plate, "Fair Mount Near Philadelphia" patt., sgn. Stubbs, two small chips on base rim, 10¼" D. **$357**
Plate, sgn. Clews, "Landing of General Lafayette" patt., 7¾" D. **$220**
Plate, "Lafayette at the Tomb of Washington" patt., unmarked but made by T. Mayer, 10" D. **$990**

A-PA Oct. 2001   Conestoga Auction Company

Historical Blue Staffordshire
Soup Plate, "American Villa" patt., sgn. B.B. & B., 10" D. **$220**
Picturesque Scenery Plate, "Fulham Church, Middlesex" R. Hall, 8½" D. **$220**
Plate, "A View Near Philadelphia" patt., unmkd., 10⅜" D. **$990**

A-PA Oct. 2001   Conestoga Auction Company

Salopian Ware
Row 1
Handleless Cup, "Urn of Flowers" patt. blue & shite w/ rosette border. **$165**
Coffeepot, w/ Oriental decor., spout chips & 1" hairline on body, 11" H. **$990**
Miniature Mug, w/ lion & cave decor. chip & repr., 2" H. **$330**
Pitcher, bulbous form w/ transfer decor. 5½" H. **$495**
Row 2
Teacups & Saucers, three w/ Oriental boat & pagoda scenes. **$495**
Waste Bowl, w/ exotic bird & floral transfer decor. & Greek key border, 3" H. **$385**
Handleless Cup & Saucer, "Stag" patt., w/ floral border, base rim ships on cup. **$385**
Row 3
Plate, w/ exotic bird & fruit decor., 6¼" D. **$220**
Plate, "w/ exotic bird & fruit decor. 7" D. **$275**
Plate, "Stag" patt. w/ floral border, 7¼" D. **$302**
Cup Plate, w/ sheep herding scene, cottage & castle, 4½" D. **$330**

POTTERY / PORCELAIN

A-OH Nov. 2001   Garth's Auctions, Inc.

Redware

First row

Pitcher, attrib. to NJ., mask spout, glaze has br. daubs, repr. handle, rim chip & minor wear, 7¾" H. **$220**

Jar, attrib. to PA., ovoid w/ raised rim, br. daubed glaze, sm. glaze flakes, 4" diam., 4½" H. **$192**

Creamer, attrib. to Anthony Baecher, VA, applied rose & two doves, rosette on handle, pinpoint glaze flakes, 4¾" H. **$715**

Pie Plates, two, coggled rims w/ rich amber glaze, faint impr. circles in center, both w/ minor rim flakes, 7" diam. **$302**

Jar, ovoid w/ incised lines under raised lip, two tone glaze w/ wide br. vertical bands, glaze on rim is worn, 5¼" diam., 6¼" H. **$275**

Second row

Turk's Head Food Molds, two, both have glaze mottled w/ dark br., one on int. & one on the rim, glaze flakes, 7¼" diam., 2⅜" H., & 7" diam., 1½" H. **$192**

Pie Plates, two, coggled rims, one has three sets of lines in yel. slip & two areas of gr., surface wear & damage, 9¾" diam., one darker in color w/ two sets of yel. slip lines, two glaze flakes, 8" diam. **$247**

A-OH Feb. 2001   Garth's Auctions, Inc.

First Row

Stick Spatter Plates, two, lg. w/ paneled rim, blue border & red, gr. & mustard flower in center, 8½" diam., sm. has blue stripes, lt. red & gr. spatter floral rim & red & gr. sprig in center, 7⅛" diam. **$165**

Cup & Saucer, "Adam's Rose", blue stick spatter flowers w/ red rose & dk. teal gr. leaves, saucer impr. "Edge Malkin & Co.", cup has two pinpoint flakes. **$100**

Gaudy Plates, four, sim. designs w/ red, blue, yel. & gr. floral borders w/ red stripes & purple stick spatter flowers, plate w/ indistinct blue label, hairline, 9" diam., bread plate "Maastricht" light stains, 6½" diam., & two toddies, stains, 5¾" diam. **$49**

Second Row

Spongeware blue & white, 3 pcs., two plates & one oval platter, one plate has dk. ground color & has English "Warranted" label, 9" diam., 2nd plate, 9¼" diam. & platter, 13" L. **$412**

Spongeware Jug, sm. blue & white, molded vintage around shoulder, 4⅝" H. **$440**

Yellowware Pitcher, East Liverpool, OH, br. stripes & white bands w/ blue mocha seaweed dec., spout chipped & glued., 6" H. **$605**

A-OH Apr. 2001   Garth's Auctions, Inc.

New Geneva Pitcher, tanware w/ dk. matte glaze on int., floral design, applied handle 7 tooled lines at neck, 7" H. **$467**

New Geneva Pitcher, reddish tanware w/ shiny br. glaze on int., wavy lines & brushed flourishes, applied handle, minor rim flakes, 5⅝" H. **$522**

New Geneva Pitcher, tanware w/ dk. br. matte glaze on int., floral design w/ stripes on applied handle, few shallow chips & glaze wear on rim, 6⅝" H. **$440**

A-OH Apr. 2001   Garth's Auctions, Inc.

White Clay Dog, OH, short ears & tail w/ long jowls, br. glaze, chip & sm. flake, 8⅛" H. **$110**

A-OH Nov. 2001   Garth's Auctions, Inc.

Corner Plant Stand, pine w/ old br. ref., square & round head nails, splits & edge damage, shelves 17½" W. to 51" W, 47½" H. **$220**

Rockingham, two pieces, oval serving dish, (illus.) 9" W, 7" diam., 2" H. & canning jar, rim chips, 7¼" H. (not illus.) **$82**

Figural Dog Pitcher w/ Rockingham glaze, open mouth pouring spout, 8⅝" H. **$165**

Treen, five pieces, three bowls w/ scrubbed int. surfaces, one w/ dark ext., old splits, 9" diam., 8⅛" diam., 8¼" diam. & two porringers, w/ tab handles, matching but one later, 8" diam. **$275**

Rockingham, four pieces, two plates, 9¾" diam., deep bowl w/ footed base, rim chips, 7" diam., 3½" H, bowl w/ tapered sides, 7⅞" diam., 2¼" H. **$220**

Carved Duck Decoys, two, duck w/ bright dec. by Gary Crossman, MD. Unsigned, 14¼" L. and a Merganser w/ gr. head, red bill, grey, br. blk. & white body, unsigned, 17" L. **$137**

A-OH Feb. 2001   Garth's Auctions, Inc.

Carpet Balls

Row 1, Left to Right

Sponge decorated in red & dk. gr., 3" diam. **$110**

Overall Design of Concentric Blue Circles, minor wear, 3⅛" diam. **$176**

Plaid w/ black stripes & blue/gr. bands, wear, 3" diam. **$121**

Row 2, Left to Right

Small Blue & White Overall Star Design, 3" diam. **$143**

Light Red & White Overall Star Design, minor wear, 3" diam. **$99**

Small Light Swirled red w/ crossed blk. stripes, 2½" diam. **$79**

A-OH Apr. 2001   Garth's Auctions, Inc.

First Row

Soft Paste Plate, grape vine border in dk. purple, shades of gr., yel. & red, floral center w/ red rose, dk. purple columbine & yel. & blue flower, minor stains, 8⅞" diam. **$110**

Stick Spatter Plate, gr. double loops w/ red stripes & purple & yellow violet in center, surface scoured w/ some additional wear, colors good, 8¾" diam. **$49**

Spatterware Saucer, br. w/ yel. band w/ bl. "leaves", white center, crazing, 6½" diam. **$100**

Stick Spatter Plate, blue border w/ red & gr. flower in center, light stains 8½" diam. **$137**

Stick Spatter Soup Plate, blue border w/ red, gr. & yel. stripes & floral center, 8¾" diam. **$165**

Second Row

Copper Luster Pitchers, two, gold band w/ molded figures of men & women, ora. gr. & purple enamel, in-the-making split in handle, 5⅝" H. And canary band w/ brown transfer scene of woman & two children, blue, yel. & gr. enamel, hairline, 6¼" H. **$110**

Stick Spatter Soup Plate, blue flowers & red open roses w/ gr., impr. "Malkin", lt. crazing & stains, 8 3/4" diam. **$60**

Gaudy Platter, purple roses w/ gr. leaves & blue & red buds, 7¼" x 10". **$110**

Stick Spatter Plate, red border w/ red, blue & gr. flowers, minor enamel imper., minor stains, 8¾" diam. **$110**

A-OH Apr. 2001   Garth's Auctions, Inc.

Sewer Tile Frog, on log, hand modeled w/ tooled bark, inscr. "H.S.", dk. br., slightly metallic glaze, traces of gold, 5¼" L, 5" H. **$412**

Stoneware Mug, applied handle & two brushed cobalt bands w/ incised edging, 3¼" diam., 4¾" H. **$247**

A-NJ May 2001   Craftsman

Fulper Corseted Vase, covered in copper dust crystalline glaze, 11½" H. **$9,000**

A-NJ Jan 2001   Craftsman

Rookwood Vase, jewel porcelain corseted by Kataro Shirayamadani, ca. 1925, w/ red & ora. flowers on yel. ground, flame mark, 8½" x 4¾". **$3,750**

A-NJ May 2001   Craftsman

Paul Revere Ovoid Vase, dec. in cuerda seca w/ glossy purple & yel. irises w/ matte gr. leaves, ca. 1938, 8¾" H. **$5,500**

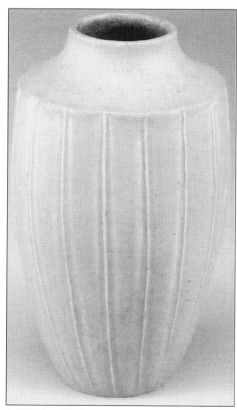

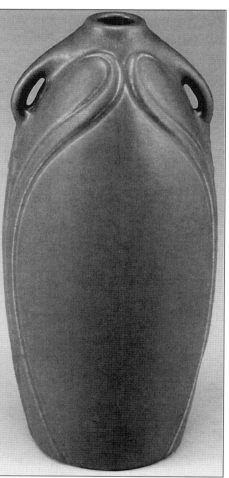

A-NJ May 2001   Craftsman

Grueby Vase, w/ corseted shoulder, incised vertical ribs, covered in glaze, stamped Faience mark, incised BA & two paper labels, 9½" H. **$6,500**

A-NJ May 2001   Craftsman

Van Briggle Vase, ca. 1904, embossed w/ trillium & covered in Persian rose matte glaze, 12" H. **$6,000**

A-NJ May 2001   Craftsman

Grueby Vase, by Marie Seaman, w/ tooled & applied full-height leaves alternating w/ buds & covered in feathered organic matte gr. glaze, minor flakes to leaf edges, stamped Faience mark /MS, 11½" H. **$4,500**

A-NJ Jan 2001   Craftsman
George Ohr Pitcher, w/ ear-shaped handle & labial rim, umber glaze, speckled w/ gunmetal, stamped G.E. OHR, Biloxi, Miss. 3" x 6". **$1,900**

A-MA May 2001   Craftsman
Weller Forest Vase, unsigned, 8" H. **$124**

A-MA May 2001   Craftsman
Weller Forest Vase, unsigned, 12" H. **$175**

A-NJ May 2001   Craftsman
Fulper Cider, set, w/ pitcher & six mugs, w/ wisteria matt glaze, incised racetrack mark, pitcher 10½" x 8" diam. **$550**

A-NJ Jan 2001   Craftsman
Rookwood Squat Vessel, by Wm. Hentschel, 1926, w/ brown branches & leaves against a matte celadon ground. Flame mark, 5" x 6½". **$800**

A-NJ May 2001   Craftsman
Mettlach China Pieces, w/ secessionist trees in blue, ochre & ivory, together w/ three-piece tea set & pitcher, chips to teapot lid, mkd. Mettlach/Made in Ger., teapot 5" H. **$650**

A-NJ Jan 2001   Craftsman
Grueby Squat Vessel, by Marie Seaman w/ tooled & applied yel. trefoils alt. w/ broad leaves, under matte gr. glaze, rest. to sm. chip at rim, stamped Grueby Pottery, 5¾" x 6½". **$11,000**

A-NH Aug. 2001   Northeast Auctions

Blue & White Chinese Canton
Row 1
Chargers, pr., 12 & 14½" D. **$1,100**
Platter, 19" L, w/ two circular veg. dishes, largest 10½" diam. **$1,100**
Shrimp Dishes, two, 10¼" L. **$600**
Platter, Well & Tree patt., 17" L. **$500**
Row 2
Water Bottles, matching pr., w/ elongated neck, 8¼" H. **$1,000**

Salad Bowl w/ cut-corners, 9" L, 5½" H. **$750**
Platters, five total (2 illus.) w/ cut-corners 10½" to 16" L. **$1,500**
Oblong Covered Sauce Tureens Illus., two matching, w/ boar's head handles & a lozenge-shaped serving dish, 7½" L. **$400**
Salt & Pepper Shakers, matched pair, 3½" H. **$3,000**
Covered Soup Tureen w/ boar's head handles, 12" L. **$700**
Square Cut-Corner Bowl, 9½" H. **$3,750**

Row 3
Reticulated Fruit Baskets, pr., w/ matching undertrays, largest tray 11¼" L, largest bowl 10½". **$1,900**
Fish Platter w/ matching pierced liner, 18½" L. **$1,800**
Scallop-Edge Bowls, pr., one Nanking, 9½" diam; the other Canton (illus.), 10¼" diam. **$850**
Covered Vegetable Dish w/ berry finial, 11" L (illus); w/ an oblong domed lid w/ finial, 11½" L. **$500**

A-SC March 2001   Charlton Hall Galleries, Inc.

Chinese Export Vases, pr., rose medallion, ca. 1850, dec. w/ panel painted figures in court scene w/ butterflies & birds. **$1,900**

A-NH Mar, 2001   Northeast Auctions

Chinese Export Famille Rose Garden Barrels, w/ floral decor. of lotus and tree peonies, 19" H. **$17,000**

A-NE Aug. 2001   Northeast Auctions

Chinese Export Porcelains
Row 1
Famille Rose Guform Vases, set of three, w/ bird, flower & butterfly decor., tallest 16" H. $2,000
Rose Medallion Baluster-Form Vases, pr., w/ gilt dragons at neck, 9" H. $400
Row 2
Mandarin Shell-Form Shrimp Dishes, pair w/ orange & gilt handles, 10½" L. $4,250
Mandarin Decor. Tablewares, three, incl. teapot, barrel-form box & covered box (not illus.). $700
Rose Medallion Punch Bowl, 14½" diam. $2,250
Mandarin Hexagonal Cache Pot & Stand, 6¼" H. $1,200
Row 3
Mandarin Graduated Rectangular Serving Dishes, pr. $3,000
Mandarin Round Covered Boxes, five, tallest 4¼" H. $4,000
Mandarin Scalloped-Edge Serving Dish, footed & decor. w/ Chinese domestic scenes, 14½" L. $1,750
Mandarin Covered Oval Hot Water Platter w/ polychrome decor. of the "Hundred Antiquities". $2,750

A-MA June 2001   Skinner, Inc.

Chinese Export Porcelain
Jars, pr., blue & white, K'ang Hsi period (1662-1722), dec. of the "Hundred Antiques", fan reserves w/ lotus borders, one w/ an artemesia leaf mark, other a fan mark, hardwood stands, 12" H. $1,495
Vases, three blue & white, pr. of 19th C. vases w/ flowering plants, 7" H, w/ a soft paste squared-body vase w/ design of children, Yung Cheng mark (1722-1735), chip, 4½" H. $690
Phoenix Dish, six-character Kuang Hsu mark (1874-1908) blue & white dec., repr. chip, 6½" diam. $300

Vases, two porcelain, China, 19th C., one w/ applied foo dogs & dragons & blue & white dec. of peonies & phoenix, one oviform w/ blue & white dec. of reserves w/ birds & flowering trees, 11¼" H. & 8" H. $172
Saucer Dish, blue & white, Ching Hua mark but K'ang Hsi period (1662-1722) deep sapphire blue dec., line, 6½" diam. $150
Phoenix Dishes, Tai Kuan mark (1820-1848) blue & white dec., of pairs of phoenix & clouds, rim frits w/ reprs.,6¼" diam. $300

A-MA June 2001   Skinner, Inc.
Blanc De Chine Figure, 18th-early 19th C., Te Hua figure of Lan Tsai Ho w/ basket of flowers, signed "Virtue extends even to Fisherman", w/ carved hardwood stand, 19½" H. $7,187

A-Aug. 2001   Northeast Auctions

Rose Medallion Tablewares

Row 1

Vases, pair w/ gilt highlights, exotic animal handes & dragons at shoulders, 14" H. **$1,250**

Five-Lobe Vase w/ central standard & lotus crown, 9½" H. **$700**

Covered Punch Pot w/ strap handles & foo dog finial, 7" H. **$500**

Deep Platter w/ alternating panels of flowers, 19" L. **$750**

Cylindrical Brush Pot, 5½" H. **$550**

Table Items, five total, incl. shell-form dish illus., cache pot, 2 condiment dishes and covered box. **$550**

Row 2

Covered Soup Tureen & Liner, w/ strap handles & berry knop, 14½" L. **$2,250**

Salad Bowl w/ cut-corners, 9½" diam. **$800**

Platter, Well & Tree patt., 19" L. **$450**

Covered Dish, oval shaped, w/ strap handles, 10¼" L. **$550**

Punch Bowl, 16" D. **$1,750**

Row 3

Fish Platter, oval, w/ mazarin, 18¼" L. **$500**

Reticulated Fruit Basket & Stand, 8½" L. **$400**

Footed Serving Dish w/ scalloped edge, 13" L. **$300**

Covered Serving Dishes, pair, 1 illus., 9" L. **$500**

Reticulated Fruit Basket & Stand, 9" L. **$450**

Covered Brush Box & Soap Dish w/ drainer. **$600**

Table Items, eight total, incl. scalloped-edge circular serving dish illus.; 3 dinner plates, 2 leaf-form dishes, handled demitasse cup & saucer & teabowl. **$300**

A-SC June 2001   Charlton Hall Galleries, Inc.

Rose Medallion Chinese Export Urn, ca. 1860, 15½" H. **$600**

A-PA Apr. 2001   Pook & Pook, Inc.

Rose Medallion Chinese Platter, 18½" diam. **$650**

A-SC June 2001   Charlton Hall Galleries, Inc.

Chinese Stoneware Storage Jar, ca. 1860, decor. in dragon designs in yellow on brown ground, 27" H. **$475**

A-CA June 2001   Butterfields
Redware Butter Tub, mkd. "John Bell" w/ spiral twist applied handles resting on three wedge formed feet, 8" diam., 5" H. **$3,525**

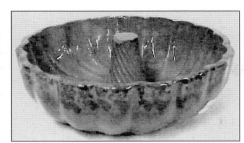

A-NY Nov. 2000   Hesse Galleries
Redware Food Mold, Shenandoah, 9" diam. **$176**

A-NY Nov. 2000   Hesse Galleries
Redware Jar, Berks Co., slip decor. 8¼" H. **$797**

A-NH Nov. 2001   Northeast Auctions
Redware Plate w/ decor. in mustard drip glaze. 11¼" in diam. **$3,000**
Stoneware Crock w/ cobalt blue decor, marked R. Seymoure, Troy, New York, w/ knopped lid, 14¼" H. **$2,100**
Redware Plate w/ yellow slip decor., 9½" diam. **$3,600**

A-NY Nov. 2000   Hesse Galleries
Redware Food Mold, tobacco splash decor. 7" diam. **$88**

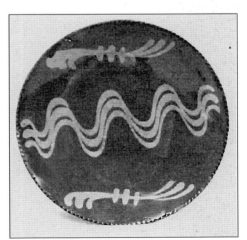

A-NY Nov. 2000   Hesse Galleries
Redware Pie Plate, slip decor. 9¾" diam. **$825**

A-NH Mar. 2001   Northeast Auctions
Redware Pitcher, Jacob Medinger 1856-1920, PA, glazed baluster-form w/ manganese splotches, ribbed handle on body w/ ringed & coggled collar, 7" H. **$1,100**
Redware Plate, ABC slip-glazed w/ cream lettering & coggled rim, 10¼" diam. **$550**
Redware Jar, baluster form w/ entwined side handles & wavy incised dec. manganese geometric & foliate motifs, attributed to David Mandeville, N.Y., overall 8½". **$6,250**

A-PA Nov. 2001   Conestoga Auction Company

Stoneware

Crock w/ applied ears, mkd. J.A. & C. W. Underwood/ Fort Edward, N.Y." w/ cobalt central decor. of flowers in basket, 13" H. **$3,025**

Jar w/ cobalt blue decor. of man in the moon variant, 3 gal., mkd. Cowden & Wilcox/ Harrisburg, PA, ca. 1860-1887. **$5,225**

Jar w/ cover, cobalt blue decor. of pair of lovebirds, mkd. "G.S. Guy & Co., Fort Edward, N.Y." , 17" H. **$2,970**

Water Cooler, attrib. to Remmy of Philadelphia, w/ cobalt blue decor. on body & around ears & spigot. chips, 13" H. **$2,640**

Jug, w/ bold cobalt blue slip decor. of a horse, by W. Hart, Ogdensburgh, 5 gal., minor chips, 18" H. **$9,350**

A-SC June 2001   Charlton Hall Galleries, Inc.

Stoneware Jar, w/ alkaline glaze, attrib. to W.F. Hahn, Edgefield, SC, ca. 1870, w/ ochre glaze, 11" H. **$300**

A-PA Sept. 2001   Pook & Pook Inc.

Stoneware

Row 1

Pitcher, early 19th C., w/ blue sunflower decor., 11" H. **$650**

Pitcher, 19th C., w/ extensive blue floral & leaf design., 12" H. **$850**

Jug, 2 gal., mkd. "Cowden & Wilcox, Harrisburg. Pa.", w/ cobalt man in the moon decor. 13" H. **$5,250**

Crock, 2 gal., 19th C., w/blue chicken pecking corn decor., 9½" H. **$650**

Row 2

Jug, 2 gal. 19th C., mkd. "Cowden & Wilcox, Harrisburg, Pa.", w/ blue floral decor.,12½" H. **$1,700**

Crock, 4 gal., 19th C., mkd. "Haxstun & Co., Fort Edward, NY", w/ cobalt blue bird decor., 11½" H. **$300**

Crock, 5 gal., mkd. "Adam Caire, Pokeepsie, NY", w/ cobalt bird decor., 12" H. **$500**

Batter Jug, w/ extensive blue fern decor, tin covers & wooden swing handle, 10" H, **$1,750**

A-PA Apr. 2001   York Town Auction, Inc.

Stoneware Water Cooler w/ cobalt, green & manganese decor. **$4,300**

A-OH Apr. 2001   Garth's Auctions, Inc.

First Row

Redware Dish, coggled edge, yel. slip dec. w/ three wavy lines, sm. rim flake, 5¼" diam. **$990**

Redware Dish, shaped like goose, hand modeled w/ few incised feathers, pinched scalloped rim, blue running glaze w/ faint gr. tinge, tail has minor edge damage, 4¾" L., 4" H. **$1,100**

Second Row

Redware Pie Plate, coggled rim, yel. slip dec. w/ three sets of wavy lines, few edge flakes, 10¼" diam. **$605**

A-OH Apr. 2001   Garth's Auctions, Inc.

Pine Bucket Bench, old worn gr. paint w/ sq. nail const., bootjack cut-outs w/ shaped top, 41½" W, 30¾" H. **$660**

First Row

Stoneware Jug, w/ cobalt bird dec., impr. "Whites. Utica", chips, good contrast, 11½" H. **$440**

Stoneware Crock, partial Woodruff mark, "Cortland", double handles w/ flared rim, cobalt tulip dec., hairline, 11" H. **$275**

Stoneware Jug, OH, impr. "T. Reed", w/ blue brushmarks over sig., & top of handle, chips & short hairline, 12½" H. **$275**

Second Row

Stoneware Canning Jars, two, both have deep blue stripe dec., rim chips, 6⅜" H., 8" H. **$467**

Stoneware Crock, partial mark for "N. Clark Jr., Athens, N.", short ovoid shape w/ double handles & fine cobalt dec., faint spider in side & shallow rim chips, 8¼" H. **$632**

Stoneware Quart Jar, w/ tulip dec., double handles & a raised rim, impr. "L. H. Yeager & Co., Allentown, PA", damage, 7" H. **$247**

Shenandoah Bowl, redware w/ cream & dk. gr. & br. running glaze, two round applied buttons on either side, crazing & minor glaze flakes, 4¼" diam., 2⅛" H. **$550**

Redware Pie Plate, coggled rim, yel. slip dec. of wavy lines & flourishes, shallow rim flakes, 8 " diam. **$990**

Stoneware Inkwell, brushed cobalt blue on top, impr. "C. Crolius… Manhattan-Wells N.Y.", chips on base, 3⅛" diam., 1⅝" H. **$3,190**

Redware Pie Plate, coggled rim, yel. slip dec. w/ wavy lines, 11¼" diam. **$935**

A-OH Nov. 2001   Garth's Auctions, Inc.

Stoneware

Crock, dec. w/ running bird, impr. "Whites, Utica, 4", deep blue bird, restr. hairline & light stains, 11½" H. **$990**

Butter Crock, blue line dec. w/ incised lines & double handles, no lid, 8¼" diam., 4" H. **$412**

Crock, w/ cobalt swirl & feather dec., impr. "Cortland", mismatched redware lid incl., 9" H. **$220**

Batter Jug, w/ bale handle & old tin lid, 11" H. **$467**

A-PA Mar. 2001   Conestoga Auction Company

Jug, 2 gal., mkd. Horkeimer Bro's, Wheeling, W. VA, w /blue stencil wine & whiskey adver., chips, 15" H. **$137**

Crock, 5 gal, mkd. Hamilton & Jones, Greensboro, PA, w/ blue stencil wreath decor., 16" H. **$522**

A-SC June 2001   Charlton Hall Galleries, Inc.

Stoneware With Alkaline Glaze
Storage Jar, Edgefield, SC, Rhodes site, ca. 1850 w/ br. glaze, 17" H. **$375**
Storage Jar, Miles site w/ dk. br. glaze, ca. 1900, 13¼" H. **$400**
Jar, Sylvanus Leander Hortsoe, Batawba Valley, NC, ca. 1850, 10¼" H. **$450**

A-PA Apr. 2001   York Town Auction, Inc.
Dressler Art Potter Vase w/ green matte glaze, 6½" H. **$150**

A-SC June 2001   Charlton Hall Galleries, Inc.

Stoneware With Alkaline Glaze
Jug, by Wm. F. Hanh, Edgefield, SC, sgn., ca. 1890, Albany-slip, 14¼" H. **$300**
Canning Jar, attrib. to Bodie, ca. 1870, w/ dk. br. glaze, 11½" H. **$225**
Jug, w/ mottled gr. glaze, attrib. to Landrum, Edgefield, SC, 12" H. **$275**
Storage Jar, SC, attrib. to Josseph G. Baynham, w/ Albany-slip, ca. 1890, 11½" H. **$180**

A-PA Apr. 2001   York Town Auction, Inc.
Sicard Pottery Vase, sgn. Weller, 6½" H. **$1,400**

A-SC June 2001   Charlton Hall Galleries, Inc.

Stoneware With Alkaline Glaze
Storage Jar, Columbia SC, w/ mottled lt. br. glaze, two handles, attrib. to Landrum, ca. 1850, 11½" H. **$385**
Storage Jar, Miles site, Edgefield, SC, ca. 1900 w/ gr. glaze, 13¼" H. **$300**
Storage Jar, SC, ca. 1910, dk. br. glaze, 8½" H. **$70**
Storage Jar, Edgefield, SC, Pottersville site, ca. 1820, lt. yel. glaze, 12" H. **$500**

A-PA may 2001   Horst Auctioneers
Spittoon w/ light brown ground w/ overall manganese mottling, mkd. "Eagle Porcelain Works, Lancaster City, PA, Henry Gast S (South) Q (Queen) St." on bottom, 7½" sq., 4¼" H. **$3,000**

A-PA Mar. 2001   Conestoga Auction Company

Stoneware
Crock, 1½ gal., w/ blue slip decor. of bird on branch, 8½" H. **$412**
Jug, 1 gal., w/ blue floral & squiggle line slip decor., chips & pit marks, 10½" high. **$192**
Jug, 1 gal., w/ blue floral slip decor., mkd. D.P. Shenfelder, Reading, PA, 11" H. **$275**
Pitcher, 1 gal., w/ slip decor., mkd. J. Burger, Rochester, NY, 11" H. **$440**

A-PA Nov. 2001   Conestoga Auction Company

Stoneware
Jug, mkd. "Harrisburg" w/ cobalt blue decor., base chip, 12" H. **$1,210**
Pitcher w/ cobalt blue decor., mkd. "Cowden & Wilcox/ Harrisburg". **$3,410**

A-PA Mar. 2001   Conestoga Auction Company

Stoneware
Crock w/ blue slip decor, hairline & chip on bale, 11¼" H. **$495**
Crock, 2 gal., w/ blue slip floral decor., dated 1851 above "2" on reverse, chip on rim, 13½" H. **$385**
Crock, 3 gal. w/cobalt blue floral & foliate designs, chips & cracks, 14" H. **$1,115**
Pitcher, w/ floral blue decor., attrib. to Remey, Phil., chips, 11" H. **$1,130**

A-PA Nov. 2001   Conestoga Auction Company

Stoneware
Crock w/ coblt blue decor., mkd. "J. & E. Norton/Bennington, VT", 11½" H. **$1,540**
Pitcher w/ cobalt blue decor. by Richard C. Remmy, ca. 1860-1880, 11" H. **$1,375**
Chicken Waterer, attrib. to Remmy, w/ cobalt blue decor. body, 12" H. **$4,290**

A-SC June 2001   Charlton Hall Galleries, Inc.

Stoneware With Alkaline Glaze
Jug, Shaw Creek, Edgefield, SC, ca. 1850 w/ lt. br. glaze, 9¾" H. **$250**
Canning Jar by Jesse P. Bodie, Edgefield, SC w/ mottled br. glaze, ca. 1870, 8¾" H. **$130**
Pitcher, attrib. to J.W. Seagler, Pinehouse site, Edgefield, SC, ca. 1880 w/ mottled br. glaze, 8¼" H. **$150**
Canning Jar, attrib. to William F. Hahn, ca. 1870, w/ lt. gr. glaze, 9" H. **$250**
Canning Jar, Pottersville, ca. 1830, mkd. "Y", w/ celery gr. glaze, 7¾" H. **$530**
Buggy Jug, Shaw Creek, ca. 1850 w/ dull yel. glaze, 8" H. **$425**

A-PA Mar. 2001   Conestoga Auction Company

Stoneware
Crock, 4 gal., mkd. Hamilton & Jones, Star Pottery, Greensboro, PA, w/ blue stenciled floral decor. **$577**
Jug, 3 gal., mkd. James Hamilton & Co., Greensboro, PA, w/ blue stenciled grape & leaf decor., hairlines, 15½" H. **$302**
Crock, 5 gal., mkd. Hamilton & Jones, Greensboro, PA, w/ blue floral stencil decor., hairline, 13" H. **$330**

A-OH Feb. 2001   Garth's Auctions, Inc.

Appliqué Quilt, w/ trapunto grapes & vining leaves, red blocks w/ gr. & red leaves on corners, all white ground, attrib. to Ashtabula City. OH, ca. 1840, stains, considerable wear to appliqué, 91" x 91" **$330**

A-OH Feb. 2001   Garth's Auctions, Inc.

Crib Quilt, PA, pieced, robbing Peter to pay Paul in red & white w/ gr. border, hand stitched, ready to hang, 37" x 43". **$275**

A-OH Apr. 2001   Garth's Auctions, Inc.

Crazy Quilt, pieced & embroidered, various materials w/ multi-colored stitching in-between, incl. animals, girls & "Lottie Seely", burgundy velvet border & reddish br. velvet back, minor wear & stains, 62" x 62". **$605**

A-OH Apr. 2001   Garth's Auctions, Inc.

Appliqué Quilt, grape vine border & medallions w/ gr. leaves & lt. br. puffed grapes, hand stitched, diagonal quilting, cross stitched initials, "H.P.", lt. stains & wear, 90" x 102". **$1,155**

Quilt Top, cotton, pieced & appliquéd, 2nd qtr. 19th C., 7'9" sq.
$6,462

Quilt, "Star & Eagle" patt., cotton, pieced & appliquéd, 7'5" x
7'2". $1,880

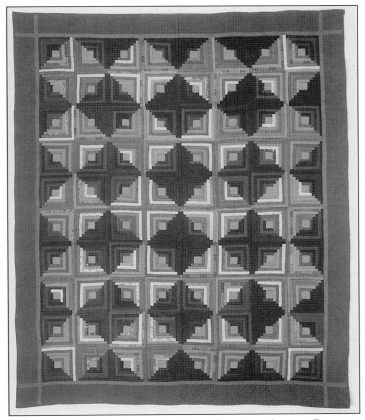

Quilt, "Log Cabin" patt. w/ green printed backing, Lebanon
Co., PA Mennonite Wool, 76" x 94". $2,860

Quilt, pieced & appliquéd, 2nd qtr. 19th C., 8'1" x 7'3".
$6,462

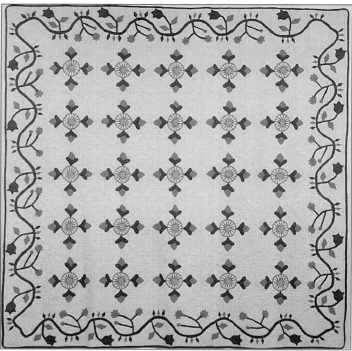

A-PA Nov. 2001   Conestoga Auction Company

Patchwork Quilt, Compass & Acorn patt., red, green & yellow, w/ vine border & plume quilting, 88" x 86". **$2,310**

A-PA Nov. 2001   Conestoga Auction Company

Appliqué Quilt, Urn & Flower patt., red, yellow & green, 78" x 82". **$3,300**

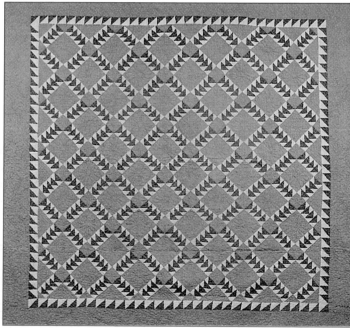

A-PA Nov. 2001   Conestoga Auction Company

Patchwork Quilt, Diamond & Sawtooth patt., w/ printed pumpkin color & green, 83" x 88". **$632**

A-PA Nov. 2001   Conestoga Auction Company

Patchwork Quilt, Diamond & Clover patt., red & white w/ bar border, sm. hole, 83" x 83". **$274**

A-NJ May 2001   Craftsman

Circular Linen, embroidered w/ amaranth in gold & blk. w/ 1½" scalloped crocheted border, minor staining, 38¼" diam. **$275**

A-NJ May 2001   Craftsman

Circular Table Linen, cotton, embroidered w/ red Glasgow roses & purple ribbon, w/ 4" crocheted edge, 41" diam. **$80**

A-OH Apr. 2001   Garth's Auctions, Inc.

Appliqué Quilt, four floral medallions w/ extra flowers in red, gr. & golden rod, hand-stitched, diamond quilting, stains, darker on back, sm. area of edge damage, 84" x 84". **$1,210**

A-MA Feb. 2001   Skinner, Inc.

Embroidered Wool Coverlet, ca. 1849, tile pattern of floral designs worked in silk, chenille threads and wood yarns in multiple shades of red, blue & green on black ground, 99¼" x 86½". **$17,250**

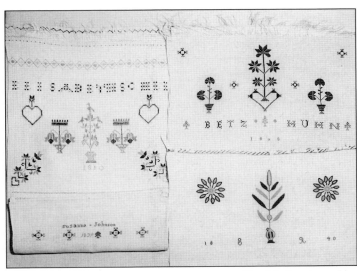

A-OH Apr. 2001   Garth's Auctions, Inc.

Show Towel, homespun w/ colorful cross-stitch needlework in pink & two shades of blue, urns of flowers, one w/ birds, hearts, diamond & fretwork lines by "Elisabeth Schli 1810". Fringed ends, few sm. holes, repr., 15¾" x 54". **$440**

Show Towel, homespun w/ finely stitched needlework in dk. br., urns of flowers, by "Betz Huhn 1808", woven dec. bands w/ pulled work fringe at end, 19" x 61". **$247**

Show Towel, strong blue & dk. pink cross-stitch geometric designs by "Susanna Johnson 1839", 14½" x 40". **$192**

Show Towel, colorful yarn crewel work flowers & potted tree in red, pale blue, pink & yel., dk. blue cross-stitched "ER 1840", dec. woven bands, yarn border has wear & stitch loss, minor stains & added fringe, 19½" x 58". **$385**

A-MA Feb. 2001   Skinner, Inc.

Pictorial Hooked Rug, early 20th C., two "kissing" horses in field of flowers, 31" X 42". **$3,738**

A-PA Apr. 2001   York Town Auction, Inc.
Album Quilt, York County, PA., ca. 1860. **$5,900**

A-Feb. 2001   Skinner, Inc.
Rugs
Pictorial Hooked Rug, New England, ca. 1860, multicolored figures of birds, flowers, stars, etc. w/ scallop borders, 44½" x 77". **$10,350**

A-NH Mar. 2001   Northeast Auctions
Pictorial Hooked Rug w/ veranda in yel., enclosed by floral & tree designs in polychrome yarns, mounted on stretcher, 24" x 40". **$5,200**

A-NH Aug. 2001   Northeast Auctions
Album Quilt w/ motifs commemorating a marriage in 1873. Worked in sixteen pieces & appliquéd blocks within a wide red swag and bowknot border, 94" x 94". **$38,000**

A-CA June 2001   Butterfields, Inc.
Quilt, pieced & appliquéd "Flower & Eagle" patt., cotton, 8'2" x 6'9". **$4,406**

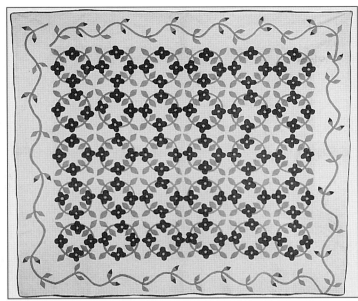

A-MA Feb. 2001   Skinner, Inc.
Appliquéd Quilt, Am. mid-19th C., red & green rose wreath patt. w/ red binding, fading, 79" x 68". **$460**

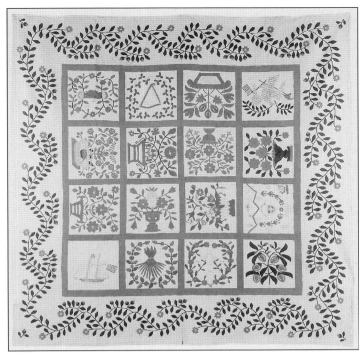

A-NH Aug. 2001   Northeast Auctions
Baltimore Album Quilt commemorating a marriage on January 23, 1848. Worked in sixteen pieced and appliquéd blocks in a red grid within a wide red rose meander vine border, 190" x 109". **$17,000**

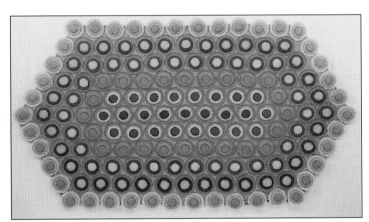

A-Pa Mar. 2001   Conestoga Auction Company
Penny Rug, multicolor w/ shaped ends, felt, 27" x 47". **$440**

A-Pa Mar. 2001   Conestoga Auction Company
Show Towel, Lancaster Co., PA, w/ embroidered urn of flowers, birds & geometric motifs, signed "Maria Weber 1824" & "When This You See, Remember Me", 16" x 54½". **$2,310**

A-MA Feb. 2001   Skinner, Inc.
Hooked Rug, Am. 19th C., w/ eight black & gray chickens surrounded by red & pink flower blossoms, a brown and a black horse below, fading. 27½" x 36". **$690**

A-MA Feb. 2001   Skinner, Inc.
Hooked Rug, Duchess Co., NY, late 19th C. earth tones, black ground, **$18,400**

A-MA May. 2001   Skinner, Inc.

Dolls

Back Row

Kestner Bisque Turned Shoulder Head, late 19th C., brown sleeping eyes, mohair wig, kid body, 16½" H. **$460**

Front Row

Kestner Bisque Turned Shoulder Head, late 19th C., brown sleeping eyes, mohair wig, kid body, 15" H. **$431**

Kestner Bisque Socket Head, late 19th C., brown sleeping eyes, mkd. Made in Germany. Fully jointed composition body, 10½" H. **$575**

Kestner Bisque Shoulder Head, early 20th C., brown sleeping eyes, kid body, mkd. Made in Germany, brown human hair wig, 15" H. **$287**

A-MA May. 2001   Skinner, Inc.

Dolls

Wax Over Papier-mâché Shoulder Head, Germany, late 19th C., blue sleeping eyes, mohair wig, 20" H. **$115**

Wax Over Papier-mâché Shoulder Head, Germany, ca. 1880s, cobalt blue stationary glass eyes, molded hair, 23" H. **$517**

Wax Over Papier-mâché Shoulder Head, Germany, late 19th C., bulgy dark pupil-less stationary glass eyes, molded hair, 20" H. **$373**

Gans + Seyfarth Bisque-head, Germany, early 20th C. Blue sleeping eyes, brown mohair wig, fully articulated composition body, 24" H. **$258**

Kestner Bisque Turned Shoulder Head, early 20th C. Blue sleeping eyes, brown synthetic wig, ultra jointed kid body, 25" H. **$488**

Front Row

Armand Marseille Bisque Socket Head, early 20th C., brown sleeping eyes, mohair wig, articulated wood & composition body, 21" H. **$431**

A-MA May. 2001   Skinner, Inc.

Dolls

Back Row

Armand Marseille Bisque-head, early 20th C., blue sleeping eyes, brown human hair wig, fully jointed composition body, repainted, 24" H. **$230**

A-MA May. 2001   **Skinner, Inc.**

Dolls

Top row

Bisque Turned Shoulder Head, Germany, late 19th C., 22½" H. $575

left to right

Bisque Turned Shoulder Head, Germany, human hair wig, 18" H. **$632**

Solid Dome Bisque Turned Shoulder Head, Germany, late 19th C., blue-lined oval eyes, kid body, 17" H. **$546**

Bisque Turned Shoulder Head, Germany, late 19th C., blue sleeping eyes, mohair wig, 16" H. **$517**

Bisque Turned Shoulder Head, Germany, ca. 1880s, solid ball-head, paperweight eyes, mohair wig, 17½" H. **$1,035**

A-MA May. 2001   **Skinner, Inc.**

Dolls

Top to bottom, left to right

English Poured Wax w/ wire-operated eyes, mid 19th C., human hair wig, 27" H. **$747**

Pierotti-type Poured Wax, England, mid 19th C., 17" H. **$632**

Montanari-type Poured Wax, blue glass sleeping eyes, cloth body, 22" H. **$546**

Wax Over Papier-Mâché Shoulder Head, Germany, ca. 1880s, blue sleeping eyes, org. mohair wig, 11½" H. **$316**

Jumeau Bisque Head Bébé, France, late 19th C., paperweight eyes, human hair wig, 22½" H. **$1,380**

Front Row

Bisque-head Belton-Type Closed Mouth, late 19th C., stationary eyes, mohair wig, composition body, 17" H. **$2,070**

Francois Gaultier Bisque Socket Head Bébé, France, late 19th C., paperweight eyes, human hair wig, 18" H. **$2,300**

A-MA May. 2001   **Skinner, Inc.**

Dolls

Back Row

Jumeau Bisque Head Bébé, France, ca. 1890s, paperweight eyes, human hair wig, 25" H. **$1610**

TOYS/DOLLS

A-MA May. 2001   Skinner, Inc.

Dolls

Kestner "A.T. Face" Bisque Head, late 19th C., brn. sleeping eyes, mohair wig, early chunky articulated Kestner composition body, 15" H. **$9,775**

French Mascotte Bisque Head Bébé, ca. 1890s, paperweight eyes, mohair wig, fully articulated body, 20" H. **$3,737**

A-MA May. 2001   Skinner, Inc.

Dolls

Back Row

Kestner Bisque Socket Head, early 20th C., sleeping eyes, mohair wig, fully jointed composition body, 18" H. **$1,035**

German Bisque Socket Head, blue glass eyes stationary, mohair wig, fully articulated composition body, 20" H. **$316**

German Bisque Socket Head, early 20th C., stationary glass eyes, replaced human hair wig, fully jointed body, 19" H. **$172**

Front Row

R. B. Bisque Socket-head, Germany, early 20th C., sleeping eyes, mohair wig, fully jointed body, 16½" H. **$460**

Simon Halbig Heinrich Handwerck Bisque-head, early 20th C., sleeping eyes, mohair wig, fully articulated, 16½" H. **$862**

Armand Marseille Bisque-head, early 20th C., stationary eyes, human hair wig, straight wrist jointed body, 18½" H. **$230**

Front Row

Kestner Bisque Head, late 19th C., blue sleeping eyes, mohair wig, straight wrist articulated composition body, 15" H. **$2,185**

Belton-type Closed Mouth Bisque Head, late 19th C., brown stationary eyes, human hair wig, straight wrist jointed compositon & wood body, 14½" H. **$1,495**

Kestner Bisque Head, late 19th C., brown sleeping eyes, mohair wig, orig. fully articulated early chunky body, 16½" H. **$1,610**

A-MA May. 2001   Skinner, Inc.

Dolls

Back Row

Kestner Bisque Turned Shoulder Head, late 19th C., brown glass stationary eyes, mohair wig, 22" H. **$575**

A-MA May. 2001   Skinner, Inc.

Dolls

Top to bottom, left to right

Simon Halbig Bisque Socket Head, ca. 1890, brown sleeping eyes, human hair wig. Straight wrist composition & wood articulated body, 18" H. **$690**

Simon Halbig Bisque Head, Germany, late 19th/early 20th C., sleeping eyes, mohair wig. Fully articulated comp. body, 17" H. **$402**

Bisque Head, Germany, late 19th C., stationary eyes, human hair wig, straight wrist articulated wood & comp. body, 15" H. **$345**

Kestner Bisque Swivel Neck, late 19th C., blue sleeping eyes, human hair wig & jointed kid body, 18½" H. **$2,070**

A-MA May. 2001   Skinner, Inc.

Dep Bisque Head Doll, late 19th/early 20th C., w/ orig. brown human wig, fully jointed French composition body (Jumeau), old cotton undergarments & dress w/ lace insertion, & pink fabric shoes, mkd. 15 Paris DEPOSE w/a bee, 27" H. **$2,070**

Belton-type Bisque Head Doll, w/ brown eyes, orig. blond mohair wig, straight wrist jointed comp. & wood body, white cotton dress & old pink fabric shoes, 17½" H. **$2,185**

F.G. Bisque Socket Head Doll, France, late 19th/early 20th C., replaced brown human hair wig, fully articulated wood & composition body, old white cotton undergarments, new aqua dress, mossy green shoes & old green velvet hat, 28" H. **$2,760**

F.G. Bisque head Bébé, late 19th C., tiny flake to one ear hole & light speckling around nose. Brown human hair wig, fully articulated comp. & wood body (some repairs), old white undergarments, green velvet coat & almost matching bonnet, & black leather high button child's shoes, 28" H. **$6,325**

A-MA May. 2001   Skinner, Inc.

Top to bottom, left to right

Kammer & Reinhardt Bisque Head Character Doll, Belton-type Closed Mouth Bisque Head, early 20th C. w/ blue glass eyes, orig. blond mohair wig, fully articulated composition body, one finger broken, period white cotton dress, mkd. K*R Simon Halbig, 16" H. **$1,035**

Armand Marseille Bisque Head Doll, ca. 1920s w/ blue sleeping eyes, brown mohair oversized wig w/ pigtails, mkd. Germany, commercial dress, 10¾" H. **$1,380**

Simon Halbig in Original Regional Outfit, Germany, late 19th C. w/ blue sleeping eyes, fully articulated compostion & wood body, orig. brown mohair wig, Swiss costume w/ chains, silk apron & lace-trimmed cap, 8" H. **$373**

Brown Kestner Bisque Socket Head Doll, late 19th/early 20th C. w/ dark brown sleeping eyes, coral pink lip coloring, new black wig, jointed compostion body, period eyelet dress & pinafore (stains), 13½" H. **$862**

Heuback Bisque Socket Head Pouty Boy, early 20th C. w/ blue eyes, painted hair, articulated wood & composition body w/ crack from neck to front, painted over, wearing hat only, 6½" H. **$258**

Top Row

Clark Chemical Pumper, pressed steel & wood, friction drive, 11" L. **$431**

Buddy L. Fliver Pickup, ca.1920, pressed steel, overpainted, 12" L. **$431**

Buddy L. Steam Shovel, ca.1920, pressed steel, orig. paint. **$316**

Street Lamp w/ Mounted Fire Alarm Box, battery operated, pressed steel w/ wooden finial. Corner of State & Main Gong Bell Mfg. Co., one glass panel missing. 12" H. **$144**

Second Row

Clark Steam Pumper, pressed steel & wood. No driver, 10½" L. **$316**

Kiddie Cyclist, red suit, blue shoes, working, ca. 1930, 9" H. **$172**

Steel Windmill, 12 blade wheel powers continual pump, some rust, vane mkd. "Empire", 21" H. **$86**

Third Row

Sand Toy, "Bowler Andy Mill" by Wolverine pat. 1919, 20" H. **$144**

Kiddie Cyclist, key wind, red overall & blue & white stripe shirt. Working, ca. 1939-1949" H. **$201**

Ferris Wheel, pressed steel with yellow cast iron seat & passengers, clockwork by Hubley, ca.1905, 6 gondolas, wheel 14", 17" H. **$2,185**

Guntherman "Tango Dancers", tin wind-up, very minor paint loss, working. **$1,265**

United Electric "Spirit of St. Louis", pressed steel w/ two airplanes circling a pylon. Excellent condition, 22" H. **$1,610**

Gong Bell Co. Gas Pump 900, pressed steel, no nozzle, 13" H. **$316**

Marx Climbing Fireman Tin Wind-up, fireman climbs ladder, good paint, 23" H. **$172**

Fourth Row

Buddy L. Fliver Roadster, pressed steel, overpainted, 11" L. **$460**

Popeye Wind-up Tin Litho Figure, w/ two suitcases, 8" H. **$259**

Foxy Fido the Mystery Dog, by "Fullatrix Toys" Paul S. Jones Co. Brockton, MA. w/ orig. box, pat.1925, 8" H. **$144**

Gibbs Service Station, ca. 1930, pressed steel & wood, 15" L. **$374**

Tin Wind-up Toonerville Trolley, copyright 1922 by Fontaine Fox, complete & running condition, 90% paint, 7" H. **$460**

Gunthermann Vis-a-Vis, ca.1910, hand painted litho tin, missing 1 rubber tire, headlamps and front fender, key supports broken. Very good paint, 10" L. **$3,680**

Climber Sheet Metal Horse, on platform, drive wheel in back, horse's head moves up & down, paint loss, 6½ H", 10½" L. **$201**

Pressed Steel Coupé, friction drive inoperative, orig. paint, 8" L. **$144**

Fifth Row

Hoge Fire Chief Car, pressed steel, wind-up, orig. paint, electric headlights, 14" L. **$374**

Teddy Bear Bell Ringer, cast iron, orig. paint, 5¾" L. **$431**

German Touring Car, tin, marked G&K, working, 6" L. **$230**

Penny Toy Pool Player, excellent condition, 4" L. **$144**

Tin Wind-up Ship, "Made in US Zone Germany", black, red & white, 14" L. **$69**

Lionel Mickey & Minnie Mouse, w/ orig. box, some repair to engine, 9" L. **$862**

Tin Wind-up Boat, single stack, US Zone Germany. **$57**

Cast Metal Toonerville Trolley, copyright 1923, Fontaine Fox, 3½" H. **$195**

Clark Touring Car, pressed steel & wood, friction drive, 10¼" L. **$345**

Kingsbury Auto Dump Truck, early, pressed steel, clockwork not operating, 8¾" L. **$230**

Tin Wind-up Ship, "Made in US Zone Germany", black, red & white, 14" L. **$57**

A-MA May. 2001   Skinner, Inc.

Steiff Giraffes on Wheels, three, c. 1913, airbrushed felt, mohair manes, some moth damage & fading, 11¾", 14" & 15". **$2,185**

Teddy Doll, blue mohair, w/ celluloid face, c. 1908, 9" H. **$373**

Feather Tree & Ornaments, partial strings of glass beads, assorted tree candle holders, figurals, tinsel, etc., tree 45" H. **$632**

Steiff Clownies & Mohair Animals, w/ some wear. **$460**

Top Row

Arcade Red Baby Dump Truck, old repaint, no driver, 10½" L. **$115**

Arcade Weaver Wrecker, cast iron, orig. paint & decal, no driver, 8½" L. **$747**

Arcade Andy Gump, cast iron, orig. paint, 7" L. **$1,725**

Cast Iron Gas Pumps, pr., one red, one blue, 7" H. **$719**

Second Row

Arcade Fageol Bus, cast iron, orig. worn orange paint, 12" L. **$316**

Lead Soldiers, set of 7, ca. 1930, steel helmets, 3½" H. **$69**

Hubley Motorcycle w/ Sidecar, cast iron, missing figures, 8½" L. **$489**

Cast Iron Touring Car, overpaint, chrome spoke wheels & spare, 7" L. **$690**

Cop Motorcycles w/ Sidecars, pr., cast iron, orig. paint, rubber wheels, both 3⅞" L, one has chip on side car brake. **$259**

Tin Litho Wind-up Girl, by Lindstrom, 8" H, overwound. **$138**

Third Row

Cast Iron Motorcycle "Crash Car", by Hubley, white rubber tires on wooden rims, 4½" L, 2½" H. **$144**

Arcade Sedan, cast iron, orig. paint & decal w/ some overpaint, 4¾" L. **$149**

Hubley Harley Motorcycle, cast iron, orig. paint, 5½" L. **$316**

Arcade Double Decker Bus, cast iron, blue w/ gold striping, driver silhouette, 7¾" L, 3" H. **$489**

German Penny Toy Touring Car, litho tin, very colorful, missing 1 rear fender. **$316**

German Penny Toy Sedan, litho tin, very colorful, 4¼" L. **$431**

Indian Motorcycle "Crash Car", cast iron, by Hubley. Orange paint, some rust, missing rubber tires, 6" L, 3½" H. **$316**

Arcade Wrecker Truck, cast iron, orig. paint decal, no boom, 5⅞" L. **$172**

Hubley "Speed" Motorcycle, cast iron, orig. paint, #5 on back, 4¼" L. **$287**

Fourth Row

Motorcycle Policeman Rider, cast iron, orig. paint w/ some over paint, rubber tires, 4¾" L. **$230**

Marx Tin Litho Drum Major, w/ googly eyes, working, 9" H. **$86**

Occupied Japan Puzzle Car, in box, red, tin wind-up, no key. **$34**

Occupied Japan Puzzle Car, green, pressed steel, wheel loose, 6" L. **$23**

Iron Bell Toys, pr. one w/ a pair of riders & 6 bells, one w/ 2 wheels on bell. **$34**

Arcade Gas Pump, cast iron, orig. paint, no nozzle, 4¼" H. **$144**

Kenton Sulky Cart, cast iron, orig. paint, 8¼" L. **$172**

Police Motorcycle, tin litho, marked Japan, friction, not working. **$46**

Fifth Row

Penny Toy Baby Buggy, marked Germany, cloth cover torn. **$17**

Arcade Sedan, cast iron, orig. paint, 3¾" L. **$144**

Airplane, cast iron, embossed "Champion" on wings with Army Air Corp star, 4½" L. **$86**

Airplane, cast iron, embossed "Lindy" on wings, 4" L. **$126**

Arcade Wrecker, cast iron, orig. paint, partial decal, rubber tires, 5½" L. **$172**

German Touring Car, tin, incomplete, mech. intact, but not working, 5¼" L. **$34**

Chein Wind-up Bear, tin litho, w/ some rust & paint loss. **$23**

"Schuco Examico 4001" Auto, made in U.S. Zone Germany, windshield & part of steering wheel missing. **$52**

Wind-up Truck, tin litho, by Minic, "Dust Cart" marked Tri-ang, made in England, 5" L. **$92**

Toledo Counter Scale, cast iron, made by Arcade, 5" H. **$86**

Shuco Motordrill Motorcycle, litho tin, no key, 5" L. **$172**

Sixth Row

Wind-up Boats, set of 4, tin, maroon base & white super structure, mkd. "Made in U.S. Zone Germany". Minor paint loss, 8" L. **$230**

A-MA May. 2001   Skinner, Inc.

Sewing Bird, bronze colored, hvy. embossed, 5" H. **$143**

Trim & Fabric, 3 boxes, velvet, satin, lace & brocade trim. Remnants of silk, muslin & cotton. Includes some modern trim. **$402**

Toy Sewing Machines, three, one cast-iron Singer, two black-painted steel w/ polychrome decor. **$546**

Sewing Machine, Singer Featherweight w/ case, 1951. **$402**

Top Row

Doepke "Model" #2001, Barber Greene high capacity bucket loader, some minor rust, 13" H. **$144**

Doepke "Model" Jaeger #2002, Cement Mixer, 15" L. **$230**

Buddy L. Concrete Mixer, good played with condition, 9½" L. **$374**

Buddy L. Sand Loader, pressed steel, orig. paint, 20" H. **$460**

Second Row

Turner Fire Pumper, pressed steel, 15" L. **$144**

Mechanical Football Player, cast iron & steel, orig. paint, 8"x7". **$115**

Republic Roadster, pressed steel wind-up, repainted. **$288**

Structo Auto Builder #12, pressed steel, orig. box & instruction, some paint loss, 15½" L. **$1,150**

Schieble Roadster, pressed steel, 18" L. **$431**

Mencel "Miss America" Boat, ca. 1930, wood & steel, key wind works, 18½" L. **$230**

Third Row

Structo Steam Shovel, pressed steel, nice orig. paint, 12" H. **$115**

Hill Climber Bus, red w/ gold striping, 12" L, 7" H. **$230**

John Deere Manure Spreader, cast iron, w/ Vindex label. All orig. w/ 90% paint, 10" L. **$1,092**

Gondola Toy by Hubley, cast iron, ca. 1905. Clockwork drives cast wheels, 20" L, 11" H. **$1,380**

Locomotive & Tender, pressed steel, friction drive, 19" L. **$144**

Arcade Chester Gump Cart, cast iron, orig. paint, 7½" L. **$402**

Structo Tractor, pressed steel, kit piece, 9" L. **$144**

Fourth Row

Wind-up Trapeze Artist, by Toyland Toys, celluloid performer, orig. box, 9" H. **$201**

Marx Big Parade, in box, tin wind-up toy in pristine condition, box is in pieces & incomplete, 24" L. **$287**

Buddy L. Coca-Cola Truck, w/ bottles, white wall tires, half windows & chrome hubcaps, minor rust on bumper, 15" L. **$172**

Hook & Ladder Wagon, cast iron, white open wagon, red ladders, 30" L. **$604**

Marx Main Street Wind-up, tin, 24" L. **$172**

Fifth Row

Structo Caterpillar Tractor, pressed steel, wind-up works, 8½" L. **$287**

Marx Car Carrier, ca. 1935, red & gray, 3 copper wind-up cars w/ red wheels ride on red trailer, 22" L. **$2,012**

Fire Pumper, cast iron, black & yellow steamer, 10" L. **$115**

German Wind-up Auto, tin, early 20th C., marked G&K L., works, 5½" L. **$402**

Tin Elephants, set of 3, one large, two small, hand painted. **$195**

Cast Iron Surrey, w/ 2 horses & driver & lady passenger, 11" L. **$69**

Fire Pumper, cast iron, yellow carriage & steamer, black horses. Heavy paint loss, 22" L. **$489**

Kingsbury Ladder Truck, pressed steel, wind-up, orig. paint, missing steering wheel. **$230**

Schieble Fire Truck, pressed steel, 14½" L. **$195**

Lehmann Naughty Boy, early 20th C., hand painted & litho tin. Mech. intact but bound up, 5" L. **$747**

Carette Limousine, lithographed tin, w/ clockwork, tin wheels & beveled glass window, hand painted tin driver, orig. head & side lamps, hand brake, some paint loss on arms, 16" L. **$6,050**

Jep Alfa Romeo Racer, painted tin, clockwork, rubber tires, all orig., very minor paint flaking near filler cap, 20" L. **$7,150**

Lehmann Balky Mule, lithographed tin w/ cloth dressed clown, clockwork, replaced donkey ears, 7" L. **$385**

Lehmann Express porter, lithographed tine w/ inertia wheel drive, 6" L. **$220**

Row 1

Pre-war Japanese Limousine, lithographed tin, clockwork, serious wear on hood, 7" L. **$138**

G & K Town Car, lithographed tin, friction drive, 5" L. **$358**

Center

Issmayer Vis-A-Vis, lithographed tin, w/ clockwork, mech. needs work, 4" L. **$495**

Row 2

Issmayer Vis-A-Vis, lithographed tin, friction drive, 4" L. **$330**

Issmayer Vis-A-Vis, lithographed tin, w/ clockwork, mech. not working, driver loose, 4½" L. **$193**

A-PA Nov. 2001   Noel Barrett Antiques &
Auctions Ltd.

Orobr Ford Tourer, lithographed tin, w/
w/ clockwork 6" L. **$248**
EBO Limousine, lithographed tin,
clockwork, glass windows, orig. driver,
missing one door, 8" L. **$248**

A-PA June 2001   Noel Barrett Antique & Auctions Ltd.

Hubley Transitional Ladder Wagon, painted cast iron, orig. figures & ladders, some
paint wear on wheels, 27½" L. **$3,300**
Transitional Pumper, companion piece to ladder wagon, orig. figures & one pair orig.
hose ends, some paint wear to wheels, 14" L. **$2,970**

A-PA Nov. 2001   Noel Barrett Antiques &
Auctions Ltd.

Orobr Rear Entry Tonneau, lithographed
tin, w/ clockwork, 8" L. **$495**

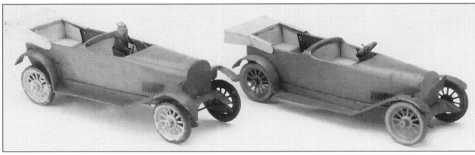

A-PA June 2001   Noel Barrett Antique & Auctions Ltd.

Open Touring Car, red, heavy tin, w/ wind-up mechanism & brake, tin driver, missing
steering wheel, 13" L. **$413**
Open Touring Car, green, heavy tin w/ spoke wheels, 13 " L. **$468**

A-PA June 2001   Noel Barrett Antique &
Auctions Ltd.

Express "Triporteur", embossed
lithographed tin, by Meier, 3" L. **$880**
Horsedrawn Sulky with Rider, embossed
lithographed tin, 4" L. **$253**

A-PA June 2001   Noel Barrett Antique & Auctions Ltd.

First row
Schieble Sedan, painted pressed steel, friction drive, 17½" L. **$220**
Dayton Coupe, painted pressed steel, friction drive, missing right rear fender, some
corrosion, 18½" L. **$193**
Second row
Schieble Roadster, painted pressed steel, friction drive, tires brittle, 18½" L. **$358**
Schieble Roadster, painted pressed steel, friction drive, some paint wear on wheels,
17½" L. **$440**

A-PA June 2001   Noel Barrett Antique &
Auctions Ltd.

Ostrich drawn Sulky with Rider,
embossed lithographed tin, w/ surface
wear to wheels, 3½" L. **$413**
Horsedrawn Trap with Driver, embossed
lithographed tin, by Meier, 3¾" L. **$303**

A-PA Nov. 2001   Noel Barrett Antiques & Auctions Ltd.

Clockwise from top
Lehmann Autobus, lithographed tin, w/ clockwork, wear on wheels, needs cleaning, 8" L. **$880**
Lehmann EHE Truck, lithographed tin, w/ clockwork, 7" L. **$358**
Lehmann Motor Coach, lithographed tin, w/ clockwork, 5" L. **$303**

A-PA June 2001   Noel Barrett Antique & Auctions Ltd.

Row 1
Hillclimber Runabout, wood & cast iron w/ 2 cast iron figures, 7" L. **$550**
Hillclimber Open Touring Car, painted pressed steel, friction drive & 2 cast iron figures, 7" L. **$193**

Row 2
Hillclimber Touring Car, wood & painted pressed steel, w/ 2 cast iron figures, 8" L. **$248**
Hillclimber Open Touring Car, painted pressed steel, w/ friction drive & 3 cast iron figures, paint flaking, 8" L. **$248**
Hillclimber Runabout, painted pressed steel and wood, w/ friction & cast iron driver, 7" L. **$330**

A-PA June 2001   Noel Barrett Antique & Auctions Ltd.

"Triumph" Motorcycle, embossed lithographed tin, w/ clockwork by Meier, 2¾". **$1,210**
"Velocette" Motorcycle, embossed lithographed tin, detail on motor, by Paya, some plating wear on wheels, 4" L. **$468**

A-PA June 2001   Noel Barrett Antique & Auctions Ltd.

"Cito" Tricar, embossed lithographed tin, by Kellermann, 3¾" L. **$578**
Motorcycle with Sidecar, embossed lithographed tin, by Distler, some areas of wear, 3¼" L. **$1,100**

A-PA June 2001   Noel Barrett Antique & Auctions Ltd.

Auto, highly detailed embossed lithographed tin, w/ inertia drive, by Meier, some wear, 3½" L. **$495**
Race Car #10, embossed lithographed tin, by Distler, 4" L. **$798**

A-PA June 2001   Noel Barrett Antique & Auctions Ltd.

Race Car, embossed lithographed tin, by JVF, wear on high spots, 3½" L. **$1,045**
Race Car, embossed lithographed tin, by Distler, 2½" L. **$935**

A-PA June 2001   Noel Barrett Antique & Auctions Ltd.

First row

Schoenhut Clown, orig., printed, cloth costume, jointed wood, 2 part head, no cone in hat, 8″ H. **$550**

Second Row

Arabian Camel, glass eyes, painted jointed wood, leather ears, rope tail, 9″ L. **$176**

Platform Horse, glass eyes, painted jointed wood, string tail, leather ears, 9″ L. **$319**

Bactrian Camel, painted eyes, painted jointed wood, rope tail, 7″ L. **$220**

Third row

Schoenhut Clown, orig. 4 color cloth costume, 2 part head, no cone in hat, 8″ H. **$550**

Pig, painted eyes & jointed wood, leather ears & tail, 7″ L. **$220**

Lion, painted eyes, painted jointed wood, rope tail, 7½″ L. **$440**

Ostrich, painted eyes, painted jointed wood, 8½″ H. **$275**

A-PA June 2001   Noel Barrett Antique & Auctions Ltd.

First row

Goat, glass eyes, painted jointed wood, leather horns, ears, etc., missing 1 ear, 8″ L. **$72**

Lion, glass eyes, painted jointed wood, laced tail, 7½″ L. **$1,100**

Second row

Donkeys, two, glass eyes, painted jointed wood, fabric mane, 1 w/ missing ears & tail, other possible replaced ears, 9″ L. **$39**

Elephant, glass eyes, painted jointed wood, leather ears & tusks, rubber trunk tip, rope tail, some paint wear on legs, 8″ L. **$413**

Donkey & Elephant, reduced size, painted jointed wood, donkey missing ear & tail, 8″ L. **$28**

Third row

Dude, redressed in cloth, jointed wood, 2 part head, orig., 8½″ H. **$143**

Lady Acrobat, bisque head, cloth clothing is orig., jointed wood, 8″ H. **$413**

Ringmaster, bisque head, cloth dressed, jointed wood w/ arm joints, orig. undergarments, missing outer wear, small chip on head, 8″ H. **$39**

Clowns, two, orig. clothing, cloth dressed, jointed wood, 1 part heads, missing ears 8½″ H. **$50**

Lady Acrobats & Ringmaster, two, cloth redressed, jointed wood, acrobats are restored, 8″ H. **$44**

A-PA June 2001   Noel Barrett Antique & Auctions Ltd.

Schoenhuts

First row

Chief Type II, cloth dressed, jointed wood, scarce figure from the Teddy Roosevelt Safari Set, missing jacket & hat cover, damage to pants on one leg, 9″ H. **$688**

Hobo, cloth dressed, jointed wood, orig. clothing except for hat, face repainted, 7½″ H. **$176**

Clowns, 2, cloth dressed, jointed wood, orig. clothing, 1 hat cover missing, paint wear to face, 1 pair ears missing, 8″ H. **$110**

Delvan Grouping, incl. cowboy, elephant, barrel, ball ring, pedestal, & tub, missing cowboy hat. **$39**

Second row

Clowns, three, reduced size, cloth dressed, jointed wood, orig. clothing, 7″ H. **$61**

Bareback Riders, 2, cloth dressed, jointed wood, 1 w/ bisque head, 1 missing arms, painted head has paint loss, 8″ H. **$28**

A-PA Nov. 2001   Noel Barrett Antiques & Auctions Ltd.

German Noah's Ark, painted w/ applied paper decorations and twenty-four composition animals, 27″ L. **$2,750**

A-PA June 2001   Noel Barrett Antique &
                                    Auctions Ltd.

First row

Wyandotte Humphrey, w/ orig. box, lithographed tin & clockwork. Some wear on box, 7" H. **$605**

Marx Charlie McCarthy Drummer Boy, orig. box w/ lt. staining, high luster lithographed tin & clockwork, 8" H. **$1,760**

Marx Porky Pig and Lasso, w/ orig. box, lithographed tin & clockwork, ©1949 Leon Schlesinger, crack in plastic hat, 8" H. **$550**

Second row

Marx Lone Ranger w/ Box, lithographed tin & clockwork, orig. box, ©1938, classic radio toy, box has some damage, 8" H. **$880**

Marx Dagwood the Driver, w/ orig. box, lithographed tin w/ clockwork, box has slight damage, 8" H. **$1,815**

Marx Rocket Fighter, w/ orig. box, lithographed tin and clockwork, 12". **$990**

Marx Donald Duck Duet w/ orig. box, lithographed tin, clockwork, and some edge wear to box, 10½" H. **$1,100**

A-PA June 2001   Noel Barrett Antique & Auctions Ltd.

First row

Marx Popeye the Champ, w/ orig. box, lithographed tin, w/ clockwork, & celluloid figures. Minor damage to 1 corner of box, 7" sq. **$2,640**

Marx Popeye & Olive on Roof, w/ orig. box, lithographed tin, clockwork, light scratches where arms hit Popeye's body. Box has small hole on border of one side, 9" H. **$1,540**

Marx Popeye Eccentric Airplane, w/ orig. box, lithographed tin & clockwork. The later version of this toy w/ patriotic colors, box. Complete but damaged, 7" H. **$770**

Second row

Chein Popeye in Barrel, w/ box, lithographed tin, clockwork, Depression era, box needs restoration, 7" H. **$633**

Marx Popeye Airport Express, w/orig. box lithographed tin and cardboard and clockwork. Toy has some missing pieces, 9" diam. **$1,155**

A-PA Nov. 2001   Noel Barrett Antique &
                                    Auctions Ltd.

Rocking Horse, painted wood w/ orig. oilcloth saddle & blanket, 46" L. **$275**

A-PA Nov. 2001   Noel Barrett Antiques &
                                    Auctions Ltd.

Express Wagon, stencil deco. wood wagon, metal tires w/ wood spoke wheels & opening tailgate w/ decor. on one side faded. Body of wagon: 33" x 17". **$495**

TOYS/DOLLS

A-PA June 2001   Noel Barrett Antique & Auctions Ltd.

Distler Mickey Mouse Organ Grinder, lithographed tin w/ clockwork & "plink-plink" musical accompaniment. When Mickey turns crank, Minnie dances, 8" H. **$5,720**

A-PA Nov. 2001   Noel Barrett Antique & Auctions Ltd.

"Rambling" Mickey Mouse, celluloid figure w/ internal clockwork, mkd. "Made in Japan", 7½" H. **$880**

A-PA June 2001   Noel Barrett Antique & Auctions Ltd.

Linemar Clarabelle Acrobat, lithographed tin, w/ clockwork. 5" H. **$220**
Topo Gigio Doll, painted molded vinyl w/ arms, mkd. "©1963", 12" H. **$44**

A-PA Nov. 2001   Noel Barrett Antiques & Auctions Ltd.

Mickey Mouse Riding Pluto, celluloid figures on wood base w/ clockwork mech., mkd. "Made in Japan", paint wear on Mickey's trousers, 8" L. **$1,760**

A-PA Nov. 2001   Noel Barrett Antiques & Auctions Ltd.

Linemar Mickey Mouse Carousel, lithographed tin, w/ clockwork toy w/ celluloid figures, small area of touch-up paint on canopy, 7" H. **$2,530**

A-PA June 2001   Noel Barrett Antique & Auctions Ltd.

First row
Lehmann Ikarus, lithographed tin plane w/ paper wings, clockwork, paper wings complete but brittle & damaged, 11" L. **$1,100**
Lehmann Garage & Sedan, embossed lithographed tin, sedan has clockwork, garage 6" D. **$413**
Lehmann Alabama Coon Jigger, lithographed tin, w/ clockwork, 9" H. **$275**
Second row
Lehmann Tut Tut, painted & lithographed tin, w/ clockwork, all orig., makes honking noise, 7" L. **$578**
Lehmann Motor Coach, painted and lithographed tin, w/ clockwork, 5" L. **$187**
Lehmann Zulu, embossed lithographed tin, w/ clockwork, 7" L. **$523**
Lehmann Low Angeles Zeppelin, lithographed tin, w/ clockwork, and orig. fins, 9" L. **$468**
Third row
Lehmann Heinkel Airplane w/ Box, lithographed tin, box complete w/ tin pull-never used, also extra underbelly assembly, 5½". **$440**
Lehmann Also, lithographed tin, clockwork, 4" L. **$385**
Lehman Quack-Quack, lithographed tin, w/ clockwork, 7" L. **$209**

A-PA June 2001   Noel Barrett Antique & Auctions Ltd.

First row
Old Curiosity Shop Bank, colorful embossed lithographed tin, missing base plate, 3″ W. **$39**
Alpine Chalet Bank, finely detailed embossed lithographed tin w/ locking rear door, some edge wear, 2½″ L. **$55**
Swiss Chalet "Barometer" Bank, embossed lithographed tin, highly detailed, a rare form, 2¼″ H. **$550**
Punch and Judy Show Candy Box, lithographed tin, 2 levers activate the puppets, sliding lid in rear for candy box, some surface wear, 3″ H. **$523**
Clock w/ Glass Dome, lithographed tin, clock tabbed to base, 2″ W. **$61**
Wall Telephone, embossed lithographed tin by Meier, light surface wear to ear pieces, 4¾″ H. **$165**
Second row
Partridges on Platforms, two, embossed tin, 1 painted (some paint loss), 1 on lithographed base, 2¾″ L. **$28**

Frog With Butterfly Box, embossed lithographed tin, frog jumps toward box which has removable lid, by Fischer, 3″ L. **$1,540**
Large Dog on Platform, embossed lithographed tin, by Meier, P-18, 3¼″ L. **$347**
Cow on Platform, embossed lithographed tin, by Meier, 3¼″ L. **$303**
Small Dog on Platform, embossed lithographed tin, by Meier, 3″ L. **$275**

A-PA June 2001   Noel Barrett Antique & Auctions Ltd.

Unique Art, w/ orig. box, slight damage, lithographed tin, w/ clockwork. Last of the U.S. made piano/dancer toys, mkd. on base "© Bob Smith", piano 6½″ L. **$2,200**
Ideal Howdy Doody Doll, wood & composition jointed doll, orig. decal & belt, surface wear & crazing to back of head, face restored, 12″ H. **$66**

A-PA Nov. 2001   Noel Barrett Antiques & Auctions Ltd.

Wood Sled, w/ wrought iron runners. Stenciled image of horse w/ added hand painted flourishes decorate the bed, 19th C. **$1,540**
Wood Sled, w/ side handles & scenic motif surrounded by flowers decorate bed. Runners are wrought iron, 49″ L. **$825**

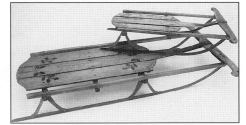

A-PA Nov. 2001   Noel Barrett Antiques & Auctions Ltd.
Top
Firefly Sled No. 8 G, stained wood w/ metal runners, stencil decor., finely crafted early repair to one handle, 26″ L. **$94**
Bottom
Firefly Sled No. 12 B, stained wood w/ metal runners, stencil decorated, 46″ L. **$55**

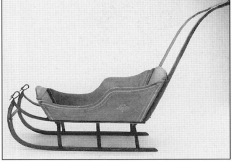

A-PA Nov. 2001   Noel Barrett Antiques & Auctions Ltd.

Push Sled, w/ wood body painted red w/ stenciled decoration. Cast iron swan heads on metal sheathed wood runners. Turned wood handle, 50″ L. **$605**

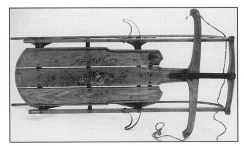

A-PA Nov. 2001   Noel Barrett Antiques & Auctions Ltd.

Flexible Flyer "Racer" Sled, stained wood w/ metal runners, strong color both in name & logo decal., 56″ L. **$138**

A-PA Nov. 2001   Noel Barrett Antiques & Auctions Ltd.

Flexible Flyer Sled, stained wood, stenciled decor, metal foot rest, paint loss on metal runners, decal somewhat faded, 50″ L. **$110**

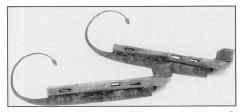

A-PA Nov. 2001   Noel Barrett Antiques & Auctions Ltd.

Early Ice Skates, painted wood w/ brass & steel. Blades mkd. "C. W. Wirths" w/ original leather straps, 12″ L. **$604**

TOYS/DOLLS

A-PA June 2001   Noel Barrett Antique & Auctions Ltd.
Clockwise from top

Marklin Station, embossed lithographed tin w/ etched and stained glass window, 4 opening doors, furnished interior, 2 electric lights loosely installed, light crazing. Station identification signs are over painted, base 13-½" x 9", 13" H. **$4,620**
Marklin "Ankunft/ Abfahrt" sign & Signal Bell, enamelled tin. Bell has iron base & crank operated bell, sign 7" H. **$660**
Marklin Passenger Gate w/ Destination Flags, enamelled tin, flags incl. Prag, Berlin, Paris, Koln, etc., 10½" H. **$1,980**
Marklin Ticket Kiosk, enamelled tin, back opens for insertion of tickets, 7½" H. **$385**

A-PA June 2001   Noel Barrett Antique & Auctions Ltd.
Left side

American Flyer 4000 Engine Passenger Set, #4040 baggage, "Pleasant View" coach. Missing roof component on engine. **$302**
Right side

Lionel #33 Engine Passenger Set, NYC baggage car, Pullman & Observation coaches. **$440**

A-PA June 2001   Noel Barrett Antique & Auctions Ltd.

Lionel Station No. 134, w/ box, minor dulling on 1 side. **$468**
Lionel Illuminated Platform. $468
Lionel Mansion & Flag Pole Base, 15" W. **$990**

A-PA June 2001   Noel Barrett Antique & Auctions Ltd.
Top row

Lionel 256 Passenger Set, early rubber stamped engine, 2-710's & 1-712 passenger cars, replaced pantagraph. **$1,430**
Second row

Lionel 256 Brass Plate Electric Loco, new wheels, possibly an older restoration. **$468**
Lionel No. 35 & 36 Passenger Cars, late unusual cars. **$231**

A-PA June 2001   Noel Barrett Antique & Auctions Ltd.

American Flyer 3115 Passenger Set, engine w/ 3 passenger cars, 2-3281, 1-3282. **$825**
Lionel Mohave 253 Set, passenger cars. **$220**

A-PA June 2001   Noel Barrett Antique & Auctions Ltd.
Lionel 402 Mohave Passenger Set, 3 pcs., incl. 431 diner & 418 passenger car w/ orange inserts. **$1,045**

A-PA June 2001   Noel Barrett Antique & Auctions Ltd.
American Flyer No. 3015 Passenger Set, 4 pc. Illini set w/ box & instruction manual. **$1,210**

A-PA June 2001   Noel Barrett Antique & Auctions Ltd.
Lionel #42 Engine Passenger Set, gray 2 motor electric engine 42, 3-18, 19 and 190 passenger cars. **$1,265**

A-PA June 2001   Noel Barrett Antique & Auctions Ltd.
Lionel Passenger Cars, 3 pcs., #'s 428, 429 and 430, one restored bottom. **$413**

A-PA June 2001   Noel Barrett Antique & Auctions Ltd.
Lionel Standard Gauge Blue Comet, all orig. castings, w/ repl. wheels & handrail brackets, light scratches, missing some window frames. **$3,850**

A-PA June 2001   Noel Barrett Antique & Auctions Ltd.
Lionel Black 42 Single Motor, w/ 3 cars, No. 18 Pullman, 19 Baggage, 190 Observation. **$825**

A-PA June 2001   Noel Barrett Antique & Auctions Ltd.
Ives Train Set # 1071 with 3236 Engine, orig. boxes, engine wheels bad, some paint flaking, minor parts missing, **$1,760**

A-PA June 2001   Noel Barrett Antique & Auctions Ltd.
Ives Passenger Cars, 3 pcs., #184 baggage, #185 Coach and #186 Observation, some packing paper residue on roofs. **$209**

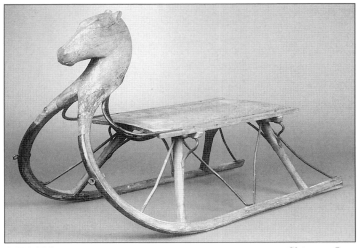

A-MA Feb. 2001   Skinner, Inc.
Carved Oak & Wrought Iron Sled, 19th C. w/ carved horse head, traces of polychrome decor., 20" H, 12¼" W, & 12¼" L. **$3,105**

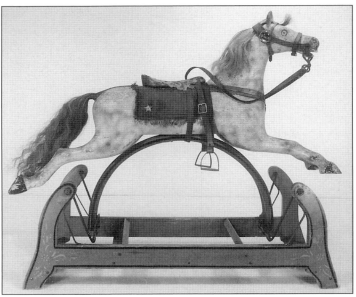

A-PA Apr. 2001   York Town Auction Inc.
Hobby Horse, untouched condition. **$1,500**

A-PA June 2001   Pook & Pook, Inc.

Doll Cradle, pine, late 19th C., w/ cutter rockers. **$400**

Child's Country Table, ME, w/ orig. blue painted surface, 14½" H, 19" W. **$375**

Stepback Cupboard, miniature, late 19th C., walnut w/ sliding doors, orig. knobs, 18¾" H, 11" W. **$300**

Miniature Marble Top Chest, pine & poplar, ca. 1850, retains red stained surface, 9½" H, 12½" W. **$500**

Child's Ladderback Rocking Chair, ca. 1800, w/ overall gilt stenciling & floral decor., 20½" H. **$250**

Child's End Table, N. Eng., Sheraton, ca. 1840, w/ orig. black painted surface, 19½" H, 13¾" W. **$1,600**

Doll Bed, PA, w/ canopy, ca. 1850, w/ overall red & yellow grain painted surface, 34" H, 24½" L. **$375**

Doll Bed, Federal, maple, ca. 1820, 12" H, 20" L. **$325**

Child's Dutch Cupboard, PA, retaining comb decor. surface, 28" H, 22¼" W. **$850**

Child's Jelly Cupboard, poplar, ca. 1850, 18" H, 12½" W. **$500**

Rocking Horse, Am., ca. 1850 w/ red seat flanked by 2 painted dapple gray horses, 17" H, 33" L. **$1,000**

Miniature Stove, Kent, cast iron, late 19th C., w/ iron pots & pans, painted blue/green, 9½" x 9½". **$350**

A-NH May 2001   Northeast Auctions

Mirrors, two, each rectangular w/deep arched crest, the larger 17″ x 10″ illus. **$1,000**

Chandelier, Continental, brass, eight-light w/scrolled candle arms & spherical pendant drop, 22″ H, 27″ diam. **$1,800**

Courting Mirror, Continental w/ églomisé panel, 25″ x 14″. **$1,100**

Portrait of an 18th C. lady, oil on canvas, 30″ x 25″. **$1,000**

Q. A. Two-Part Looking Glass, green painted & japanned, beveled mirror plates. 47″ x 20½″. **$5,000**

Country Slat-Back Dining Chairs, assembled set of six, New England w/ sausage turnings, in black paint, comprising five sides and an armchair. **$2,750**

Hutch-Table, New England country, 26½″ H, 46″ diam. **$3,250**

Dutch Plates, five blue & white, 9″ diam., various marks, 2 illus. **$1,300**

Candlesticks, 2 similar, brass, Dutch, 9½″. **$1,600**

Candlesticks, pair, early Spanish brass, 9½″. **$1,600**

Candlesticks, pair, English, Q.A., 6½″. **$650**

Blanket Chest, Wm. & Mary, New England w/2 false drawers over 2 long drawers, 39½″ H, 35½″ W, 20″ D. **$1,500**

Andirons, Am. knife-blade, sgn., w/ brass urn finial & penny feet, 23″ H. **$1,300**

Candleholder, double-arm, early, hardwood w/ circular shelf, splayed legs, 35″ H. **$700**

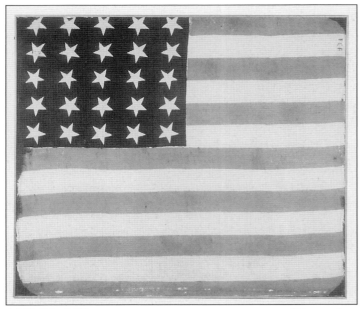

A-MA Feb. 2001   Skinner, Inc.

Woven Wool American Flag Blanket, ca. 1836-37 w/ 25
stars, mkd. "FBC" in ink in upper left-hand star & right-hand
corner, wear & losses, mounted and framed, 62½" W, 70" L.
$12,650

A-NH Aug. 2001   Northeast Auctions

Early American 13 Star Flag. This unusual pattern is know as
"quincuncial", based on the repetition of a motif of 5 units. Size: 58" x
108". **$1,100**
American Carved Pine Pilot House Eagle on Ball, 21" wingspread, 19"
H. **$5,500**
Pilot House Carved & Guilded Eagle w/ open beak, 31" H, 34" L.
$17,000
American Weathered Carving of an Eagle's Head w/ carved feathers,
mounted on a board, 17" L. **$650**

A-OH Apr. 2001   Garth's Auctions, Inc.

Officer Sword Belt, rect. brass eagle buckle, good patina, black
leather belt w/ stitched designs retains the orig. sword hangers.
$660
Early Relics, two, a Civil War era leather cap box, loose stitches
on belt loops, 3¼" H., tin drum canteen w/ worn plating & some
resolder, 6½" diam. **$330**
Bull's-eye Canteen, Civil War era w/ orig. woven cloth strap,
pewter spout sig. "Hadden, Porter & Booth, PA", 7⅝" diam.
$302
Brass Spurs, pr., Confederate, Leech & Rigdon style, 4". **$110**
U.S. Cartridge Box, Civil War w/ cross belt & eagle plate,
"Calhoune N.Y.", maker's stamp on inner flap, incl. tin liners &
oval U.S. plate. **$880**

A-CA June 2001   Butterfields

Powder Horn, Am. dated Sept. 27, 1750, typical form w/
carving all around incl. scrolls, cannon & sailing ship, 13" L.
$3,525
Carved Horn & Silver Cup w/ Horn Salt, Eng., late 18th/ early
19th C. Cup has silver rim & base w/ portrait of King George III,
& inscribed: God Save the Queen, dated 1797; the salt is
carved w/ a deer & other carvings inscribed: M. Belcher, salt,
dated 1807, max. 4½ " H. **$2,937**

A-OH Apr. 2001   Garth's Auctions, Inc.
Tintype, soldier wearing shell jacket, sixth
plate, seated wearing slouch hat w/
feather, lt. pink tinting on cheeks, half
case. **$247**

A-OH Apr. 2001   Garth's Auctions, Inc.
Tintype, soldiers in a half case, quarter
plate, two men seated cross-legged, minor
bends. **$302**

A-OH Apr. 2001   Garth's Auctions, Inc.
Confederate Officer's Coat, w/ VA
buttons, double breasted & made of blue-
gray wool, 12 lg. & 3 sm. buttons mkd.
"Scovill Mfg. Waterbury", pr. Captain's
bars for collar, sleeves 10" deep at elbow,
minor moth damage, otherwise very
good. **$39,600**

A-OH Apr. 2001   Garth's Auctions, Inc.
Tintype, Civil War soldier in half case,
sixth plate, seated wearing forage cap,
frock coat & vest, very rich, unusual liner
w/ classical designs. **$247**

A-OH Apr. 2001   Garth's Auctions, Inc.
Tintype, enlisted man, sixth plate, very
clear image w/ minor scratches, half
case. **$385**

A-MA Oct. 2001   Skinner
Snare Drum, Civil War Period, 19th C.,
hand dec., U.S. Eagle above shield &
flags w/ scrolls, initialed D.C.B., painted
in red, white, blue & gold colors w/ black
band on natural wood ground, peep hole
w/ no label on inter., pewter keepers &
pair of drumsticks, replaced rope,
crackled fin., 17⅝" diam., 14" H. **$1,150**

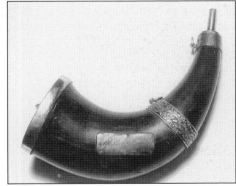

A-OH Apr. 2001   Garth's Auctions, Inc.
Presentation Powder Horn, TX, buffalo
horn w/ sterling silver bands & cap, silver
panel on either side w/ engraving
"…killed by Col. John Darrington…
Brassos, 1835", other side "Pres. by J.
Darrington to Col. Wade Hampton",
engraved scene on the end cap of hunter
w/ long rifle, few insect holes & brass end
appears to be later, 10½" L. **$9,900**

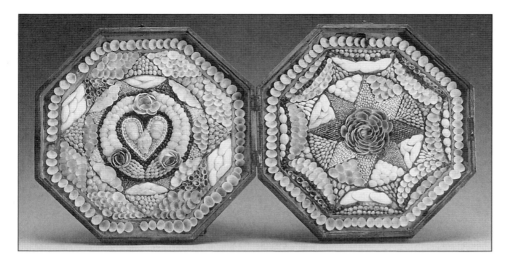

A-NH Aug. 2001   Northeast Auction

Row 1

Sailor's Shellwork Double Valentine, hinged octagonal case w/ a variety of shells w/ inscrip. "From a Friend", 14" H. **$7,500**

Nantucket Basket w/ swing handle, by W.D. Appleton (1918), 8" L. **$2,000**

Sailor's Shellwork Valentine, mounted in an octagonal oak frame, 16½" diam. **$10,000**

Row 2

Nantucket Purse Basket w/ carved ivory whale on lid, sgn. S.P. Boyer, 10½" L. **$12,000**

Nantucket Baskets, three, the first w/ bail handle, sgn. J.H. Robinson Adams, Dorchester, 6½" diam.; second round & sgn. Alice Gibbs, No. 16th 1870; third, a larger example, 12" diam.; last basket illus. on Row 3 **$1,800**

Sailor's Shellwork Valentine w/ central heart & rose within an 8-point star, in an octagonal frame, 13" x 13". **$6,500**

Nantucket Purse Basket w/ rosewood insert & carved ivory whale on lid, dated 1972, & sgn. Elder, 8½" L. **$1,500**

Nantucket Basket w/ swing handle, w/ oak trim & pine base, 7" diam. **$2,000**

Nantucket Oval Purse Basket by Sayle, 1979, top w/ caring of a half-hull, 7" H, 10½" L. **$2,250**

Row 3

Nantucket Basket w/ shaped swing handle, 10" diam. **$3,000**

Sailor's Shellwork Valentines, pair, each w/ octagonal frame enclosing shellwork of flowers within geometric borders w/ pink shells & outer border w/ curlicues, frame 19¼" H, shellwork 12½" H. **$15,000**

Sailor's Shellwork Double Valentine w/ variety of shells, inscrip. "A Present from Barbados", 10" H. **$4,000**

Nantucket Basket, description above w/ group of 3 baskets in Row 2.

A-CA June 2001   Butterfield

Sailor's Valentine, wood & shellwork, second half 19th C., one side in form of a star & wreaths, the other side centering a heart within geometric border, open–27½" W., 3½" H. **$5,287**

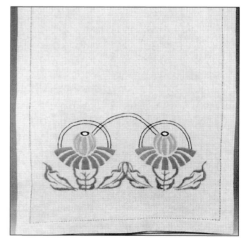

A-NJ May 2001   Craftsman

Table Runner, Arts & Crafts, embroidered w/ amber cornflowers on oatmeal ground, few minor stains, 19½" x 53". **$100**

A-NJ May 2001   Craftsman

Table Runner, Arts & Crafts, embroidered w/ geometric flowers in red, blue, yel. & gr., on buff linen w/ crocheted ends, 53" x 19½". **$350**

A-NH Mar. 2001   Northeast Auctions

Candlestick, 17th C., brass dome-base, Spanish or Scandinavian, circular spreading foot below conforming mid-drip pan, urn-turned stem, 8½" H. **$1,000**
Burl Bowl, w/ molded rim & mid-band, 15" diam., 6½" H. **$1,300**
Drop-leaf Table, New England, Q.A., maple w/ scrubbed surface, shaped apron, cabriole legs on pad feet, top 15" x 42", 28" H. **$4,500**

A-OH Nov. 2001   Garth's Auctions, Inc.

Early Hutch Table, w/ old dry red surface, pine w/visible handplane marks. Cyma curved cut-outs on ends, three-board top w/ old pegs that hold the base to top, 62½" W, 35" D, 30½" H. **$2,970**
Treenware, 2 pcs., poplar charger 11½" diam., & plate w/ turned foot, 7" diam. **$220**
Burl Bowl, w/ old dry scrubbed surface, 15½" W, 5¼" D. **$605**
Folk Art Eagle, sgn. by Daniel Strausser, ca. 1980, 11½" H, contemporary. **$220**
Decorated Box, pine w/ orig. dec., incl. houses & trees, peg const., 13¼" W, 8½" D, 6½" H. **$412**

A-NH Mar. 2001   Northeast Auctions

Burl Bowl, oval w/ raised cut-out handles, 13¼" L. **$800**
Tea Table, New England Q.A., painted blue, rect. top above base w/ apron joining turned legs on pad feet, top 21½" x 25", 27" H. **$6,750**
Armchair, New England Q.A., maple Spanish foot, oxbow crest & vase splat above rush seat on block & vase turned frontal legs, bulbous stretcher. **$4,250**
Hooked Rug, Clamshell design, red, blue gr. & grey within bl. border, 34" x 55". **$950**

A-NH Aug. 2001   Northeast Auctions
English Table Globes labeled Edward Stanford Geographical Publisher, London. The celestial globe sgn. Malby's. Each w/ brass circumference ring & fitted on stands, 18" H. **$9,000**

A-NH May, 2001   Northeast Auctions

Wall Boxes, the first a double candlebox in red wash, 20" H.; the second w/ sliding lid, pair **$800**

Quilt, Am., pieced & appliquéd w/ 20 blocks of stylized flower baskets in red w/ navy & green calico fabrics within a red grid & border. **$900**

Needlework Picture, early Am. w/ basket of flowers flanked by peacocks, 11" x 10" frame size. **$700**

Memorial Picture, early Am., watercolor w/ lady watering flowers, 18½" x 15½" frame size. **$1,000**

Two New England Banister-Back Chairs, the first a Portsmouth armchair in Spanish brown w/ cupid's bow crest above five split banisters, the second a side chair w/ yoked crest & paintbrush feet (not illus.) **$1,500**

Butter Stamps w/ carved American eagle, 4½" diam., pair **$600**

English Whieldon Tortoise Shell Plates, three, octagonal, 8¼", including a pair w/ green highlights (not illus.) **$700**

Salt Glaze Pierced-Edge Deep Plates, four 9" diam., & two 8" examples. **$1,400**

Tavern Table, New England, William & Mary w/ black paint, w/ rectangular breadboard top above a base w/ drawer, vase-turned legs joined by a box stretcher, top 37½" x 22", 26½" H. **$1,500**

Wagon Seat, double chairback ladderback of small size, 34" L. **$600**

Sackback Writing Arm Windsor Chair, Am. in black paint. **$1,000**

Brass Andirons, NY, Chippendale, 17" H. **$300**

Chippendale Andirons, Am. each w/ an urn top above tapered post & plinth on cabriole legs w/ ball & claw feet, 21" H. **$500**

Q.A. Miniature Yoke Back Armchair, Hudson River Valley, 14" H. **$8,000**

English Salt-Glaze Chargers, pair, 16" diam. **$1,500**

Q.A. Brass Andirons, w/ lemon top, cabriole legs & penny feet, 12½" H. **$300**

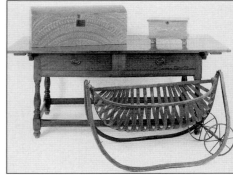

A-PA Nov.-Dec. 2001   Pook & Pook, Inc.

Tavern Table, PA, walnut, ca. 1780, rect. batten top over 2 drawers, block & baluster turned legs w/ ball feet, joined by stretchers, 73" L. 32½" W, 30" H. **$3,250**

Dome Lid Box, PA, painted, ca. 1840, w/ overall yel. sponge dec. on a vibrant red ground, 32¾" W, 13½" H. **$4,000**

Mini Blanket Chest, New England, painted pine, ca. 1830 w/ rect. molded top, molded base & turned feet, retaining overall ochre grain dec., 13¼" W, 9" H. **$600**

Cradle, painted boat shaped, dated 1876, stave const., swinging on frame w/ 2 wheels, retains orig. blue painted surface & salmon striping, Oct. 17th '76, 42" L, 24" H. **$950**

A-SC Sept. 2001   Charlton Hall Galleries, Inc.

Tea Caddy, MOP, Eng., ca. 1850, hinged lid opening to lidded compartment, ivory bun feet, 4" H, 5½" W, 3½" D. **$475**

A-OH Jan. 2001   Garth's Auctions, Inc.

Pewter Teapots, two, both unmkd. four ball feet & blk. painted wooden handle & repl. finial, damage & wear, 7" H. One w/ scrolled handle, polished w/ reprs., lt. pitting, 8½" H. **$165**

Pewter Measures, set of seven Euro. "Centilitre" to "Litre", some wear, 1⅝" to 7¼" H. **$220**

A-OH Feb. 2001   Garth's Auctions, Inc.

Dry Sink, poplar scraped to orig. putty-white color, bracket feet w/ arched aprons, one nailed drawer, well w/ zinc liner, chips, 48¼" W, 18¾" D, 32" H. **$1,375**

Stoneware Pitcher & Bowl, assembled set w/ variation in color, blue sponge dec. w/ stripe, pitcher glue repr., bowl is worn on rim & chip, 12" H, bowl 15" diam. **$275**

Figural Sprinkler, cast iron, wood duck w/ yel., ora. & gr. paint, wear but very good detail. **$660**

Spice Cabinet, poplar & oak w/ gr. paint, lt. staining, inset turnings around pulls, scalloped arched crest, two pulls repl., 18" H. **$357**

Six Textiles, blk. & white plaid, two lg. mattress covers, machine stitched, 42" x 67" & four lg. pillow covers 27" x 28", 28" x 55", 26" x 30", 28" x 30", minor stains. **$110**

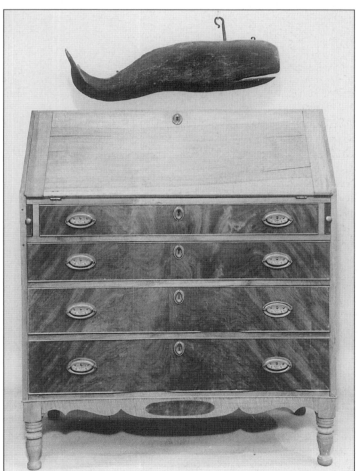

A-OH Apr. 2001   Garth's Auctions, Inc.

Sheraton Slant Lid Desk, ref. birch & cherry, flame veneer & pine secondary wood, tiger maple front w/ oval mahogany medallion inlay, 4 dov. drawers w/ applied beading & orig. oval thistle brasses w/ figured mahogany veneering, 8 int. dov. drawers w/ brass knobs & 10 pigeon holes, 7 have scalloped tops, dov. case, int. candle burns at back of the writing surface, age splits, lid hinges repl., chips & rest. to beading, 39½" W, 47" H. **$1,320**

Folk Art Trade Sign, carved whale, w/ old dry red paint over an earlier white, sq. head nail eyes & wrought iron hangers, dk. stain to touch-up wear around mouth, possible tail rest., 30" L. **$935**

A-OH Feb. 2001   Garth's Auctions, Inc.

Hepplewhite Chest, 19th C., cherry & tiger maple w/ inlay, minor restor. & repl. hardware. Case 41¾" W, 62¾" H. **$4,400**

Stoneware Crock, w/ cobalt blue decor., mkd. N.G. Hornell, Newport, Ohio. Small repr. to base, 15" H. **$550**

MISCELLANEOUS

A-IA May 2001　　　Jackson's International
Auctioneers

Top Row

American Electric Wall Phone, oak case, orig. condition w/ cantilevered mouth piece, 32" H. **$345**

Kellogg Wall Phone, oak case, orig. condition, 25" H. **$259**

Wall Phone, walnut case, 39" H. **$287**

French Candlestick Phone, ca. 1933, 11" H. **$69**

Second Row

Kellogg Candlestick Phone, 11" H. **$126**

Wall Phone, oak, 32" H. **$230**

Wall Phone, oak, 21" H. **$115**

Wall Phone, central oak, 28" H. **$184**

Third Row

Western Electric Cradle Phone, 9" L. **$57**

Kellogg Candlestick Phone, 11" H. **$138**

Brass Candlestick Phone, nickel plate finish, 11" H. **$69**

A-VA Sept. 2000 Green Valley Auctions, Inc.

Westward Ho

Covered Compote, 7" diam., 10½" H **$175**

Covered Compote, 6" diam., 9½" H **$110**

Covered Compote, oval, 5½" x 8¾", 11½" H **$175**

A-PA Oct. 2001　　　Conestoga Auction
Company

Baskets

Row 1

Splint Work Basket, 16" H, 15" diam. **$82**

Splint Basket, w/ diamond re-enforced handle, red & blue dyed design, 10½" H, 17" L. **$341**

Splint Oval Basket, 6" H, 7" L. **$385**

Row 2

Splint Round Basket, small, 4" H, 5½" diam. **$176**

Splint Oval Basket, small 4" H, 5¼" L. **$264**

Splint Miniature Basket, tightly woven, sgn. and dated July 22, 1917, 2½" H, 3" diam. **$1,650**

Splint Basket, oval w/ red dyed band decor., 6" H, 8" L. **$385**

A-MA Feb. 2001   Skinner, Inc.

Double Sided Gameboard, Am., 19th C, w/ deep blue-green & red & black backgammon & checkers surfaces, 14¼ x 15¼". $2,530
Comb-Back Windsor Armchair, New England, ca. 1810, bamboo turnings, 46½" H. $4,025
Pine Paneled Wall Cupboard, New England, late 18th C., w/ old blue paint, minor imper., 33" W, 75½" H. $24,150

A-NH Nov. 2001   Northeast Auctions

Stoneware Crock, w/ cobalt blue glaze, 3 gal., 14½" H. $100
Q.A. Tea Table, country, New England pine & figured maple, 25½" H, top 25" x 38". $7,000
Q.A. Armchair, Quebec transitional, maple & birch, 41¼" H. $4,000

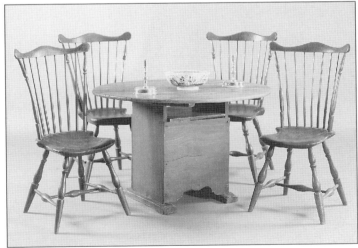

A-NH May 2001   Northeast Auctions

Windsor Fan-Back Chairs, set of five (four illus.) $4,500
Hutch-Table, New England, w/ shoe feet, pivoting top, 41" diam., 26¼" H. $6,250
Candlesticks, English brass w/ dome bases, 8" H. $2,250
Liverpool Delft Punch Bowl, blue & white w/ polychrome landscape decor. 10½" diam. $950

A-NH Nov. 2001   Northeast Auctions

Delft Jars, Dutch, blue & white w/ ribbed bodies, 14½" H. $3,800
KAS, Chippendale, walnut , VA, 82" H, 76" W, 23½" D. $28,000

A-NH May 2001   Northeast Auctions

Windsor Armchairs, two similar sackbacks. **$1,100**
Candlesticks, brass, pair of Eng. Q.A., 6½″ H. **$650**
Firebucket, MA, leather, decor. & dated 1838, 12½″ H. **$1,100**
Desk on Frame, NY, Wm. & Mary, pine w/ ball feet, 34″ H, 25″ W. **$2,800**
Candlesticks, brass, pair, Q.A., 8″ H. **$1,100**
Tavern Table, New England, pine w/ red paint, top 24¼ x 32½″. **$2,000**
Windsor Armchairs, sackback, three, w/ black paint, two illus. **$2,200**

A-PA Feb. 2001   Pook & Pook, Inc.

Tall Case Clock, Chippendale, PA., walnut, ca. 1770, 8-day brass movement, boss engraved "B. Chandlee, Nottingham", 97″ H. **$16,000**
Portrait, Am., oil on canvas, 19th C., two brothers, PA, 36″ x 28½″. **$600**
Chest of Drawers, PA, Chippendale, walnut, ca. 1770, 32½″ H, 33″ W. **$16,000**
Mantel Clock, PA, mahogany pillar & scroll, ca. 1810, dial inscrib. John Scharf, Selinsgrove, PA, 27½″ H. **$6,500**
Chinese Export Blue & White Garnitures, 11½″ H, & 6 pcs. not illus. **$1200**

A-PA Feb. 2001   Pook & Pook, Inc.

Dutch Cupboard, PA, 2-pc., ca. 1815, cherrry w/ 2 candle drawers, 82½″ H, 54½″ W. **$7,300**
Gaudy Welch Tea Service, ca. 1820, Sahara patt., w/ teapot, sugar, cream pitcher, waste bowl, 2 cake plates & 12 cups & saucers. **$1,400**
Stoneware Crock by Haxstun Ottman & Co., Fort Edwards, NY, w/ blue decor., 13″ H. **$300**
Stoneware Jug, early 19th C., inscrib. "Vinegar 3g", 16″ H, losses. **$375**
Theorem, water color on paper of basket of fruit & bird, sign. "D. Ellinger", 5¾″ x 7¼″. **$900**

A-PA Feb. 2001   Pook & Pook, Inc.

Pole Screen, George III, mahogany, late 18th C., w/ round shirred needlework & bead work, 18½" D, 56½" H. **$700**

Q.A. Tea Table, PA, ca. 1760, w/ circular dished rim top on a birdcage support, 29¼" H, 36" D, battens added to underside top. **$1,200**

Pole Screen, Chippendale, mahogany, ca. 1780, w/ rectangular needlework coat of arms, over orig. silk screen, 51½" H, 7" W. **$1,100**

A-P June 2001   Pook & Pook, Inc.

Quilt, PA, appliqué, four block Princess Feather patt. blue, red & mustard on quilted ivory ground. **$1,300**

Dry Sink, PA, grain painted, mid 19th C., 35" H, 60" W, 19" D. **$2,200**

Stoneware Jar, Remmey, ca. 1860 w/ cobalt blue decor, stamped "RCR.Phila", 8¾" H. **$375**

Stoneware Two-Handled Crock, Remmey, ca. 1840 w/ cobalt leaf decor., stamped "RCR, Phila.", 9½" H. **$550**

Stoneware Pitcher, PA, ca. 1830 w/ cobalt blue decor., 9" H. **$800**

Stoneware Crock, Remmey, ca. 1840, w/ cobalt blue decor. stamped "RCR, Phila", 9¾" H. **$550**

Trencher, N. Eng, maple painted red (backside), early 19th C., 7" H, 28" L, 16¾" W. **$1,500**

Redware Storage Jar, 2-handled, ca. 1820 w/ manganese splash decor., 9½" H. **$450**

Redware Flowerpot w/ mustard swirl decor. **$260**

A-PA June 2001   Pook & Pook, Inc.

Mirror, New England, ca. 1830, w/ decor. half column, églomisé panel & stencil corner blocks, 27" H, 14¼" W. **$2,900**

Bellows, Am. Federal, painted, ca. 1820, w/ yellow house inside a heart, vine decor. & spread winged eagle, 19½" long, leather restored. **$1,200**

Child's Desk, Wm. & Mary, maple, ca. 1740 w/ fitted interior, restoration, 22½" x 18½". **$3,200**

Courting Mirror, New England, Queen Anne, walnut veneered, ca. 1740, 12¾" x 7½". **$1,400**

Highchair, New England, ca. 1760, w/ rush seat, retains orig. red painted surface, 30½" H. **$850**

Hearth Broom, ca. 1820, w/ red & black rings on cream ground, 27" L. **$100**

Q.A. Table, New England, maple, ca. 1760, retains old finish, top repl., 26¾" H. **$1,900**

Pole Screen, mahogany, ca. 1790 w/ oval needlework, 59½" H. **$1,100**

A-NH Aug. 2001   Northeast Auctions

Pine Hooded Cradle, RI, dovetail const., 47" L. **$1,000**

A-NH Aug. 2001   Northeast Auctions

William & Mary Tuckaway Table, Boston, walnut base w/ an asso. 18th C. oval maple top, 32" x 24", 24" H. **$8,000**
Candlesticks, two capstan that are similar, brass, 6" H. **$1,100**
Squat Bottles, blown dark-green squat, one illus. tallest 7½" H, **$1,750**

A-PA June 2001   Pook & Pook, Inc.

Q.A. Chest of Drawers, Chester Co., PA, walnut, ca. 1770, feet restored, 53½" H, 39" W. **$5,500**
Chippendale Miniature Blanket Chest, VA, cherry, ca. 1775 w/ till. Dovetailed case rests on ogee bracket feet, 9½" H, 12" W. **$10,000**
Chippendale Miniature Blanket Chest, PA, cherry, ca. 1775 w/ till. Dovetailed case rests on ogee bracket feet, 11¼" H, 17¼" W. **$2,700**
Bible Box, Chester Co. PA, walnut, dovetailed case, ball feet, repairs, 8½" H, 19½" W. **$2,800**

A-NH Aug. 2001   Northeast Auctions

Bedstead, Sheraton, MA, birch, rope bed, 84½" H, 78½" L, 54" W. **$2,000**

A-NH May 2001   Northeast Auctions

Q. A. Side Chairs, New England, four, maple, each w/ oxbow crest rail. **$2,250**
Whale Oil Lanterns, two, tallest 17". **$200**
Burl Wood Bowl, early Am., 16¼" diam. **$1,200**
Hutch Table, New England, birch w/ pivoting top & drawer, 28" H, 47" diam. **$1,250**
Onion Lanterns, three, Am. tin & glass, tallest 11" H. **$800**
Lanterns, tin, 2 circular w/ mica panels, tallest 18" H. **$700**
Candle Lanterns, four, early Am., hexagonal, tallest 16" H. **$1,000**

A-PA Feb. 2001   Pook & Pook, Inc.

Child's Windsor Side Chair, PA, ca. 1810 w/ saddle seat, bamboo turnings, retains old varnish surface, 21½" H. **$600**
Stand Table, Hepplewhite, PA, tiger maple, ca. 1800., restored, 27" H. **$1,000**

A-NH Aug. 2001   Northeast Auctions

Brass Candlesticks, English, mid-drip matched pair, 7½" H. **$7,500**
Punch Strainer, New England carved applewood, concave pierced bowl continuing to tapering ends, 15-1/4" L. **$2,100**
Delft Punch Bowl, English, blue & white w/ floral decor., 8" H, 13½" D. **$7,500**
Silver Punch Ladle w/ shell-form bowl & turned handle, 13½" L. **$500**

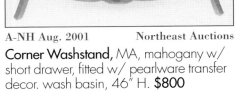

A-NH Aug. 2001   Northeast Auctions

Corner Washstand, MA, mahogany w/ short drawer, fitted w/ pearlware transfer decor. wash basin, 46" H. **$800**

A-OH Jan. 2001   Garth's Auctions, Inc.

Slant Lid Desk, ref. tiger maple w/ good figure & pine secondary wood, dov. case, turned feet threaded into case, dov. drawers have incised beading w/ repl. brass bale pulls & 7 dov. drawers are fitted into int. & have brass pulls. Molding along base is an old repl. & one loose foot, 37½" W, 40" H. **$3,850**

Pewter Teapot, Am., two line "Boardman & Hart, N. York, no. 5" mark, scrolled handle & domed lid w/ wafer finial, minor dents, 7½" H. **$357**

Pewter Baptismal Bowl, footed, "Roswell Gleason" touch, MA, ca. 1822-1871, bowl is 8⅛" diam., 5" H. **$1,265**

Pewter Teapot, "A. Porter" touch mark, ME, ca. 1830-1840, restor. on base & lid, 7¼" H. **$330**

Pewter Charger, early touch marks for John Danforth, Norwich, CT, ca. 1773-1795, scratches & minor dents, 12⅛" diam. **$1,265**

A-Feb. 2001   Skinner, Inc.

Pictorial Hooked Rug, Am. ca. 1900 w/ pair of blue horses & tree in abstract landscape, 43" W, 31" H. **$2,990**

Bow-Back Windsor Side Chairs, pr., New England, late 18th C., w/ old red over green paint, imper., 38" H. **$6,325**

Windsor Footstools (or Crickets), pr., New England, mid. 19th C., orig. dark red surface, imper., 8½" H **$6,900**

Painted Fireboard, ca. 1840, w/ square shadowbox frame and central portrait of large chained dog & small seated man w/ hat at base of post, old surface, losses, 31½" W, 18" D, 32" H. **$4,600**

A-OH Jan. 2001   Garth's Auctions, Inc.

Chippendale High Chest, ref. maple & pine secondary w/ high bracket feet & molded base, dov. drawers w/ beaded trim, repl. batwing brasses & lock escut., stepped & molded cornice, restor., 35¼" W, 47½" H. **$1,540**

Treen Jar, covered, varnished fin. w/ traces of old paint dec., turned foot & rim w/ slightly domed lid, minor chips, 6" diam., 5" H. **$137**

Tin Lantern, w/ cobalt globe, base has removable font, globe blown w/ rolled edges, bale handle, punched designs w/ sm. chips along edge top, brass burner repl., 10½" H. **$577**

Bowl, bird's eye maple, turned w/ mellow varnished finish, thin raised lip rim, sm. hole drilled for hanging, 15" diam., 4" H. **$220**

MISCELLANEOUS

A-PA Sept. 2001   Pook & Pook Inc.

Pembroke Table, New England, ca. 1805, Federal, figured maple, w/ scalloped drop leaves, 27½" H, 33" W. **$4,500**

Q.A. Side Chair, Boston, MA., ca. 1760, slip seat. **$6,500**

Candlestand, New England, Federal, ca. 1800, 26" H, 16½" W. **$1,600**

Canton Soup Tureen, ca. 1800, blue & white w/ boar's head handles. **$1,200**

Canton Scalloped Serving Dish, early 19th C., 10½" L, w/ 3 small creamers not illus., all blue & white. **$350**

Rectangular Canton Platter, blue & white, early 19th C., 16¼" L. **$400**

Canton Sauce Tureen, 6½" L, together w/ blue & white export bowl, 8" diam. **$425**

Canton Water Pitcher, early 19th C., 8½" H. **$1,900**

Northeast Auctions

A-NH Aug. 2001

Tin Shoe & Architectural Bracket, 11¼" H. **$2,200**
Theorem, Am. School, w/ colorful fruit on velvet, 15" x 20¼". **$7,750**
Tin Sconces, each w/ sunburst above rectangular backplate & drip pan. **$1,800**
Windsor Chair painted black w/ carved saddle seat. **$4,500**

Country Console Table, painted black w/ gold line decor., top 16" x 28½", 28½" H. **$1,500**
Tole Basket w/ yellow & black decor. containing approx. 23 pcs. stone fruit. **$3,250**
Country Chippendale Chair, N.H., attrib. to the Dunlap School. **$3,750**
Plow, iron, Am. builder's model, 20" L. **$2,200**

MISCELLANEOUS

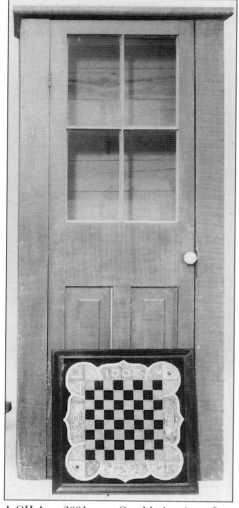

A-OH Apr. 2001   **Garth's Auctions, Inc.**

Chimney Cupboards, pr., dec., poplar w/ pine shelves & ash backboards, orig. dk. red over a lighter red dec., one door w/ two raised panels, four panes of glass, white mullions, white porcelain knobs, surface wear, rest. hinges, ea. has opening at back to accommodate baseboard molding (one illus.). **$2,365**

Fraternal Gameboard, w/ reverse painted dec., bl. & gold metallic sq. bordered by "I.O.O.F." chain links & other symbols, flaking, bl. oak frame, 20½" x 20½". **$330**

A-NH Mar. 2001

Northeast Auctions

Hooked Rug, w/ boat flying Am. flag & red pennant, frame height 15½". **$500**

Two-Masted Fishing Boat Weathervane, first half 20th C., w/ b/w paint, 27" H, 36" L. **$400**

Assorted Wrought Iron Eeling w/ ten other spearing tools, some w/ handles, longest 6' (part illus.) **$400**

Two-Masted Schooner Weathervane w/ rigging, ca. 1930, copper w/ old varnish on yel., 31" H, 40" L. **$1,600**

Diorama w/ "The Puritan," Am. Grand Banks Schooner fitted w/ crew & dories, painted background w/ harbor & lighthouse, 18" x 30". **$2,400**

Diorama w/ three-masted vessel on textured gr. sea, 24" x 30". **$1,600**

Lap-Desk, cedar, brass-bound, fitted w/ lift-out tray & ink bottle, together w/ ephemera incl. an 1865 letter w/ Civil War contents. **$500**

Valuables Box, walnut, dovetailed const. w/ diamond escutcheon, top 8" x 12" **$400**

Diorama, w/ three-masted vessel "Lizzie" flying red pennants w/ gr. case, 18" x 31". **$600**

Hooked Rugs, three w/ marine motifs (one illus.) **$650**

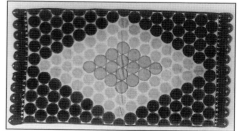

A-OH Apr. 2001   **Garth's Auctions, Inc.**

Child's Sleigh, w/ painted dec., old repaint incl. scrollwork & foliage on red ground, yel. line borders & a blue int., edge wear, 29" W, 13½' D, 18" H. **$385**

A-OH Apr. 2001   **Garth's Auctions, Inc.**

Penny Rug, lg., bl. lt. gr. & br. wool circles on lt. ora. ground, scalloped ends have gr. & pink embroidery, minor holes, 27¾" x 48" **$55**

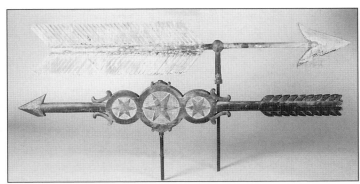

A-MA Feb. 2001   Skinner, Inc.

Weathervanes

Copper Arrow, American, late 19th C., w/ all-over verdigris surface, imper., 9½" H, 56½" L. **$2,530**

Carved & Painted Arrow, American, 19th C., w/ six-pointed stars carved in relief w/ carved scrolls & feathers. Traces of blue/ white & gilt polychrome decor., imper., 19" H, 54" L. **$3,220**

A-Feb. 2001   Skinner, Inc.

Game Boards

Row 1, Left to Right

Double-Sided Board, Am. early 19th C., black, white & green paint, w/ initials, 14" x 11½". **$1,725**

Parcheesi Gameboard, New England, ca. 1870-80 w/ red, green & yellow paint, 17½" square. **$5,750**

Checkerboard, Am., 19th C., w/ red, pink, green, white, yellow & black paint, w/ rose blossoms and leafy stems on border, 15½" x 15¾". **$2,185**

Double-Sidded Board, New England, ca. 1850-70, black & red paint, the obverse w/ checkers, the reverse with Old Mill, applied molded edge, 14¼" square. **$4,887**

American Checkerboard, ca. 1849-50, w/ brown & yellow paint, the obverse w/ checkers, the reverse w/ a caricature of President Zachary Taylor, 14½" square. **$3,105**

A-PA Nov.-Dec. 2001   Pook & Pook, Inc.

Globes, pr. Georgian celestial & terrestrial, ca. 1780, ea. w/ paper covered globes by "Ferguson", spiral fluted & urn carved mahogany pedestals w/ cabriole legs, snake feet, losses, 12" globes, 24" H. **$4,250**

Canterbury, George III, mahogany, ca. 1800, w/ 4 compartments over single drawer, turned feet w/ caster, 19½" W, 19" H. **$350**

Table, Georgian mahogany, ca. 1740 w/ rect. top w/ 2 drop leaves, straight skirt & turned legs, pad feet, 36" L, 28" H. **$600**

A-IA Aug. 2001   Gene Harris Antique Auction Center, Inc.

Slot Machine, Mills five-cent Token Bell. **$1,250**
Slot Machine, Mills ten-cent Token Bell. **$1,100**
Slot Machine, Mills twenty-five-cent Token Bell. **$1,600**

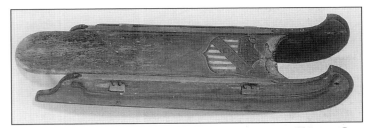

A-MA Feb. 2001   Skinner, Inc.

Pine & Wrought Iron Sled, late 19th C., "Victor" model w/ carved & painted eagle & shield patriotic motif, red painted sides, black painted runners, hand holds & bracing, minor imper., 6½" x 46½" x 13". **$3,450**

A-MA Feb. 2001   Skinner, Inc.

Shorebird Decoys
Left to Right

Black-Bellied Plover w/ black, white & brown paint & glass eyes, NJ, ca. 1890, w/ stand 9" H. **$1,840**

Curlew, decoy by Dan Leeds, Pleasantville, NJ, 1880-1900, w/ brown paint, w/ stand 13" H. **$2,415**

Carved Shore Birds, pr., New England, ca. 1910 w/ brown & white paint, wear, w/ stands 12¼" high. **$1,725**

Carved Wood & Root Egret Decoy, Southern, ca. 1890, root head white w/ black bill, weather surface, w/ stand 13" H. **$3,335**

Shorebird w/ white paint, New England, ca. 1930, w/ stand 10½" L. **$977**

Carved & Painted Peep, ca. 1900, 7" L. **$2,300**

Shorebird, Townsend Inlet, NJ, 20th C, w/ iron bill, paint wear, 9" L. **$1,150**

Root-Head Shore Bird, Eastern shore of MD, ca. 1900, weathered paint, 12" L. **$4,025**

Yellowlegs Decoy, NJ, ca. 1890, painted, 11" L. **$2,185**

A-PA May 2001   Horst Auction Center

Decoys, 20th C.
Row 1, Left to Right

Greater Scaup, female, brown head, mottlled brown body, w/ patch of white at base of blue bill, applied yellow & glass eyes & wings tipped w/ white. 15½" L. **$65**

Shorebird, mkd. W.E.K. on underside, 5½" H. **$20**

Shorebird, mkd. W.E.K. on underside w/ glass eyes, light brown w/ black & white spotting, 7½" H. **$45**

Row 2

Old Squaw Decoys, pair w/ black & white paint, male 14½" L, female, 13½" L. **$60**

Row 3, Left to Right

Redhead w/ yellow & black eyes, blue bill, gray body. 15½" L. **$35**

Canvasback w/ dark red head, black bill, white body, black breast, 15½" L. **$60**

A-NH Aug. 2001   Northeast Auctions

Decoys
First row

Lesser Scaup w/ inset glass eyes & in use wear, 13½" L. **$500**

Elder Drake w/ incised details, 14½" L. **$400**

Golden-Eye Drake w/ glass eyes, 12¼ L. **$300**

Black Mallard w/ glass eyes, 17" L. **$500**

Red-Head attrib. to H. Keyes Chadwick, inscribed on underside in pencil & branded TSH, 14" L. **$1,200**

Second row

Red-Head w/ elaborate painted feathering & glass eyes, 13½" L. **$500**

Black Duck w/ tack eyes & flat head, 16½" L. **$1,100**

Mallard Hen, attrib. to Mark McNair, 18" L. **$6,500**

Preening Red-Breasted Merganser by Mark McNair, 1995, w/ brand on underside, 19" L. **$2,800**

Brant attrib. to Joseph Lincoln, 20" L. **$3,000**

Third row

Redheads, pr., w/ incised details, 14½" L. **$1,100**

Red-Breasted Merganser w/ red glass inset eyes, mkd. "Deke" on underside, 18" L. **$5,000**

Black Duck, attrib. to Mason Factory w/ glass eyes, 16" L. **$500**

Black Duck w/ glass eyes, probably Mason, challenge grade. 16" L. **$500**

Black Duck, hollow, Mason Factory premier grade, weighted & branded L. Minot, 17" L. **$500**

A-Feb. 2001   Skinner, Inc.

Cast Iron Windmill Weights
Rooster, by Elgin Wind Power & Pump Co., early 20th C., w/ raised numbers on tail, painted silver w/ red details, surface imper., 16" x 16½". **$1,495**
"Hummer" Rooster, by Elgin Co., w/ raised lettering on tail, traces of white & red paint, 13¼" x 10". **$863**
"W", weight by Althouse-Wheeler Co., early 20th C., 9" x 16½" on stand. **$978**
Rooster, one of two, attrib. to Elgin Co., w/ white paint, red & yellow details, surface imper., 19½" x 18". **$2,990**

A-Feb. 2001   Skinner, Inc.

Cast Iron Windmill Weights
Squirrel, by Elgin Wind Power & Pump Co., Elgin, IL, early 20th C. w/ brown, gold & green paint, 19½" H. **$3,737**
Rooster, by Elgin Wind Power & Pump Co., late 19th C., w/ painted white body w/ red details, surface imperfections, 18" x 20½". **$5,175**
Horse, one of 3 flat weights by Dempster Mill Manu. Co., Beatrice, NE, early 20th C., one unpainted, one white, and one green, surface imper., 16½" x 17¼". **$1,495**
Bull, flat weight, early 20th C., painted red w/ white highlights, surface imper. 18¼" x 24". **$863**

A-MA Oct. 2001   Skinner, Inc.

Checkerboard, painted wood, Am., late 19th-early 20th C., applied molded frame, bl. & natural squares, yel., red, & gr. linear dec., minor wear, 8¼" x 23¾". **$1,380**
Checkerboard, painted oak, Am., 19th C., bl. & gilt sq. outline in red w/ yel. & bl. border, joinery separation, wear, 18⅞" x 18¼". **$1,610**

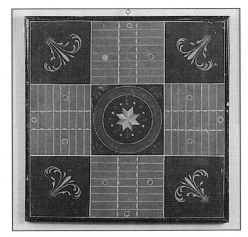

A-MA Oct. 2001   Skinner, Inc.

Parcheesi/Checkerboard, polychrome painted, fourth qtr. 19th C., centered w/ eight pointed star, scrolled foliate motifs, linear border dec. on checkerboard, applied frame, 23¾" x 24¾". **$4,025**

Framed Theorem, on velvet, contemporary by "Ellinger", still life w/ colorful fruit in blue compote, comb dec. frame w/ raised corner blocks, 21" x 17½". **$2,310**

Folk Art Carved Frame, cherry w/ old finish, carved relief of eagle, "U.S." within star & acorns on one side, incised geometric line detail, opening 11⅛" x 8½", overall 22" x 19¼". **$770**

Windsor Side Chair, branded signature "J. Appleton", old dry red paint w/ evidence of later colors, splayed bamboo base w/ shield seat, pierced & scalloped crest, front rung old repl., 34¼" H. **$275**

Stand, decorated one drawer, attributed to Schoraie County N.Y., orig. dk. red paint w/ stenciled leaves & flowers in gold & copper paint, traces of gesso on base, bold turned legs w/ dovetailed drawer w/ brass pulls, one-board top, leg restrored. 21¼" W, 30" H. **$495**

Small Box, w/ leather covering & brass tack dec., pine w/ blue & white wallpaper lining, w/ brass pull on lid, wear, 6" W, 4" D, 3½" H. **$110**

Hanging Wall Box, pine, 19th C., lid restored, 15" W, 23" H. **$800**

Half-Column Frame, PA, 19th C., w/ yellow & orange grained decoration enclosing a printed birth & baptismal record by G.S. Peters, 19½" x 17¼". **$2,600**

Trade Sign, New England, made from saw, inscribed "Arkwrights Timber". **$300**

Painted Dower Chest, PA, ca. 1800, lid w/ traces of 2 panels flanking a star above a case decoration w/ two light blue panels w/ red & white arched border, small central arched panel w/ red bird, bracket feet. Sides w/ red, white & blue stars, orig. tulip form wrought iron strap hinges, 48" W, 23¼" H. **$8,000**

Windsor Bowback Armchair, MA, late 18th C., w/ brass plaque inscribed "property of Philip Freeman…in 1775…", minor loss, repairs. **$475**

Stoneware Crock, four-gal., marked "Cowden & Wilcox, Harrisburg" w/ blue floral decoration, hairline crack, 14½" H. **$1,300**

Parade Axe, New England, pine, 43½" L. **$450**

Federal Sewing Table, mahogany & mahogany veneer w/ pine secondary & old ref., dov. drawers w/ leather covered writing surface top, veneer repairs, 28½" H., 23" W. **$2,475**

Battersea Candlesticks, pr., blue enameling on copper w/ white panels, floral detail, matching bobeches have chips, sm. flake, 9" H. **$2,530**

Tea Caddy, mahogany veneer over pine w/ old finish, brass ball feet, divided int. is missing lids, liner worn, 7½" W, 5½" H. **$715**

A-MA Oct. 2001   Skinner, Inc.

Wooden Shoes & Snuff Boxes, 24 assorted, Am., Eng., Euro., 18th & 19th C., incl. bl. lacquered pair w/ silver metal inlay, one w/ sliding carved whalebone cover, one copper, several studded w/ copper or bronze inlay, 2½" - 6¾" L., ½" - 6" H. **$2,645**

A-MA Oct. 2001   Skinner, Inc.

Doctor's Box, paint dec., ME, 19th C., w/ copper and brass trim, rope handles, painted gr. w/ red & white eagle, flag & shield motifs, white lettering, opens to compartments w/ walnut flame veneered hinged door, wear, 14" W, 15" H. **$1,092**

A-PA May 2001   Horst Auctioneers

Coverlet, sgn., "Peter Leisey, Cocalico Twp., Lancaster Co., Penna", wool & linen, w/ center seam, 76" W, 96" L (ex. fringe), very minor staining. **$2,200**

Redware

Row 1

Bowl, 19th C., w/ slip decor., ear shaped handles, some glaze wear & loss of slip decor., 15" diam., 5½" H. **$825**

Jug, late 18th C. w/ overall lead & manganese glaze resulting in a dark brown ground, glaze wear & chip on base, 15" H. **$450**

Charger, early 19th C. orange ground decorated w/ yellow slip, coggle rim, 13½" diam., 5¼" H, chips & nicks. **$900**

Row 2

Pie Plate, 19th C., w/ orange ground & yellow slip decor, 7½" diam. **$600**

Plate, 19th C., w/ orange-brown ground & yellow slip decor., chips & nicks round rim, 9" diam. **$850**

Plate, 19th C., w/ orange-brown ground & yellow slip decor., 9½" diam. **$775**

Pitcher, early 20th C., by Jacob Medinger, Montgomery Co., PA, w/ orange ground w/ trace of green splotches, sgn. "Medinger", 6½" H. **$1,450**

Blanket Chest, early 19th C., painted red w/ black trim. **$400**

A-OH Aug. 2001   Garth's Auctions, Inc.

Pie Safe, hanging w/ punched tins on both sides, pine case has thin red wash, white porcelain pull on door, two int. shelves, edge damage to tins, mortised const., 31" W, 31" H. **$990**

Grease Lamp, wrought & cast iron, circular font w/ a rooster finial, bale top w/ long hanger and brass ring, old dk. pitted surface, 23" H. **$440**

A-NC July 2001   Robert S. Brunk Auction Services, Inc.

Pima Basket, woven as hat, shades of blk./br. on straw-colored fields, 3¼" x 12½" x 11½". **$1,600**

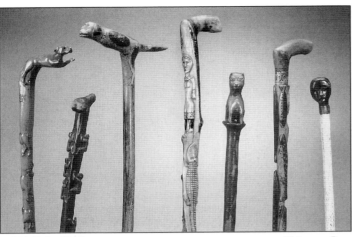

A-MA Feb. 2001   Skinner, Inc.

Carved Wooden Canes

Left to Right

Pennsylvania German, 19th/ early 20 C., handle in form of full bodied leaping dog on tapering shaft w. carved animals, chicken, goose & duck. 36½" L. **$805**

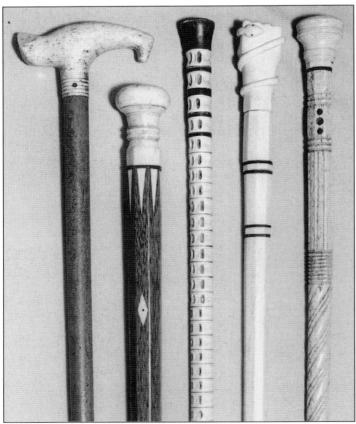

A-OH Jan. 2001   Garth's Auctions, Inc.

Cane, whale bone w/ ring, reeded & twised carved detail, turned ivory knob, blk. baleen inlaid dots & ring, drilled hole, 35" L. **$2,200**

Cane, whale bone w/ carved ivory handle in the form of a hand holding a snake, inlaid rings of blk. paper like material, minor wear, 37½" L. **$1,760**

Cane, made from fish vertebrae w/ knob & inlaid rings of baleen or horn, sm. chip on knob, 34" L. **$137**

Canes, 2, wood w/ turned ivory knob & dart & diamond inlay, age cracks, 35½" L, cane w/ bone handle, chipped 31" L. **$935**

Carved & Painted Wood w/ dog's head knob handle-shaft decor. w/ four-legged creature & snake in high relief, old paint, wear, 32½" L. **$575**

Hound Cane, VT, 19th C., w/ spotted dog form handle, orig. paint, cracking, wear. 35½" L. **$546**

Carved Applewood Figural Cane, Southern U.S., early 20th C., bark covered shaft w/ carvings of a woman, squirrel and animals highlighted w/ glass eyes, green & black coloring, 37" L. **$1,150**

Figural Cane, PA, 19th C., handle carved in form of full-bodied seated male dog on tapering shaft, 34½" L. **$920**

Figural Cane, dated 1900, probably MI, handle on tapering shaft decor. w/ polychrome trout & bait in high relief, 35½" L. **$2,185**

Carved Figural Cane, New England, ca. 1820-40, knob handle of ebonized wood in form of woman's head joined by copper riveted brass cuff tapering to narwhale bone shaft, wear, minor loss to nose, 34½" L. **$2,185**

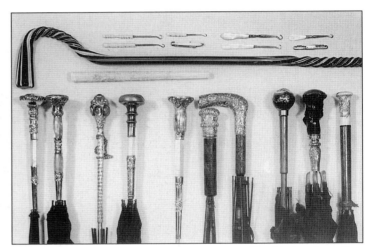

A-OH Mar. 2001   Garth's Auctions, Inc.

First Row

13 Button Hooks, 2 Pen Knives, 2, all w/ MOP handles, some rust, 2⅛" to 4¾" L. **$110**

14 Button Hooks, 1 Pen Knife Button Hook, all w/ bone or ivory handles, some rust, 2¼" to 4¼" L. **$27**

Cane, glass, deep amber w/ white threading, four sided w/ twist detail at handle & end, end broken off, 35" L. **$55**

Umbrella Handle, carved oriental ivory, fair scene w/ musicians & people wearing masks, artist sig., "53" carved in sm. end, age cracks, 9½" L. **$92**

Second Row

Umbrellas, 2 w/ ornate handles, both gold colored w/ embossing & set w/ either abalone or MOP, both mono., MOP set has no cloth covering, 36"L & 37" L. **$137**

Umbrellas, 2 w/ ornate handles, white metal w/ raised roses & set w/ MOP, some battering 36" L, & a silver colored cane w/ stem & knob set w/ lt. purple glass, ribs only 32¼" L. **$55**

Umbrellas, 3 w/ ornate handles, one emb. gold colored & set w/ MOP, minor dents, 12½" L. Two carved wood w/ dk. stain & gold colored knobs, battering & one has hole, ribs only, 35" L. & 37" L. **$137**

Umbrellas, 3 w/ ornate handles, emb. gold colored metal & burl, 32" L. Porcelain knob, burgundy w/ gilding, & handpainted cherubs w/ flowers, 34½" L, & an ivory cane w/ carved roses, wear & cloth is in tatters, 36½" L. **$165**

A-OH Apr. 2001 Garth's Auctions, Inc.

First Row

Creamer, sm. white clay w/ dk. br. shiny glaze, applied animal face under spout, sm. flakes on spout & base, 2⅝" H. **$100**

Lamps, three wrought iron, two betty lamps, one missing lid but has hanger & chain w/ wick pick, 5" H., larger has old black paint, hanger but pick is missing, paint wear, 4⅞" H. Double crusie lamp stamped "JB", hanger w/ twisted detail, may be later addition, lt. rust, 5⅞" H. **$302**

Buckets, two mini., turned wood, lg. w/ alligatored dk. yel. paint w/ bl. stripes, sm. has varnished finish w/ bl. stripes, wood & wire bale handles, both have wear, 2⅞" diam. 2⅜" H., 2⅝" diam. 2" H. **$220**

Second Row

Pottery Grease Lamp, overall Albany glaze, saucer base, applied strap handle & two small spouts on round open font, 4⅞" diam., 5¼" H. **$1,870**

Pincushion, lg. strawberry, red fabric w/ gr. & br. shaded velvet top, velvet has minor wear, 5½" L. **$82**

Wooden Bowl w/ double horse head, incised eyes & carved ear, mouths, & forelocks, wear from use, some edge damage & scorch marks, good color, 6¼" W, 2½" D, 4" H. **$440**

Shaker Bentwood Boxes, two w/ finger const. w/ two on base & single on lid, copper tacks, one has lt. varnish finish w/ traces of mustard paint, 5⅜" W, 3⅜" diam., 2" H. & other has natural finish, split on end, 5¼" W, 3¼" diam., 2" H. **$385**

Wax Figural Valentine, in glass dome, attrib. to PA Dutch, long, br. haired woman in blue trimmed dress holding flowers, surrounded by gold foil paper & cloth flowers, orig. cardboard base is worn w/ added bl. velvet, 3½" W, 7½" H. **$220**

A-OH Apr. 2001 Garth's Auctions, Inc.

First Row

Bentwood Box, oval, prob. by C. Hersey, MA, single finger const., old gr. paint w/ traces of earlier gr., 5¾" W, 4¼" D, 2³⁄₁₆" H. **$467**

Shaker Bentwood Box, oval, finger const. & copper tacks w/ two fingers on base & one on lid, reddish stain, 7½" W, 5⅓" D, 2½" H. **$302**

Bentwood Box, oval, single finger const. on base & lid, copper tacks, old varnish, minor wear & few old splits in lid, 5½" W, 4⅛" D, 2⅛" H. **$110**

Shaker Bentwood Box, oval, finger const. w/ two on base & one on lid, brass tacks, old dark green (black) repaint over traces of earlier green, minor wear, 6⅛" W, 4" D, 2" H. **$687**

Second Row

Shaker Bentwood Box, oval, finger const. w/ two on base & single on lid, copper tacks, natural patina, wear, minor edge damage, 7¼" W, 4⅝" D, 2⅞" H. **$110**

Shaker Bentwood Box, oval, finger const. w/ two on base & single on lid, copper tacks, old gr. repaint, wear, 5½" W, 3½" D, 2⅛" H. **$852**

Shaker Bentwood Box, oval, finger const., two on base & single on lid, copper tacks, old blue paint, wear, 9½" W, 7" D, 3¾" H. **$1,485**

Shaker Bentwood Box, oval, finger const. w/ two on base & single on lid, copper tacks, lid has cherry stain, rim & base has varnish w/ a yel. tinge, 4½" W, 3⅛" D, 1⅝" H. **$110**

Shaker Bentwood Box, oval, finger const. w/ two on base & single on lid, copper tacks, natural finish, oval ghost image on lid, 7¼" W, 4¾" D, 2⅞" H. **$137**

Shaker Bentwood Box, oval, similar to above w/ darker finish, lid has faint ghost image, 6" W, 3⅞" D, 2½" H. **$165**

A-NH Aug. 2001 Northeast Auctions

Agateware Seated Cat, English, w/ brown on cream ground w/ blue highlights, 5" H. **$2,400**

A-NH Aug. 2001   Northeast Auctions

Tea Caddies, fruitwood pear & apple, tallest 6". **$6,500**
Tea Caddy, miniature mahogany box in form of chest, lift top, 11" H. **$1,900**
Chippendale Tea Caddy, mahogany w/ bracket feet, 7¼" L. **$100**
Classical Tea Caddy in form of sideboard, mahogany, 8" L, 14" H. **$2,500**
Box, decor. w/ floral panels & striped ends, 12" L. **$500**
Tea Caddy, fruitwood pear-form, w/ lock & key, 6½" H. **$3,250**

A-PA Feb. 2001   Pook & Pook, Inc.

Gaming Table, George III, mahogany ca. 1760, w/ open fretwork brackets, lift top, 28¾" H, 34½" W. **$2,500**
Reverse Paintings, two French portraits of women, 12¾" x 9¼". **$1,200**
Chinese Export Canton Platter, blue & white, 19th C., 18¼" L. **$375**
Tea Caddy, English, rosewood, ca. 1810, fitted interior, 7" H, 12¼" W. **$300**

A-NH Nov. 2001   Northeast Auctions

Courting Mirror in original box, Continental w/ mirror plate surrounded by painted floral decor., overall 17¼" x 13". **$850**
Stepback Cupboard, MA, pine, 78" H, 64" L, 18" D. **$13,000**
Chinese Export Canton, assembled set of 25 assorted pieces. **$3,000**
Colonial Revival Brewster-Style Armchair w/ carving, 45" H. **$800**
Child's Oak Armchair, English Jacobean w/ carving, 35" H. **$2,000**
Joint Stool, English w/ black painted surface, William & Mary style, 20" H. **$1,700**
Armchair, Pilgrim-century w/ four slats & sausage turnings, black paint. **$1,100**

A-OH Jan. 2001   Garth's Auctions, Inc.

Sheraton Sewing Stand, mahogany & mahogany flame veneer, poplar & butternut secondary wood, dov. drawers have old embossed brass pulls, divided int., minor veneer damage w/ reprs., 17½" W, 28½" H. **$1,760**
Nantucket Basket, swing handle w/ lid, natural finish w/ tapering oval sides & wooden panel base, w/ carved ivory whale on lid, cloth lined, 9¾" W, 10" H. **$330**

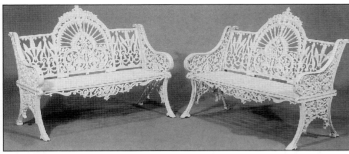

Garden Benches, pr., cast-iron, Eng., 37¾" H, 46¾" W, 24" D. $1,700

A-OH Apr. 2001   Garth's Auctions, Inc.

Stepback Wall Cupboard, one-piece in tiger maple w/ mellow golden color, attrib. to PA, turned legs, five dov. drawers, two-board top w/ high pie shelf, mortised & paneled doors, one int. shelf, brass pulls repl., one glued break, 44½" W, 60¼" H. **$8,525**

Stoneware Jug, OH, ovoid shaped w/ impr. sgn. "T. Reed", cobalt tulip on one side w/ raised rings around the spout & appied strap handle, shallow base chip, 10¾" H. **$770**

Burl Bowl, ash w/ old scrubbed surface, incised ring detail around base & ext. w/ a raised rim, rim split, 11½" diam., 4" H. **$880**

Stoneware Jug, impr. sgn. "Orcutt H-miston & Co. Troy", NY, deep cobalt leaf dec., applied handles, shallow rim chips, 9⅞" H. **$385**

Ovoid Stoneware Jug, two-gal., impr. sgn. "Harrington & Burger, Rochester", lg. cobalt blue floral dec. has good contrast, 13½" H. **$605**

A-OH Apr. 2001   Garth's Auctions, Inc.

Pie Safe, w/ 12 punched star tins, poplar w/ old finish, high legs w/ 3 tins in ea. side & matching door on front, dov. drawer in base w/ turned wooden pulls, pitting on some tins, surface front lightly cleaned, 41½" W, 57¼" H. **$1,100**

Weathervane, arrow, iron w/ old gr. repaint on tip & feathers, traces of an earlier gilt beneath, enameled steel base contemporary, 39" L. **$935**

Stoneware Crock, partial maker's mkd. "Fort Edward, N.Y.", signed, deep blue stylized floral dec. w/ double handles, 10" H. **$330**

Stoneware Crock, dec., impr. "John Burger, Rochester", cobalt blue wreath surround "2", double handles w/ flared rim, minor hairlines, 11¼" H. **$110**

Stoneware Crock, dec., impr. signed "S. B. Bosworth, Hartford, CT, 2", double handles w/ incised line detail & raised rim, cobalt flower design, imper. & flake, 9" H. **$110**

A-OH Nov. 2001 Garth's Auctions, Inc.

Work Table, PA, cherry w/ old finish, dov. drawer has divided int., beaded edges & orig. shaped pull, three-board pin top w/ breadboard ends, edge chips & insect damage, small patch in top, 55" W, 36¼" D. 29" H. **$1,265**

Lighting Device, wrt. iron, tripod base, two candle sockets, scrolled center finial, two dec. loops on base & two missing, 13" H. **$275**

Goose Decoy, w/ carved, initial "R", w/ br. & white paint on body, blk. neck & bill, glass eyes, wear & a few splits, 22" L, 12" H. **$1,815**

Bentwood Pantry Boxes, assembled set of four, all have iron tacks & old ref., 3" H; 2½" H; third has traces of old red, 1¾" H, fourth has chips & age splits, 1¾" H., longest 9½". **$192**

Woven Splint Baskets, two, round w/ raised centers, Taconic swing handle w/ good br. patina & carved initials "R.B.R.", splint breaks, 15½" diam., 18" H. and a market basket w/ dry natural finish & arched handle, 15" diam., 16" H. **$385**

A-OH Jan. 2001 Garth's Auctions, Inc.

Hepplewhite Drop Leaf Table, ref. birch w/ mellow reddish color, 42" W, 11½" leaves which are bowed, attrib. to N.H. **$385**

Sauce Pans, six graduated copper, all are dov. & have "H.P." stamped along w/ "Harrods Stores Ltd., London", cast iron handles & tin wash int., smallest missing lid, 8¾" diam. to 4¾" diam. **$1,100**

Figural Andirons, pr., cast iron, "George Washington" w/ blue, yel. & blk. repaint, 15" H. **$220**

Eagle Finial, lg. cast iron, cast in two sections w/ old gold repaint, 15½" W, 9" H. **$110**

A-OH Jan. 2001 Garth's Auctions, Inc.

Christmas Ornaments, five, clown, boy, accordian, harmonica & horse in silvered red, pink, blue & yel., some wear, 2¼" to 4¼" L. **$192**

Christmas Ornaments, five birds, three pictured, silver, red, yel. blue & gr. w/ white or pink fiber tails, 4" to5" L. **$165**

Christmas Ornaments, two lg. birds, white w/ silvered pink & blue wings, & pink & chartreuse wings, wear & tails missing, 4½" to 5½" L. **$38**

Santa Claus Ornaments, four cotton batting & Victorian scrap, some wear, 4⅞" to 10¼" H. **$247**

Christmas Ornaments, eight assort., six silvered glass Santas in red, white & some blue, 2½" to 3¼" L. One celluloid Santa, 4" L, & one free form silvered ball, 7" L. **$385**

Tin Candle Holders, three, w/ weighted gold glitter balls, minor wear, 5½" L. **$148**

A-KS Aug. 2001 Woody Auction

Oriental Vase, "Foil Cloisonné", dark green background w/ scene. sgn. 11" H. **$402**

Cloisonné Vase, elaborate & colorful, 6" H. **$236**

Cloisonné Vase, deep red background w/ pink rose decor. 7" H. **$344**

Cloisonné Vase, multicolored decor. on blue background, 10" H. **$275**

Oriental Vase, w/ scene of Mt. Fuji. "Wireless Cloisonné", 4"W, 6" H. **$450**

Oriental Vase, Cloisonné, cobalt blue w/ white storks, 3"H, 2¼"W. **$275**

Oriental Vase, enameled w/ raised white floral motif, 6" H. **$700**

Oriental Vase, raised enameled floral, light blue w/ pink & white, 3½" H. **$225**

Oriental Vase, black w/ raised green & white enameled floral, 5" H. **$650**

A-NH Mar. 2001   Northeast Auctions

Staffordshire Tableware, marine patt. w/ dark-blue transfer dec. centering a ship in harbor, incl. 2 oblong platters, View of Dublin, Erith on the Thames, ea. mkd. "Wood", a coffeepot & teapot, sauce tureen, companion stand & eagle head ladle, gravy boat, two 9" plates, 10" soup plate, tea bowl & saucer. **$10,500**

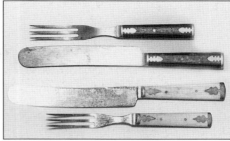

A-OH Apr. 2001   Garth's Auctions, Inc.

Flatware, set by "J. Ward", four knives & four forks w/ wooden handles, orig. box, box has wear & some damage, knife 8⅞" L. **$82**
Flatware, 21 pcs., set of eight knives & forks, w/ bone handles, knives 9¾" L., plus four forks & one mismatched knife w/ wooden handles, knife 9¼" L, marked "Landers, Frary & Clark, Aetna Works". **$82**

A-PA Nov.-Dec. 2001   Pook & Pook, Inc.

Portrait, Eng. oil on canvas, ca. 1820, boy wearing blue frock w/ hand on dog, 37½" x 29½" **$1,200**
Dutch Cupboard, OH, ca. 1840, upper w/ walnut molded cornice w/ scalloped trim over a maple case w/ two 6-light doors above pie shelf, lower w/ 3 drawers over 2 cupboard doors w/ walnut panels & scalloped trim, all supported by cut-out bracket feet, 50" W, 82" H. **$4,750**
Windsor Sackback Armchair, N.Eng., ca. 1790, w/ 7 spindle back, sawed arms, oval seat & baluster turned legs. **$500**
Gaudy Tea Service, 26 pc., ironstone, ca. 1840, "Scroll" patt. by E. Walley. **$500**
Watercolor, by David Y. Ellinger, Am., 20th C., velvet theorem of rooster, sgn. lower left "D. Ellinger", 13¾" x 14". **$1,900**

A-PA Nov.-Dec. 2001   Pook & Pook, Inc.

Double Portrait, New England, oil on canvas, 19th C., boy in bl. coat w/ white collar & girl in red dress, 29½" x 23½". **$2,200**
Desk, CT, Q.A., ca 1770, w/ fall front, fitted int. w/ carved center drawer, 4 graduated thumb molded drawers on frame w/ scrolled skirt & banty legs w/ modified animal paw feet, 37" W, 43¾" H. **$2,200**

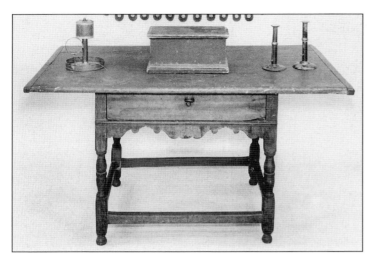

A-OH Apr. 2001   Garth's Auctions, Inc.

Tavern Table, Q.A., ref. maple & pine, turned feet & legs, stretcher base, dov. drawer w/ wrought iron loop over remnants of other wooden pull, pegged const. w/ few rosehead nails, two-board top w/ bread board ends, rest., minor splits, 47¾" W, 28" D, 27" H. **$1,980**

Petticoat Lamp, tin, round pan base w/ lg. ring handle, sm. pick & chain are attached to handle, 9" H. **$247**

Blanket Chest, mini., dov. case w/ old dk. gr. paint, molded base & lid, int. till is missing lid & has hidden compartment, edge chips, 13" W, 7½" D, 6¼" H. **$495**

Hogscraper Candlesticks, two, both have applied brass "wedding rings", lt. overall pitting & one ring is resoldered, 7⅞" H., 7½" H. **$440**

A-PA Sept. 2001   Pook & Pook Inc.

Rye Straw Basket, PA, early 19th C., 26½" L, minor wear. **$200**

Spaniel, 19th C., w/ brown & yellow mottled glaze. **$300**

Child's Ladderback Chair, VA, ca. 1790, w/ splint seat, 22½" H. **$1,200**

Hanging Box, PA, retains yellow & ochre grain painted decor., 15½" H, 12" W. **$4,750**

Oval Wallpaper Box, mid-19th C., 9½" H. **$275**

Wallpaper Box, New England box w/ state views. **$2,200**

Q.A. Tavern Table, PA, ca. 1790, 29" H, 78" W, together by association. **$1,500**

Hanging Apothecary, ca. 1860, w/ 12 drawers, pine, 17½" H, 14" W. **$900**

Large Hat Box (bottom row), York Co., PA, w/ green & yellow wallpaper decor. **$1,500**

Redware Canister, 19th C., w/ black manganese splash decor., 10¼" H. **$500**

Redware Pitcher, early 19th C., w/ black splotches, 9¼" H. **$600**

Mortar & Pestle, 18th C., burlwood. **$280**

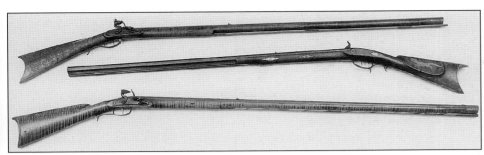

A-PA 2001   Pook & Pook, Inc.

Rifles
Long Rifle, tiger maple, full stock, PA, ca. 1800, sgn. "H. Humberger" in script on barrel, mkd. London Warranted w/ elaborately pierced & engraved patchbox w/ inlaid spread winged eagle, 44" barrel length, 54" overall. **$3,750**
Half Stock Rifle, figured walnut, PA, ca. 1830, lock sgn. J. Fordney, Lancaster, w/ engraved patch box, percussion mechanism, octagonal barrel & silver alligator inlay, overall length 54½" overall. **$4,000**
Rifle, tiger maple, York Co., PA, by C. Zorger, w/ brass butt & silver inlay, percussion mechanism by Small & Sons, 60" L, 44½" barrel. **$2,000**

A-OH Nov. 2001   Garth's Auctions, Inc.

Civil War Artillery Drum, w/ orig. eagle dec. & int. paper label for "C&F Soistmann, No. 458, PA", old ropes are threaded through hoops. Several leather tabs remain, 3 sticks incl. 17" diam., 15⅝" H. **$11,555**

A-NH Mar. 2001   Northeast Auctions

Shaker
Canterbury Child's Ladder Back Chair, w/ tilters & caned seat. **$1,900**
Canterbury Child's Ladder Back Rocker, w/caned seat. **$1,900**
Dry Sink & Cupboard, N.Y. honey pine w/ shaped gallery w/ corner shelf above well. Case has a short drawer & recess panel cupboard door, & the side w/ similar cupboard door. Remnants of red. 34" H, 31" W. **$6,250**
Oval Box, w/ finger-lap construction & natural patina, 12" diam. **$850**
Seed Box, Mt. Lebanon w/ red & gold label "genuine garden seeds"; together w/ two Shaker cardboard candy boxes, one E. Canterbury Sugared Nuts, and the other Sabbathday Lake Shaker Sweets. The seed box is 11½" x 23½". **$750**
Horsehair Sieve, marked #9, 9⅜" diam. **$400**
Bucker, w/ turned lid, Enfield, teal-blue, w/ metal bands & diamond-form plates joining the swing handle, 12" diam., 9½" H. **$700**
Carrier, circular w/ copper tacks & stationary center handle, 6" diam., 3½" H. **$650**

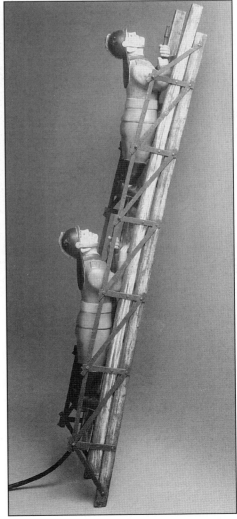

A-NH Mar. 2001   Northeast Auctions

Folk Art Carved & Painted Firemen on Ladder, Eng. or Fr., 75" H. **$4,000**

MISCELLANEOUS

Corner Cupboard, Am., painted & grain decor. Panels w/ faux tiger graining 84" H. **$5,000**

Hooked Rug, Am. w/ facing roosters. Threads on camel ground within a wide striated border w/ abstract motifs. Purple & blue accent colors, 27" x 45". **$2,300**

Treen Bowl w/ blue paint, 17" diam. **$1,800**

Spatter Pitcher w/ blue decor. 12" H. **$600**

Mortars & Pestles, two, the first is barrel-form w/ rings, 8" H; the second is plain w/ foot rim. 7½" H. **$150**

Spice Box, Am. w/ red & black painted decor., wooden knobs & double arched moulding, 13" H, 17" W. **$2,700**

Pottery Kitchenware, 3 pcs., including redware colander w/ russet & black glaze, 10" diam.; a brown glazed redware storage container w/ knopped lid, 9½" H, and a molded baluster form cookie jar w/ blue & ochre band, 8" H, (first illus.) **$750**

Dry Sink, Am., salmon painted & decorated, 31" H, case 20" x 44". **$2,500**

Chopping Bowl, w/ blue-green paint, oblong, 19½". **$1,300**

Wooden Utensils & Tools incl. a turned & leaf decor. treen bread plate w/ screen dome, 11" diam.; scoop; mallet; leaf carved undertray; niddy-noddy dated 1794; child's violin bow; two spoons w/ wool yarn; and 4 implements incl. a pair of scissors. (First three illus.) **$200**

Treen Trencher, rect. w/ extended side handles 20" L; and a circular treen bowl, 11" diam. (Second illus.) **$175**

Tap Table, New England country Chippendale, maple w/ scrubbed top & breadboard ends above an apron w/ long drawer. Tapered legs, 28" H, top 29" x 43". **$2,800**

Stoneware Crocks w/ floral decor. One five gallon w/ applied handles. The other a 3 gallon by Whites, Utica, NY. together w/ a stoneware pitcher w/ cobalt stylized leaf decor., 14½" H. **$1,300**

Hearth Stool w/ 3 legs (illus.) & a bamboo turned example. **$650**

A-NH Mar. 2001   Northeast Auctions

Currier & Ives Lithograph, "The Farmer's Home – Winter", large folio, handcolored, pub 1863. **$1,600**

A-NH Mar. 2001   Northeast Auctions

Currier & Ives Lithograph, "Winter In The Country – A Cold Morning", large folio, handcolored, pub. 1864. **$4,750**

A-PA Feb. 2001   Pook & Pook, Inc.

Live Steam Locomotive Model of George V, together w/ its tender & sections of track, made by Basset Lowke, Ltd., 24½" H, 89½" L. overall. **$3,400**

INDEX

A

ABC Plate, 149
Acoma, 15
Adam's Rose, 178
Advertising, 8-13, 30
Agata, 88, 93, 105
Alabaster, 97
Amberina, 88, 95, 102
American Indian, 14-17
Amethyst, 88, 104, 110
Amphora Pottery, 149
Andirons, 223, 228, 248
Anna Pottery, 149
Apothecary Chest, 64
Armorial China, 166, 175
Art Glass, 88-111
Arts and Crafts, 120, 132, 226
Aurene, 92
Axe, 32, 33, 242

B

Banks,
    Mechanical, 18-19
    Still, 18-19, 219
Banner, 10
Barometer, 26, 28
Basket, 14, 16, 84, 115, 117, 226, 230, 243, 246, 248, 250
Battersea Enamel, 149
Bedroom Suite, 82
Beds, 73, 234
Belleek, 149, 159
Bellows, 233
Bench, 195, 247
Bennington, 149
Blanc De Chine, 191
Blanket Chest, 51, 54, 55, 223, 234, 243
Bloor Derby, 149
Bohemian Glass, 88, 95
Bookcase, 67, 83, 85
Bottle, 108, 113, 234
Bowl, Wooden, 114, 118, 227, 233, 235, 247, 253
Boxes, 20, 21, 104, 105, 114, 145, 228, 242, 245, 248, 250
    Bible, 234
    Doctor's, 243
    Enamel, 169
    Painted, 227
    Sewing, 37
    Shaker, 245
    Wall, 242
    Wallpaper, 250

Bucket, 251
Bucket Bench, 195
Buffalo Pottery, 149
Burmese, 88, 93, 97, 101, 105, 107
Butter Molds, 114, 116
Butter Paddles, 116
Butter Prints, 114-116, 118, 228
Button Hooks, 244

C

Cabinets, Spice, 229
Cambridge Glass, 88
Cameo Glass, 88, 93, 95, 98, 99, 101, 104-106, 108
Canary Luster, 149, 178
Candle Box, 114
Candle Molds, 127
Candle Sconce, 127
Candlestand, 76, 78, 237
Candlestick, 135, 143, 223, 227, 232-235, 242
Cane, 97, 244
Canterbury, 74, 239
Canton, 149, 183, 190, 237, 246
Capo-di-Monte, 151, 165
Carlsbad, 149
Carpet Balls, 187
Carvings, 35-37, 224, 227
Castleford, 149
Celadon, 149
Cellarette, 74
Chairs,
    Arm, 38-46
    Arrowback, 81
    Brewster, 246
    Chippendale, 39
    Commode Chair, 39
    Corner, 40
    Duncan Phyfe, 39
    Easy Chair, 38
    Hepplewhite, 39
    High Chair, 41, 43, 45, 233
    Ladder Back, 40, 43, 45, 81, 246
    Lolling, 39
    Morris, 87
    Office, 46
    Rocker, 41, 44, 46
    Shaker, 251
    Side, 44-46, 98, 223, 235
    Stickley, 87
    Victorian, 41
    Wicker, 86
    Windsor, 42, 43, 45, 46, 228, 231, 232, 235-237, 242, 249
    Wing Back, 38

Chandelier, 127
Chelsea, 149, 159, 170
Chests,
    Blanket, 51, 54, 55, 223, 234, 243, 250
    Spice, 64
Chest of Drawers, 47-52, 54, 65, 66, 229, 232, 234
China Closet, 61
Chinese Export, 61
Chocolate Glass, 88
Christmas Items, 209, 248
Civil War Items, 224, 225
Clarice Cliff, 149
Clews, 149
Clifton, 149
Clocks, 9, 22-28, 232
Cloisonné, 248
Coalport, 149
Coffee Mill, 115, 116
Coin Glass, 113
Cookie Cutters, 133
Copeland, 149
Copper Luster, 149, 155
Coralene, 88, 107
Corday, 149
Coverlets, 201, 243
Cowan, 149
Crackle Glass, 88
Cradles, 14, 228, 234
Cranberry, 88
Creamware, 182
Crown Ducal, 149
Crown Milano, 88, 95, 101, 103, 104
Cupboards, 56-62, 64, 232
Custard Glass, 89

D

Daum Nancy, 89, 92, 93, 98, 105
Davenport, 149
Decoys, 114, 187, 240, 248
Dedham, 149, 151
Deldare, 157
Delft, 149, 231, 235, 236
Desk, 66-68, 70, 71, 229, 232, 249
    Lap, 238
    Sugar, 67
Desk Set, 132
Diorama, 238
Dolls, 10, 204-207
Doll Furniture, 222
Doorstops, 140-141
Dorchester, 149
Doulton, 149

Dower Chest, 242
Dresden, 149, 159, 161, 173
Dresser, 84
Dressler Pottery, 196
Drum, 15, 225, 251
Dry Sink, 229, 233, 251, 253

E

Etagere, 74

F

Famille Rose, 161, 190, 191
Figural Groupings, 165
Figurines, 160, 164
Findlay Onyx, 89, 102
Fireboard, 236
Fire Fighting Equipment, 29-34
Fire Marks, 30
Flags, 224
Flatware, 249
Flint Glass, 112
Flow Blue, 149, 155, 171
Folk Art, 35, 251
Footstools, 73, 236
Fraktur, 146
Frames, 37, 242
Fulper, 189

G

Gallé, 89, 93, 99, 106, 107, 149
Game Boards, 231, 238, 239,
    241
Gaudy Dutch, 149
Gaudy Ironstone, 149
Gaudy Welch, 149, 181, 232
Globes, 227, 239
Gouda Pottery, 149
Grueby, 151, 188, 189
Gunderson Peachblow, 89, 106

H

Haeger, 151
Hampshire, 151
Harper, 151
Haviland, 184
Heisey, 102
Helmets, 31, 32
Highboy, 47
Historical Blue, 177-180, 185, 249
Hobnail, 89
Holly Amber, 89
Hopi, 15
Horn Ware, 224
Horse Collar, 15

I

Ice Cream Freezer, 115
Indian, North America, 14-17
Iron, Cast, 141, 144
Ironstone, 151, 173, 176, 249

J

Jasperware, 151, 161
Jelly Cupboard, 62
Jugtown Pottery, 151

K

Kas, 54, 231
King's Rose, 151
Kitchen Utensils, 144, 145
Kugels, 108

L

Lamps,
    Banquet, 124
    Betty, 127, 129
    Bracket, 125
    Cut Glass, 122
    Desk, 123
    Electric, 120-123
    Finger, 120, 123
    Fluid, 120, 123
    GWTW, 94, 119, 124
    Hanging, 121, 122
    Kerosene, 120, 125, 126
    Lace Maker's, 128
    Oil, 108, 124, 130
    Peg, 125
    Student, 128
    Table, 121, 122, 126
    Tiffany, 120, 122
    Whale Oil, 127, 130
Lamp Shades, 121, 122, 126
Lanterns, 29, 30, 130, 145
Latticino Glass, 108
Leeds, 151, 170, 173, 178
Legras, 89, 99
Lenox, 159
Limoges, 151
Linen Press, 52, 53
Lion Glass, 112
Liverpool, 151, 166
Locks, 142-144
Loetz, 89, 93, 107
Lohunda, 151
Lotus Ware, 151
Luster, 151, 155, 175, 178
Lutz, 89, 102

M

Majolica, 151, 165-169, 172
Mary Gregory, 89, 97, 102
Meissen, 165
Mettlach, 165, 189
Milk Glass, 90, 111
Mirror, 37, 73, 233, 246
Mocha, 180
Model, 237, 253
Molds, 114
Mortar and Pestle, 250, 253
Moser, 90, 95, 101, 103, 104
Mother-of-Pearl, 90, 92, 98
Music Box, 74

N

Nailsea, 90
Nanny Bench, 44
Needlework, 228
Nippon, 159, 161, 163
New Geneva, 186

O

Ornaments, Christmas, 108, 209, 248
Oyster Plates, 167

P

Paintings, Pictures, Prints,
    Currier and Ives, 253
    Lithographs, 29-31
    Mourning Pictures, 147, 228
    Paintings, 146, 147
    Portraits, 148, 223, 232, 249
    Reverse Paintings, 246
    Sampler, 146
    Taufschein, 242
    Theorem, 146, 232, 237, 242, 249
Paperweights, 98
Parlor Set, 41
Paul Revere Pottery, 188
Peachblow, 91, 93, 97, 102, 105, 107
Pearlware, 182, 184
Pease Jars, 118
Pelaton Glass, 103
Pewter, 134, 135-137, 139, 141, 143,
    227, 236
Piano, 74
Picard China, 159
Pie Safe, 54, 62, 243, 247
Pincushion, 245
Pole Screen, 233
Porch Swing, 86
Poster, 10, 11, 13
Powder Horn, 225
Pressed Glass, 101, 109, 110, 112, 230

Q

Quezal, 93, 102, 103
Quilts, 198-203, 228, 233
Quimper, 153

R

Railroad Ware, 138, 139
Redware, 153, 174, 186, 193, 195, 233, 243
Redwing, 153
Ridgway, 153
Rifle, 15, 251
Rockingham, 153, 159, 161, 163, 190-192
Rolling Pin, 109
Roly-Poly Tins, 9
Rookwood, 153, 170, 188, 189
Rosalene, 90, 103
Rose Medallion, 153, 159, 161, 163, 190, 191, 192
Roseville, 153, 165
Royal Bayreuth, 153, 161
Royal Bonn, 153, 171
Royal Doulton, 103, 153, 165, 171
Royal Flemish, 104
Royal Rudolstadt, 153, 161
Royal Worcester, 153, 155, 157, 163
Roycroft, 132, 153
RS Germany, 153, 159
RS Prussia, 153, 161
RS Tillowitz, 161
Rubina, 90, 102
Rubina Verde, 90
Rugs, 14-17, 201-203, 226, 236, 238
Rush Light, 129

S

Sailor's Valentine, 226
Salopian, 185
San Ildefonso, 15
Santa Clara, 15
Santa Domingo, 15
Satsuma, 154, 170
Saturday Evening Girls, 184
Scales, 128
Schrank, 53
Sconces, 120, 237
Secretary, 68, 69, 71
Server, 80, 81
Settee, 41, 44
Settle, 87
Sewerpipe, 165, 181, 183
Sewing Bird, 211
Sewing Machine, 211
Sewing Stand, 246

Shaker, 20
Shore Birds, 240
Show Towel, 201, 203
Sideboard, 63, 81, 83, 85
Signs, 12, 13
Silver, 131, 235
Slag Glass, 91, 95, 102
Sled, 219, 222, 239
Sleigh, 238
Slot Machine, 239
Snuff Box, 172, 243
Sofas, 39, 40
Spatterware, 154, 176, 177, 179-183, 186, 187
Spongeware, 154, 229
Spice Boxes, 250, 253
Spool Cabinets, 8, 9, 66
Staffordshire, 151, 174
Stein, 165, 184
Steuben, 91, 92, 103
Stickley, 132
Stoneware, 194-197, 229, 232, 233, 242, 247, 250, 253
Stool, 246, 253
Stove, 124
Strainer, Wooden, 235
Sunderland Luster, 175

T

Tables,
    Banquet, 75
    Card, 77, 78
    Dining, 75, 76, 81, 84
    Drop Leaf, 79, 81, 227, 233, 239, 248
    Games, 246
    Harvest, 79
    Hutch, 79, 223, 227, 231, 235
    Library, 81
    Pembroke, 78, 237
    Sewing, 242
    Stand, 78, 235, 242
    Tap, 253
    Tavern, 79, 80, 228, 250
    Tea, 75, 79, 80, 227, 231, 233
    Tuckaway, 234
    Work, 80, 248
Tea Caddy, 21, 228, 242, 246
Tea Cart, 84
Tea Leaf, 154, 168
Telephone, 230
Textile, 198-203, 226, 229
Tiffany, 91, 93, 95, 100, 102
Tin Types, 225
Tobacco Cutter, 144

Tobacco Tins, 9, 116
Toleware, 133, 134, 145, 237
Torch, 32
Totem Pole, 15
Toys,
    Airplane, 209, 211, 213, 217
    Animals, 209, 211, 213
    Boat, 209, 211
    Car, 209, 214, 215, 218
    Dolls, 10, 204-207, 218, 219
    Motorcycle, 208, 211, 214, 215
    Noah's Ark, 216
    Pull, 209
    Rocking Horse, 217, 222
    Schoenhuts, 216
    Soldier, 211
    Train, 220, 221
    Truck, 210, 212-215
    Wagon, 211, 214, 217
Trade Sign, 229
Trammel, 133
Treenware, 114-116, 118, 236
Trumpets, 33, 34

U

Umbrellas, 244
Uncle Sam, 10, 11

V

Van Briggle, 154, 171
Vasa Murrhina, 91
Victorian, 41, 65, 69, 71, 73, 78, 81
Villeroy and Boch, 54

W

Wagon Seat, 228
Wardrobe, 53, 66
Washboard, 141
Washstand, 46, 235
Waste Basket, 84
Watches, 24, 28
Wavecrest, 91, 92, 97
Wax Jack, 129
Wax Valentine, 245
Weathervanes, 238, 239, 247
Wedgwood, 93, 154, 161, 171
Weller, 154, 172, 189
Westward Ho, 109
Whieldon, 228
Whimseys, 35, 251
Whirligigs, 35, 36
Windmill Weights, 241
Witch Ball, 109
Wooden Utensils, 252
Woodenware, 114-118